MOBILIZING MAINSTREAM ISLAM

Religion and Conflict

A series edited by Ron E. Hassner

A list of titles is available at cornellpress.cornell.edu

MOBILIZING MAINSTREAM ISLAM

THE POLITICS OF
ORTHODOXY IN INDONESIA
IN COMPARATIVE
PERSPECTIVE

SASKIA SCHÄFER

CORNELL UNIVERSITY PRESS
Ithaca and London

Copyright © 2025 by Saskia Schäfer

All rights reserved. Except for brief quotations in a review, this book, or parts thereof, must not be reproduced in any form without permission in writing from the publisher. For information, address Cornell University Press, Sage House, 512 East State Street, Ithaca, New York 14850. Visit our website at cornellpress.cornell.edu.

First published 2025 by Cornell University Press

Librarians: A CIP catalog record for this book is available from the Library of Congress.

ISBN 9781501785245 (hardcover)
ISBN 9781501785252 (paperback)
ISBN 9781501785269 (pdf)
ISBN 9781501785276 (epub)

GPSR EU contact: Sam Thornton, Mare Nostrum Group B.V., Mauritskade 21D, 1091 GC, Amsterdam, NL, gpsr@mare-nostrum.co.uk.

For Levin, Lila, and Clara

Contents

List of Abbreviations   viii

Note on Transliteration   x

Introduction   1

1. Between Homogenization and Decentralization: The Rise of "Mainstream Islam"   31

2. The Making of Mainstream Islam: Ahmadiyya and Shi'a to the Margins   73

3. Patterns of Othering: Blasphemy, Classifications, and Political Homophobia   111

4. Bottom-Up vs. Top-Down Centralization: Indonesia and Malaysia in Comparative Perspective   165

Conclusion   191

Acknowledgments   197

Notes   201

References   203

Index   243

Abbreviations

ABI	Ahlul Bayt Indonesia
ABIM	Angkatan Belia Islam Malaysia (Muslim Youth Movement of Malaysia)
AKP	Adalet ve Kalkınma Partisi (Justice and Development Party)
Bakorpakem	*Badan Koordinasi Pengawasan Aliran Kepercayaan Masyarakat* (Coordinating Body to Monitor People's Beliefs)
BN	Barisan Nasional (National Front)
DDII	Dewan Dakwah Islamiyah Indonesia (Indonesian Islamic Propagation Council)
FPI	Front Pembela Islam (Islamic Defenders Front)
Golkar	Partai Golongan Karya (Functional Party)
HRC	Human Rights Campaign
HTI	Party of Liberation—Indonesia
ICMI	Ikatan Cendekiawan Muslim Indonesia (Indonesian Association of Muslim Intellectuals)
IJABI	Ikatan Jamaah Ahlulbait Indonesia (**Association of the Ahlul Bait Jama'ah of Indonesia**)
JAI	**Jamaah Ahmadiyah Indonesia** (Indonesian Ahmadiyyah Congregation)
JAKIM	**Jabatan Kemajuan Islam Malaysia** (Department of Islamic Advancement of Malaysia)
JIL	Jaringan Islam Liberal (Liberal Islam Network)
KPHI	Komisi Pengawas Haj Indonesia (Hajj Supervisory Commission)
KUA	*Kantor Urusan Agama* (Office of Religious Affairs)
Masyumi	Majelis Syuro Muslimin Indonesia (Consultative Body of Indonesian Muslims)
MUI	Majelis Ulama Indonesia (Council of Indonesian Ulama)
NKRI	Negara Kesatuan Republik Indonesia (Unitary Republic of Indonesia)

NU	Nahdlatul Ulama (Renaissance of the Ulama)
PAS	Parti Islam Se-Malaysia (All-Malaysia Islamic Party)
PBB	Partai Bulan Bintang (Motherland Party)
PKB	**Partai Kebangkitan Bangsa** (National Awakening Party)
PKS	Partai Keadilan Sejahtera (Prosperous Justice Party)
TIS	Turkish-Islamic Synthesis
UMNO	United Malays National Organisation

Note on Transliteration

This work generally follows standardized Indonesian and Malaysian spelling conventions for Arabic-derived terms, reflecting the orthographic norms of *Bahasa Indonesia* and *Bahasa Malaysia* as codified in their respective national contexts. Readers familiar with Arabic may notice that certain phonetic and orthographic forms have been adapted to align with Southeast Asian usage. Where appropriate, I have simplified spellings for accessibility. In particular, I use widely recognized English renderings for terms that have entered common English usage (e.g., *sharia* rather than *syariah*).

MOBILIZING MAINSTREAM ISLAM

Introduction

In February 1955, the government of Indonesia sponsored a nationwide competition to design a national monument, a national bank, and a national mosque. President Sukarno, the successful revolutionary and canny convener of the Bandung conference, placed great importance on symbolic and architectural matters, personally overseeing the jury for the competition. He also insisted that the national mosque be built near the Jakarta Cathedral and the Immanuel Church, to symbolize religious harmony. The chosen architect was a Protestant from northern Sumatra, Friedrich "Frits" Silaban. Sukarno approved of the architect's vision of adding Middle Eastern and Javanese accents to the International Style then dominant in the West. The construction of the Istiqlal—"Independence"—Mosque took seventeen years. In 1978, Sukarno's successor, General Suharto, inaugurated the national mosque. For more than forty years, it has stood as the largest modern religious edifice in Southeast Asia, with an interior space of some forty thousand square meters.

Today, in central Jakarta the Istiqlal Mosque still stands as a grand representation of one of the anchors of early Indonesian nationalism. In its own way, it also still demonstrates the country's unity: During Friday prayer, some of the mosque's worshippers use the cathedral's parking lot and vice versa on Sundays. The mosque reminds onlookers of the postindependence vision of harmony between modern Islam and multireligious nationalism.

In 1999, just a few weeks before the first democratic elections since 1955, the mosque became the target of a group of violent jihadists. They, and other Islamists, identified the Istiqlal Mosque with the accommodation between Islam and secular nationalist forces and with Islam's subordination to secular state power (Sidel 2006, 200).

In December 2016, the Istiqlal Mosque became a focal point for one of the largest protests in Indonesia's postwar history. It centered on the removal of Jakarta's governor, Basuki Tjahaja Purnama (Ahok), who had assumed the governorship after Joko Widodo became president in 2014 and was hoping for being reelected. The immediate catalyst for the protest was a widely circulated, doctored video of Ahok allegedly making blasphemous remarks about the Quran. Political opponents, who had long mobilized against him along identity-based lines, capitalized on this moment. The protest escalated into a mass prayer on the mosque's grounds. A coalition of socially conservative Muslims, Islamists, and politicians seeking allies among religious organizations convinced Muslims from across the archipelago to follow their call. Members of the hardline Islamist organization Islamic Defenders Front (FPI) carried the red-and-white Indonesian flag and combined it with Islamic symbols, such as white skull caps and turbans. Others carried flags commonly used by Islamists (Almanar 2016). One image circulating online at the time showed a protester wearing a white skull cap with an Indonesian flag draped around his neck as a shawl; another shows youth in clothes combining images of the Indonesian flag with large Arabic lettering. Another image shows a gigantic Indonesian flag carried over the heads of the protesters (Bourchier 2019). The flag appeared in the November and December demonstrations, illustrating the success and the scale of these merging efforts.

Many of the key actors involved did not succeed in securing positions for themselves in the aftermath of the protest, but their use of Islamist symbolism and rhetoric sent clear signals to the political leadership: Less than five months later, Ahok would not only lose the election for Jakarta's governorship but also be sentenced to two years in prison for blasphemy. He almost fully served the sentence, being released in January 2019, and rather than returning to formal politics, he took a post in the state-owned oil and gas company Pertamina. Many regarded the 2017 gubernatorial election in Jakarta as a precursor to the 2019 Indonesian presidential election. Ahok's downfall sent an unmistakable message: Hitherto marginal Islamist extremists had flexed their vast mobilization power. They showed they could topple a popular figure of the political center with relative ease. President Joko Widodo, commonly called Jokowi, now risked a similar fate. Closely associated with Ahok, he had long been accused of not being a proper Muslim, even of being secretly of Chinese origin himself.

Many of the Islamists at the rally—in particular, members of hardline Islamist organizations such as the FPI—were aligned with former military General Prabowo Subianto, the aspiring strongman Jokowi had narrowly beat out in the last presidential election in 2014 and who was likely going to challenge him again in the upcoming one in 2019. The protest forced Jokowi to revise his previous strategy of sidelining far-right Islamists and instead invited them into his own government. He chose as his vice presidential candidate, Ma'ruf Amin, the head of the semiofficial Council of Indonesian Ulama (MUI), who had played a crucial role in drafting a religious statement against Ahok that had helped foment the 2016 protest. The stratagem, however cynical, achieved what Jokowi wanted: The Islamist alliance was split. Within months, radical Islamist influence seemed to have ebbed. The outspoken hardline Islamist preacher Rizieq Shihab, whose stock had been rising in the wake of the 2016 protest that he had helped organize, took temporary refuge in Saudi Arabia. Some observers of the 2016 upheaval congratulated Jokowi on his tactical shrewdness. Others believed that it was religion that had won either way.

The 2016 protests and the 2019 elections marked the peak of a rapid rise of Islamist and extremist forces that had steadily intensified throughout the 2000s and much of the 2010s. However, contrary to the perceptions held by many Indonesian secularists and external observers, it was not "religion" itself that triumphed during this postreform period but rather a specific form of religious interpretation. In this interpretation, the formerly capacious understanding of Islam, which included a variety of practices and beliefs that arrived on the archipelago from many different regions, has been shrunk into a narrow platform called "Mainstream Islam" whose contours are determined by a small group of increasingly powerful religious authorities and their supporters. By Mainstream Islam, I do not primarily mean a group of specific organizations or discourses but rather the homogenization and bureaucratization of what is accepted as proper Islam as well as the growing importance of Islam in this homogenized form.

This book explains how a variety of religious and political actors transformed the relationship between Islam and the state in the 2000s and 2010s and how a new religious nationalism threatened the pluralistic vision of the past and inscribed the values of religious homogeneity into Indonesian nationhood in post-1998 Indonesia. This shift profoundly affected marginalized minorities, secularists, and LGBTQI people, whose place within the Indonesian nation has since been called into question.

This book analyzes the normalization of Islamist social conservatism as the result of several interconnected developments. Islamization was more than Islam's increased public visibility, as this visibility was accompanied by intensifying institutionalization, regulation, and monitoring of Muslim belief. This regulation and monitoring, conducted by a wide range of traditional and emerging religious authorities and facilitated by state authorities and civil society actors, led to a reduction of religious diversity and a drive toward specific notions of orthodoxy. I call this process the construction of Mainstream Islam and show that it relied on assimilation and othering.

I argue that in the 2000s and early 2010s, Indonesia experienced a wave of deepening homogenization of belief in the form of constructing Mainstream Islam and a push to the right. This book offers a framework for the analysis of social exclusion in an environment of highly competitive elections, a fragmented civil society, a liberalized and expanded media sphere, and a pluralized landscape of religious authority and authorities.

The Reform Period

This book analyzes these shifts in the period following the resignation of Suharto, whose New Order authoritarian regime lasted for thirty years and ended amid massive protests in 1997–98. The time after that is usually called the reform period (*reformasi*): Suharto's successors established free, democratic elections, built liberal democratic institutions, and lifted many restrictions in the realm of press freedom and the right of assembly. These new freedoms allowed Islam, which had already become more publicly visible since the 1980s due to the global da'wah movement, to further thrive in the public sphere. In the post-1998 period of electoral democracy, Indonesia's Islamist parties were not very successful at the ballot box. However, Islamists soon succeeded in normalizing many of their ideas through a combination of strategies, such as framing techniques and building coalitions with established and upcoming socially conservative politicians.

Most of the case studies analyzed in the book fall between the mid-2000s and mid-2010s. In this period, Indonesia experienced electoral democratization and the rise of liberal institutions—such as the Constitutional Court—as well as increasing intolerance and aggression toward minoritized identities, such as Ahmadiyya, Shi'a, LGBTQI people, and others. In this period, two different presidents, first Susilo Bambang Yudhoyono (2009–14) and then Jokowi (2014–24), managed the political competition from Islamists in very different ways.

Mainstream Islam and the Islamist Conservative Majoritarian Synthesis

The construction of Mainstream Islam, which has been a long-term process, is a foundation and backdrop for the changing relationship between nationalism and Islam and for what I call the Majoritarian Islamist Conservative Synthesis. The construction of Mainstream Islam essentially prepared the ideological ground for the Majoritarian Islamist Conservative Synthesis, which built on this homogenized center by infusing it with a specific political and moral agenda—one that emphasized Islamic modernity in a socially conservative form and aligned with nationalism in a majoritarian sense. The conditions that facilitated these processes was large-scale decentralization in different areas and Islamist-nationalist alliances.

In this relationship, the construction of Mainstream Islam provides the structural framework (a narrower conception of acceptable Islam), while the Majoritarian Islamist Conservative Synthesis intensified this framework, transforming it into a broader nationalist project that regulated belief and public morality, often at the expense of intra-Muslim diversity. The synthesis can thus be seen as both an outgrowth of and a driver for further mainstreaming, as it channels the homogenizing form of Islam into a politically potent ideology that reshapes Indonesian national identity. The synthesis is thus both a product and a catalyst of the mainstreaming processes.

The term *Mainstream Islam* is not my own coinage but rather a designation employed by other Indonesianists and by Indonesian policy advisors and scholars, such as Jusuf Wanandi (2002), as well as by religious authorities themselves. These commentators often use the term to describe the large Muslim civil society organizations and to distinguish their positions from hardliners, who used to be a fringe phenomenon. In my reading, however, the term captures how Islam has become more regulated and streamlined, as previously more complex and more localized sets of rules and practices have converged into a narrower spectrum of what many Indonesian Muslims view as acceptable. The way synthesis thus serves less to describe an existing set of interpretations or actors than to focus on its constructedness and its discursive productivity. My use of the words *mainstream* and *mainstreaming* is different from but related to the way the Indonesian media scholar Inaya Rakhmani (2014) uses the terms in her book on how religious TV series contributed to "mainstreaming Islam into Indonesia's post-authoritarian popular culture" because in addition to the aspect of disseminating Islam widely in the sense of Islamization, it highlights homogenization and the discursive construction of an Islamic center. This process can be traced back to at least the nineteenth century, before the formation of the Indonesian nation-state, even before the formation of large civil society organizations, and has since then experienced different waves of acceleration.

The Majoritarian Islamist Conservative Synthesis can be seen as constructing national identity through regulatory capture and normative standardization. In this view, state actors do not merely support Islam's presence in public life; they actively institutionalize a particular Islamic normativity that becomes more closely connected with Indonesian-ness. This is illustrated, for instance, by the rejected attempt to repeal the so-called blasphemy law in 2010, when the Indonesian Constitutional Court reaffirmed the authority of certain religious organizations, a decision that sparked widespread dissatisfaction among many members of religious minorities who felt increasingly under pressure (chap. 3). Rather than accommodating diverse expressions within Islam, the synthesis uses policies to delimit which religious expressions are "acceptable" as Indonesian, creating a hierarchy of belonging within the nation itself. Various state and nonstate actors, such as then President Yudhoyono (2004–14), his Minister of Religious Affairs Suryadharma Ali, the MUI, and the vigilante organization FPI, were part of this synthesis and have driven the construction of Mainstream Islam forward. Journalists, clerics, midlevel political and religious leaders, and many ordinary Indonesians further amplified the calls to define acceptable and unacceptable variants of Islam.

I refer to this discursive constellation—including the actors, their messages, and their effects—as a synthesis rather than merely an alliance for two reasons. First, this term underscores the shift in discourse: the effects of these alliances outlast the immediate political influence of the actors. Second, identity-based discourses, including those on minority rights that were intended to support the respective marginalized people, have unintentionally accelerated the construction of Mainstream Islam by differentiating minorities from what increasingly came to be seen as mainstream.

The concept of Mainstream Islam I use in this book draws on Tomoko **Masuzawa's** (2005) *discussion on the "invention of world religions"* where she critiques the nineteenth-century predominantly Western scholarly project of categorizing "world religions" that contributed to the weakening of diversity within traditions of belief and on Ashis Nandy's (1988) "imperialism of categories."

The assimilation of Muslim beliefs and practices into norms set by state and religious authorities is often called Sunnification, and scholars of different disciplinary background show how various state and nonstate authorities in various periods have driven this process forward. Sunnification typically involves marginalizing, assimilating, and directing other forms of violence at nonconforming identities, as for instance in the Ottoman Empire and the Turkish Republic (Dressler 2013). In the case of Indonesia, many of the marginalized identities are part of Sunni Islam, such as many liberal Muslims or Muslims campaigning for tolerance toward gender diversity, and hence it is more useful to talk about Mainstream Islam more generally. As I use the term to analyze the developments in the 2000s and 2010s in Indonesia, it grasps a process and highlights the constructedness of an Islamic "center" in the form of organizations, discourses, and practices and the connected marginalization of others. The following section introduces this concept briefly; chapter 1 then examines it in more depth.

For many foreign and domestic observers, Indonesia in the late 2000s and early 2010s appeared to have succumbed to the Islamist lure that the revolutionary nationalist generation had effectively resisted and contained and that Jokowi then contained again in his second term as president. How did the founding vision of multireligious nationalism, demonstrated in the placement of the Istiqlal Mosque next to the national cathedral, fall apart? The seeds for the politics of orthodoxy were already sown in the early years of the young republic, but the effects of the bureaucratization of religion would only fully break through decades later. The Jakarta Charter, which became the basis of the Indonesian constitution in 1945, had originally included a clause that would have obliged Indonesian Muslims to adhere to sharia-inspired positive laws. However, the final version of the constitution did not include allusions to the Sharia. During the anticolonial struggle, Indonesian nationalists evoked Islam as an emancipatory force, but the founding fathers integrated Islam into a broader vision of multireligious nationalism. Under the Suharto's long New Order (1966–98), the state subordinated Islam to a developmentalist agenda that deemphasized but nevertheless regulated the multireligious nation-state.

Now, in the post-1998 reform period, democratization and decentralization enabled a new intertwining of Islam and nationalism. More than sixty years after Islamists lost the struggle to amend the proposal of religious authorities to strictly regulate religion, questions concerning Islam once again came to dominate the political agenda. Islamist organizations, on the rise since the 1980s as part of the rapid expansion of the global da'wah movement, strived for restoration of the charter, which they saw as not only correcting a historical betrayal of Indonesia's Islamic struggle but also as the starting point for a thorough-going shariatization of society (Fealy 2008).

Scholars usually describe the increased public presence and influence of Islam observed in various parts of the world since the 1970s and 1980s with the term *Islamization*. This encompassed the more widespread use of modest dress (C. Jones 2010) or so-called Islamic banking (Hasyim 2023) and sometimes also the introduction of laws presented as "Islamic." I will in this book use the term *Islamization* to describe the increased visibility of piety, intensified institutionalization, regulation, and monitoring of belief. In contrast,

"Islamist" usually describes political actors, who, often inspired by the Egyptian Muslim Brotherhood, view Islam as a comprehensive political system and strive to implement Islamic principles and laws in all realms, supported by the state in an enforcing role. Islamism has only limited use as an analytical category, as it often serves as a projection foil for othering processes, but where I use it as an analytical shorthand, I draw on the sociologist Nilüfer Göle's (1997) definition of Islamism as the "re-appropriation of a Muslim identity and values as a basis for an alternative social and political agenda" to highlight the interplay of social and cultural aspects of Islam with political aspirations. Depending on their specific contexts, Islamists offer, or claim to offer, alternatives to what many see as the hegemony of Western values and practices. This pattern most explicitly emerged as part of anticolonial struggles but persisted in criticism of postcolonial or neo-imperial dependencies and unfair toll regulations, heavy consumption, and high levels of up- and downward social mobility or systems in which the winners take all. In political constellations where Muslim authorities are heavily regulated and restricted by the state, Islamists offer concrete alternatives to the government in the form of draft legislation and policy suggestions. Some Islamist actors, such as the Egyptian Muslim Brotherhood, have also famously been key actors in disaster relief and other areas in which many postcolonial states have disappointed the expectations of their citizens, and thereby expanded their credibility. It is often useful to analytically distinguish between sociocultural Islamization and state-oriented Islamism, but the phenomena share significant common ground such as the greater visibility of Islam in the public realm, the sharper distinction of gender roles, and the risen influence of religious authorities.

In the 2010s, Yudhoyono first facilitated the rise of Islamist forces. From 2014 onward, Jokowi then tried to disengage with these forces and ignore them in his coalition-building efforts, but this strategy ultimately failed, embodied in the fall of his ally Ahok in 2017. Since then, the knowledge that Islamist rhetoric and protest can be mobilized on a large scale has informed political decision-makers. As part of Jokowi's reelection campaign, he initiated a new phase of religious regulation, combining both authoritarian measures against certain religious authorities along with the political embrace of others. These actions curtailed the influence of hardline groups, marking a distinct shift from the simultaneous democratization and rising intolerance dynamic of the preceding years. Whether such selective repression of religious authorities is sustainable remains an open question. But in order to understand the long-term preconditions required for the rise of Mainstream Islam and religious nationalism in the post-Suharto period, one must look closely at the freer, less authoritarian years within the postreform era.

One of the most important dates in the early phase of this period is 2005, the year the MUI issued fatwas against the controversial Ahmadiyya congregation, interfaith marriage, and secularism, pluralism, and liberalism. These concepts were often collectively labeled with the acronym *Sepelis* or *Sipilis*—intentionally resembling the term for the disease syphilis to evoke negative connotations. This set of fatwas caused a "discourse explosion" (Foucault [1984] 1992). Around the same time, intolerance and violence against social categories deemed deviant minorities—such as the Ahmadiyya—rose, as several empirical works documented (Putra, Mashuri, and Zaduqisti 2015). Ahmadiyya Muslims consider themselves to be Muslims, but their status within the *ummah*, the transnational community of Islam, is a subject of significant controversy (Burhani 2014a, 2014b; Zulkarnain 2005). After the fatwa, a disparate assemblage of actors—including politicians across the party spectrum, Islamic scholars, and religiopolitical entrepreneurs—pushed for the convergence of inner-Islamic variance into a homogenizing version of Mainstream Islam. During this process, Mainstream Islam wrestled, and eventually merged, with Indonesian nationalism in what I call an Islamist Conservative Majoritarian Synthesis. Put differently, the construction of Mainstream Islam was at the center of the recent reconfiguration of Indonesian nationalism in the 2000s and 2010s.

This rise of Mainstream Islam and a new religious nationalism with deepened connections of religious and state authorities decreased the space for inner-Islamic diversity. A particular notion of "true Islam" (*Islam yang benar*) has become dominant, replacing in many areas the diversity and fluidity that characterized premodern belief in the archipelago. This idea of Mainstream Islam resulted in the deterioration of the situation of many Muslims who belonged to controversial congregations such as the Ahmadiyya and Shi'a, as numerous human rights reports documented (Amnesty International 2011, 2018; Human Rights Watch 2013). It also contributed to the rising importance of religious categories, as the individual case studies in this book illustrate. During my fieldwork, in a conversation I had with Ahmadi students about a novel dealing with the persecution of a group of Ahmadiyya members, one young Ahmadi student said to me: "When I read the novel, it made me feel different. I used to just be a normal Indonesian, and reading it makes me feel . . . different (*berbeda*)."[1]

Religious identity has become more important in the post-1998 period. The new religious nationalism calls for tighter regulation in the realm of belief, prioritizes Muslims adhering to Islam as defined by the most powerful religious authorities, and marginalizes those deemed deviant. Indonesia shares this rise of religion vis-à-vis nationalism with other countries: Similar developments can be observed in Malaysia, Turkey, India, Poland, Hungary, and the United States. In a global wave of new nationalisms, right-leaning strongman politicians have appropriated the anti-elite rhetoric of the former left and combined it with locally salient identity discourses. In each of these cases, both state and nonstate actors have promoted a message favoring greater homogenization, rejecting not only normative religious pluralism (*pluralisme*) but also the acknowledgment of religious diversity or plurality (*pluralitas*) in discourse, policy, and law. This is particularly noteworthy in postcolonial states whose elites once envisioned them as multireligious, multicultural, and multilingual alternatives to the more homogeneous European nation-states, such as India and Indonesia. One key difference between Indonesia and better-studied cases such as Turkey, India, and Hungary is the volatility of alliances between political and religious leaders in Indonesia. Indonesia's post-1998 trajectory has not been determined by state actors and their allies (as was the case in Turkey, India, and Hungary). In Indonesia, the state actors played a much more limited role. The main agents of change in Indonesia consisted of a complex assemblage of actors—religious authorities, media celebrities, activists—most of whom forge fleeting alliances of convenience with specific state actors and politicians. These politicians facilitated the political developments by giving these nonstate actors a lot of room to maneuver. Jokowi's sudden embrace of a senior religious cleric as his running mate in 2019 illustrated that Indonesia's religiopolitical camps allow for spontaneous alliances at the highest level. Perhaps more important, it called into question the original national vision of multireligiosity. The lack of reliable alliances makes the necessity of identifying common enemies all the more central: political and religious leaders support and outbid each other in their search for new culprits of alleged heterodoxy or slander of values they define as Islamic. Patrolling the border of religion has become a key practice that compensates for a lack of core values and policy suggestions, and for the lack of strong, long-lasting networks.

One purpose of this book is to analyze, through the case of Indonesia, why a self-professed pluralist political leader like Jokowi in an electoral democracy struggles to withstand the mobilization potential of hardline forces, despite—and because of—formally democratic elections. The electoral democratization was accompanied by extensive decentralization, delegating political authority and fiscal powers to numerous district governments nationwide. The primary objective of this decentralization was to enhance public oversight of state authorities. However, it soon became evident that a significant unintended consequence of this decentralization was the downward shift in the locus of predatory behavior. This shift facilitated the proliferation of corruption and informal deal-making at multiple levels rather than their eradication (Hadiz 2010; Hadiz and Robison 2004; Winters 2011). Jeffrey Winters (2011, 180) aptly describes the system as an "untamed ruling oligarchy" and Edward Aspinall and Ward Berenschot (2019, 7) call it "freewheeling clientelism." These terms illustrate the high level of dynamism during this period. One of the key characteristics of the political landscape is the unevenness of the playing field, mainly due to the oligarchic structures. This clientelism also has effects on the situation of people categorized as belonging to minorities. For instance, Ahmadis—members of the controversial and at times persecuted Ahmadiyya congregation—may formally be granted particular benefits and protections of citizenship, but because political power is also executed by clientelist networks, these networks shape the ability of Ahmadis to access their rights and protections (Soedirgo 2018, 191).

At the same time, Indonesia's media landscape rapidly diversified. In this new economic and political landscape, gaining popular approval became crucial for an increasingly diverse array of actors. As in other contexts, news media and political actors competed for attention by utilizing emotional content, which often includes hostility toward out-groups (Rathje, van Bavel, and van der Linden 2021). In digital media, emotional posts on controversial issues provoke significant user reactions, shaping political attitudes and increasing engagement (Humprecht et al. 2024). This further incentivized political and religious authorities to make popular statements (Pelletier 2021).

I refer to these developments—spanning formal procedures and patronage networks, religious authorities, civil society, and media—as Indonesia's "fourfold decentralization." This process shares important elements with political developments elsewhere, such as personalized politics replacing traditional party structures, the rise of religious authorities, and the fragmentation of public spheres.

Studying the Indonesian case helps us understand how religion and nationalism work together not just in Indonesia but also in a wider, global context, at a time in which new political actors compete in a rapidly changing media landscape and questions of identity assume center stage. Indonesia holds lessons for understanding the emergence of religious nationalism in electoral democracies characterized by accelerated competition for resources. It also illustrates why a broad notion of authority and political elites is necessary to understand contemporary political developments beyond specific local contexts.

Religious Nationalism and Thin Religion

Scholarship on religion and politics typically considers Islam in Southeast Asia to be peripheral, partly because of its geographic distance from the heartland of Mecca and Medina. The focus usually lies on the Middle East, even though only 12 percent of the world's Muslims are Arabs. Most Islamic studies departments in Europe and the United States do not teach Indonesian alongside Arabic, Turkish, Persian, and Urdu. Reasons for this lie in the importance of Mecca and Medina for Islam, in the centrality of the Arab language as the language of the Quran, and in the political interests of Europe in the Middle East and the ways in which these shaped European and, by extension, US scholarship. Partly because of this regional focus, Islam has always had a special position vis-à-vis democracy in the eyes of many conservative commentators, Muslim and non-Muslim alike.

Three broad strands characterize the literature on Islam and democracy: The first claims incompatibility (Huntington 1984; Karaman 2014; Lewis 1996), the second asserts the inherently democratic aspects of Islam (Voll and Esposito 1994), and the third strand searches for conditions under which Muslims can live democratically (Bayat 2007). For the most part, political scientists and influential policymakers have been influenced by the first, discussing Islam and politics within security and terrorism discourses that experienced another boost after 9/11 (Mamdani 2004). Southeast Asia has been perceived as being on the periphery of these debates, or as exceptional. Many commentators view Indonesia and sometimes even Malaysia as secular, in the sense of not being overtly influenced by or making use of religion. However, neither Malaysia nor Indonesia have been exceptional in the larger global trend of increasing religiosity in public life. Religion is a crucial part of contemporary Indonesian and Malaysian politics on all levels and these two cases allow us to understand two different forms of religious nationalism.

After independence from Dutch colonial rule, Indonesia's founding fathers sought to establish a society that transcended racial hierarchies and boundaries while respecting the country's diversity. Islam had been a crucial driving force of the independence movement, but the leadership also wanted to ensure broader acceptance among non-Muslim communities, particularly in regions like Bali and eastern Indonesia where non-Muslims were a significant part of the population. Later, the Suharto government similarly committed to multireligious nationalism. It was partly this commitment to multireligiousity and diversity that prevented the electoral success of young Islamist parties in the post-1998 period. Another factor was the prodemocratic commitments from Islamic authorities. Anthropologists and political scientists, such as

Robert Hefner (2000) and Alfred Stepan (2000), have shown how various religious and political authorities toward the end of the Suharto era succeeded in developing a language and atmosphere of compromise and negotiation that enabled the transition period.

Within a few years, however, this atmosphere was replaced by one of fierce competition for resources and influence. Several religious authorities sought positions of political influence or monetized their followership through religious products and events (Hoesterey 2016) or private religious education (Pelletier 2021). When restrictions on public display of religiosity fell away, transnational Muslim communities such as the Hizbut Tahrir increasingly demonstrated their convictions by wearing long white gowns, face coverings, or turbans and demanded that the state implement their version of Islamic law. In this climate, Islam became more publicly important and socially conservative religious authorities dominated debates about the right interpretation of Islam. I use the term *social conservatism* less to describe actors who promote stability and tradition and more to grasp a modern political agenda that combines an emphasis on publicly visible piety, the nuclear family as the basic unit of society, national pride, and advocacy for laws and policies aligned with particular religious or moral teachings, such as patriarchal gender norms with economic liberalization and simultaneous skepticism toward multiculturalism or liberal cosmopolitanism.

Indonesia specialists across the social sciences documented and analyzed this period in rich empirical detail. In an often-cited article on what he called the "conservative turn," the anthropologist Martin van Bruinessen (2011b) asked, "What happened to the smiling face of Indonesian Islam?" He and the others (Hasyim 2023; Hefner 2019; Ichwan 2005, 2013; Sebastian, Hasyim, and Arifianto 2020) have shown how social conservatives excluded liberal Muslim leaders from the ranks of major Muslim organizations, how key organizations issued ever stricter statements concerning orthopraxy, and how the growing public visibility of Islam coincided with growing instances of antipluralist rhetoric, legislation, and pressure on minorities. Others studied the violence committed in the name of religion (Hasan 2006; Sidel 2006). Some of the scholarship has focused specifically on the key discursive elements such as fatwas (Gillespie 2007; Hicks 2012; Menchik 2016) and changes in religious communication (Alatas 2021; Slama 2018) while others have highlighted the complexity and shifts within the large civil society organizations (Menchik 2022) and broader public debates (Burhani 2014a). Several works have analyzed the legal and institutional changes that hardened identity boundaries and disadvantaged specific identities, such as, among others, Ahmadiyya and Shi'a (Buehler 2016; Crouch 2013b; Fenwick 2016). Scholars have also noted the growing collaborations between nationalists and religious conservatives (Bourchier 2019; Chaplin 2021).

From a comparative perspective, it is useful to add the concept "thin religion" by the historian and political scientist Sudipta Kaviraj (2010) to the analysis: Thin religion differs from more encompassing practices of religiosity that include complex rituals, practices, and beliefs. Instead, thin religion combines elements of religion, politics, and nationalism. Glossing over intranational regional differences and informed doctrinal discussions, it can be used in the service of nationalist mobilizations. Political leaders, be they Christian, Hindu, or Muslim, make eclectic use of religious symbols and tropes or use religion as a stand-in for an ideology rather than making substantive religious references (Ádám and Bozóki 2016; Gorski 2017). Islamist-majoritarian rhetoric by Muslim leaders in Indonesia is similarly stripped of the elaborate philosophical and legal reasoning of Islamic law and instead reduced to pragmatic and often simplistic condemnations of particular identities, such as Shi'a Muslims, and concepts like liberalism or secularism. Visible and open religion made a return to politics after decades of largely military rule, and it has made this return in its thin and identitarian variants.

For many Muslim countries, including Indonesia, observers have often viewed nationalism and Islam as separate, even conflicting, forces. Perhaps the best example of this is the dominant interpretation of Arab nationalism in the first half of the twentieth century as secular, which was later superseded by the rise of Islamism. However, Arab nationalism and Islamism have long been intertwined, connected by the unifying force of the Arab language, the mother tongue of Islam (Mackintosh-Smith 2019). Members of the classical pantheon of Arab nationalism—from Gamal Abdel Nasser to Hafez al-Assad to Saddam Hussein—often made use of Islamist imagery and tropes when it suited their purposes. In my view, it was primarily a generation of Western adherents of modernization theory and its headlong secularization thesis that blocked the view of this ongoing entanglement. Indonesia's nationalism, inspired inter alia by the promise of interwar socialist and communist parties in Western Europe, was similarly intertwined with Islam. Tan Malaka ([1925] 2019), a leader of the Indonesian Communist Party, called for intensifying collaboration with Islamists as part of the anticolonial struggle when he went to the Fourth Congress of the Communist International in Moscow in 1922. Although many party members remained unconvinced, Islam's emancipatory potential, fully activated during the anticolonial and anti-imperial struggle but later repressed, formed a major repertoire for those seeking power during and after the reform period (Kahin 1952; Sidel 2021; Subijanto, forthcoming). In other words, the repression of Islam was an important enabling precondition of the developments in the early 2000s and 2010s. Indonesia is thus not understood in this book as an outlier or as the moderate exception within an otherwise intrinsically undemocratic "Muslim World." Instead, I treat Indonesia as the world's largest Muslim electoral democracy and as a country that has provided social scientists with one of the major tutorials about modern nationalism that—only a generation ago—inspired the most widely read book on the subject, Benedict Anderson's *Imagined Communities* (1983).

Under the New Order regime that took power in 1965, the military dictatorship largely repressed religion in public space. For many Muslims, the connection to the ummah faded into the background vis-a-vis developmentalist nationalism. As part of the Pancasila, the national foundational philosophy and contained in the preamble of the constitution, the state had foregrounded Indonesia's multireligiosity rather than the numerical majority of those categorized as Muslims, even though what counted as "religious" was defined along criteria drawn from particular interpretations of Islam. After 1954, various state agencies pressed Indigenous belief systems into the nationally accepted religions (*agama*) (Ramstedt 2019) and regulated what counts as proper religion. The parallel existence of these various accepted religions leads Jeremy Menchik to the conclusion that "Indonesia's brand of nationalism is exclusively religious though not particular" (Menchik 2014). However, ten years on, despite the continued rhetoric of *Bhinneka Tunggal Ika* (unity in diversity), public non-Islamic holidays, and greater public recognition of religious diversity than in many other countries (such as the United States or western Europe, where only Christian holidays are official public holidays), Islam has—in large part—virtually become synonymous with Indonesian religiosity.

The predominant position of Islam is evident for instance in the education sector: non-Muslim students have far fewer opportunities for religious education compared to their Muslim counterparts (Harsono 2016; Nadhirah 2023). In some regions, Christians and other non-Muslims have faced difficulties obtaining permits for buildings houses of worship (Crouch 2013b). In some areas, school regulations demanded that female non-Muslim students wear a veil (Artharini 2017). Another area where non-Muslims face bureaucratic obstacles is the regulation of marriage and divorce. For Muslims, marriage registration is handled by the Office of Religious Affairs (*Kantor Urusan Agama*, KUA). According to the Law on Population Administration (Law No. 23 of 2006), Article 34, Verse 6, "muslim registration does not require a Civil Registration Certificate." A marriage registered with the KUA is sufficient for legal recognition. The KUA system is integrated with the Civil Registry Office, allowing for the seamless issuance of a marriage certificate (*buku nikah*), which is automatically recorded in the civil registry. Additionally, KUA offices are often affiliated with mosques and local imams, simplifying the process for Muslim couples. In contrast, non-Muslims do not have a comparable system. Marriages conducted in churches, viharas, or other religious institutions must be separately registered with the Civil Registry Office to gain legal recognition. This discrepancy has significant implications. For example, non-Muslims must provide a marriage certificate registered with the Civil Registry Office to obtain birth certificates for their children, a requirement that does not apply to Muslims (Heta News 2023). This disparity highlights the institutional privilege afforded to Muslims in important bureaucratic processes.

Thus, Islam as defined by state bureaucrats, occupies the center ground. Within that category of Islam, authorities will often not accept certain congregations or beliefs as Islamic, such as the Ahmadiyya. Some Ahmadis reported that state authorities initially denied them ID cards, unless they "converted to Islam" (*Tempo* 2017) . In other words, there were state bureaucrats who at one point denied these Ahmadis a crucial state document until they would concede to the view of their belief as inferior. Although they later received their IDs without such performed conversions, the initial denial illustrates how the notion of a "correct" interpretation of Islam had permeated state institutions, enforcing specific interpretations of religious identity. The media discussion of this case signaled to the wider public the tight connection between national and religious identity.

In the 2000s and 2010s, as these debates were becoming more important and thus affected more people, pluralist activists tried to counter this, for instance, by trying to reframe the Pancasila as diversity embracing and the nation as religiously neutral. More specifically, in 2009–10, a coalition of human rights activists and pluralists tried to repeal the so-called blasphemy law, arguing on the basis of a pluralist interpretation of the constitution and the Pancasila. This pluralist group lost influence in defining nationalism to others who emphasized the country's Muslim identity. As a result, nationalism and Muslim identity became intertwined once more, but in a new way. This time, without a colonial oppressor as a common adversary, the search for enemies turned inward, targeting internal others.

Political scientists working on Indonesia have connected the rise of Islamist and conservative Islam as well as "radicalization" to the stagnation and regression of democracy in different ways. While the 2010s were largely characterized by two parallel strands of perspectives on Indonesian politics, the analyses following the mass demonstrations ousting Ahok in 2016–17 began to combine approaches foregrounding cultural factors and those highlighting socioeconomic issues. Of the two strands, the predominant one emphasized the authoritarianizing steps taken by parts of the government (Aspinall and Mietzner 2019) and the importance of religio-racial divisions and their exploitability on the part of competitive elites (Mietzner and Muhtadi 2019) Another strand, most importantly represented by Vedi Hadiz (2015) and Ian Wilson (2017), focused instead on the importance of socioeconomic inequalities and the ways in which political entrepreneurs combine them in a variant of "Islamic populism." Social grievances, argues Hadiz (2015, 2021) convincingly, are often expressed in an Islamic lexicon. But if the battle for economic inequality is primarily being fought through the prism and vocabulary of Islam, what is this normative Islam to which actors on all sides make an appeal and claim to represent, and how did it develop?

The Origins of Mainstream Islam

The construction of Mainstream Islam was accelerated by the process of electoral democratization and the encompassing decentralization of the post–New Order years. However, the creation of a more unified and less diverse religiosity is in no way a new development. Instead, Mainstream Islam is one variant of the processes of homogenization and identitarian convergence that characterize modernity. The more familiar variant of this homogenization is nationalism (Gellner 1983), the best-studied area of the reduction of diversity and ambiguity (Bauman 1991).[2] The modern reduction of diversity in the realm of religion is crucial to understanding the mutually reinforcing relationship between nationalism and modern religion. Both are characterized by a growing intolerance of ambiguity. In the social sciences, one of the most striking contributions to this body of thought came from the sociologist Zygmunt Bauman. He identified the rage for order as the main characteristic of modernity as it grew out of the period of European Enlightenment. This urge to structure the world and human knowledge about it led to the rapid rise of classifying in all areas of life. This classification, in turn, relies on simplification and segregation and decreased toleration for ambivalence, defined by Bauman as "the possibility of assigning an object or event to more than one category." (1991, 1). Bauman, in turn, drew on Mary Douglas's classic *Purity and Danger*, which argued that modern subjects often struggle to assign people to multiple categories. The resulting ambiguity, Douglas argued, implicitly indicates the error of the categorization itself, which instead of being relinquished, is clung to ever more tightly by members of a community who seek to police their epistemic integrity through the means of symbolic boundaries. "Placeless" people who "may be doing nothing morally wrong," and whose status is indefinable, are particularly problematic. They form the fodder of what Arjun Appadurai (2006), has called "the fear of small numbers": Even a very small speck of "matter out of place" reminds people of the constructedness and vulnerability of their community's purity and integrity (Douglas 1966). In the modern nation state, the state classifies and structures the citizens to construct a clear homogenized "we." On the practical level this process expresses itself in taxonomy, classification, inventory, and statistics (Bauman 1991).

The historian Thomas Bauer (2021), argues that Arab societies have, over the course of the past 150 years, become increasingly intolerant of all forms of ambiguity. He locates the source of this impatience with plurality in the extended reach of Western Enlightenment thinking and its drive toward monosemy across space and time. This pressure to define oneself according to clear, unambiguous values and norms developed in the Middle East as a consequence of colonialism, in which colonial administrators sought to fit a molten world of religious affiliations into the hardened rubrics of the colonial survey, census, and revenue collection. A look into colonial censuses shows the tussle between colonial scholars striving for ever more precise classifications of "racial" groups and the more pragmatic tendencies of colonial administrators who reduced the number of categories in their censuses in order to make the population more easily administrable and governable (Hirschman 1987; Scott 1998). Middle Eastern rulers and elites then perceived the need to place themselves in a globe neatly partitioned into "world religions." From there, the monosemic impulse spread to other parts of the world, including other Muslim societies. In Turkey, for instance, the focus on Turkish identity as Sunni and secular replaced a previously more diverse landscape of more fluid identities (Dressler 2013; White 2014).

The rising intolerance of religious ambiguity was first identified by psychologists and linguists in the postwar period before the matter was taken up by political scientists, historians, and scholars of Muslim society. In the 1940s, the psychologist Else Frenkel-Brunswik (1949) differentiated between people who were tolerant of ambiguity and those who were intolerant of it and mapped a correlation between racism and intolerance of ambiguity. Later studies found similar correlations between religiosity and intolerance of ambiguity (Reis 1997).

In Indonesia, in daily life, and especially in the countryside, there continues to be a large variance of Islamic practice (Hoesterey 2022; V. Meyer 2024; Sila 2020; Sila 2021). However, in the realm of publicly vocal opinions on proper Islamic conduct and the importance of such proper conduct for Indonesian society and the nation, the acceptance of variety has been radically shrinking. It is impossible to determine the precise date that this homogenization began, but the bureaucratization that had a key role in this reduction began in prenational colonial times and has since then been accelerated at different points in history.

The origins lie in the late eighteenth century, when closer ties and more regular travel to Mecca began. In the colonial period it accelerated by means of the greater regulation and bureaucratization of Islam by Dutch colonial authorities. In 1998, this process received a new boost. If the ideal Indonesian citizen had always been a religious one (Künkler 2011; Menchik 2014), and if Islam was always central in the modeling of this modern religiosity (Ramstedt 2019), the 2000s and early 2010s saw the continuing hardening of this Islamic core and the integration of extremist and hardline positions, marginalizing those deemed deviant.

Key periods of acceleration of greater bureaucratization and homogenization were, for instance, the organized collaboration against the Dutch and the subsequent forced merging of the major Islamic organizations under the umbrella organization Masyumi by the Japanese in 1943 and the integration of religious education into the national curricula. The textbooks used in public schools have, over time, portrayed Islam in various ways, more often focusing on the unity of Indonesian Muslims than on diversity.

For many scholars and observers, including Indonesians, the process of Islamization is synonymous with Arabization (*arabisasi*). In some respects, this corresponds with the concept of *ghazwul fikri* (*al-ghazw al-fikri*, invasion of ideas), which many Arab-oriented Islamists invoke when they lament particular aspects of pop culture, decadence, and secularist or pluralist approaches to religion (Bruinessen 2015). Many claim that this concept is itself a symptom of another kind of cultural invasion from Middle Eastern Islamist sources and propagated by certain local actors backed by lavish funding from Saudi Arabia and other Gulf countries. Many Indonesians perceived the Middle Eastern influence as an Arabization endangering local practices and countering liberal interpretations. Of course, the hardening of inner-Islamic boundaries in Indonesia cannot be isolated from developments in the Middle East and elsewhere. However, the influence from the Arab region is only one of several powerful global discourses that shape Muslim Southeast Asia. The notion that Indonesia has been conquered or swept through by Arab Islam glosses over local actors (Chaplin 2021) and ignores complementary and competing dynamics that are in many respects more fundamental.

The heavy emphasis on Arabization in the hardening of Indonesian Islam is in part attributable to the rise of a security discourse in and about the country. Particularly after the Bali bombings in 2002, Arabs in the Malay world became viewed as possible threats to security, "the face of political extremism in the region" (Mandal 2017). Sumit Mandal (2017) locates this discourse in influential news media based in the United States, but it is important to acknowledge that this powerful dichotomy between moderate and extreme Islam, between "good Muslims and bad Muslims" (Mamdani 2002), not only informs the politics of the United States' strategic alliances with nation-states that have substantial Muslim populations (Mandal 2017) but also has long tinged scholarship. Mandal points to the colonial origins of associating an Islamic threat with the Arab "center" and quiescence with the "periphery." Despite being marginalized in Islamic studies and other perspectives on Islam, Southeast Asian Muslims have long maintained their own understanding of themselves as authentic Islamic centers, not peripheral appendages to Arab Islam, as evidenced by their rich traditions of local saints and scholars directly connected to the Prophet Muhammad (Sevea 2024). We must be aware of this false dichotomy between a supposedly "pure" Arab center and a "syncretic" Southeast Asian periphery without denying Arab influence on Southeast Asia's local discourses.

Most Indonesians consider Mainstream Islam as consisting of the mass civil society organizations Nahdlatul Ulama (also referred to as NU) and Muhammadiyah, which together comprise around 90 million members, as well as several other organizations. The large organizations are heterogeneous, with factions within them often debating diametrically opposed positions. In the 2000s and 2010s, heated debates about clothing and relations to non-Muslims highlighted questions of Islamic rules and which authority should oversee and enforce these rules. It was through discussions about the degree to which liberalism and pluralism are compatible with Islam, how Sunni Muslims should handle other interpretations of Islam, and what constitutes blasphemy and how it should be punished that an internally still heterogeneous *mainstream* emerged.

The idea of this constructed mainstream here does not imply the complete absence of debate or internal divergence. Instead, it refers to the process through which certain norms, discourses, and practices gain broader acceptance and are institutionalized as representative of Mainstream Islam even while contestation continues. The contestation marks the boundaries of the emerging mainstream. One organization had a particularly crucial part in boundary shaping: the aforementioned MUI, a semigovernmental body comprising representatives from the various civil society organizations, including NU and Muhammadiyah. Since its founding in the 1970s, the MUI has been a prolific source of claim making about how to represent Indonesian Muslims. Faced with its own obsolescence after the fall of Suharto, the MUI made itself heard through vocal and often provocative statements and judgments about the boundaries of "true Islam." Fatwas, disseminated through the MUI's own channels and through media, were a crucial instrument in the consolidation of the MUI's power to define Islam.

Pushing Mainstream Islam Further Right: The Islamist Conservative Majoritarian Synthesis

The Islamist Conservative Majoritarian Synthesis, of which the MUI is a key actor but by no means the only one, refers to a set of actors, discourses, and policies that has been fundamentally transforming the religiopolitical constellation of Indonesia. In this powerful synthesis, a wide range of actors draws on two main elements: First, they invoked Islam's history of emancipation and resistance, rooted in its central role in anticolonial struggles across various regions. This legacy endured through the Cold War and the era of military dictatorships that heavily regulated and policed religion— Indonesia being no exception. Second, the architects of the Islamist Conservative Majoritarian Synthesis that dominated Indonesian politics from the mid-2000s to the late 2010s embedded their vision of Islam within a narrative of Islamic modernity. This vision was embodied in the rise of an Islamic fashion industry and the proliferation of supposedly Sharia-compliant banking and finance as well as Islamic-themed social media influencers and lifestyle brands. Together, these elements promoted a distinctly modern, yet socially conservative, Islamic identity embraced by large parts of urban professionals. The architects of Indonesia's Islamist Conservative Majoritarian Synthesis combined the confidence, political integrity, and moral superiority that Islam stocked up during the colonial and later the New Order repression with this modern image and simultaneously emptied their variant of Islamism of its former socialist and democratic aspirations, emphasizing individual morality in the public sphere, especially regulating sexuality and orthodoxy.

Turkish society underwent a similar process of Islamism transforming into conservatism in the 1980s and 1990s (Tuğal 2009). This followed/built onto the Turkish-Islamic Synthesis, which had originally been formulated by right-wing nationalist intellectuals in the 1970s and then politically implemented after the 1980 coup. Similar to the Indonesian case, the notion of an Islamic modernity is crucial here, as I discuss in more detail below. A major difference to the Turkish case is that since the early days of the Turkish Republic, citizenship had been modeled after Sunni Muslim Turkish men, sidelining other variants of Islam as well as Christians, Jews, and other believers. In Indonesia, such dominance of Sunni Islam was less clear at the outset, when diversity discourses prevailed over prescriptions of orthodoxy. Although citizenship was structured in hierarchical ways, many foreign and local scholars and intellectuals ranked Muslims in varying degrees of piety, and religious authorities such as the MUI had already issued fatwas against the Ahmadiyya and other organizations in earlier periods, the intra-Muslim hierarchization was not as widely felt and did not permanently affect Muslims in the way that the post-1998 hierarchization did.

Theoretically, of course, the nation is meant to provide equal citizenship for all of its members. In a democratic nation-state, all citizens are supposed to have equal access to the law and be equally protected from harm. In reality, all national landscapes have been characterized by strong hierarchies and inequalities, from class and gender injustices to stark racialized and ethnicisized differences. Most nations center their legal frameworks and cultural practices around male-dominated norms and the majority's hegemonic, ethnicized identity—for example, White Anglo-Saxon Protestants in the United States and Australia, Sunni Muslim Turks in Turkey, and English-speaking ethnic Chinese in Singapore. There is a relatively stable, albeit contested, center, with hierarchically lower-ranked identities wrapping around the center concentrically. The center and the social categories relating to it slightly shift their characteristics and precise position over time. Those forming the center—such as, in the case of Indonesia, Sunni Muslim men—do not attempt to completely exclude other social categories but instead keep them on the margins, at a distance from which they do not challenge or threaten but rather affirm and structurally define the center.

The center uses a rhetoric of internal homogeneity and cultivates the deviant social categories as internal others. In this reading, the center relies on the existence of those on the margins for defining itself. If the center consists of competing and internally heterogeneous individuals and groups, which it does in the Indonesian case, it heavily relies on creating an image of its own homogeneity by highlighting differences to others, the identities deemed deviant. This requires delicate boundary patrolling. The case studies in this book thus analyze the most important cases of internal others as sites of patrolling the boundaries of religion. The center was, for this historical moment, occupied by what I earlier describe as the Islamist Conservative Majoritarian Synthesis, a discursive constellation including state and non-state actors, their messages, and the long-lasting effects of these messages.

This synthesis works differently in various places of the vast archipelago. Especially in the urban centers, the practice of preaching has mingled with increased consumerism and the competitive pop culture market. There has been a rapid rise of new religious authorities, many of them simultaneously present on stages and on people's mobile phone screens through personalized apps and many of them opinionated on the proper way to practice Islam. Many of them owe their rise to the way in which the media has amplified their controversial statements on allegedly deviant strands of Islam, such as Ahmadis or Shi'a: By declaring others not part of Islam, they have claimed their own place in what is constituted as "true Islam." With a political system focused much more on individuals than political parties, politicians have to consider the positions of these pop preachers when crafting their own promises and actions. Many of them forge temporary or long-lasting alliances with religious leaders. Indonesia's Islamist Conservative Majoritarian Synthesis has managed to influence and capture some state institutions by circumventing elections while simultaneously making use of the competitive electoral and economic environment.

A key element that holds the synthesis together and coheres the center in this new phase of Indonesian nationalism is the marginalization and persecution of Muslims with increasingly contested identities, such as Ahmadis, Shi'a, atheists, LGBTQI and others who have since been marginalized as internal others in the 2000s and 2010s. Local scholarship and human rights reports have analyzed many of these cases in much detail, but they have rarely been brought together in a comparative manner that detects patterns. I have identified a set of main factors that explain why some identities get attacked more than others. They are the visibility of a particular identity category and the ways in which it is framed as "foreign." The marking of some identities as foreign also lies at the core of the simultaneous homogenization and polarization of identities: Nuances are disappearing, while identities are becoming more fixed. In order to understand this, it is crucial to pay attention to regional variances: In West Java, ethnic organizations are an important part of the social structure, whereas in East Java, religious leaders of the large Muslim civil society organization NU are key authorities to which elected officials often yield during disagreements. Outside of Java, other religious and ethnic identities struggle against Java-centric notions of Indonesian identity. In each context, religion and politics operate differently.

The example of Indonesia shows how the rise of thin, yet highly regulated religion has been shaped by the introduction of electoral democratization, decentralization, and neoliberal reforms, each of which privileges competition at the core of its agenda and incentivizes political and religious leaders to showcase their own moral credentials through harsh and exclusionary judgments. New religious entrepreneurs have made their way to the center of power, from where they contribute their own statements and configure Indonesian nationalism as mainly Sunni Muslim in modernist-conservative interpretation. Those pushed toward the margins of society—Ahmadis and Shi'a Muslims, LGBTQI people, liberals, atheists, and members of smaller sects and organizations—belong to very different social categories and communities. If they were in slightly awkward positions a few decades ago, their belonging to the Indonesian nation was not questioned and contested to the degree it is now. Throughout the process of their marginalization and defense, their identities have become hardened and fixated.

The new claims to orthodoxy and the policing of boundaries of proper religion homogenize the practices of belief and the spectrum of the political discourse. After attacks against Ahmadi and Shi'a mosques and schools, and after high-profile religious authorities issued fatwas against them for alleged deviance from orthodoxy, the status of these identities as Muslims became the subject of heated public debates. Being Indonesian became increasingly defined as being a good Muslim, defined by religious authorities who have a complex relationship to the state apparatus, as for instance illustrated by the Constitutional Court's reasoning in upholding the so-called blasphemy law in 2010 (chap. 3).

The Islamist-conservative synthesis established itself during the post-1998 reform period, a time of highly competitive electoral democratization, rapid economic development, and social and political decentralization. Largely pushed by nonstate actors framing their demands in religious terms, top politicians of less explicitly religious backgrounds facilitated the rise of Islamists and offered themselves as their allies. From the perspective of many liberal observers, Indonesia was fulfilling the core demands of democratization: Media was no longer censored, the NGO landscape blossomed, and the government accepted the International Monetary Fund's (IMF) conditions for bailout after the 1997 crisis, including the privatization of all state enterprises (Lane 2001). To meet the IMF's conditions, the Indonesian state had to cut many services provided to the public. This resulted in growing household debt (TheGlobalEconomy.com, n.d.), a slow decline in poverty, and growing inequality reflected in the country's Gini index, which increased to 39.0 in 2013 from 30.0 in the 1990s (World Bank n.d.; Tjoe 2018). There was an expanding consumerist middle class, which modernization theorists expected to consolidate democratization. The military, a crucial potential veto in liberal democratization theories, was severely restricted in its actions.

Another potential threat, Islamist parties, remained relatively unsuccessful at the ballot boxes. Throughout the 2000s, however, as many liberals were hailing Indonesia as an example of a Muslim majority democracy, right-wing Islamists found alternative channels, such as online media and closed forums, to influence the legislature and the judiciary.

Understanding Politics Across the Disciplines: Approach and Methodology

The key assumptions of my analysis are that religion and the state are discursive and contingent, and that religion and politics are inseparable. Contrary to those differentiating between "secular" and "religious" forces, most state and religious authorities cooperate in order to reach locally contingent interests. Often, *local* alliances between state and religious authorities work together and against the interests of *national* political and religious authorities, as, for instance, the case of Shi'a persecution in East Java illustrates. This book thus analyzes the changing conditions under which these alliances operate and the effects they have on the reconfiguration of post-1998 Indonesian society.

This book focuses on the period between the early 2000s and the late 2010s. It is based on discourse analysis conducted between 2009 and 2014 and ten months of fieldwork conducted in 2010 and 2011 in various cities and towns in Java, Kalimantan, and Sulawesi and on the Malay Peninsula and on research trips to Jakarta and Central Java in 2012 and 2013. Shuttling between Indonesia and Malaysia enabled a comparative perspective. Comparisons to Malaysia, Indonesia's linguistic and cultural twin country (Holst 2007; Noor 2011) where the intertwinement between religion and politics is much more rigorously institutionalized, have informed large parts of the analysis. I conducted several dozen formal semistructured interviews, but more importantly I lived with local hosts and took public transport to engage in hundreds of conversations, shorter and longer. In most of these conversations, which were in either the Indonesian national language or English, I explained that I had come to Indonesia to research the debate about so-called deviant streams (*aliran sesat*). This phrase often sparked comments and conversations about religion in Indonesia, the status of minorities (*minoritas*), and Islamic authority. I found formal interviews to be of limited value because most of my interlocutors, be they from NU or from the now-banned Hizbut Tahrir, were very polite and often remained purposefully vague and affirmative in their conversations with me. Thus, I formally interviewed mostly people who are framed as minorities and less visible in the public discourses. For policymakers and religious authorities, their positions were gleaned from public communications such as mailing lists, letters, press releases, fatwas, and media interviews. In addition, I attended academic conferences and religious gatherings.

Along with my field notes, the analysis of media and public discourses was central. I used the sociolinguistic method of critical discourse analysis (Fairclough 2010; Jäger [1993] 2004) to connect my observations in daily communication and during academic conferences and religious gatherings with my daily reading of the news. I identified major discursive strands and conducted in-depth analyses of crucial "discourse fragments" that encapsulate the major positions within any discourse. I also focused on what Siegfried Jäger ([1993] 2004) calls "discourse events" and what the anthropologist Sally Falk Moore (1987) calls "diagnostic events": The kind of event that "reveals ongoing contests and conflicts and competitions and the efforts to prevent, suppress, or repress these."

Why did religious and political authorities continuously praise Ahmadis for uttering the *shahada*, the Islamic declaration of faith, in showcase conversion events, when Ahmadis actually already do that several times a day in their daily prayers? How were rumors about Ahmadis as reflected in the newspapers and on TV discussed at family dinners and during office coffee breaks? Critical discourse analysis provides a way to think about the connections between these different levels of discourse and to analytically zoom in and out from everyday conversations to legal documents and public statements.

The Foucauldian concept of discourse, on which critical discourse analysis builds, goes beyond the linguistic level and includes events and actions, assuming that they are intrinsically connected. This book offers an analysis of the discourses that ensued after the fatwa and eventually contributed to the 2019 election of Ma'ruf Amin, one of the key drivers of the 2005 fatwa, as Indonesia's vice president. Ma'ruf Amin embodies the blurred line between religion and politics. My argument is not that Islam differs from other religions in this regard but that religion and politics are shorthand terms for overlapping fields or spheres that cannot be neatly separated from each other or from other spheres, such as the economy.

Politics Beyond Formal Institutions

My framework for understanding religion and politics is rooted in an understanding of political science that values in-depth area knowledge beyond formal institutions. Neither the very narrow nor the more medium definitions of democracy that underlie the empirical and comparative democracy indices, such as Freedom House, the Bertelsmann Transformation Index, or even the more encompassing V-Dem (Varieties of Democracy) Institute, consider the importance of religious authorities. Nor do these indices analyze media beyond the mere question of press freedom, measured in terms of censorship and risks for journalists. However, it is crucial to understand how low levels of professional training and, more importantly, practices of brown envelope journalism shape Indonesian public debates: Underpaid and freelance journalists receive cash for transport and food from those they write about, a practice that significantly shapes coverage beyond questions of censorship and safety.

In the wake of the so-called third-wave democracies, some political scientists have called for more attention to be paid to informal institutions (Helmke and Levitsky 2004; Lauth 2000). Scholars who have taken up this task have mostly focused on lobbying and money politics. As Aspinall and Berenschot, as well as Berenschot and Gerry van Klinken, have convincingly argued, taking informal politics seriously requires scholars to place them at the center of analysis rather than view them as deviations, failings, or epiphenomena (Aspinall and Berenschot 2019; Berenschot and van Klinken 2018).

My analysis further expands the notion of informal politics by treating religious authorities, influential civil society organizations, and the structures of Indonesian media as central. I do not treat the shifts within these landscapes as secondary or as conditions in which Indonesian postreform democratization and authoritarianization occurred but instead view them as part of these processes.

A more encompassing notion of democracy and politics highlights four interconnected realms of Indonesian politics: formal procedures and patronage networks, religious authorities, civil society, and media. All of these were affected by the post-1998 reforms, decentralization, and competition. Between 1999 and 2001, a large-scale decentralization program began. Within a short time, the government decentralized much of its responsibility for public services to the local level, almost doubled the regional share in government spending, reallocated two-thirds of the central civil service to the regions, and handed over more than sixteen thousand service facilities to the regions (World Bank 2021). The reformers established a new accountability system at the local level, with the head of the region being elected by regional parliaments, which in turn are elected by popular vote. The decentralization was meant to ease the grip of the Jakarta elite over the whole country, but its unintended effect was to unleash corruption on a grand scale (Aspinall and Berenschot 2019;

Winters 2013). The decentralization coincided with a fast-growing media landscape, with rapid economic development and consumption, and with the fragmentation of established religious authorities and the rise of new ones. This fourfold decentralization lies at the heart of my explanation of the centrality of religion in Indonesia's postreform politics.

Book Structure and Organization

Chapter 1 focuses on the historical preconditions for the rise of Mainstream Islam and the political landscape of the 2000s and 2010s. My main argument in this chapter is that modern bureaucratization and homogenization laid the groundwork for the construction of Mainstream Islam and that the post-1998 decentralization in the realms of elections, civil society, media, and religious authority created the conditions for the formation of the Islamist Conservative Majoritarian Synthesis. I begin with this chapter because it outlines the complicated and heterogeneous constellation of actors and allows readers to understand the specificities of this period of Indonesian history.

Chapter 2 analyzes the cases of the marginalization of the Ahmadiyya and Shi'a in depth as sites for defining Mainstream Islam as part of Indonesia's reconfiguring national identity. The chapter makes three key arguments. First, it highlights **collaboration between state and religious authorities and the rise of the MUI**. Second, it analyzes the mechanisms through which **the Islamist Conservative Majoritarian Synthesis othered Ahmadiyya and Shi'a communities** and pushed them to the margins of both Islam and the Indonesian nation. These mechanisms include securitization, theological delegitimization, and the portrayal of these groups as foreign threats. Finally, the chapter also **argues that the scope of emancipatory vocabulary** was narrow and that the reliance mostly on the discourse of minorities and rights, inadvertently concretized the otherness of those labeled Ahmadiyya and Shi'a and thereby reinforced their exclusion from the mainstream rather than integrating them into the broader national and religious identity. The evidence of these cases supports the book's main argument that the 2000s and 2010s saw a strengthening of a notion of Mainstream Islam that was fuzzy at its core but hard at its boundaries. The primary sources I draw on for this chapter are my fieldwork interviews and observations from the early 2010s as well as Indonesian media debates and scholarship. That evidence supports this chapter's argument because it shows who the key actors and what the main lines of argumentation were in this discourse.

Chapter 3 adopts a broader and comparative approach to examining the construction of Mainstream Islam, focusing on a diverse range of identities that the Islamist Majoritarian Synthesis marginalized. It delves into how debates over public morality construct and police social boundaries, creating cycles of moral panic that shift focus from one marginalized group to another. This demonstrates how exclusionary processes extend beyond but connect to theological deviance debates to encompass broader sociocultural and moral boundaries. The three main arguments in this chapter are the following: First, that **visibility is a key factor of vulnerability but not a sufficient explanation for marginalization,** since even those who attempt to keep a low profile are not always shielded from persecution. The Islamist Conservative Majoritarian Synthesis can impose visibility, especially through media. Second, the cases **connect the rise of social conservatism and nationalism to broader socioeconomic grievances** and global influences, such as neoliberal inequality and resistance to perceived foreign cultural interventions. Third, while chapter 2 discusses the challenges of human rights rhetoric, chapter 3 elaborates on how advocacy toward the end of the 2010s shifted to more localized and culturally rooted approaches, like Islam Nusantara, which proved more effective in defending inner-Islamic diversity. Again, for this chapter my fieldwork interviews and observations from the early 2010s, as well as Indonesian media debates and scholarship, serve as my evidence.

Chapter 4 compares Indonesia to neighboring Malaysia and moves beyond the micro-level analysis of specific groups and theological debates to provide a broader view on political systems and the role of the state in the construction of Mainstream Islam. The chapter contrasts Malaysia's model of state-driven control over Islam with Indonesia's more decentralized dynamics. The central argument is that in Indonesia, the pressure of competitive electoral logic, rather than the opening of the public sphere, has accelerated the mainstreaming of Islam. By removing the variables of free speech from the Malaysian case—where political participation and speech are heavily restricted—the analysis demonstrates that open public discourse is not a necessary condition for the mainstreaming of Islam and the rise of religious nationalism. Instead, both cases suggest that competition over state resources and public support drove the construction of Mainstream Islam: bottom-up and decentralized in Indonesia and top-down and centralized in Malaysia.

The conclusion places Indonesia's Mainstream Islam in a global development of rising nationalism drawing on thin religious interpretations, as seen in, for instance, the White Christian nationalism propagated by the Fidesz Party in Hungary and Donald Trump in the United States; the resurgence of the Hindutva in India, and the emergence and evolution of the Justice and Development Party in Turkey. The conclusion discusses Indonesia's lessons for understanding the conditions under which not only authoritarian strongmen but also outwardly liberal democratic institutions can slip into an atmosphere of violence and increasing autocratization.

CHAPTER 1

Between Homogenization and Decentralization

The Rise of "Mainstream Islam"

In 1975, Siti Hartinah, President Suharto's wife, invited Indonesians to stroll through a miniature of their seventeen-thousand-island archipelago. She had built the Taman Mini Indonesia Indah, a national theme park, in the east of Jakarta. The park, which has since been refurbished several times, is open from sunrise to ten o'clock at night. With an entry fee of around 35,000 rupiah—only slightly more than the cost of a plate of fried rice—it is very accessible to the public. Taman Mini is like a 3D-version of Benedict Anderson's *Imagined Communities* (1983), or at least its Indonesian components: It enables visitors to imagine a unified national community through the physical representation of the country's diverse cultures and regions in a shared space. A small cable car carries the curious visitor across the artificial Archipelago Lake, over the octopus-shaped island of Sulawesi, the bulky miniature of Borneo, and the long green patch of Java. After the ride, visitors can stroll to the park section devoted to native houses and religious buildings. Each of the at the time five officially acknowledged religions of Indonesia is represented here—Islam, Protestantism, Catholicism, Hinduism, and Buddhism—with replicas of mosques, churches, and temples neatly and peacefully lined up one after another. From there, it's a short walk to the section devoted to Indonesia's regions, where costumes and various headpieces are on display.

The forms and patterns of the country that Indonesians have grown up with come to life in the park. From the boat-shaped houses of the Torajans in Tana Toraja in South Sulawesi to the costumes with handwoven ikat fabrics from the eastern island of Flores, all the elements of Indonesia's diversity found in the national curriculum are on display. They are bite-sized, manageable, and preserved under the comforting and sturdy umbrella of the Indonesian nation-state (Pemberton 1994). The cable car, the park's monorail, and the more recently added science-oriented "Discovery Center" also showcase Indonesia's ability to combine tradition (*tradisi*) and modernity (*modernitas*). In a tacit concession to the tastes of the modern Indonesian middle-class tourist, the restaurant section of the park does not trouble itself with reflecting the archipelago's culinary diversity but instead features a branch of the Indonesian-owned fast-food chain California Fried Chicken.

In Taman Mini Park, the Indonesian nation-state is a serene arrangement of miniature islands, houses, mosques, and costumes. Unlike the displays of the National Museum at the National Monument, where the bloody fight for independence is commemorated, Taman Mini portrays Indonesia as timeless, self-evident, and natural. This display illustrates the tendency to streamline religious identities into simplified frameworks, as grasped by Sudipta Kaviraj's (2010) concept of thin religion. In *Imagined Communities*, Anderson considered the country a model through which the techniques of modern nation-state making could be clearly grasped. And yet many observers were astonished that after the fall of Suharto's strictly centralized system in 1998, the archipelago did not disintegrate. They had anticipated balkanization, and, at first, local politics seemed to confirm this. When East Timor's secession loomed after the 1999 referendum, the struggles for an independent Papua and Aceh also gained new momentum. East Timor's independence in 2002 further nurtured their hopes. But more than twenty years afterward, these struggles have been silenced—negotiated in the case of Aceh and suppressed in the case of Papua. Indonesia's borders seem stable for now. But as resolute as the nation-state's geographical boundaries may appear, the nation—any nation—is never safe and secure. Its internal boundaries continue to quake and shift. Indonesia's diversity is not only apparent in its geographic vastness. Comprising more than seven hundred languages and myriad religious and ethnic backgrounds, beliefs, and practices, the country has led many observers to wonder how it has managed any form of unity at all.

From a comparative and global perspective, the Indonesian nation does indeed seem well integrated and unified. Even the neighbors' skeptical whisperings and rumors about foreign allegiances of this and that religious group are expressed in Bahasa Indonesia, that unlikely national language—Malay rather than Javanese—that Suharto's regime managed to spread among the more than two hundred million Indonesians. In the 2000s and 2010s, listening to these conversations, one might have overlooked Indonesian's role as a unifying language, as discussions among religious authorities, intellectuals, and everyday citizens on public transport often mirrored the divisive, identity-based rhetoric seen elsewhere. This trend was not merely a product of the era's free speech—which flourished from 1998 until Joko Widodo's (Jokowi) authoritarian shift in the late 2010s—but was both a continuation of earlier identity politics and amplified by the new dynamics of an electoral democracy.

The Suharto regime simultaneously suppressed and promoted Indonesian diversity, as illustrated by the Taman Mini Indonesia Indah, where regional subidentities of the Indonesian nation were displayed side by side. Similar to the situation in Soviet satellite states, where governments cultivated particular national identities amid their apparent suppression (Brubaker 1994), the Indonesian nation-state groomed and refined religious and ethnic identities behind the national screen. The tension between national, regional, and other identities is inherent to the political concept of the nation-state, and Indonesia, despite its multicultural and multireligious ambitions, is no exception. Article 32 of the Indonesian Constitution, for instance, called for a national Indonesian culture (*budaya Indonesia*) but also to "respect and preserve local languages as national cultural treasures" (Ramstedt 2019). Teachers took children to the Taman Mini national theme park to discuss how they needed to prevent potential conflicts, frequently characterized as SARA (an acronym standing for ethnic group, social group, and religion). The most visibly suppressed and simultaneously highlighted ethnicized identity was Chinese-origin Indonesian. When Suharto fell, violence turned against members of this ethnic group, with hundreds of shops destroyed and Indonesians of Chinese origin attacked.

The violence and tensions between the different officially recognized categories of identity subsided in the early 2000s, as Indonesians eagerly used their new opportunities of political participation to build a new era and the government made various efforts to curb violence. As president, Islamic scholar Abdurrahman Wahid, often referred to as Gus Dur, worked to advance minority rights, for instance, issuing a presidential decree on Chinese culture that paved the way for Chinese New Year to become a national holiday. After a period marked by violence framed as conflicts between Muslims and Christians, as well as other non-Muslims in various regions of the archipelago—such as Maluku, Central Sulawesi, and Bali—the nature and scale of identity-based violence shifted (Bertrand 2004; Redman 2008). Following the early 2000s, Indonesia experienced a decline in large-scale religious violence, particularly after the Maluku and Central Sulawesi conflicts. However, incidents of religious intolerance persisted, often targeting non-Muslims but also Muslims whose practices and belief deviated from those of established Muslim authorities. For instance, the Setara Institute, which monitored religious freedom in Indonesia, documented 220 cases of violent attacks on religious minorities, including Christians, Ahmadiyah members, and Shi'a Muslims in 2013, up from 91 such cases in 2007 (Kine 2014).

This chapter expands the theoretical concepts from the introduction and examines the conditions of rising identity politics and Muslim majoritarianism in Indonesia during the 2000s and 2010s. It explains the acceleration of the construction of mainstream Islam and the gradual drift toward social conservatism and religious nationalism. This chapter thereby lays the groundwork for the empirical chapters that analyze how the marginalization of particular identities framed as minorities relates to the rise of majoritarianism and the shift in the relationship between nationalism and Islam in Indonesia.

How did authorities and believers regulate religion in post-1998 and thereby create the conditions for accelerating the construction of Mainstream Islam and tying it more closely to nationalism? I argue that in many ways, the homogenization of Islam in the 2000s and 2010s was a continuation of processes that began in the colonial era. Some of the foundations for the marginalization of members of particular strands of belief stem from much earlier periods, such as the regulation of religion and belief that have been part of the nation-state since its early days.

In addition, I argue that the already existing tendency toward more homogenization received a new boost after 1998. The increasing intolerance of ambiguity along the spectrum of Islamic belief contributed to growing polarization between formerly compatible positions. This boost for homogenization and polarization was the product of a fourfold decentralization process in the realms of elections, civil society, media, and religious authority and authorities.

As part of Indonesia's modernization, as elsewhere, belief became more regulated and bureaucratized. The tightening regulation, paired with increasing nationwide and transnational communication, has privileged those whose knowledge is certified and approved by established authorities. The processes of increased certification and regulation contributed to the homogenization of belief, identity, and religious practices. The increased regulation has weakened local practices and interpretations vis-à-vis imported ones backed by powerful and financially strong institutions, many of which are located in Saudi Arabia and the United States and its close allies. In a race for influential positions in the state apparatus, a certificate of the famous Al-Azhar University in Cairo will likely outweigh the recommendation letter by a local Javanese scholar, as will a degree from a North American or Australian university. The increased regulation also suppresses ambiguities and compels believers to tick only one of several boxes available on a given form. Further, such choices become fixed and permanent.

The postcolonial Indonesian state heavily regulated religion. This, especially against the background of the mobilizational power of Islam in the anticolonial struggle, helps explain the appeal of Islamist rhetoric. Islamist rhetoric, understood as claiming to offer an alternative to the predominant political structures, thrived in Indonesia in the late 1990s and early 2000s, just as it thrived in other societies when many people found the political elites morally corrupt and insufficiently pious, while at the same time placing restrictions on religious authorities, such as in Egypt and Turkey before the early 2000s and Tunisia before Ben Ali's fall in 2011.

In 1990s and early 2000s Indonesia, Islamist parties and movements were sometimes vocal in demanding transparency, fighting corruption, and championing social welfare reforms. Through these principles, the emancipatory potential of Islam became prominent. At that time, there was also growing advocacy within Indonesian Islamic movements for women's rights and gender equality, often led by Muslim women's organizations such as *Fatayat* Nahdlatul Ulama and *Aisyiyah* (the women's wing of Muhammadiyah), who worked to improve women's access to education, health care, and political participation (Rinaldo 2013). This internal reformist movement highlights the emancipatory potential of Islam to challenge patriarchal norms and promote gender justice within the framework of Islamic ethics. This emancipatory potential and the promises of Islam lingered and became part of the repertoire of political actors. At the same time, the rising halal industry portrayed Islam as modern and cosmopolitan, and neoliberal privatization and individualization placed the responsibility for a good life—both morally and materially—on the individual believer.

Regulating Religion in the Modern State

This section shows discusses how the Indonesian nation-state regulated religion, laying the groundwork for the hierarchization of variants of belief and practice. The architects of the young republic tried to establish an inclusive state and counter the racial hierarchies of their oppressors, but they institutionalized and later perpetuated a differentiation between religion proper (*agama*) and local beliefs in a very clear hierarchy in which the monotheistic religions formed the top and the blueprint for how religion and belief should be structured. The young Indonesian republic was not an exception as nation-states consolidated as the primary political order worldwide, each with their own complex relationship to religions and belief systems. The concept of "world religions" (Fitzgerald 2000; Masuzawa 2005), largely modeled after nineteenth-century European attitudes towards Protestantism, had been exported to the European colonies at the same time as modern state bureaucracies were built.

Early on after Indonesian independence, it was mostly through the Ministry of Religious Affairs (MORA) that the state regulated religion and beliefs. The MORA has never had as far-reaching competences as the Turkish Directorate of Religious Affairs or the Malaysian Islamic bureaucracy, whose officers have the task of writing the Friday sermons for all state-approved mosques, but the MORA inter alia separated religion proper from mere belief and tradition and determined the definition of religion. The MORA initially only recognized three religions: Islam, Protestantism, and Catholicism (the latter two remain categorized as separate religions today). The MORA referred to nontheistic belief systems, including Hinduism, Buddhism, Confucianism, and Indigenous beliefs, as "dogmatic opinions that belonged to tribes which were still backward" (Ramstedt 2004). In 1952, the MORA passed regulation No. 9 of 1952, Article VI, spelling out the requirements for a belief to qualify as a religion (*agama*): It had to profess an internationally recognized monotheistic creed with a holy scripture, embrace the idea of prophethood, and adhere to universal ethical teachings (Atkinson 1983; McDaniel 2010; Ramstedt 2004). If adherents of older spiritual practices and beliefs wanted to become full members of the modern Indonesian nation, they had to homogenize and rationalize their belief systems along monotheistic lines. In this way, they would come to be officially recognized religions as part of the first pillar of the Pancasila, the principle of "belief in the one and only God (Ketuhanan Yang Maha Esa)." Hindu, Buddhist, and Confucian religious leaders adjusted the official narratives of their belief systems accordingly, and the MORA recognized Hinduism in 1958 and Buddhism and Confucianism (for the time being) in 1965, after each had undergone "reforms" along monotheistic lines (Howell [1982] 2011). The example of Balinese Hinduism illustrates how the monotheistic religions served as the model: intellectuals and bureaucrats crafted a Balinese belief system fulfilling the MORA's criteria. They emphasized the "oneness of God" by promoting Brahman to the "supreme god" and reducing other gods to his "angel and saints and declared the Vedas to be the counterpart of the Quran and the Bible (Ramstedt 2019). This process of massaging local beliefs into the system of five and later six official religions has aptly been described as *agamaisation*, or religionization (Cederroth 1996).

This process of religionization involved excluding and marginalizing traditional beliefs. In 1954, the MORA established the Inter-Departmental Committee for the Supervision of Faith Movements in Society (Bakor Pakem) whose main task was the monitoring of adherents of the wide range of traditional belief systems outside the formally recognized religions. This wide range became later subsumed under the term *aliran kepercayaan* (literally "streams of beliefs," often translated as "belief systems") (Ropi 2017). The term encompasses *kebatinan*—"the science of the inner" or "inwardness," derived from the Arabic *bāṭin* (meaning "inner" or "hidden")—as well as *kejawèn* ("Javanism"), which refers to the culture, spirituality, and practices of the Javanese people in Central and East Java, along with other local spiritual traditions (*kerohanian*). In 1961, the Indonesian government transferred Bakor Pakem to the Attorney General's Office to centralize control over *aliran kepercayaan* and enforce national security laws. The state reframed religious deviance as a legal issue, empowering the Attorney General's Office to prosecute groups or individuals seen as threats to Pancasila, or national unity. A few years later, the 1965–66 antileft massacres (G. B. Robinson 2018) put further pressure on adherents of nonreligious beliefs because of the danger of being accused of being Communist, and many of their leaders organized in more formal structures. The massacres marked the end of Sukarno's Guided Democracy period and ushered in Suharto's New Order regime. In 1978, the New Order regime finally decided to categorize traditional beliefs as "culture" and transferred their management to the Ministry of Culture. The odd and marginalized position of *aliran kepercayaan* resulted in disadvantages and a legal limbo for citizens who were not officially registered as followers of a recognized religion, especially in areas of inheritance rights, child legitimacy, and divorce settlements. For instance, many faced difficulties officially registering their marriages without identifying with one of the official religions (Künkler 2018; Künkler, Madeley, and Shankar 2018; Ramstedt 2019).

During the New Order regime between 1966 and 1998, Islamic practice and piety were neither particularly visible nor encouraged. However, Suharto realized that he would not be able to ignore Islam, even before modernist Islamist currents became more influential internationally during the 1980s and '90s. In 1975, the government facilitated and greeted the founding of the Council of Indonesian Ulama (Majelis Ulama Indonesia, MUI), comprising delegates from the Nahladul Ulama, Muhammadiyah, Persatuan Islam, Syarikat Islam, Mathla'ul Anwar, Persatuan Tarbiyah Islamiyah, and several others. The MUI's first National Congress held its closing ceremony at the newly opened Taman Mini Indonesia Indah. The government stated three main goals for the MUI: strengthening monotheistic religion in the sense of the Pancasila to ensure national resilience, participation of the Islamic scholars in national development, and maintenance of harmony between the different religions in Indonesia (Bruinessen 1996). Suharto envisioned the MUI as a supplement to the MORA, not a competitor; however, Suharto's attempt to coopt Muslim leaders came too late and was insufficient: "Islamic study groups" were already mushrooming all over the country, especially in the universities. The military government had continued the Dutch attempt to distinguish between political and cultural groups and granted believers the freedom to practice their religiosity under the condition that the study groups didn't become cells of political discussion. Political demands were, however, simmering in the study groups and elsewhere. Islam, which had long offered a challenge to the powers-that-be, first against the colonial state and then against the authoritarian New Order, increasingly became a political force that Suharto could not ignore, especially after the fall of the Berlin Wall, when his US support waned. In 1990, the government tried its hand at policy making in the name of Islam by allowing the founding of the Indonesian Association of Muslim Intellectuals (*Ikatan Cendekiawan Muslim Indonesia*, ICMI). Its first president was Bacharuddin Jusuf Habibie, a close adviser and then-minister of technology and research. ICMI consisted mainly of scholars and intellectuals who aimed to cooperate with the government. One goal was to reduce the influence of some of Suharto's close business associates, because according to the Muslim leaders, there were too many Christians and Chinese among them. Islam's rising influence became clearer in Suharto's attempts to cast himself as a faithful Muslim. In 1991, he performed the hajj and adopted the name Haji Mohammed Suharto. He had pictures of his freshly discovered piety published in the Indonesian media. But it was too late to protect his position for long. After violent street protests during the economic crisis of 1997, Suharto eventually, albeit reluctantly, stepped down. In 1998, his vice-president, Habibie, replaced him, ushering in the hopeful and tumultuous reform era.

The post-1998 reform era was never the system overthrow that many liked to see it as, but it did bring important changes, for instance allowing the press to blossom into one of the freest in Asia and the establishment of a range of liberal democratic institutions. Most importantly perhaps, it included a thoroughgoing decentralization process during which a newly vocal range of Muslim religious leaders and politicians highlighting Islam emerged. They quickly learned to adapt to the new rules of competition for supporters, which now included declaring strict positions on corruption, collusion, and nepotism (*korupsi, kolusi*, and *nepotisme*), and marketing one's piety to showcase moral credentials. At first, some outside and local observers feared an Iranian-style uprising of modernist Islamist forces, but it would become more complicated than that. New Islamist parties like the Prosperous Justice Party (*Partai Keadilan Sejahtera*, PKS) and the Crescent Star Party (*Partai Bulan Bintang*) focused on implementing Islamic law and moral reforms. Many admired their commitment to lifting the country's political morality. Perhaps most of all, initially, the parties symbolized the hope of curbing corruption. For many, they also stood for contemplating alternatives to Western hedonism within a new democratic framework. It didn't take long until corruption and sex scandals destroyed the Islamic parties' images as moral purists. Islamist parties soon lost their appeal and used up their bonus as hitherto noncorrupted and morally "clean" newcomers into the party landscape. Since the Islamists at the time formed the only alternative within a system otherwise consisting mainly of leftovers from the old military regime, these scandals also destroyed the hope that the political system could become a force for fundamental change. Everyday discussions of morality descended into debates about the acceptable length of a skirt and homophile emojis (see chap. 3). Nevertheless, the disenchantment of the Islamist political parties left unscathed the promise of Islam as a better way of organizing society. Despite failing to sway electoral majorities, Islamists influenced the political agenda and contributed to a broader rightward shift in Indonesian politics. The discourse of morality would continue and Indonesia eventually entered a new era of regulating religion. The initial push for those regulations that resulted in a reconfiguration of nationalism and religion would now come mainly from religiopolitical entrepreneurs outside the state apparatus.

Religious Nationalism

The 2000s and 2010s saw a major shift in the imagination of Indonesia as a country in which Islam was just one religion among others. Islam and nationalism were never as separate as outside observers often thought and as Indonesian secularists wished, but the 2000s and 2010s saw an increasing overlapping and partial merging of these two imaginaries in different phases and in different ways. Three actors were key in this process: the Indonesian president Susilo Bambang Yudhoyono (2004–14), who cultivated friendly ties with socially conservative Muslim leaders seeking political influence; the already mentioned MUI; and the Islamic Defenders Front (FPI), an organization of vigilantes frequently responsible for acts of violence against religious minorities (Dwi et al. 2012; Halili 2016; Wilson 2015). The FPI demanded that the state implement and enforce its version of Islamic law, including a heavy regulation of alcohol consumption, sexuality, and gender relations. All of these actors drove forward a greater regulation of religion through state actors and thereby changed the relationship between Islam and nationalism.

Also, as previously discussed, many urban professionals, after decades of regulation and suppression under Suharto, came to view religion as modern, cosmopolitan, and morally superior. Consequently, very few politicians resisted the temptation to position themselves in the proximity of religion. In a rise of identity symbolism, most of all pertaining to race and religion, Islamic symbols such as headscarves and turbans became an important part of increasingly personality-centered election campaigns, particularly in religiously diverse areas (Fox and Menchik 2011).

Groups such as the Salafi-influenced Wahdah Islamiyah exemplify the increasing overlap between Islamic conservatism and nationalist ideologies in contemporary Indonesia. Advocating for political leadership to be placed exclusively in the hands of Muslims, Wahdah Islamiyah also demanded that basic citizenship rights should apply only to adherents of Indonesia's other officially recognized religion who submit to the practices and political precedence of the Sunni Muslim majority (Chaplin 2017). This example illustrates the homogenizing pressures that have reshaped Indonesia's religious and national imaginaries in recent decades. This trend, while positioned as a defense of national unity, contrasts sharply with earlier pluralist visions of Indonesia championed by figures like Abdurrahman Wahid for whom religious diversity was part of Indonesian nationalism.

In previous decades, the omission of the Jakarta Charter—the proposed preamble to Indonesia's 1945 Constitution requiring Muslims to follow a state-defined Islamic law—and the emphasis of Indonesia's multireligious character created a perception of division between nationalism and Islamism. After 1998, the scholar and public intellectual Azyumardi Azra tried to reinforce this perception and to breathe new life into the Pancasila, which Suharto had used for his own authoritarian agenda. Hoping to counter sectarianism and violence, much of it framed in religious terms, he and others tried to resuscitate the Pancasila in a new form as a common ideological platform and a symbol of tolerance and pluralism (Bourchier 2019). In this interpretation of the Pancasila, the focus was on diversity and the coexistence of various practices of belief. The idea was to counter Islamist voices that saw the new democratization as their chance to finally press forward their vision of a society in which the state would enforce what they perceived to be proper Islamic conduct. The ways in which people around Azyumardi Azra envisioned the post-Suharto Pancasila gave Islam a central place but accepted that this interpretation of Islam would share the center with other religions and beliefs. Ultimately, the group of Muslim scholars, human rights lawyers, and Christian religious leaders was unable to protect this project of breathing new life into the Pancasila in a new pluralist and democratic way. They could not save their interpretation, as incoming President Yudhoyono, himself of military background, disseminated his own interpretation of the Pancasila in public discourse and the education curriculum, eventually blurring the distinction from earlier New Order use (Bourchier 2019). This thwarted the attempt to establish the Pancasila's interpretation. Around the same time, Yudhoyono was strengthening his ties with right-leaning and socially conservative religious leaders whose dedication to tolerance, let alone acceptance and inclusion, was dubious. During the presidencies of Yudhoyono's predecessors Habibie, Megawati Sukarnoputri, and Abdurrahman Wahid, the MUI, once founded by Suharto to control religious leaders and now committed to saving its own skin, had remained in the background and languished. In wise foresight, Abdurrahman Wahid even tried to not let the MUI rise above other fatwa-giving councils (Hasyim 2013). Abdurrahman Wahid, who was the grandson of Nahdlatul Ulama (NU) founder Hasyim Asy'ari, also headed the organization from 1984 to 1999 and briefly served as president between 1999 and 2001. Abdurrahman Wahid, successfully connected NU to the discourse of nationalism to a greater degree than Muhammadiyah was able to do. Abdurrahman Wahid used the discourse of nationalism to defend local Islamic traditions—and with them, the organization itself—against claims of authentic Islam. He emphasized that Indonesians did not need to use Arabic phrases to wish each other good morning, but that Indonesian language expressions were perfectly Islamic and fine. Presumably, Abdurrahman Wahid wanted to preserve a variety of opinions, and he was suspicious of centralizing too much interpretative power in one institution, especially one that was so close to political power.

Contrary to his predecessors, Yudhoyono embraced the MUI. In his speech during the opening ceremony of its 2005 National Congress, he affirmed that his government and the MUI shared the mission to curb evils such as crime and pornography (Hasyim 2013). He said that not all matters related to state affairs could be resolved through formal legal channels and that this was where the MUI could be important for his government: "We want the MUI to play a central role with regards to Islamic doctrine . . . and for matters where the state should listen to the fatwa from MUI and the ulama" (Suaedy 2016). Yudhoyono's support of the MUI was not his only contribution to the phase of nationalist-Islamist alliance building under his time as president. In his second term, he appointed Suryadharma Ali as head of the Islamist United Development Party (Partai Persatuan Pembangunan). Suryadharma Ali was a major voice of intolerance, inflaming community tensions targeting minority groups such as the Ahmadiyah and Shi'a (Bush 2015). In addition, Suryadharma Ali was a strong and vocal supporter of the extremist nonstate organization FPI. Another defender of the increasingly bold FPI was Home Affairs Minister Gamawan Fauzi, who, in response to increasing calls for him to disband the FPI after multiple acts of violence were attributed to the group, called the FPI a "national asset" and asked political leaders to work with the FPI (Parlina 2013). Yudhoyono, through his personnel decisions, remarks, actions, and frequent inaction, actively fueled a political atmosphere that enabled and encouraged right-wing conservative politicians to form alliances with extremists. This environment tolerated attacks against minorities, with reprimands rarely occurring. In short, Yudhoyono helped pave the way for the shaping of a new kind of religious nationalism in Indonesia. Islamist organizations were keen to use this newly gained space.

When Jokowi took over power from Yudhoyono in 2014, the hopes of many pluralists and human rights activists rested on his shoulders. They expected that he would counter the climate that allowed anti-minority positions to thrive under Yudhoyono. However, Jokowi inherited a political system where nationalists had become accustomed to relying on religious legitimization and alliances with right-wing Islamists. Extremists had learned that politicians at every level were willing to lend them an ear and a platform. In his first term (2014–19), Jokowi tried to cut off the extremists' oxygen by ignoring them and keeping his distance. However, this strategy failed. Their networks had spread too far to simply fade away. By the mid-2010s, the religious right and their alliance with extremists had already grown so powerful that Jokowi had little ability to counter their mobilizational strength.

Jokowi's opponents accused him of being secretly non-Muslim, concealing his Chinese origins, and being pro-Communist and anti-Islam. Spurred in part by the ambitions of competing contenders for the position of governor, the 2016 protests against Jokowi's political ally Jakarta Governor Basuki Tjahaja Purnama (Ahok) marked the culmination of resentment among influential right-wing conservative politicians and extremist identitarian organizations. Ahok's opponents referenced Ahok's careless remark about using the Quran for one's own purposes, which he made during his campaigning tour, to bring him down and thereby seriously injure Jokowi's rule. In 2017, Jokowi stated at a minor public event that religion and politics should remain separate. MUI Deputy Secretary General Tengku Zulkarnain immediately criticized the statement and accused Jokowi of promoting secularism and liberalism, which belonged to Western countries, not to Indonesia (La Batu 2017). Around the same time, Islamists and majoritarians reinterpreted the first pillar of the Pancasila in ways that supported their views (Ichwan and Slama 2022).

The Islamist Conservative Majoritarian Synthesis

The homogenizing of beliefs and practices goes back to before the bureaucratization within the nation-state at least to the nineteenth century. One important development was the opening of the Suez Canal in 1869, after which travel to the Middle East became more widespread and the subsequent import of ideas prevalent in the Hejaz at that time became more frequent and influential in Southeast Asia, among other places. The intensified contact with Mecca resulted in a phase of Islamic knowledge production in Southeast Asia that existed parallel to greater European influence and colonialism in the Middle East and Southeast Asia. Across Java, many *pesentren*—Islamic boarding schools—standardized their curricula (Alatas 2021). Many of the processes originating in that period are still ongoing, including the bureaucratization of religious knowledge, authority in modern state structures, and the anti-imperial impetus to use Islam to challenge state power.

Another factor was colonial scholar-bureaucrats assessing Islam against their own largely Protestant or Calvinist backgrounds and Orientalist-tinged education. Some of them looked back at previous appointments in or travels to the Middle East as well. These two groups overlapped in their conviction that there was a pure form of Islam and that traditional Islam in Southeast Asia was a deviation from it.

Among many Muslims in Java, *ijtihad*, individual interpretation of the Quran and the Sunnah, became more widespread, as opposed to *taqlid*, the acceptance of the interpretations offered by the traditional ulema. Some of these reformists or modernists formed the Muhammadiyah organization in 1912. In response, several Muslim traditionalists felt compelled to react and established the NU organization in 1926, with the goal of preserving the chains of transmission and taqlid.

The formation of these organizations and their initial competition were key milestones in the long-term process of the ongoing Islamization of Southeast Asia. Islamization here describes the increased visibility of piety and the intensified institutionalization, regulation, and monitoring of belief. The actors in these processes are the believers themselves as well as civil society organizations, religious authorities, and the state. In the period since 1998, it is particularly the latter two that have pushed Islamization and shaped it in ways that I suggest amount to the creation of Mainstream Islam. Even when speaking Indonesian, *"Islam Mainstream,"* with the adjective placed behind the noun and pronounced with a trilled or rolled *r* using the tip of the tongue, is a term that Indonesian intellectuals use to refer to the most influential Islamic organizations and schools of thought and practice as they formed at the beginning of the twentieth century.

Part of this process of homogenization as part of modernity has been the explicit marking of variants of belief that is also visible in other parts of the world. What observers label Islamization in some places is closely related to what others describe as Sunnification or Sunni privilege in other places such as Turkey or South Asia (Barkey, Kaviraj, and Naresh 2021; Shaikh 2018; Talbot 2016). The reasons for the specific constructions of mainstream interpretations and the rise of "world religions" (Masuzawa 2005) are complex and differ in their specific details across regions and periods, but one key factor in the Indonesian case have been political alliances. In the 2000s and 2010s, a range of actors together formed what I call the Islamist Conservative Majoritarian Synthesis. I use this term rather than merely alliance to highlight two key aspects of this constellation: First, the long-lasting effects that the discourse had, going way beyond particular temporal and often fleeting political alliances such as that between Islamists during the anti-Ahok protests in 2016–17 and political candidates at the time. Since then, politicians consider the mobilizational potential of Islam in their decision-making, an effect that has gone way beyond the particular alliances of that moment. Second, the term highlights that not only Islamists and social conservatives have driven forward the construction of Mainstream Islam but that the distinction between majorities and minorities itself has also contributed to this notion. This effect, which scholars have usually discussed as part of studying modernity, the diffusion of norms, and globalization (Appadurai 2006; Hurd 2015; Massad 2008), has meant that defenders of identities constructed as minorities have also—however inadvertently and paradoxically—contributed to the notion of Mainstream Islam by drawing on discourses of minority rights in their attempts to counter increasing pressure, discrimination, and persecution of those viewed as different from the majority. The empirical chapters will demonstrate how minority rights discourses have inadvertently strengthened mainstream Islam, further marginalizing the very groups they aimed to protect. Here, the focus lies on the alliances between Islamists and conservatives, and their consequences amid Indonesia's fourfold centralization in the 2000s and 2010s.

For the term, I draw on scholarship on the Turkish-Islamic Synthesis (TIS), a strategy crafted by a group of rightist Turkologists in 1973, adopted and implemented by the military in 1980 and then maintained by the center-right Motherland Party (MP) rule in the 1980s. This short excursion allows throwing the circumstances and political opportunity structure in post-Suharto Indonesia into relief. The mixture of Sunni Islam and Turkish nationalism replaced rigid repression of public religiosity with the notion that Turkish and Sunni Muslim identity naturally belonged together and strengthened each other. Institutionally, the outcome of this mixture was reflected in greater budgets for state institutions regulating religion, more state-controlled religious education, and the increasing influence of nonstate Sunni organizations. Since 1980, the synthesis has allowed the right-wing governments to embrace, use, and control the permanent enlargement of the religious field that had begun in the mid-1970s (Şen 2010). Some scholars have argued that the dominant element of the synthesis is Islamism rather than nationalism (Dursun 2003). Mustafa Şen concludes that the success of the Turkish Justice and Development Party (Adalet ve Kalkınma Partisi, AKP) was thus an exception explicable not by the narrative that the periphery rose against the center but by the one that suggests its rise instead is "the latest product of the political trend started with the [National Front] governments of the 1970s that united different currents of the right." One of the functions of the TIS was to define social and political problems as cultural issues (Şen 2010). The intellectuals behind the original formulation of the TIS were critical of Western imperialism, Westernization, and consequently also of the Western orientation of Kemalism. Here, they shared some arguments with leftist criticisms of many pro-Western governments at the time. Drawing on Cihan Tugal's analysis of the absorption of religious activists critical of the state into the emerging pro-state AKP in the 1990s and early 2000s, one may add that the synthesis also allowed leftist Islamists to split from center-right and rightist Islamists, who now found a more potent partner in the previously more Kemalist military. The TIS, boosted by the admiration that many Muslims worldwide held for the Iranian Revolution and by the influx of Saudi capital, laid the foundation for the AKP's electoral success. This development holds lessons for religio-identitarian politics elsewhere.

To describe Indonesia's recent collaboration between right-wing Islamists and right-wing nationalists as a synthesis is not so much to emphasize the parallels between the Turkish and the Indonesian case—the differences are glaringly obvious. Instead, this description proposes a perspective that analyzes individual actors in their relationships with each other and previous constellations to explain the ways right-wing Islamists forge alliances that draw on and appropriate traditionally leftist demands, such as curbing Western imperialism and its local allies, and how these discourses shape political developments in the long run. The Turkish case demonstrates how bridging two hitherto rival frameworks (nationalism and Islamism) can function in the interests of both extreme right and center-right conservatives, minimizing the differences between them.

The most obvious difference between the Turkish and Indonesian cases is that in the Indonesian case, religion and publicly visible forms of piety have from the beginning been a central pillar of the nation. Already during the independence struggle, Sukarno merged *nationalism* (nationalism), *agama* (religion), and *komunisme* (Communism) in his term *Nas-A-Kom*. The second main difference is the historical moment in which the respective new Islamist-nationalist alliances were forged: In Indonesia, the main historical development shaping the merger is the increased competition in the electoral arena and other socioeconomic realms amid decentralized elections and the continuing spread of neoliberalism as well as the expectation of economic recovery after the financial and economic crisis of 1997. The phase of neoliberalism that shapes the Indonesian Islamist Conservative Majoritarian Synthesis differs from the neoliberalism that shaped Turkey in the 1980s: Rather than selling more of its national infrastructure to international investors, Indonesia has been following inward-oriented economic policies and protectionism. Neoliberalism manifests itself most importantly as increased competition among individuals and in the permeation of competition throughout all realms of life, including religion. Companies, for instance, used religiously framed motivational programs to reconfigure religious practice as conducive to business success and personal growth. This training combined Euro-American management texts, self-help manuals, and life-coach meetings with a religious twist so that followers could aspire to be like the prophet Muhammad, who is imagined as the model CEO (Rudnyckyj 2012).

Popular Islamic preachers thrived in this new atmosphere, in which Indonesians were willing to shift the expectations of economic growth from the nation's shoulders to their own. Indonesian Islamic discourse increasingly framed piety as a form of self-regulation compatible with market rationality, turning moral discipline into both a spiritual and economic asset in the wake of economic crisis (Rudnyckyj 2010). This shift turned public piety as a pathway to upward mobility and personal stability in a volatile economy. The best example of the ways in which pop preachers combine entrepreneurship, preaching, and political messages is the famous Abdullah Gymnastiar, better known as Aa Gym. With his self-help advice of Manajemen Qolbu

(Management of the Heart), the former student of electrical engineering became a religious celebrity without any formal Islamic education. At the peak of his success in 2006, millions of viewers watched his weekly television shows, hundreds of thousands made pilgrimages to his Islamic school, and several political parties quietly courted Aa Gym to run as their vice presidential candidate in 2009. According to polling data, Aa Gym was the most adored Indonesian (Hoesterey 2016). Other preachers enjoying different levels of popularity were Yusuf Mansur, Arifin Ilham, Abdul Somad Batubara, Khalid Basalamah, and those who preached to national or specific regional audiences. Some of the new popular preachers stressed their hadrami Arab descent or their Chinese origins. A well-known example is the controversial young preacher Felix Siauw, a convert to Islam from Catholicism who attracted several million Twitter followers. He became known for his hardline positions and his sympathy for the Islamist Hizbut Tahrir organization.

In the 2000s and early 2010s, the influence of NU and Muhammadiyah, the giant Muslim civil society organizations that shaped Indonesia since before its independence, suffered significantly from, among other developments, the rise of these pop preachers. NU and the Muhammadiyah comprise around 60 and 40 million members, respectively (Nashrullah 2019) and stretch from the top-level way down to the grassroots, functioning as charitable bodies funding schools, hospitals, and, in the case of Muhammadiyah, universities. Religious practice, outward display of piety, and social and political engagement are closely intertwined. A meeting organized by one of these institutions might begin with prayers, continue with discussions on fundraising to support members, and end in a debate on recommendations for changing a school curriculum that may be submitted to politicians. Both organizations internally negotiate vast diversities and ambivalences, and as large organizations, they faced difficulties keeping up with the fast developments and the rearranging of the political and medial landscape of the 2000s.

Before they tied themselves closer to the government in the late 2010s (NU) and early 2020s (both organizations), they were not as prolific and influential as other institutions and individuals. Earlier, in the 1950s and 1960s, the NU had temporarily functioned as a political party and one of its most prominent leaders, Abdurrahman Wahid, briefly served as president between 1999 and 2001. NU membership only partly translated into the support of particular parties: Although the National Awakening Party has remained the main NU-affiliated political party, NU leaders have also supported other politicians, and NU members vote for other parties. Abdurrahman Wahid's followers today still admire him for his pluralist and diversity-embracing conception of Islam, but some critics do not easily forget his loyalty to stability under Suharto or his own undemocratic inclinations. After he got caught up in accusations of corruption and had to step down, many members renewed their call for staying out of messy political questions and instead focusing on religious and social activities. The debate on the relationship between religious, social, and political activities characterized many of the meetings in the 2000s. In many important areas, such as digitalization, NU and Muhammadiyah lagged behind smaller organizations, especially Islamist ones who professionalized quickly.

In the mid-2000s, right-wing-conservative voices came to dominate the influential boards of NU and Muhammadiyah organizations. In 2004 and 2005, NU and Muhammadiyah held their national congresses (which are held every five years), and both saw what Martin van Bruinessen calls a "purge" of liberal leadership (Bruinessen 2015). NU reelected Hasyim Muzadi, partly for his support of the MUI's fatwa against liberal Islam. This fatwa also attacked Ulil Abshar-Abdalla, a lifelong member of NU from a central Javanese family of Islamic scholars who cofounded the Liberal Islam Network in 2001. His followers perceived the network as the rightful inheritors of Abdurrahman Wahid's legacy of an inclusive and tolerant Islam, but others strongly opposed the usage of the term *liberal*. The network was one of the main targets of the MUI's fatwa against liberalism, pluralism, and secularism. However, only five years after that fatwa, in 2010, Abshar-Abdalla ran for membership of the board and attracted a small but nevertheless vocal number of supporters. He did not come close to collecting enough votes to near membership on the board, but his popularity probably contributed to the election of the relatively progressive Said Aqil Siradj as the chairman. Said Aqil Siradj wanted to steer the organization away from Hasyim Muzadi's framing of Islam as NU pursued in the Quranic terms of *rahmatan lil alamin*, and he would soon promote his own ideas of branding Islam.

In the 2014 presidential election, when Jokowi and his running mate Jusuf Kalla competed against Prabowo Subianto and Hatta Rajasa, several senior NU figures, including former NU Chairman Hasyim Muzadi, voiced support for Jokowi-Kalla. Then-Chairman Said Aqil Siradj and former Constitutional Court Chief Justice Mahfud MD supported Prabowo-Hatta, significantly increasing Prabowo's votes and contributing to the tight result of 53 percent to 47 percent of the overall vote.

During his time as president, Jokowi further deepened his relationship with various groups within NU, whose votes he knew he needed to counter opposition against his rule framed in Islamist terms. In 2015, the quinquennial congress took place in Jombang, East Java, where the NU was originally founded. During his presidency, Jokowi strengthened ties with NU groups whose support he needed to counter Islamist opposition. At NU's 2015 quinquennial Muktamar congress in Jombang (NU's birthplace), Jokowi opened the event wearing a black suit and red sarong, signaling Javanese-Western fusion rather than Arabic leanings. The congress became contentious over leadership elections, particularly for the Spiritual Guide (*rais 'aam*) position. Progressive leader Ahmad Mustofa Bisri (Gus Mus) initially led the vote count but withdrew his candidacy, enabling conservative Ma'ruf Amin—who had placed second—to assume the role. This created an ideological tension within NU's leadership, as Ma'ruf Amin was one of the key architects of the punitive 2005 fatwas and represented controversial hardline views. Shortly after this victory, Ma'ruf Amin further consolidated his influence by being elected chairman of Indonesia's Ulama Council (MUI) in August 2015, succeeding Din Syamsuddin. These dual appointments positioned Ma'ruf Amin as a key religious authority, foreshadowing his later rise to vice-presidency (Saat 2015).

In the same year, NU clerics around Said Aqil Siradj proposed the concept of Islam Nusantara, meaning archipelagic Islam or Indonesian Islam. The success of this concept and the political alliances it soon facilitated brought to a halt the era in which the MUI and others continuously narrowed the corridor of acceptable Islamic beliefs and practices and posed new questions. The concept was wrapped as a contribution to soft diplomacy as a counter to the violent pictures disseminated by a militant group that at the time had seized large swathes of territory in eastern Syria and across northern and western Iraq and called itself the Islamic State. The group managed, partly due to its professional PR office and obliging tabloids worldwide, to dominate global headlines for several months.

More importantly, Islam Nusantara was part of the ongoing struggle over the privilege to define Islam and of the ongoing effort of tying NU to the discourses of nationalism and Islam. The concept became the subject of heated controversy and deepened frictions within the NU. Followers of the late Hasyim Muzadi continued to remain loyal to the concept of Islam Rahmatal lil Alamin (Islam as a universal blessing for all creations of God) and formed the True Path NU grouping. A rift ensued, with the West Sumatra branch of the MUI issuing a fatwa against the concept (Hasyim 2018). Senior ulama Misbahussalam argued that Islam Nusantara as a concept accommodates "Shi'a, Liberal Islam, and other ideologies that contradict the basic tenets of Islam" (Arifianto and Wanto 2015).

Jokowi embraced the concept and furthered his support for NU as a whole by introducing in his opening speech at the 2015 congress the yearly National Santri (Islamic boarding school students') Day (Hari Santri Nasional) (Kholid

2015). In 2014 at a campaign event in a pesantren boarding school, Jokowi had promised to create this new public holiday (Tribunnews.com 2014). Jokowi designated October 22 as National Santri Day in order to commemorate October 22, 1945, when the founder of NU Hasyim Asy'ari initiated the Jihad Resolution (Amiq 1998) to call Muslims in the country to fight against allied forces to defend the country's independence (Akuntono 2015). Jokowi explained that the National Santri Day "was created as a form of respect and appreciation from the state to the ulama, kiai, ajengan, santri, and all components of the nation who follow their example" (Florentin 2018). Since then, on every October 22, the MORA has organized a media-effective "Santriversary" with thousands of pesantren students participating in, for example, writing events. The NU also organizes numerous smaller events, such as the Santripreneur Awards, to support start-ups created by santris. Muhammadiyah leaders, likely worried about the NU's close ties with Jokowi's government, have rejected the National Santjri Day, reasoning that it would cause polarization among Indonesia's Muslims along "santri" and "non-santri" lines (Firmansyah 2015). While its elite discourses are well-studied, the sheer size of NU makes evaluating its internal breadth and the variety among its grassroots members difficult. Attempts to measure attitudes and values among its members remain sporadic and thin. Jeremy Menchik's (2016) survey on political attitudes among NU leaders, conducted in 2010, led him to the conclusion that they are "tolerant" but not liberal, while Marcus Mietzner and Burhanuddin Muhtadi (2020) found in their 2019 survey that NU followers have significant tendencies toward intolerance, although their definition of tolerance resembles that of liberalism to such a high degree that their findings confirm those by Menchik more than they challenge them.

Muhammadiyah is more stringently organized than NU, and the differences between various groups are not as stark. The chairman Amien Rais had been a key figure during the democratization period that brought down Suharto. From 1998 until 2005, the chairman was Syafi'i Ma'arif, a supporter of prodemocracy activism within the organization. In 2005, he was replaced with the more conservative Sirajuddin Muhammad "Din" Syamsuddin, who served for two terms (from 2005 to 2010 and 2010 to 2015), after which Haedar Nashir took over. In the period of increased identity politics surrounding the 2016 gubernatorial election and leading up to the 2019 presidential election, Muhammadiyah leadership offered a platform to right-wing Islamist organizations and individuals, such as Felix Siauw (Burhani 2019a), while some NU campaigners for Jokowi-Amin stressed the defense of Islam against "rightists" (*Islam kanan*) (Aspinall and Mietzner 2019). One explanation for the lack of hesitation toward friendly ties with more radical actors is competition between NU and Muhammadiyah: The former's success in presenting itself as the main force of Islam and nationalism and its use of the notion of "Islam Nusantara" put Muhammadiyah leaders under pressure (Burhani 2019b). Muhammadiyah also faced pressure from Islamist groups, which gained public support by quickly sharing images and videos of their disaster relief efforts, while state responses were slow or inadequate. Liberal and pluralist organizations often lack large-scale charity efforts, and even more important, they lack the image of being grassroots-oriented and caring.

The influence of both the NU and the Muhammadiyah was said to be waning over the last decades, largely due to the improvement of state infrastructure in education and health and the subsequent reduction in these areas on the part of the organizations (Hicks 2012) as well as the rise of other religious authorities such as the aforementioned pop preachers. The election of Ma'ruf Amin as vice president, however, halted this development. Some interpreted his election as a revival of the NU and its political ambitions. At the same time, depending on the perspective, Ma'ruf Amin may be viewed as the representative not so much of the NU but of the MUI.

The MUI is situated between the state and civil society: Although the council receives substantial amounts from various ministries, many Indonesians consider it to be a civil society body that is independent of the government. Without a doubt, the leaders within the MUI are the most successful political figures of the post-1998 era, having not only rescued but also significantly raised the profile and influence of their organization. Under Suharto, the MUI had been perceived as his rubber stamp, despite a few statements here and there that contradicted state policy (Mudzhar 1993). Faced with obsolescence after the fall of Suharto, the MUI was quick to grasp the new competitive situation and managed to reinvent itself. It shook off the reputation of being a rubber stamp of the regime and became a force of its own, perceived as autonomous and influential on the government. The MUI embodies the dual rise of increased punitive regulation and competition in the post-Suharto period: While the leaders in the council were quick to play to the rules of the new competitive system after Suharto's fall, they also called for and benefited from the tighter state regulation of the religious field, for instance, the increase of Sharia-inspired positive law. The MUI benefited from its "semi-officiality" and "semi-representative" status (Ichwan 2012), partly state funded but not under any particular state authority. It successfully cast itself as an adviser to a morally precarious government. In reality, the government rarely consulted the MUI outside the issues of Islamic banking and finance,[1] but what mattered more was public perception. In this perception, the MUI's practice of proactively offering advice predominated, along with news of corruption and favoritism. At the end of the 2010s, the MUI held a near monopoly on fatwas related to Islamic creed (Fenwick 2016; Hasyim 2013; Ichwan 2005; Lindsey 2012; Schäfer 2019). The MUI succeeded in becoming the representative voice of mainstream Islam in Indonesia or, in other words, a kind of semiofficial state mufti. In this capacity, the council turned into a quasi legislature. Partly informed by the Islamic principle of "commanding right, forbidding wrong," which had been predicated on a right and duty to social intervention of a kind but more importantly widely disseminated in a free and competitive media landscape, some fatwas heavily influenced public debates. In this case, other than in national versus international law, "soft law" proves at least as powerful as "hard law."[2]

The MUI is made up of members from Muhammadiyah and NU as well as other organizations. It presents itself as a large tent (*tenda besar*) of Muslim organizations (Hasyim 2014). It has a national umbrella chapter, thirty-three branches at the level of provinces, and more than four hundred district-level branches. Various government actors have been inviting MUI members to be part of law-drafting processes and to discuss policies. Fatwas are the council's most visible tool. In Islamic law, fatwas are legal opinions, usually formulated by individual scholars on request. In the case of Indonesian Muslim civil society organizations, it has often been councils that formulate fatwas. Fatwas form the basis of all discursive and legal influence that the council exerts (Menchik 2022). For fatwas to be as powerful in this way, the MUI has transformed the traditionally more personal legal advice into a new form. One can view fatwas as links between complicated legal formulations and public understanding (Hallaq 1996) or between legal theory and social practice (Caeiro 2006). The council has used fatwas to circumvent the parliament and the government and manages to influence positive law through agenda setting, such as exemplified in the 2008 decree restricting Ahmadiyya activities that several ministries jointly issued three years after the council's fatwa declaring the Ahmadiyya outside Islam.

Fatwas are not legally binding in Indonesia outside the realm of sharia finance and banking, but the influence of some of them has nevertheless been enormous. The council has several ways of issuing fatwas and other genres of advice on a range of issues, often without specific requests. The practice of issuing collective fatwas is a novelty of the modern state structure (Kaptein 2004). The council widely disseminates its statements via its own media outlets and via the press. Most of the Indonesian press has willingly accepted the MUI's offer to serve as the main authority on core Islamic matters. MUI spokespeople often dominated media commentary on anti-minority violence, while minority representatives were sidelined.

The various provincial and local branches are involved in their own political dynamics and their respective fatwas sometimes differ from other provincial- and national-level fatwas. According with most interpretations of Islamic law, fatwas do not cancel out one another. In practice, the near equality of fatwas has contributed to a limited division of labor between various religious authorities: The MUI succeeded in becoming the main authority on questions of creed, *akidah*. While NU and Muhammadiyah retained their own fatwa committees, these have "allowed [the] MUI to take the lead" (Hasyim 2013), and the MUI's fatwas are perceived as the most authoritative and almost official (Fealy and Hooker 2006). The political influence of fatwas can be traced on three levels: in law and policy making, in the judiciary, and in shaping public attitudes. In law and policy making, the 2005 fatwa against the Ahmadiyya congregation is a prominent example. It not only declared the Ahmadiyya congregation non-Muslim but also demanded that the state act, which it eventually did. On the level of the judiciary, the Ahok case of 2016–17 illustrates the strong correlation between the MUI's fatwa or other statements and the judiciary's outcome. Judges have conferred with religious authorities, partly to demonstrate their intention to be "fiercely protective of their independence" (Crouch 2017b) from the government. In the Ahok case, judges even pronounced a sentence that far exceeded what prosecutors had asked for.

In the reshuffling landscape of the 2000s and against the fresh memory of the insecurities of the end of Suharto's rule and widespread skepticism toward political leaders, the MUI offered clarity and guidance with its firm stance and punitive demands, supported by Susilo Bambang Yudhoyono. Harking back to the Indonesian Muslim Community Congress (Kongres Umat Islam Indonesia) in November 1998, when MUI scholars first agreed that Sharia-based arguments were to help the council create a new image and position, the council's strategy rested on four main pillars (Schäfer 2019): monopolizing the industry of halal certifications to ensure its financial independence; positioning the council's statements as always slightly more restrictive than NU and Muhammadiyah; creating distance from the government through a rhetoric of demands and critique while publicizing its advice to the government as demands; and establishing a rhetoric of "mainstream Islam" and "true Islam" and claiming to represent it.

Several encounters between MUI leader Ma'ruf Amin and National Police Chief Tito Karniavan in the context of the Ahok protests in December 2016 illustrate the tug-of-war between religious leaders and state actors and how fatwas function as a kind of über-law in contemporary Indonesia. After mass mobilization against Jakarta's Governor Ahok following an MUI statement in

2016, a debate on the place of fatwas in Indonesian society ensued between National Police Chief Tito Karniavan and MUI leader Ma'ruf Amin. Tito Karniavan had emphasized the nonbinding status of MUI fatwas (Putro 2016). Ma'ruf Amin responded that while fatwas indeed were not part of the positive law, they could be the basis of regulations (Sodikin 2016). Some reporters reproduced this statement more forcefully. The respective report in the widely disseminated Jakarta daily *Poskota*, for instance, stated that Ma'ruf Amin had once again called attention to the fact that despite being provisional, a specific fatwa must be perceived as a regulation (*Poskota News* 2016). Other news portals featured the latter part of the quote as their headline, thereby underlining the importance of fatwas as quasi regulations or regulations-to-be (VOA ISLAM 2016). In this brief power struggle between Tito Karniavan and Ma'ruf Amin, the latter had the final say.

Even more telling was Tito Karniavan's agreement to hold a press conference with elders of the so-called National Movement to Safeguard the Fatwa of the Indonesian Ulama Council (Gerakan Nasional Pengawal *Fatwa*, GNPF-MUI) ahead of the large December protest (Peterson 2020). On November 28, 2016, Tito met radical Islamists, such as Rizieq Shihab and Bachtiar Nasir, a Salafi Islamist and chairman of the newly founded group National Movement to Guard Ulama's Religious Edicts (Ketua Gerakan Nasional Pengawal *Fatwa*) at the MUI Headquarters in Menteng, Central Jakarta (CNN Indonesia 2016). Rizieq Shihab had been imprisoned for hate speech for a few months several years earlier but was just crafting his political comeback. Bachtiar Nasir had only recently become widely known due to his leadership in the GNPF-MUI. Tito then sat at a table with Ma'ruf Amin, the widely popular Islamic preacher Aa Gym, Rizieq Shihab, Bachtiar Nasir, and Police Inspector-General Boy Rafli Amar. Behind them were six other men, one of whom was Muhammad Zaitun Rasmin, the chairman of Wahdah Islamiyah, a Salafi organization based in Makassar whose leaders are known for political lobbying and influence (Chaplin 2021). Tito explained that the police were keen to avoid a repeat performance of the demonstration in November and expressed the police's willingness to assist with the logistics necessary to make the demonstration peaceful. Tito did not believe Ahok was guilty and yet here he was, at a nationwide televised press conference, placating a group of people calling for Ahok's conviction, one of whom, Rizieq Shihab, had been convicted of inciting violence against peaceful protestors in 2008. Rizieq made full use of this moment. He made demands of law enforcement officials and insisted that the police and attorney general and general prosecutor work together to finalize Ahok's case as quickly as possible and that the case then be provided to the court immediately as

Ahok's remarks had "already caused a national furore [*kegaduhan nasional*], even an international uproar [*heboh internasional*]." Rizieq then stated that since its establishment, GNPF-MUI's self-declared position has been "that MUI fatwas must be implemented by the state." Nobody raised the point that the issued statement in question was technically not even a fatwa but only a genre of advice called a "religious opinion and stance" (*pendapat dan sikap keagamaan*) and had therefore not been subjected to the usual processes and level of scrutiny of a MUI fatwa as prescribed in MUI's Organisational Administrative Guidelines (Peterson 2020, 146). The naming of the movement as "GNPF" (Guardians of the Fatwa) was thus strategic and symbolic, and lent religious and moral authority to the protests. This blurring of boundaries between formal religious edicts and political mobilization was part of GNPF's mobilizational power.

Tito Karniavan concluded the press conference flanked by the GNPF-MUI top brass, posed for photographs, and, at one point, even held hands with Rizieq Shihab and Ma'ruf Amin.

During the protest, Tito Karniavan ascended the stage, joining the GNPF-MUI personnel (Ichwan 2016). He told the crowd, "We have been in dialogue with GNPF-MUI for this event, as well as the legal process, and, praise be to God (alhamdullilah), two days ago, we handed the case file (berkas) over to the attorney-general and general prosecutor (kejaksaan), and yesterday we charged Basuki Tjahaja Purnama [with blasphemy]" (Wijaya 2016). Tito Karniavan conceded that the decision to charge Ahok was the result of the police bowing to public pressure.

The MUI—and those who later jumped on the bandwagon—used similar strategies and tactics as right-wing populist actors of the same period elsewhere, such as European nationalists demanding purification and homogenization along nationalist ideas. One of the MUI's first strategies was to make controversial provocative remarks to ensure its place in the headlines. Cherian George 2017, in his study of outrage-entrepreneurship, calls the MUI the "most influential purveyor of intolerance" (George 2017). Most importantly, the MUI pronounced "eye-catching punitive judgements" (Davies 2017) to spiral itself up in the public debates. William Davies's discussion of punitiveness and the rising popularity of far-right parties in Europe can be used for understanding Indonesian development as well. In this reading, a sense of injustice informs a yearning for punitiveness: "Many people ready to vote for populists have the feeling that in our society the innocent are punished and the guilty get away unpunished." This interpretation can be transferred to Indonesia's flawed legal system and growing socioeconomic inequalities. In 2005, the harsh fatwas against the Ahmadiyya, interfaith marriage, and secularism, pluralism, and liberalism gained the MUI its desired publicity. Whereas the leadership of the NU and Muhammadiyah had until then issued more nuanced opinions on these matters, the MUI now claimed much more restrictive positions. With these fatwas, which sparked much public debate, the council managed to dominate the political discussion for several weeks. As many political entrepreneurs elsewhere before them, they had successfully employed their controversial suggestions and demands to boost their significance.

The MUI's second main strategy was to create the public perception of autonomy of the government. It ensured that the public perceived it as an actor who challenges the government. It framed its positions as criticism, demands, and advice. What helped the council were not only its competitors' weakness but also the apparent simplicity and clarity of its own judgments. Despite internal disagreements and frictions (Hasyim 2013), the council conveyed an image of unity and offered crisp judgments on complicated matters. Believers were able to rely on clear guidance. Unlike the complex and often contradictory opinions coming from the NU and the Muhammadiyah, the MUI's statements were brisk and sharp. Again, the anti-Ahok fatwa is a case in point: The MUI fatwa confidently declared Ahok's statement blasphemous. It stated that the Surah Al-Maidah explicitly prohibited Jews and Christians from becoming political leaders. In the explanatory part of the fatwa, the council did not refer to other possible or existing interpretations of the Surah. The council thus set itself in sharp contrast to a political system perceived as murky and entangled in contradictions.

The MUI's third strategy lies in the realm of political economy. In a triple stroke, the MUI outwardly underlined its independence, gained actual financial means outside state funding and with donations from the large civil society organizations NU and Muhammadiyah (which constitute a large part of funding of the MUI), and put its foot on another marker of morality when it gained the monopoly on halal certification. To ensure its independence, or at least its perceived independence from government funding, the MUI seized the growing trend of halal certification. It became the single most respected inspector and certifier for halal labels on Indonesian products and foreign products in the Indonesian market (Hasyim 2013; Lindsey 2012). Lawmakers collaborated closely with the MUI in the lucrative commercial areas of pilgrimage management and halal certification, allowing them the accumulation of symbolic and financial capital. After 1989, the council held a near monopoly in halal certification for nearly three decades. In October 2017, the MORA eventually handed this authority to the newly established Halal Products Certification Agency. However, the agency still depended on MUI fatwas to issue halal certificates, and the MUI retained the authority to certify halal auditors (Sapiie 2017). Also in 2017, the MORA handed the management of pilgrimage funds to the new Hajj Fund Management Agency. This implemented a 2008 law on hajj administration (Alfitri 2018) that confirmed the minister of religion as the sole organizer and chief coordinator of the government's "national duty" to assist pilgrims as well as introduced two new bodies that dilute the ministry's once comprehensive authority in this area (Lindsey 2012). A second new body was the Indonesian Hajj Supervisory Commission (Komisi Pengawas Haj Indonesia, KPHI). Separately funded from the state budget, it monitors the ministry and reports annually to the president and the parliament. Of the KPHI's nine members, three are appointed by the ministry and six must be members of MUI or another Muslim social organization. Thus, in the key areas of halal certification and haj management, the government became the sole authority, but it conceded important roles to the MUI.

Finally, the MUI assumes the role of the overall representative of Muslim organizations and thus "acts as the arbiter of mainstream Islam in Indonesia" (Hasyim 2015). The MUI benefits from the notion of Mainstream Islam and from the discursive connections to the notion of true Islam.

In combination, these four strategies have ensured that many Indonesians perceive the MUI as both autonomous of and influential on the state. For the first time in Indonesian history, there is one centralized Muslim authority acknowledged both by the state apparatus and large parts of civil society. At the end of the 2010s, the MUI held the monopoly on representing so-called Mainstream Islam that it has helped nurture. This monopoly was uncontested between 2005 and 2016. In 2016, however, in the wake of the Ahok rallies, hitherto marginal extremist organizations employed the strategies of the MUI and have since been acting side by side with the MUI in a complicated mix of cooperation and competition for the domination over defining what Islam is.

Indonesia's Fourfold Decentralization in the Post-1998 Period

In the post-1998 period, decentralization and reregulation shaped political developments. In this section, I highlight four intersecting areas in which authority fragmented and decentralized: elections, civil society, media, and religious authorities. The last of these four areas is the most important to understand in the context of the construction of Mainstream Islam, partly because much of the excellent ethnographic work on religious authorities is most starkly disconnected from scholarship on formal politics.

Patronage Democracy: Elections Between Oligarchy and Neoliberal Competition

Despite the global popularity of the term *democracy* and the rapid spreading of elections, scholars have documented a global wave of authoritarianization. So, then, "why bother with elections?" asked the political scientist Adam Przeworski (2018). He discusses the various meanings and uses of elections across a range of regimes. According to Przewosrski, elections do indeed matter, because when elections are competitive and the result hard to predict, it does make a difference who wins. This argument is important in Indonesia, even if elections are only one among many political practices, and even if money politics crucially shape these elections and turn them into something far from the ideal of being free and fair. Elections matter. But they do not, as Przeworksi also states, deliver rational or just policies. Elected governments neither outperform authoritarian ones in terms of wealth creation, nor do they tackle economic inequality in a better way. But, Przeworksi argues, we should nevertheless value elections for two other instrumental reasons: They minimize popular dissatisfaction with laws, and they allow societies to regulate conflicts peacefully. In Przeworksi's view, elections have pacifying qualities, even in authoritarian regimes.

One could make the case that for large parts of the electorate in a patronage democracy such as Indonesia, elections amount to what scholars of workplace participation and management call pseudoparticipation, offering the illusion of openness in a realm of top-down decision-making. Edward Aspinall and Ward Berenschot (2019) have offered a detailed analysis of the way regional elections in Indonesia work through networks and brokers who organize votes for candidates. They built their argument on a body of literature that had shown to what a large degree the old New Order elites were still in power (Winters et al. 2000), just as after many other political transitions (Albertus and Menaldo 2018).

Civil Society

The ease of restrictions and the possibilities of relatively unrestrained political activism coincided with a shift that had elsewhere been referred to as the NGOization of social movements: the professionalization, bureaucratization, and institutionalization of social movements (Choudry and Kapoor 2013). Scholars and observers often subsume a great variety of religious actors under the term *civil society*, despite their close relationships with state actors and institutions.

Mary Kaldor (2003) groups conceptions of civil society into five categories: those based entirely on the rule of law and civility (*societas civilis*), those with all social life organized between the state and the family (*bürgerliche Gesellschaft*), those based on social movements and civic activism, those based on charities and voluntary associations, and those based on various movements, including ones that pursue nationalism and fundamentalist goals (a range of organizations that others have called "uncivil society"). To understand the developments of postreform Indonesia, it is not sufficient to focus on the third group of social movements and civic activism, nor is it particularly valuable to simply denounce some actors as "uncivil," especially given the complex internal dynamics of many religious organizations.

Initially, in the young republic of the 1950s and 1960s, still carried by the spirit of hard-won independence and collective developmentalism, Indonesians engaged in labor unions, women's organizations, peasant associations, and religious organizations. In those years, civil society was highly polarized, reflecting and deepening sociopolitical cleavages in the country's political life. Most large civil society organizations were affiliated to political parties that had strived to maximize their political power and had differing ideological visions for the Indonesian society (Mujani 2020).

In the following decades of authoritarian rule, the state became the common enemy for many associations. Even though restrictions during the authoritarian rule seriously hampered the development of civil society, the number of civil society organizations grew in the late New Order. The number of NGOs grew from only a handful in the 1970s to about three thousand in the 1980s and approximately six thousand in the 1990s (Beittinger-Lee 2013). Various international foundations, such as the Ford Foundation, Asia Foundation, and the German political party–associated foundations Friedrich Naumann Stiftung and Friedrich Ebert Stiftung, had long-standing presences in the country and began to fund human rights organizations and other Indonesian NGOs from the 1980s onward.

In the mid-1990s, bilateral donors such as the US Agency for International Development and Australian Agency for International Development (AusAid) began launching democracy assistance programs; the main beneficiaries were NGOs (Fox and Menchik 2011; Fox 2018). In that decade, public discourse on civil society in Indonesia grew and became more divisive. Public intellectuals and politicians, often having returned from overseas education, such as Abdurrahman Wahid, Amien Rais, Arief Budiman, Azyumadi Azra, A. S. Hikam, Nurcholis Madjid, and Ryaas Rasyid, promoted their own notions and terms of civil society. Nurcholis Madjid popularized his idea of civil society, named *masyarakat madani*, through the Paramadina Foundation

(Ramstedt 2019). Abdurrahman Wahid and A. S. Hikam initiated and formed NU's civil society discourse (Künkler, Madeley, and Shankar 2018; Ramstedt 2019).

Indonesia was part of a global rise of NGOs, usually founded and supported under the label "civil society." The biggest donors worldwide are international agencies such as the World Bank, International Monetary Fund, and USAID (Choudry and Kapoor 2013). The term *civil society* as used and supported by donor agencies, such as governments and NGOs, usually refers to a small set of organizations: professionalized NGOs engaged in advocacy or civic education on public interest issues (Ottaway and Carothers 2000). Short-term and decentralized donations have incentivized social movement groups to professionalize, meaning to demonstrate managerial and technical capabilities to signal capacity and accountability to donors (Alvarez 2009; Smith and Jenkins 2011; Ungsuchaval 2020). Previously loosely organized, horizontally dispersed organizations transformed into more professionalized "vertically structured, policy-outcome-oriented NGOs focusing on generating issue-specific and marketable expert services or knowledge," a process that has been called NGOization (Lang 2013). These incentives for greater professionalization excluded groups with low levels of managerialism (Choudry and Kapoor 2010). Critics highlight the proximity to power and raise questions concerning the representativeness, legitimacy, and accountability of NGOs (Jordan and van Tuijl 2012). Many NGOs are urban-based and elitist, distanced from the people on whose behalf they advocate (Okafor 2006). Heavy reliance on foreign donors carries significant risks, particularly the tendency to reduce social movements to liberal values that align with economic restructuring—evident in neoliberal programs, as seen in Indonesia's case.

For Indonesian Islam, scholars usually identified two camps in debates on the term and concept of civil society: the "traditionalists" such as NU sympathizers, who mostly used the English term "civil society" or its direct translation, *masyarakat sipil*; and the "modernists," mostly Muslim intellectuals and members of Muhammadiyah, who preferred the term *masyarakat madani* (Noer 1973). While the latter term can have different interpretations, it usually refers to an Islamic-inspired vision of civil society, although the distinctly Islamic character often remained nebulous. *Masyarakat* is an Indonesian word meaning "society." *Madani* refers, according to some modernist scholars, to the Arabic word *madaniyah* meaning "civility," and, for others, to the society of Medina in the seventh century. Even though some traditionalist scholars have accused modernists of being Islamist, and the latter have criticized NU of being too Western influenced, the main difference between the two streams is less about religion, which plays a role in both concepts, and more about the relation between civil society and the state. Whereas for many NU scholars and activists, civil society was meant to be autonomous from and external to the state, in the view of many modernists, civil society and the state could have strong links and overlaps (Baso 1999). In line with the importance of religion in these concepts, part of the revival of independent associational life in the 1990s came in the form of Islamic study groups, or so-called Campus Islam. They quickly turned political. The Tanjung Priok Massacre is often cited as a turning point near the end of the New Order: The brutal attack in 1984 against angry citizens who were protesting because a neighborhood security officer was said to have stepped into a mosque without removing his shoes saw several dozen people killed. This and similar acts of violence and the tireless work of civil society actors to point them out contributed significantly to the destabilization of Suharto's regime (Hasyim 2013; Suaedy 2016).

After the fall of Suharto, Habibie lifted most restrictions on civil society and citizen participation. He publicly embraced the idea of a strong masyarakat madani in the new democratic order (Bush 2015). Greater civil and political freedoms resulted in an unmatched civil society boom. The freedom of assembly and association paved the way for countless new NGOs, labor unions, student associations, networks, and newspapers. NGOs were the big winners of the time because international aid agencies promoted them as partners in their programs to overcome the social and economic impacts of the 1998 economic crisis and to support democratic actors, institutions, and processes (Dwi et al. 2012; Halili 2016). Between 1996 and 2002, the number of NGOs grew from approximately ten thousand to seventy thousand (Parlina 2013). Abroad and at home, expectations were high that Indonesia would transform into a liberal democracy.

International donor agencies were estimated to make up 85 to 90 percent of funding for NGOs (McGlynn Scanlon and Alawiyah 2015). A report commissioned by the Australian government in 2013 estimated the total donor assistance to the NGO sector overall in Indonesia during that year at approximately USD 340 million. The report found the revenue highly concentrated in the hand of a relatively small group of organizations based in urban centers. Organizations located outside of provincial and district capitals have since had little access to international donor agencies. According to the report, the richest quartile of national NGOs received USD 1.6 million in 2013, whereas the poorest quartile of subnational NGOs, including provincial level ones, obtained less than USD 125,000. The largest parts of USAID's democracy assistance went to civil society organizations (USAID 2018, 136).

After a peak of USD 60 million in 2002, the funding by USAID to Indonesian civil society organizations steadily declined, with brief rises during election years (USAID 2018, 136). In the election year 2019, the funding amount increased to USD 5.9 million and in 2020 declined to USD 1 million (www.foreignassistance.gov, n.d.). AusAid, which was the largest donor in Indonesia in 2010 with a USD 450 million program, is particularly keen to avoid conflict with the Indonesian government and therefore instructed its staff to avoid politically sensitive activities (Mietzner 2012). AusAid also refuses to promote civil society groups that are critical of the Indonesian government (Aspinall and Mietzner 2010). However, Aspinall (2013) also emphasizes that local NGOs have a high degree of agency, sometimes directing foreign agendas as much as being appropriated by them.

The remaking of Indonesia was, according to the criteria of the international donors, relatively successful: Aspinall finds that donors increasingly aligned their programs with those of the Indonesian government and moved away from the civil society support that characterized their programs earlier on. They partly did so because they regarded Indonesian democracy as stable and ranked the efficacy of government institutions highest on their agenda (Aspinall 2010). This, predictably, clashed with experiences on the ground: He quotes a USAID staffer in Jakarta as saying that "it's a constant struggle in the field to make the case to Washington that it's important to keep support levels high. The "success story" view is the prevailing view in headquarters . . . , but not in the field here in Indonesia" (Aspinall 2010). Mietzner points out the Australian government's desire to avoid conflict: "[AusAid], whose US$450 million program made it the largest donor in Indonesia in 2010, was particularly anxious about avoiding conflict with the Jakarta government and thus instructed its employees to shun politically sensitive activities" (Mietzner 2012).

Some scholars had been skeptical from the outset. Verena Beittinger-Lee contends Indonesia's civil society played a relatively insignificant role, pointing to a lack of professionalism among the civil society organizations, competition among various actors, and segmentation of civil society along primordial lines as evidence. She also highlights the important role of what she calls "un-civil society" organizations (Beittinger-Lee 2013). Of course, such attempts to differentiate analytically between "civil" and "un-civil" illustrate the intertwinements of scholarship and political decision-making. In this area, the most important donor has been Saudi Arabia. Although much has been written about the influence of the Saudi government on Islam abroad through funding of educational institutions, publishers, and organizations, reliable numbers are impossible to obtain. Vedi Hadiz's

(2021) perspective sophisticates the narrative that Indonesia is merely a battleground between Western liberalism and Saudi Wahabi Islam: He argues that some of the popularity of Islamic discourse is built on the ashes of the Indonesian left and that "social grievances related to endemic issues like social injustice are increasingly being framed through Islamic cultural references."

In all these accounts, the dependence on the part of local civil society from international donors and influence is evident, as is the stark difference between internationally funded NGOs and local organizations without access to such funding. Indonesia's civil society is fragmented in various ways: separated vertically largely along operating in different frameworks, for instance, those using a religious framework versus those working with a focus on pluralism and human rights, and horizontally depending on their proximity and distance to the powers-that-be, either national or international. The high level of political competition and the digital divide in the use of media further enhanced this fragmentation, which adds to the fleeting character of many alliances.

Media

The end of authoritarian rule in 1998 ushered in an exhilarating but unsettled period of democratization in Indonesia that very much concerned the public sphere. When elections were first held in 1998, television had already long been an important medium for the urban middle classes, and it continued to spread rapidly to rural areas where whole neighborhoods would gather around a single TV set. A politician's appearance, charisma, and screen performance were still secondary to his or her personal networks in the early 2000s, but by the time Jokowi ran for the governorship of Jakarta in 2012, he was able to make ample use of the media to increase his popularity and beat his well-connected contender Fauzi Bowo. Similar to some Latin American leaders and to the Thai politician-cum-businessman Thaksin Shinawatra, Jokowi engaged in a relationship with media that was very productive for him (Hamid 2014). This was a subtler and more sophisticated way of using media coverage than simply using his own TV and radio stations, as the Italian media magnate and politician Silvio Berlusconi had done in the early 1990s and early 2000s, but it followed some of the same principles. Scholars in media studies and political science have used terms such as *media democracy* or *mediocracy* (T. Meyer and Hinchman 2002), and videocracy (Mazzoleni 1995) to analyze the influence of mediatization on processes of political representation.

In Indonesia, since electoral democracy was reintroduced in 1998 simultaneously with the rise of digital information networks, political processes have been shaped even more strongly by the importance of visual and online media (Strassler 2019). The success and failure of individual politicians can often be traced back to their relationship with the media: Before Jokowi ran for governorship he served as the mayor of Surakarta, and during this period, he developed his signature *blusukan*—unannounced spot checks at offices, accompanied by media. He also paid impromptu visits to slums, during which he wore simple, informal clothes, listened, and witnessed firsthand issues addressed by residents such as the price of food, housing difficulties, flooding, and transportation. The media coverage of these visits significantly contributed to his popularity. Several scholars have tried to explain this phenomenon by describing Jokowi as a populist (Mietzner 2015), but the importance of mediatized politics tells us more about how during the information age, the outcomes of elections and other political processes must be analyzed with view to the respective media dynamics.

During the New Order and under its heavy censorship, Indonesians used creative techniques for criticizing the government and developed a mediascape that was "stretching the Indonesian state's capacity to control" (Hill and Sen 2005). After 1998, most censorship laws were dropped and basic media freedom was legally enshrined. Indonesia's press became one of the freest in Asia. However, several limitations on press freedom passed at the time still remain active: those enshrined in the so-called blasphemy law and the Law No. 11/2008 on Information and Electronic Transactions Law. The use of both laws increased in the 2010s. Beyond the legal realm, Indonesia continues to be one of the most dangerous countries for journalists. Observers and human rights organizations report that authorities rarely prosecute attacks against journalists, including those by state security forces (Human Rights Watch 2017).

In addition to these limitations, which are covered in detail in press freedom reports and liberal democracy indices, two main developments shape postreform media in Indonesia: the increasing commercialization of an already oligarchic ownership structure and a dramatic shift toward electronic media. None of these characteristics are unique to Indonesia. Berlusconi's capture of Italian democracy through his private media empire was one of the early examples of the ways in which concentrated media ownership affected elections (Curran 2011). In various democratic theories and in empirical democracy studies, the importance of free and open debates has always been central. Several European languages refer to the press as the Fourth Power or the Fourth Estate (German: *Vierte Gewalt*; Spanish: *cuarto poder*; French: *quatrième pouvoir*) that complements the legislative, executive, and judicial branches. Free and open debates are at the center not only of minimalist liberal but also of deliberative and agonistic notions of democracy. Yet, the spread of TV and later the rapid digitalization of communication challenged many assumptions of these theories and highlighted the incompleteness of the dominant ways of gauging freedom of expression (Fleuß and Schaal 2019). While governments continue to constrain freedom of expression, the larger threats to democracy arise from ownership structures and commercial orientations.

In Indonesia, privatization in the 1980s and 1990s paved the way for a boom in commercial broadcast media. The accumulation of power and capital also affects the media sector (Dhakidae 1991; Sudibyo and Patria 2013; Tapsell 2014). Indonesia's hundreds of newspapers and television and radio stations and thousands of online media sites are in the hands of a small group of owners (George 2017; M. Lim 2012; Tapsell 2017). Some of these are media focused, such as Kompas Gramedia Group and the Jawa Pos Group, but other owners are oligarchs who include media as part of their wealth and power accumulations, such as Golkar Party Chairman Aburizal Bakri, who owns Visi Media Asia; Nasdem Party founder Surya Paloh, who owns Media Group; and Perindo founder Hary Tanoesoedibjo, who owns Media Nusantara Citra Group (George 2017; Dhyatmika 2014). Ross Tapsell (2017) describes these owners as media oligopolists who rely on multiplatform portfolios or "digital ecosystems" that increasingly connect news to event management and travel as well as to housing, job, and communication portals. Advertiser-friendly decisions have transformed many media outlets into more consumer-oriented, lifestyle, and entertainment venues. This has come "at the expense of news and information required for the country's civic health" (Tapsell 2017) and "journalism's public service mission" (George and Venkiteswaran 2019). Any subscriber to *The Jakarta Post* will have noticed the regular invitations to events on financial and investment consultancy. A perhaps obvious consequence of this ownership structure is that some owners use or offer their media outlets as campaign vehicles that only print favorable information about the owner (George and Venkiteswaran 2019). An example of suppression of negative coverage is the environmental disaster in 2006 involving an oil and gas company owned by Aburizal Bakrie, who was then welfare minister. He bought a newspaper in the region, which subsequently covered the company more favorably (Tapsell 2010). Joko Widodo's election campaign also relied on a network of oligarchs and their media to turn him from an outsider into a frontrunner (Tapsell 2014). He maintained the strategy in 2019 to defend his position.

The lack of public support for journalism as a key element of democracy also results in a low level of professional training for most journalists. Funding for the establishment and maintenance of quality journalism is difficult to come by in most societies and even more so in postauthoritarian ones and those characterized by precarious labor. Without social safety nets in place, it is easier for politicians and civil society actors to offer incentives like cash transfers and employment opportunities for favorable coverage. These widespread practices are less discussed in the literature on media in Indonesia but studied in more detail in several African countries under the key phrase *brown envelope journalism*. This term describes cash secretly given to a journalist on a reporting mission; other types of incentives, such as meals and freebies; and, to some extent, institutional corruption (Skjerdal 2003). In Indonesia, journalists are often offered compensation for their "transportation costs" and then receive a higher amount in cash if they commit to favorable coverage. This makes it easier for actors with respective funds to influence reporting. Not all media employ salaried journalists but often encourage freelancing. The economic dependencies add to practices of self-censorship (Tapsell 2012). One Shi'a activist noted in a conversation with me that many journalists she talks to were not trained in ethical questions and therefore were unaware of the problematic of discrimination and biased coverage. She says she often persuades journalists to soften their coverage. She would explain to journalists the plight of members of targeted groups and also offer them modest compensation for their troubles.

The other major development that has shaped Indonesian public discussions is rapid digitalization. Indonesians began using the internet in the second half of the 1990s. Even in smaller towns, many embraced the new connection to the rest of the world and spent hours in ubiquitous internet cafés (*warung internet / warnet*) (Hill and Sen 2005). In dark and stuffy rooms promising sweet instant coffees and anonymity, they would spend hours reading and contributing to mailing lists. These mailing lists played their part in bringing down Suharto. Soon after that, smart phones became widely popular (Hill and Sen 1997; M. Lim 2012; Y. Nugroho et al. 2012; Purbo 2017). They were key status symbols and contributed to the rapid mobilization of online communication. Users and observers held high hopes for the internet to democratize: Everyone would be able to chime in, and every voice would be heard now! This optimism was not unique to Indonesia or other postauthoritarian societies but characterized public debates on the internet everywhere. Even as late as 2011, long after the internet had been commercialized, global media celebrated the Arab Spring as a "Twitter Uprising" and "Facebook Revolution."

After a period of enthusiasm and "technological utopianism" (M. Lim 2018) in the 1990s, a more sober and even bleaker view of the effects of the increasing presence of digital networks began to dominate scholarly and public debates (Pariser 2011; Sunstein 2003). In the late 2010s, many observers connected the global surge of right-wing nationalism on digital media (Fuchs 2020; M. Lim 2017; Schroeder 2019). Public debates and studies in various fields and disciplines discussed the ways in which digital networks (usually referred to as "social media") in recent political events in the United States and Europe contributed to the weakening of democracy. They argue that social networking platforms and their algorithms provide a fertile ground for the growth of nationalist and right-wing populist rhetoric by doing any of the following: serving as a direct link to people and allowing populists to circumvent traditional journalistic and political gatekeepers (Engesser et al. 2017; Schroeder 2019); exacerbating the polarization of society (Wirz 2018), particularly via echo chambers and "filter bubbles" (Spohr 2017; Sunstein 2018); assisting the proliferation of hate speech and racist/discriminatory messages (Cleland, Anderson, and Aldridge-Deacon 2018); and facilitating the spread of mis- and disinformation and amplifying populist and extremist voices (Govil and Baishya 2018; Marwick and Lewis 2017). A well-known example was the case of the British company Cambridge Analytica. The political consulting firm harvested some 87 million Facebook profiles and used the data to sway voters during the 2016 campaign. Many observers concluded that the company significantly contributed to the election of Donald Trump in 2016. Putting aside questions of cybersecurity and the use of digital network bots (automated programs mimicking human users), it is clear that previously marginal right-wing political actors successfully developed strategies that allowed them to benefit from the omnipresence of digital communication.

One strategy of right-wing populists in the United States and the United Kingdom has been to make a great sway of attacking elites, regardless of the challengers' own elitist backgrounds (Davies 2018). Combining politics and daily news with entertainment, their styles rely on making strong, eye-catching quasi-violent judgments, as discussed in explaining the rise of the MUI. The most well-known example is Trump's tagline for his competitor Hillary Clinton during the 2016 presidential campaign: "Lock her up!" Trump's successful candidacy as an outsider can to some degree be explained by the media giving him a platform: The media will return to these figures because they know they will get the stark judgments that ensure attention in an economy of too much data and heavy competition for attention (Davies 2018).

In Indonesia, those taking up arms are not only politicians but also religious authorities and others using and enhancing the popularity of Islam in popular culture (Rakhmani 2016). Indonesia offers some superlatives for those interested in the politics of digital media in terms of sheer numbers, but in this deeply unequal society, many lack accesses to digital media. In some areas, whole neighborhoods regularly gather around a single TV set. In a village on an island in northern Sulawesi, I once watched a young man climb a tree and raise his arm up into the air: He was, his neighbors explained to me, sending off an SMS text message from the island's only spot with network coverage. Others describe similar scenes in different parts in the archipelago (Pisani 2014). The internet, then, exacerbated many of the more general problems of the post-Suharto period but also led to renegotiations (Slama 2021). What David T. Hill and Krishna Sen (1997) have discussed as an effect of digital media in the newly democratizing country in the late 1990s did characterize large parts of the political developments in the 2000s and 2010s: "the Internet may be at best yet another index of inequality, at worst yet another impediment to equal participation in an emerging democracy."

Yet the digital divide goes beyond the mere question of access. In the 2020s, with a global mobile phone penetration of more than 90 percent, the divide concerns access to more bandwidth, skills to participate in the exchange of information, and the education to digest the available information (Purbo 2017). This kind of specific digital literacy (Rheingold 2014) is not sufficiently prioritized in most education systems, including the Indonesian one (Jurriens and Tapsell 2017). Stark differences in levels of education result in stark differences in the abilities to digest available information and to be able to identify "fake news." Rumors thrive under such circumstances, and they contribute significantly to creating an environment in which violence perpetrated by small groups against some identities becomes acceptable to silent majorities. In the Indonesian cases discussed in the following chapters, it becomes clear that politicians often fan rumors rather than try to curb them. In addition to the obvious consequence of adding to the resentments against marginalized identities, another consequence of this is a general atmosphere of mistrust.

Another development that the Indonesian experiences highlight is the focus on individual candidates and their media representations. Scholars have been debating "the personalization of politics" and its relationship to "the rise of the electronic media and their insatiable appetite for visual images" (McAllister 2012). Given the near indistinguishability of promises, platforms, and policies of Indonesian parties (with the exception of the Islamist PKS), the rhetoric and media representation of individual authorities is especially important. Nowhere has this become more visible than in the realm of religious authority, where preachers and religious entrepreneurs have in the 2000s and 2010s developed various ways of cultivating online and offline followership (Alatas 2021; Akmaliah 2020; Fakhruroji 2019; Pabbajah et al. 2021; Slama 2017; Solahudin and Fakhruroji 2020).

Diversification and Pluralization of Islamic Authority and Authorities—but Not of Opinions

Muslims seeking religious advice are flooded with different options via a variety of channels. Before the arrival of European colonialists and concepts, a Muslim in distress had relatively few options: a local Islamic cleric of authority would readily dispense moral advice. He, or in some rare cases, she, would know the circumstances of the advice-seeker's life and take them into account. Clerics would base their advice their own interpretations of the Quran and the hadith. If the believer had doubts, they theoretically had the option of seeking the advice of another learned scholar, and then the advice seeker would use this and their own wisdom to form a conclusion. For the more immobile among the advice-seekers, the local imam was the main and perhaps sole authority. Today, a pious believer who wants to find out the right thing to do will most likely be torn between several options, such as consulting their local *kyai*, (Islamic religious teacher or scholar) browsing through the latest issue of their favored Islamic organization's news bulletin and websites, or searching online for the advice of a famous ulama abroad. There are thousands of lectures and Q&A sessions with Islamic scholars on YouTube and other websites to choose from. Where to turn? Or, to put it differently, who speaks for Islam?

Religious authority in late modernity is characterized by the tension between the increased bureaucratic regulation of the modern nation-state and simultaneously increased competition, marketization, and individualization. *Authority* and *authorities* are terms often used interchangeably, but they denote different aspects within an analysis of power. Authorities are actors who hold concrete positions. They relate to other actors in terms of interest, dependency, and competition. Religious authorities are men and women who claim, project, and exert religious authority within a given context (Krämer and Schmidtke 2006). The way authorities argue and engage or avoid engagement with one another influences their authority. "Religious authority can assume a number of forms and functions: the ability (chance, power, or right) to define correct belief and practice, or orthodoxy and orthopraxy, respectively; to shape and influence the views and conduct of others accordingly; to identify, marginalize, punish or exclude deviance, heresy and apostasy and their agents and advocates" (Krämer and Schmidtke 2006). Authority, on the other hand, denotes a form of definitive ability and power, and it can come in different forms. "Religious authority . . . may be embodied in certain notions, in texts, in individual persons, in groups of persons, and in institutions in the widest sense of the word" (Kaptein 2004). It is also not static but built and cultivated (Alatas 2021). The respect held for ulama in a society for centuries depended on their lineage, interpretative skills, education, and relationship to the ruler. "The worst of scholars is he who visits princes" begins an often-quoted hadith (F. Robinson 2009). To what degree this holds true for a democratically elected government after a dictatorship is one of the many questions that Indonesians have been debating with renewed rigor since 1998.

The shapes that Muslim authority and authorities have taken in the twentieth century illustrate the simultaneous increased regulation and decentralization that have contributed to developing Mainstream Islam. Radio, tapes, and electronic media fixed some interpretations of religion and diversified others. Formal religious education became more important: those returning from Al-Azhar and other famous Middle Eastern institutions of Islamic learning proudly brought their certificates with them; national institutions and religious organizations began to issue their own certificates and further regulated religious authority (Feener and Cammack 2007; Hallaq 2009; M. B. Hooker 2003; M. B. Hooker and V. Hooker 2006). On the other hand, scholars trained in traditional ways now also competed with other figures who lack formal education but excelled in new media, such as radio, TV, and later digital media. In late modernity, individual believers have come to pick and choose from a wide range of possible sources of religious guidance. Decentralization and simultaneous regulation developed in close connection and influenced each other. Echoing the seemingly contradictory double developments of the MUI—increased competition and simultaneous increased regulation—the MORA signaled in the 2010s that it might favor and work toward a stricter regime of supervision and control in the form of certifying particular preachers (Millie, Syarif, and Fakhruroji 2019). This would be a significant shift and enhance the tendency of tighter competition and regulation. We see here the paradox of homogenization of belief and at the same time increasing heterogenization. In the liberalized environment and the rapidly expanding field of religious consumption and popular preaching, old and new religious authorities began to compete for devotees and clients and for access to political decision-makers. Particularly urban Indonesians changed the way religious authority operated. They transformed the loyal allegiances their parents and grandparents held to particular religious authorities into shorter periods of followership for exchangeable candidates.

These followerships came to matter politically in the highly competitive landscape of the 2000s and 2010s (Saat and Burhani 2020). The best-studied example of a successful alliance of a popular preacher and a politician is that between the aforementioned Aa Gym and Yudhoyono (Hoesterey 2016). Aa Gym, an influential Islamic preacher known for his emphasis on Manajemen Qolbu (Management of the Heart), became a household name in the early 2000s, particularly among Indonesia's growing middle class. His sermons blended Islamic teachings with motivational self-improvement themes, appealing to urban, modern Muslims who sought a synthesis of religious piety and personal success. Yudhoyono recognized Aa Gym's growing influence and strategically aligned himself with the preacher to bolster his credibility among pious Muslim voters. Religious entrepreneurs like Aa Gym and those who imitated his methods significantly contributed to normalizing socially conservative values and tying them closely to Islam while simultaneously offering political elites a pathway to secure religious legitimacy. Aa Gym's influence waned after his polygamy scandal in 2006, which alienated much of his modern, middle-class audience, particularly women. This highlights the volatility of preacher-politician alliances in Indonesia's competitive media and electoral landscape.

Highly connected middle-class Muslims, many of them women, organize Islamic study gatherings (*majelis taklim*), often independently from the established Islamic organizations and Islamic political parties. Observers have highlighted the "ideological flexibility" of these gatherings, and the broad variety of preachers a particular group can host (Slama 2019). This flexibility allows religious and political leaders to mobilize religious attachment and followership in a highly competitive political landscape. This mobilizational power materialized in the demonstrations against Ahok in 2015 and 2016.

Jokowi himself did not initially seek the proximity of religious leaders in a comparable way when he assumed office in 2014 but religion had by then already become so important that the anti-Ahok protests in 2016–17 eventually overwhelmed him and prompted him to craft a new strategy of facing and handling the Islamist Conservative Majoritarian Synthesis.

This chapter has examined the rise of *Mainstream Islam* in Indonesia as part of a broader trend toward religious homogenization. Far from being a rupture, this trajectory builds on processes of regulation, bureaucratization, and the marginalization of religious diversity that began in the colonial era and were later institutionalized by the postcolonial Indonesian state. The MORA played a pivotal role in defining "religion" in monotheistic terms, leading to the exclusion and marginalization of local beliefs, while the New Order regime further entrenched these hierarchies under its authoritarian control.

I have argued that the post-1998 period amplified these earlier dynamics, driven by a **fourfold decentralization** of elections, civil society, media, and religious authority. This new competitive environment empowered nonstate actors, including Islamist groups and popular preachers, to shape public debates and influence policy. The MUI, which reinvented itself after Suharto's fall, emerged as a central authority promoting punitive fatwas and moral regulation, while individual preachers like Aa Gym leveraged media and neoliberal discourses to align piety with modern aspirations.

The chapter highlights the instabilities of the 2000s and 2010s. Compared to countries of the Organisation for Economic Co-operation and Development, Indonesia has been characterized by more income mobility over shorter time spans at the top and especially at the bottom of income distribution (OECD 2018). Income mobility translated into more opportunities but also into greater risks of hard falls down the ladder. The resulting insecurities had effects on the political culture. The rise of opportunity and risk for individuals, reflected in a rise of household debt and greater social mobility, incentivized politicians, religious leaders, and others in the public realm to outbid each other with public statements and policies that attracted attention. In the postreform era, in which religion enjoyed the image of being modern, moral, and cosmopolitan, statements pertaining to religion were particularly popular, and many political leaders sought the proximity of religious leaders. The chapter introduces the concept of the **Islamist Conservative Majoritarian Synthesis**, drawing on parallels with Turkey's TIS but highlighting that the Indonesian variant has been more bottom-up than the Turkish variant.

In Indonesia, the convergence of religious regulation and political competition has contributed to the construction of Mainstream Islam. This chapter has shown how national and religious homogenization intertwine, laying the groundwork for the more explicit policing of orthodoxy discussed in the following chapters. The term *synthesis* rather than merely *alliance* underscores the long-lasting effects of discourses that outlive temporal political alliances, such as those seen during the anti-Ahok protests of 2016–17. Politicians since then routinely factor in the mobilizational power of Islam, demonstrating how these alliances have reshaped decision-making processes well beyond their immediate context. Moreover, this synthesis highlights the role of unintentional discursive effects and points out that minority-rights discourses, in countering majoritarian pressures, have inadvertently reinforced the notion of *Mainstream Islam*, further marginalizing the very minorities they aim to protect.

CHAPTER 2

The Making of Mainstream Islam
Ahmadiyya and Shi'a to the Margins

On June 1, 2011, a coalition of activists—human rights advocates, Christians, Ahmadis, and Shi'a Muslims—who on any other day would have passionately disagreed about their beliefs took to the streets in central Jakarta to defend themselves against attacks and accusations that had been leveled against them. The diverse coalition called itself the National Alliance for Freedom of Faith and Religion. They had joined forces to demand that the state protect religious minorities from attacks on their religious sites, schools, and homes. Various vigilantes, most of all members of the Islamic Defenders Front (FPI), were responsible for the attacks, and the state had done little to prevent the violence or prosecute the perpetrators. The protesters chose June 1 because it was Pancasila Day in Indonesia, when the country's founding national motto is celebrated. The protestors wanted to resuscitate pluralist interpretations of the Pancasila. Azyumardi Azra, reformist Muslim scholar and public intellectual, had proposed this strategy just after the fall of Suharto as way of countering violence framed in religious terms. The idea was to turn—or return—the Pancasila into a common ideological platform and a symbol of tolerance and pluralism (Bourchier 2019, 719). The idea failed to win over large crowds, partly because Suharto had also used the Pancasila and the concept was too slippery and versatile to spark real enthusiasm. On June 1, FPI members and others violently attacked the protest and injured several activists. Police officers stood by, either unable or unwilling to curb the violence. Nine days after the attack on the Jakarta protest, three state ministries issued a joint decree banning the activities of the Ahmadiyya, one of the minority groups the protesters sought to protect from discrimination. What exactly the decree meant by "activities" was left vague. Established in India in 1889 by Mirza Ghulam Ahmad, who claimed to be the awaited Mahdi (redeemer) and *mujaddid* (renovator), the Ahmadiyya soon split into two groups after Ahmad's death: the Ahmadiyya Anjuman Ishaat-i-Islam (Lahore Ahmadiyya Movement) and the Ahmadiyya Muslim Community. After the first Ahmadis arrived in Java in the 1920s, their initially amicable relations with the modernizing Islamic organization Muhammadiyah broke down in 1929 due to differences regarding the status of Mirza Ghulam Ahmad. The mass Muslim civil society organizations have shunned the Ahmadiyya ever since (Beck 2005). In South Asia, many Muslim groups accused the Ahmadis of dividing the *umma* and thus of weakening the anticolonial struggle. In 1974, the Saudi-led Muslim World League issued a fatwa declaring the Ahmadis non-Muslim. Ahmadis were accused of claiming Mirza Ghulam Ahmad as a prophet, distributing corrupted versions of the Quran, and seeking to abolish jihad as a concept and practice. This latter charge was connected to the political accusation of being agents of imperialism and Zionism. In Southeast Asia, similar fatwas were issued by the Malaysian National Fatwa Council and by the Council of Indonesian Islamic Scholars (MUI) in 1980. The original 1980 fatwa by the MUI states: "In accordance with data and facts found in nine books about Ahmadiyah, the MUI decides (*memfatwakan*) that the Ahmadiyah is a congregation outside of Islam, deviant and misleading (*sesat dan menyesatkan*). In order to deal with this problem, the MUI hopes to be in constant contact with the government" (Majelis Ulama Indonesia 2005). This fatwa formed the basis for a request by the Ministry of Religious Affairs that the Ministry of Justice reconsider the legal status of the Indonesian Ahmadiyya Congregation (Jemaah Ahmadiyah Indonesia, JAI) in 1984 (Hasyim 2016). Yet no legal restrictions followed. On the contrary, the JAI's legal status was later further strengthened by the Directorate for Relations with Political Institutions (Alfitri 2008). This was partly due to the relative dormancy and marginality of the MUI during Suharto's reign. The national fatwa was taken up by regional MUI branches in North Sumatra in 1980, Aceh in 1984, and Riau in 1994. Although occasional outbursts of local violence against Ahmadis took place, no nationwide debates ensued until the reform period.

Administratively, the JAI acquired legal status as a social organization in 1953, and once more in 2003 from the Directorate for Relations with Political Institutions of the Ministry of Home Affairs (Alfitri 2008). It has been most active in West Java. The JAI is a globally centralized organization oriented toward and in many ways organized and held together by the Caliphate in London. When believers enter the Ahmadiyya community, the Caliph gives them a new name; he also approves of marriages, and Ahmadiyya communities gather on Fridays to watch the sermon delivered by their Caliph. Where allowed, they hold such meetings in mosques. In countries where they are officially banned, they often hold their meetings in people's homes or in spaces they rent. In Indonesia, Ahmadiyya mosques do not visually differ from other mosques, but they also do not make any effort to hide their existence in backyards; they are often marked as Ahmadiyya mosques by public signs. When they receive funds from their organization, local Ahmadis build proud and spacious mosques for their community, such as the An-Nur Mosque in Manislor in West Java.

The scale of accusations of heresy and physical attacks against them has sharply risen in the reform period, despite the Ahmadiyya being a numerically small congregation: in the mid-2000s, the government cited 50,000 members, while the JAI claimed 400,000 (International Crisis Group 2008). Several of their mosques have been attacked by groups of opponents and then have often been "sealed" by police, with the support of religious authorities. Some of them have been erected with funding from the central organization in London and thus are known by their neighbors to be part of the congregation even if the respective sign declaring the mosque to be Ahmadi is missing or hidden due to fear of attacks. We owe most of our information about the rise in anti-Ahmadiyya rhetoric and violence to human rights reports and scholarship based on qualitative research (The Asia Foundation 2016). A small number of mid- and large-N surveys exist on questions of tolerance toward Ahmadis, but none of them were conducted regularly enough to reliably document a large-scale trend. The Wahid Institute, a research-oriented NGO founded in 2004 by former President of Indonesia Abdurrahman Wahid and led by his daughter Yenny Zannuba Wahid, documented violations against the right to religious freedom and belief in their annual reports from 2009 to 2013. The reports found that Ahmadis were the most targeted group across the years but also documented a rise in attacks against Shi'a Muslims. In 2011, the institute's researchers counted 47 incidents targeting Ahmadis and only 2 targeting Shi'a, but in 2012, they counted 27 incidents against Shi'a, and 19 against Ahmadis (Wahid Institute 2011, 2012). In 2013, they found 128 incidents targeting individual Ahmadis and only 6 incidents targeting Shi'a but also 11 incidents involving Ahmadiyya groups and 10 incidents targeting Shi'a groups (Wahid Institute 2013). These numbers are hardly reliable, particularly because various communities adopted different strategies of involving human rights organizations and reporting incidents, but they illustrate that the Ahmadiyya and also Shi'a Muslims have become primary targets. The Jakarta-based Setara Institute for Democracy and Peace, another human rights organization, founded in 2005, documented violations of religious freedom against Ahmadis and Shi'a in their annual reports between 2007 and 2019. In the reports, the Setara researchers included a wider set of actions under the umbrella of violations of religious freedom: unjustified surveillance, intimidation, banning or interrupting religious activities, prohibiting the construction of places of worship, destroying or damaging places of worship, and similar incidents. Most cases, according to the reports, involved citizens, but many also involved state actors. Many of the attacks against Ahmadiyya and Shi'a communities were reported in a particular year but had long-lasting effects on the involved people: Very often, people fled their homes in the wake of the attacks and have since not been able to return (Gaffar 2013; Pamungkas 2015). The rapid spread of anti-Ahmadiyya legislation across the 2000s confirms the complicity of state actors in the discrimination and marginalization of Ahmadis. After 1998, local governments issued more than forty regulations across Indonesia that ban the Ahmadiyya in various locales. Several of these regulations use the same or similar wording, and local government heads issued these regulations in most cases without the parliament being involved and without any immediate societal pressure preceding the decisions (Buehler 2023).

Most Muslims I spoke to during my time in Indonesia were familiar with the Ahmadiyya controversy and had formed strong opinions of their own, often based on very little information. They were skeptical of the state's ambivalent and shifting positions on the matter, often trusted the MUI's judgments, and warily kept a distance from the Ahmadiyya. Typically, they might consider but eventually decide against inviting Ahmadis to podium discussions for fear of attacks by the FPI. Other congregations—such as Shi'a Muslims and smaller organizations—suffered similarly from rumors and attacks. Even if in some cases, such as that of Shi'a Islam, high-ranking religious authorities came to their defense, they nevertheless suffered from discrimination. Turning one's attention from the relatively small organization of the Ahmadiyya to the large variety of practices subsumed under the category Shi'a illustrates how quickly the debates on deviance developed and how similar the processes of othering are. When I began my research in 2008, many educated and theologically knowledgeable observers shook their heads and emphasized that the Ahmadiyya and the Shi'a were entirely different and incomparable. Such a view is understandable from a theological perspective. The Ahmadiyya, which came into existence only in the

1880s in then British India, is a relatively tightly structured, transnationally well-connected, and somewhat secluded and exclusive community. Unlike the Ahmadiyya, Shi'a Islam has been an integral part of Islam since its early days. Due to Indonesia's pluralist Islamization, driven by Muslim traders from many different regions of the world, Shi'a Islam has been part of the Indonesian social fabric for hundreds of years and only became more visible as a category in the late twentieth century (Formichi 2015; Sofjan 2016). The Iranian revolution in 1979 contributed to this visibility and cast the image of Shi'a Islam as a critical and potentially revolutionary variant of Islam. Conversion to Shi'ism became a "double protest against the political regime and the Sunni religious establishment" (Zulkifli 2013). As elsewhere, those who newly identified with Shi'a Islam found the antigovernment aspect appealing (Luizard 2002). Many read anti-imperialist Iranian intellectuals like Ali Shariati alongside neo-Marxist writings and referred to the Qum School as an important supplement to the Frankfurt School (Al-Tanwir 2017). Forty years after the Iranian Revolution, many Indonesians still associated Shi'a Islam with Iran, sometimes seen as a last bastion of Islam in a US-dominated global landscape. Many Indonesians I spoke to nodded in approval of Iran's braveness when our conversation would move to global politics and the tensions between the United States and Iran. Indonesia's most prominent Shi'a-sympathetic public intellectual, the late Jalaluddin Rakhmat, explained this period to me in an interview: "It was post-1965 Indonesia: You wouldn't consider becoming communist anymore if you wanted to change the world. Another option was to become Shi'a."[1] Some Shi'a consequently try to emphasize their Indonesian identity and avoid associations with Iran (Formichi 2020).

The public discourses on the two identities reflect their vast differences to some degree: Powerful voices defended Shi'a Muslims against accusations of heterodoxy. Due to the very different shapes of these identities and their very different places in Islamic history, it may seem far-fetched to group them together, and some observers argue that the cases are entirely different (Soedirgo 2020). One key difference is the dissonance among various branches of the MUI, illustrating the various competing interests within the organization. The fatwa issued by the East Java branch of the MUI illustrates this. Another difference is the historical position of Ahmadis and Shi'a during the New Order: While Ahmadis remained very much under the radar of the military regime, Shi'a Islam and its references to the Iranian Revolution posed a threat to the regime. The rebellious potential of Shi'a Islam is thus more obvious, and one might therefore expect greater caution on the part of the government.

However, studying the cases of the Ahmadiyya and Shi'a together reveals important patterns. The cases show how the Islamist Conservative Majoritarian Synthesis absorbed theological debates and transformed them in a political and productive way that resulted in the omnipresence of the questions of what constitutes real Islam, who should hold the defining power over it, and how it should be policed and implemented. The cases also show how religious and state authorities collaborated and how theological nuances mattered less than the integration and translation of theological arguments into security discourses, often connected to accusations and constructions of particular kinds of foreignness. In this way, both cases illustrate the influence of international conflicts on Indonesian politics. The accusation that Ahmadis and Shi'a Muslims are supported by and potentially loyal to foreign forces appear in either crude or subtle forms, in official statements and rumors, always accompanied by headlines. Implied in these discourses is the suggestion that one cannot simultaneously be part of a transnational group identity and of the mainly Indonesian nation whose variant of Islam is defined by its key religious organizations.

Many of my interlocutors during my time in Indonesia—for instance, fellow passengers on public transport—would routinely mention Ahmadiyya and Shi'a in the same sentence. This was not entirely new: In 1984, the MUI had already released a first public recommendation (*tawisya*) warning against Shi'a Islam, together with its warning against the Ahmadiyya (Hasyim 2011; Zulian 2018). Then still largely in line with government policies, the MUI warned that many Shi'a Muslims were developing a direction that fundamentally differed from Sunni Islam. It stopped short of judging Shi'a Islam as deviant. In its release of controversial fatwas in 2005, the MUI did not include Shi'a Islam, and the central MUI never declared the sect outside Islam; however, local MUI branches held different views on particular Shi'a groups, and public debates included questioning their belonging.

In processes of group formation, small numbers often yield the greatest controversy. In his analysis of what he aptly calls "fear of small numbers," Arjun Appadurai draws on his fieldwork in India and Pakistan and on Mary Douglas's book *Purity and Danger* (1966) to argue that violence framed in ethnic or religious terms is a response to the uncertainties caused by globalization. It springs from the earlier discussed modern desire to create certainties. Appadurai argues that the classical liberal idea of temporary, issue-based minorities has in the homogenized nation-states morphed into the protection of fixed, identity-based minorities. These minorities, often by the mere fact of their existence, challenge national narratives of social cohesion and homogeneity. They remind the constructed and imagined majorities of their impurity and constructedness and thus cause fear: the smaller the numbers and the smaller the differences, the greater the fear. This fear of the other, however, does not spontaneously and organically grow but develops and spreads from fanning by specific actors, as studies of group violence and exclusion mechanisms have shown across different times and locales. In the case of Indonesia after Suharto, religiopolitical entrepreneurs claiming the center of Islam in Indonesia stirred fears and skepticism by spreading wrong information and through assimilation and othering. The construction of Mainstream Islam is the logical continuation of modern homogenization tendencies. During the 2000s, the process of homogenization gained speed. Assimilation and othering were crucial elements of the vigilant border patrol in the competition for defining and representing Islam. The Islamist Conservative Majoritarian Synthesis pushed Ahmadis and Shi'a to form the religious other at the margins so that those who defined themselves as the internally divergent mainstream or core, would occupy the center of Islam in Indonesia without having to define themselves other than through what they are *not*.

Jessica Soedirgo (2020) argues that the Ahmadis were "a constitutive threat to Muslims in Indonesia because their beliefs and practices challenged those that allowed a diverse people to belong to a single category" and that "political entrepreneurs were incentivized to amplify these visible constitutive threats for their own interests." I somewhat agree, but my analysis stresses that the Ahmadiyya were not a threat to Muslim identity but developed into a, in some ways necessary, component of Indonesia's increasingly Islamized nationalism that emerged during the phase of increasing decentralization and socioeconomic insecurities. Styled as a potential threat, the deviant category was a key component of the category of dirt that allowed the numerical majority its purity. In other words, the threat was to a crucial degree fabricated and cultivated.

One important similarity is the way in which theological arguments get reduced and translated into and connected to arguments within security discourses. In both cases, the theological arguments were supplemented with simplistic accusations aiming at the very core of Islamic belief and practice. Their attackers accused Ahmadis and Shi'a of abolishing the hajj and replacing the five daily prayers with alternative prayers. These accusations suggest that Ahmadis and Shi'a hurt Islam at its very core. Rumors often widely disseminated these narratives. In both cases, visibility and alleged foreignness were key aspects in the process of othering.

Members of the Ahmadiyya and Shi'a experienced violence, usually conducted by nonstate actors but tolerated by state actors such as police. In both cases, police often just watched violence against the minorities unfold rather than protecting them. Among controversial social identities, the Ahmadiyya were attacked more often but attacks against Shi'a did occur and the media also widely reported on them. These cases illustrate how various actors intertwine theological arguments with security discourses as illustrated in the media coverage of a fatal attack against Ahmadis in 2011. The cases also show how political leaders in various cases performatively othered Ahmadis and Shi'a to enhance their own pious image, as for instance illustrated by the staging of conversion rituals of Ahmadiyya members by the then–Minister of Religious Affairs Suryadharma Ali.

In the case of the Shi'a, an intrinsic and largely uncontroversial identity and practice was singled out, discriminated against, and eventually transformed into an internal other on the margins of the nation. Of all the cases, the Shi'a case shows most clearly how the discourse of heterodoxy and deviance has infused society with permanent insecurity about what is permissible and what is not. In addition to assimilation and othering through violence and through theological and security-related discourses, the other key phenomenon that the Ahmadiyya and Shi'a cases show is that the arguments used to defend members of marginalized identities in that period were internally homogeneous. After decades of repression under the New Order, Indonesians were now developing new frameworks, vocabularies, and repertoires to defend pressured and attacked individuals and groups. The anti-Communist past continued to tinge the political atmosphere and kept leftist emancipatory repertoires from blossoming, and at the same time, large amounts of funds channeled into Indonesia by Western governments and international agencies shifted discourses of defense toward religious freedom, human rights, and liberalism. As a result, in the early 2000s emancipatory vocabulary was not very diverse, as the cases of the Ahmadiyya and the Shi'a identities, among others, illustrate.

Earlier, in the mid-1990s, the discourses of Islam and of rights had largely operated together, first against the rule of Suharto and then for the democratization of the newly reformed system. Several initiatives focused their activities on interpretations of Islam that highlighted its compatibility and comfortable relationship with human rights, as expressed in the works of Abdullahi An-Na'im, a Sudanese-born Muslim scholar who lives in the United States and whose work is very popular in Southeast Asia. I have often seen quotes from his writings cited in brochures and even on campaign posters.

In the 2000s and early 2010s, the public debates on the Ahmadiyya and Shi'a, and by extension on issues of pluralism and religiopolitical authority, occurred within four distinct sets of arguments: religion, security, human rights, and nationalism. Religious and security concerns largely predominated the debates and supported arguments for placing restrictions on the Ahmadiyya and Shi'a. For many years, human rights and nationalist rhetoric served as the main repertoires used to protect and defend Ahmadiyya and Shi'a Muslims. However, over time, human rights discourse faded, while nationalism merged with religion, security, and appeals to public order or social harmony. Discursive actors pitched these frameworks against each other and combined them in different ways. At the end of the 2010s, only nationalism and Islam were left as predominant discourses, and they had grown into each other.

The discourse of human rights dominated the defense frameworks in the discourses on allegedly deviant identities. It was only in the late 2010s that defenders of Ahmadis and Shi'a Muslims would shift their strategies. The analysis of the attacks against and defense of the Ahmadiyya and Shi'a shows how various actors using different discursive repertoires talked past each other.

Violence Against Ahmadis and Its Media Coverage

The actors that made attacking the Ahmadiyya one of their main goals included smaller organizations of known perpetrators of violence, such as the FPI, and the nonviolent but nation-state-renouncing Hizbut Tahrir. Most important, the MUI, claiming to represent the sixty-million-member Nahdlatul Ulama (NU) and the forty-million-member Muhammadiyah, turned against the Ahmadis early on (Nashrullah 2019). Politicians chimed in, both from explicitly religious and so-called secular parties. Each of them had their arguments for attacking the Ahmadiyya, usually citing a combination of social order and references to the MUI's theological reasoning. The sticking point of anti-Ahmadiyya rhetoric and legitimization of violence is Mirza Ghulam Ahmad's alleged status as a prophet. This heresy, opponents argue, is a threat to Muslims whose faith may stumble (Burhani 2014a). In this rhetoric, particularly in online debates, metaphors of disease present the Ahmadis as a threat to the umma as a whole and to the piety of individual Muslims (Burhani 2014a). Like many tropes in the Ahmadiyya case, the image of "cancer" too had its predecessors in Pakistani public debates (Gualtieri 1989). The evoked images are powerful, and they blend with the motif of endangered social order.

Those attacking the Ahmadiyya were unified in their rhetoric but divided on the means of curbing Ahmadiyya activities, meaning mostly their proselytizing efforts. The Ahmadiyya congregation strives to invite new members and actively disseminate pamphlets and brochures. Proselytization among Muslims has been a sensitive topic in Muslim Southeast Asia since the arrival of the first Europeans, and the Indonesian state early on established legal tools to curb it (Crouch 2014). The proselytizing activities of the Ahmadiyya likely contributed to the wrath against them (Soedirgo 2018, 2020), but it would be a mistake to make this the only or even the main explanation.

One of the key actors benefiting from and breathing fire into the controversies surrounding those it deemed not part of Islam was the MUI. After the end of the New Order, the MUI began replacing the pejorative term *splinter movement—gerakan sempalan*—with the even harsher term *aliran sesat*—"misled stream" (Bruinessen 1992). In the mid-2000s, the MUI made it the key term for describing teachings and organizations that deviated from what it accepted as Islamic. Some fatwas and statements used the double phrase *sesat dan menyesatkan*, literally "deviant/misled and misleading." This alludes to the oft-cited danger of leading others astray and can be traced back to a hadith: "'Abdullah bin 'Amr bin Al-'As (May Allah be pleased with them) reported: I heard the Messenger of Allah (PBUH) saying: 'Verily, Allah does not take away knowledge by snatching it from the people, but He takes it away by taking away (the lives of) the religious scholars till none of the scholars stays alive. Then the people will take ignorant ones as their leaders, who, when asked to deliver religious verdicts, will issue them without knowledge, the result being that they will go astray and will lead others astray'" (Nawawi 2014). The Indonesian term *aliran sesat* is not legally defined, but officials regularly use it in their communication; in the 2000s, it became a household term. During my fieldwork, I used it in casual conversations on public transport and when strolling through book fairs looking for material to observe my interlocutors' reactions and their interpretation of the term. Upon my asking whether they had any books or magazines on aliran sesat, not once did a seller not know what I might be referring to. In almost all cases, they reached into their piles and boxes and produced books or magazines about Ahmadiyya and in some cases about Shi'a Muslims. Their responses to my question embodied the state of the debate: Ahmadis were without question identified as deviant by the authorities I interviewed. About Shi'a Muslims most of my interlocutors were less sure. Some would mention Shi'a among those deemed deviant without hesitation; others said they were obviously an important and perfectly legitimate part of Islam. In the hierarchy that the MUI and its allies crafted in the late 2000s and early 2010s, the MUI formed the center. Around it were the masses of the members of the NU and Muhammadiyah as well as those of more hardline organizers that had since 2005 been represented by the MUI. Beyond them were the thin rings of identity categories whose status was contested: Christians, Hindus, Confucians, adherents of *aliran kepercayaan*, and, pushed further to the perimeter, Shi'a and Ahmadiyya. This concentric order of belonging, ranked according to piety and religious identity was not new, nor was the term *aliran sesat*. State institutions, such as the Ministry of Religious Affairs and the Bakor Pakem, which was established in 1952 under the Ministry of Religious Affairs to monitor Indigenous beliefs, "mysticism," and new congregations, have also used *aliran sesat* in their internal and external communication. Often, the usage is loose and not defined in any detail, and it partly derived its powerful effect from this vagueness. In 2007, the MUI issued a list of ten criteria for identifying aliran sesat (Detiknews 2007; MUI Digital 2024). This attempt to define Islam did not provoke significant public controversy among major Muslim organizations or the broader public—likely because debates still lingered over the MUI's 2005 fatwas against Ahmadis, interreligious marriage, secularism, pluralism, and liberalism.

The MUI's ten-point manual (*pedoman*) would serve as a doctrinal benchmark for the next decade and beyond, declaring a religious teaching or group deviant if it:

1. Denies one of the pillars of faith or the pillars of Islam.
2. Follows a creed unsupported by sharia evidence.
3. Believes in any revelations after the Qur'an.
4. Rejects the Qur'an's authenticity.
5. Interprets the Qur'an contrary to established exegetical rules.
6. Denies the hadith as a source of Islamic teachings.
7. Insults or rejects the Prophet Muhammad.
8. Denies Prophet Muhammad's status as the final prophet.
9. Modifies core acts of worship as prescribed by sharia.
10. Declares other Muslims unbelievers solely for not belonging to their group.

By issuing this list, the MUI clarified two things: It assumed the central authority in defining what Islam is, and it announced that several more declarations of beliefs and organizations as deviant would follow. In a way, it also delivered a postscriptum legitimization or at least explanation of the MUI's 2005 series of fatwas. While the MUI denied any causal link between its fatwa and anti-Ahmadiyya violence (Panggabean 2016) and some Ahmadis also doubt that the fatwa was responsible, many observers discern such a link, even if the details of the causality remain difficult to assess (Assyaukanie 2009a; Burhani 2014a; Olle 2009).

The 2005 fatwa and the joint ministerial decree of 2008 constitute key references for those attacking the Ahmadiyya and penetrators and commentators often cited them to excuse or legitimize violence. In February 2011, brutal video footage circulated in various newsgroup mailing lists and TV channels in Indonesia and beyond, documenting the most brutal attack against an Ahmadi community in this period. Within two days, nearly everyone I spoke to had seen it. Filmed with a mobile phone, the footage showed the killing of several Ahmadis during an attack in the village of Cikeusik in Banten, a province in the western part of Java. Stripped of their clothes, three men were clubbed to death. In the background were dozens of onlookers—including police in uniform—amid shouts of "Allahu Akbar." The chant here functioned as a claim to moral righteousness. The presence of uniformed officers who did not intervene further amplified the message that the state's ambivalence, the ulama's delegitimization, and the crowd's invocation of the divine had together rendered such violence not only permissible but publicly affirmed.

Media reports suggested that the attackers were locals who were fed up with their Ahmadi neighbors and cited the 2005 fatwa issued by the MUI that declared the Ahmadiyya to be "outside Islam." However, at least one of the main instigators of the violence had traveled several hours by car (Detiknews 2011c; Harsono 2011) to confront the Ahmadis, who themselves had also invited support from outside.

The day after the attack, the MUI announced it "regretted the incident" and condemned the violence, but at the same time, the council confirmed its fatwa: It still considered the Ahmadiyya to be deviant (*sesat*) and outside Islam. The MUI elder Amidhan was quoted as saying, "This fatwa already came out in 1980 and then was reaffirmed in 2005. This stream (aliran) deviates from the teachings of Islam. There is no need to debate this any further" (*Viva News* 2011).

Two days after the incident, the province's Governor Ratu Atut Chosiyah of Golkar, a party considered nonreligious and part of the ruling coalition since 2004, reportedly said the attack was a disaster "beyond human power" and called on the Ahmadis to "return to the right and true Islamic teachings" (*kembali mengikuti ajaran Islam yang benar*). While thousands of Indonesians watched the footage of the brutal killing of several Ahmadis on news channels and YouTube, Ratu Atut Chosiyah was quoted as saying, "There are currently 1,117 Ahmadis in six areas. We [Provincial Government of Banten], together with the MUI and the Regional Consultative Council on the level of regency observe and influence them [*melakukan pengawasam serta pembinaan*]. To this date, 24 members of their flock have already become aware [*insaf*] and have returned to follow the teachings of true and right Islam. I hope that the others also can do that. We will continue this until they really 'become aware' [*betul-betul insaf*]." This quote captures several central issues of this chapter: First, the narrative of "true and right Islam" (*ajaran Islam yang benar*) is explicitly evoked. Second, there is a strong focus on the

Ahmadis themselves rather than on the perpetrators of the attack. Third, the Ahmadis themselves are held responsible indirectly by placing conversion right after the commenting on the assault on them. Fourth, what others frame as "attack" or "assault" is called a "disaster," and it is stated that it is "beyond human power." This removes responsibility from any other individual or group besides the Ahmadis. Last, the governor of Banten does not seem to see it as her government's task to prevent or punish the violence. At least she does not think it is expected from her. Nor does she find it necessary to explain the inactivity or inefficiency of the police officers present at the scene who are visibly passive in the widely circulated footage. Furthermore, she sees the government's task as influencing and religiously educating the Ahmadis. This is especially noteworthy since she represents Golkar, a not explicitly religious party. We observe here the growing alliance between nationalism and Islam. The governor also included the MUI in her scheme of "influencing" and educating the Ahmadis, stressing the collaboration between state institutions and the MUI in the process of assimilation.

MUI members, politicians, and media coverage ignored the specific backgrounds of the perpetrators and, instead of reporting those, framed the attack as a "clash" by Ahmadis with "true Islam" (*Islam yang benar*) or as anger of the masses (*amuk massa*). Commenting on the Cikeusik attack, the parliamentarian and Islamist United Development Party (Partai Persatuan Pembangunan) politician Ahmad Dimiyati Natakusumah stated that he worried that a "clash" (*bentrok*) with Ahmadis such as in Cikeusik would happen again unless the Ahmadiyya were disbanded. He emphasized that if Ahmadiyya wanted to be left alone, they should return to the true Islam (*Islam yang benar*) (Suryanto 2011).

Two distinct exclusionary mechanisms pushed the Ahmadis away from the center of the Indonesian umma: The first mechanism was that of the increasingly hard-line mass media depriving Ahmadis of their own voice, leaving a significant gap that few, if any, religious voices were ready to fill in a defending way. The second mechanism was the filling of this gap with the language of human rights, which distinguished the Ahmadis as a clear-cut religious minority from an imagined Muslim mainstream.

The media depiction of the Ahmadis throughout the 2000s is telling: Mainstream media reports portrayed Ahmadis as a faceless and nameless social category that both caused and experienced trouble. The culmination of this type of portrayal was the 2011 Cikeusik attack (Harsono 2016; Nugroho et al. 2013; *Tempo* 2011c). In the subsequent media coverage, the news items about the attack featured local politicians, police, religious authorities, and human rights activists but almost no Ahmadis. An example of this is the first press report after the Cikeusik attack, issued by the Indonesian news agency Antara and later picked up and modified by various newspapers. It cited MUI representatives, politicians, police, and witnesses but no Ahmadi voices. Later reports added comments by human rights activists defending Ahmadis. This was the first mechanism: The media diminished possibilities for Ahmadi self-representation. The images of the dead bodies of killed Ahmadis were displayed without comments of sadness or care; instead, the images recalled the descriptions of nameless corpses in the massacres of 1965, when Communists were forcibly excluded from national self-conception. The effect was to exclude Ahmadis from the nation (Burhani 2013). This nation was increasingly imagined as Muslim in a particular way, and its ideal citizen was a Muslim whose variant of Islam would find approval by the leading religious authorities. Despite this absence of Ahmadi voices in mainstream media, some members of the community—particularly Ahmadi women—were already making efforts to assert themselves as active participants in the discourse. They defended their rights against mosque closures, challenged discriminatory restrictions, and spoke publicly about the enmity they faced (Noor 2017).

It took some time before media outlets began to cite Ahmadi spokespeople and to invite some of them to talk shows. Eventually, Ahmadis were able to speak for "the Ahmadiyya" rather than be represented by human rights activists advocating on their behalf. This is when the second, subtler mechanism set in: The reports portrayed Ahmadis as a religious minority, distinct from other Indonesian Muslims. Letting Ahmadis speak as individuals rather than have human rights activists represent them gave a face to the hitherto faceless category of Ahmadiyya.

Although these efforts to slowly rehabilitate the Ahmadis successfully contributed to preventing a further weakening of ligatures between Ahmadis and the rest of Indonesian society, they also unintentionally ended up portraying the Ahmadis as a minority that is fundamentally different from the Indonesian mainstream, and in this way concretized their difference. An example is the commentary two weeks after the Cikeusik attack by Ahmadiyya spokesperson Mubarik Ahmad, who pointed out that the Ahmadiyya had been officially accepted in the 1950s and recalled Ahmadi contributions to the nation. Despite Mubarik Ahmad's efforts to stress the Indonesian-ness of Ahmadis, the media continuously stressed the otherness of the Ahmadis. An example is the often-repeated phrasing in media reports that the Cikeusik attack was a "clash between Ahmadis and locals [*warga sekitar*]," or between Ahmadis and "villagers" (*warga desa*). In forums and blogs, common formulations are "people against Ahmadis" and "Ahmadis and Citizens / Townspeople/villagers clash (National Human Rights Commission of the Republic of Indonesia 2015) The Cikeusik case had in fact involved local villagers as well as outsiders on both sides (Detiknews 2011c; Schäfer 2018), but the media reports entirely glossed over this.[2] This coverage portrayed the Ahmadis as outsiders and others.

Intimidations and restrictions of Ahmadis were framed in similar ways: for instance, when media reproduced images of banners that unknown motorcyclists hung up in Depok, near Jakarta, in June 2017. The banners read, "The people of [the village of] Sawangan reject the Ahmadiyya!" (Dipa 2017). Newspapers reproduced the claim without emphasizing that the unknown perpetrators may have traveled from afar (Dipa 2017; Schäfer 2018). The presentation of the Ahmadis as outsiders opposed to and by local villagers fed into an Islamist narrative of an Indonesian umat defending itself against dangerous outsiders.

The media also repeatedly reported demands that the Ahmadiyya discontinue identifying as Muslim, as in Pakistan. Shortly after the Cikeusik killings and four years after an Ahmadi community was evicted from their village on the eastern island of Lombok, Golkar parliament member H. M. Busro suggested that the government relocate the Ahmadis to an uninhabited island: "Indonesia has 17,000 islands, many of which are uninhabited. So why not move them to an island that is not inhabited" (Fikreatif 2011).

In much of the coverage of anti-Ahmadiyya violence, especially in the years leading up to the Cikeusik attack, the background of the perpetrators remained vague and unclear. Few journalists questioned the claims of the perpetrators to represent "true Islam." Research on the biased coverage of topics pertaining to Islam and minorities suggests that many journalists also agree with the accusations against the Ahmadiyya. A survey among six hundred Indonesian journalists conducted in 2010 found that most media workers identified closely with an Islamic and nationalist identity. Asked to complete the sentence, "Above all, I am a(n) . . . ," the primary identity cited by about 40 percent of respondents was "Indonesian" (40.3 percent) and "Muslim" (39.7 percent). Only 12 percent said they were a "journalist" first. When asked if they supported banning the Ahmadiyah sect, 64 percent of the surveyed journalists said yes (Pintak and Setiyono 2011). These findings partly explain the lack of critical distance to positions disseminated by politicians and religious authorities.

Other studies found sensationalist reporting that largely portrayed the Ahmadiyya as the culprits in this conflict (Andarini 2014). Examples are a news piece on *KOMPAS.com* that repeats statements on the deviance of the Ahmadiyya as voiced by the MUI leader Ma'ruf Amin in 2011: While Ma'ruf

Amin's opinion that "Islam mainstream" cannot tolerate the theological differences with the Ahmadiyya is given a lot of room, no alternative voice is cited (Aziz 2011). A 2010 piece in the Indonesia section of Voice of America summarizes that "followers of Ahmadiyah [are] considered a deviant sect in Indonesia, [and] continue to face pressure from some mainstream Muslim groups" (Dewan 2010). The press coverage about anti-Ahmadiyya attacks is also a testament to the success of the narrative of Mainstream Islam, which has further entrenched itself through uncritical use of the term on the part of journalists and academics.

Theological debates found their way into politically useful rumors. An example of anti-Ahmadiyya literature is Dede Nasrudin's book *Koreksi Terhadap Pemahaman Ahmadiyah Dalam Masalah Kenabian* (Correction of the Ahmadiyya's understanding within the problem of prophethood) (2008), published by a small Wahabi-oriented press, Irsyad Baitus Salam, based in Bandung. The book's short preface is by Hafizh Utsman, an NU member, senior MUI leader in West Java, and member of the Central Fatwa Commission. He served as chairman of MUI in West Java for three periods from 2000 until 2014 as well as a member of the Fatwa Commission in Central MUI from 2009 to 2010 (Sunandar 2011). The book opens with a chapter entitled, "Prophet Muhammad, the Last Prophet and Messenger." The first paragraph states that even though the verses on the finality of the prophethood have been explained to Ahmadis many times, the Ahmadis still continued to twist the meaning of those verses. Dede Nasrudin cites Ahmadiyya publications, summarizes their interpretation of verses and hadiths, and offers "corrections."

Scripture-based arguments against the Ahmadiyya would usually take the form of rumors in this period. Politicians would often subtly refer to them in official statements on religious issues. The most significant and widely disseminated rumor has been that the Ahmadis have an alternative testimony of faith (*shahada*) and holy book and thus are heretics. Yet most Ahmadis who regularly pray typically pronounce the shahada at least five times daily. Nevertheless, they are widely rumored to have substituted Mirza Ghulam Ahmad for the Prophet Muhammad in the shahada. These rumors emphasize the Ahmadis' dissimilarity by exaggerating existing differences and inventing new ones. Nearly all my interlocutors, whether during fleeting conversations on buses or at street food stalls or among the parents of my more educated friends, cited this rumor when I asked them what they thought was problematic about the Ahmadiyya. While telling me this, some of them pronounced the distorted sentence: "There Is No God but God and Ahmad Is His Messenger" and stressed the altered ending with facial expressions of hurt and disgust. Such a line does not exist among Ahmadis. It is pure but powerful fiction and rumor. Politicians and media outlets have further propelled these rumors in the manner of their coverage of the Ahmadiyya question. Since 2012 in Kuningan, Manislor village, Ahmadiyah members have needed to sign a formal letter stating that they are Muslims and declare the shahada before they can receive their electronic ID card that confirms their status as Muslims.

Conversion ceremonies are another bureaucratization and manifestation of the rumor that the shahada is new to Ahmadis. Such ceremonies were organized by individual mosques, by the FPI, and also by the MUI in collaboration with other local authorities. One such ceremony was held on the symbolically loaded date of June 1, 2009, on the square surrounding the National Monument, Monas, a year after the brutal Monas Tragedy. Seventy Ahmadis declared their repentance in front of a thousand people from various groups, including FPI, the Islamic Society Forum (Forum Umat Islam, FUI) and Gerakan Reformis Islam. FPI General Secretary Ahmad Sobri Lubis oversaw the ceremony, which was followed by chants of Allahu Akbar from the audiences. The converted Ahmadis had come from Tasikmalaya in West Java (Antara News 2009). In March 2011, an Ahmadi family converted in the Al-Ukhuwah Mosque in Bandung, and Ahmad Sobri Lubis reportedly repaid a loan the family had received from an Ahmadiyya group (Detiknews 2011a). Around the same time, eighteen people declared their repentance in the Agung Cimahi Mosque in West Java, witnessed by Hilmi Rifai, the head of the local Office of Religious Affairs (Kepala Kantor Urusan Agama) and a board member of the Regional Leadership Coordination Forum (Musyawarah Pimpinan Daerah, Muspida); members of the MUI Cimahi; and Muhammad Hilman Firdaus, the head of the Shura Council of the FUI (JPNN 2011).

Shortly after, thirty-eight Ahmadis living in Kecamatan Cisurupan, Kabupaten Garut, and Jawa Barat declared their repentance. Afterward, the local head of MUI stated that there were no longer any Ahmadis around; all of them had "returned to Islam" (Pitakasari 2011). Two weeks later, in April 2011, in the West Javanese town of Purwakarta, thirty-one of the local eighty-nine Ahmadis undertook a similar ceremony, held in the Agung Purwakarta Mosque and witnessed by the *bupati* (regent) Dedi Mulyadi, the local MUI representative, and the mosque administrators (Pitakasari 2011). Several similar ceremonies were organized, mostly in West Java but also in East Lombok. In March 2016, ten families converted in the village Dasan Bangik in East Lombok. They declared their shahada in the village's office (Kantor Desa), witnessed by the head of the village, religious leaders, and the community. Head of District Sambelia H. Bukhari stated that "with their return to Islam, there are no more problems" (*Lombok Today* 2016).

A prominent example of a widely covered ceremony is one held in Tasikmalaya, West Java, in May 2013. Then–Minister of Religious Affairs Suryadharma Ali was in attendance, together with representatives from the Director General for Guidance of the Islamic Community (Direktorat Jendral Bina Masyarakat Islam) and local community leaders who were not further named in the reports. The event was widely covered in the media. A *KOMPAS* reporter quoted Dadang Romansyah, the head of the local branch of the Ministry of Religious Affairs, as saying, "Today twenty people have uttered the shahada" and quoted Suryadharma Ali saying, "I honestly saw [people] cry and shed tears the moment dozens of Ahmadis officially entered Islam" (Nugraha 2013). *Suara Islam* quoted the minister as saying, "I cried the moment they uttered the shahada" (Syaiful 2013). *Republika* reported that a group of twenty Ahmadis had "repented" (*bertobat*), "returned to pledging the two sentences of the shahada," and "return[ed] to the lap of Islam" (Nashih 2013). On the website of the Ministry of Religious Affairs, a photograph of the ceremony depicted the minister shaking the hands of the converts with this caption: "Suryadharma Ali providing assistance to the Ahmadis after they have affirmed their return to their Islam by reading the two sentences of the shahada" (Menteri Agama Republik Indonesia 2013). This media emphasis on the novelty of the shahada for Ahmadis suggested that they do not already hold the shahada at the core of their belief system. The coverage of this event confirms the previously mentioned comment of Cikeusik Governor Ratu Atut Chosiyah: Conversion is constantly presented as an option, thereby shifting the focus in the Ahmadiyya debate onto the Ahmadis rather than the perpetrators.

In his efforts to publicly support the conversion of Ahmadis, Suryadharma Ali also financially supported Ahmadis who chose to leave the Ahmadiyya congregation and affiliate themselves with an organization called Victims of the Heretic Ahmadiyah Society Association (Ikatan Masyarakat Korban Aliran Sesat Ahmadiyah) (Nashih 2013. Its members were treated as originally non-Muslim converts to Islam (*mualaf*) who were now entitled to zakat. Part of the IDR 1 billion in zakat funds donated to the Tasikmalaya converts was for supporting businesses, and other parts were going into religious education for the newly converted, conducted inter alia by the local MUI (Amrullah 2013).

In Banten, the head of the subdistrict, district military personnel (Komando Distrik Militer, or Kodim), and members of the city's MUI organized a similar although much smaller ceremony in April 2011 in Banten (*Liputan6*

2011a), most likely in reaction to the Cikeusik killing. Several FPI leaders applauded the alleged return to Islam, such as Ustad Awi of the FPI Jakarta branch (*Liputan6* 2011b) and Harun, the head of the MUI in Parigi District (*SINDOnews* 2019).³ In Banten, the head of the MUI Cikeusik Haji Amir, who was also a community leader in Desa Umbulan, Banten, made repentance and a formal "return to Islam" a condition for Ahmadis who wanted to return to their homes, seven years after the 2011 attack (Bonasir 2018). In total, at least seven hundred Ahmadis publicly read the shahada, which the authorities framed as repentance and return to Islam (Ichsan 2013).

A key aspect that these examples illustrate is the close collaboration between political and religious authorities. The Ministry of Religious Affairs subsequently showcased the 2013 Tasikmalaya ceremony on its official website. Other examples go beyond symbolism. In early March 2011, shortly after the Cikeusik attack, Banten Governor Ratu Atut Chosiyah released a regulation (Peraturan Gubernur Banten Nomor 5 Tahun 2011) prohibiting any Ahmadiyya activity. The regional secretary of Banten, Muhadi stated, "This Governor's Regulation was issued as a response to the pressure of clerical leaders, Islamic organizations, MUI and a number of elements of the Islamic community [masyarakat Islam] who asked the Provincial Government to immediately issue a regulation on prohibiting the activities of Ahmadiyah congregations in Banten Province." Afterward, the local MUI regularly cited this regulation (VOA ISLAM 2011).

The close collaboration between political and religious authorities is not restricted to Java. In Jambi, Sumatera, the MUI held a four-hour meeting in the hall of the office of the ministry of religious affairs. The result was a recommendation to the governor of Jambi and the central government to forbid Ahmadiyah in Jambi and in Indonesia. The head of the local MUI branch, Hadri Hasan, explained that their rejection was based on several legal and religious references: Law No. 5 of 1969, the MUI fatwas issued during the 1980 and 2005 national congresses, and a circular letter from the Directorate General of Islamic Guidance at the Ministry of Religious Affairs (No. D/BA/01/3099/1984, dated September 20, 1984) (Regional Office of the Ministry of Religious Affairs, Jambi Province, 2011). Later that year, the governor of Jambi did release the respective regulation (Governor of Jambi Regulation No.27 2011) and forbade any Ahmadiyya activities in the province. These examples show the eagerness of some political leaders to enhance their own moral credibility by embracing the positions of religious authorities.

Another theological argument used against the Ahmadis is the aforementioned allegation that they possess a new, corrupt Quran. The spread of this rumor prepared the ground for Suryadharma Ali's call to ban the Ahmadiyya in August 2010, when he said that the Ahmadis "do not even believe the Koran is the last Holy Book, among other things" (*The Jakarta Post* 2010). This rumor references the Ahmadiyya Tadhkirah, a collection of divine revelations received by Mirza Ghulam Ahmad, but among Ahmadis, the status of this work does not approach that of the Quran. Another important concept that appears in the public discourse on Ahmadis is "repentance." Critics of the Ahmadis call for them to "repent" (*taubat*) and return to the "right path." Most journalists do not critically discuss this call for "repentance" but simply quote religious authorities who offer "repentance" as a solution to the larger problem that the Ahmadis cause by existing. An example is an article in the newspaper *Republika* titled "Thank God, Ahmadis in the Subdistrict of Cisurupan Have Repented" (Pitakasari 2011). The image accompanying the article is a picture of a man signing a document that is labeled the "process of repentance." This process was overseen by Garut Agus Solehudin, an MUI member. The Ahmadis confessed, pledged their faith, and read the shahada, witnessed by the regent, representatives of the regional administration, religious authorities, and other invited guests. One of the Ahmadis is quoted as emphasizing that they had not been forced to repent. The word stems from the Quranic Arabic word *tawbah*, meaning "repentance, penitence, or contrition." In both the Quran and the hadith, the word is used to refer to the act of abandoning what God has prohibited and returning to what God has commanded. In sharia law and Islamic scholarship, it means to turn or retreat from past sinful and evil activities and to decisively refrain from them in the future.

The theology-based discourse against the Ahmadis usually has come intertwined with security concerns. Securitization is particularly popular among politicians and police. Reminiscent of the defenders of the blasphemy law, they present the Ahmadis as a security threat and a source of social unrest. They have argued that curbing their activities is an urgent duty. An example is a comment by Ahmad Heryawan of the Prosperous Justice Party and governor of West Java Province, when he banned Ahmadiyya activities there in March 2011, shortly after the Cikeusik incident. The reason, he explained, was to "protect public order and safety" (Suprapto 2011). Ahmadis are also accused of "provoking" attacks. An article published on NU's website the day after the Cikeusik attack quoted national police spokesman Boy Rafli Amar: "We suspect that there was a provocation in bringing a large number of people to Cikeusik" (*NU Online* 2011). Ahmadi Dede Sujana was sentenced to six months in prison after the attack for allegedly having provoked the violence by not leaving the house that had been threatened, arming himself in preparation for the previously announced attack, and punching one of the assailants (Tampubolon 2011). The head of the Serang Prosecutors' Office, Jan Maringka, said, "We have collected enough evidence. . . . We found several sharp weapons in Dede's cars. It showed that Dede intended to fight the attackers" (*The Jakarta Post* 2011b). This official approach is also reflected in media coverage. According to one report, Alex Fauzy Rasyad, the Cikeusik chief of police, "explained that the attack on part of the residents of Cikeusik against the Ahmadiyya Community was triggered by the attitude of the members of the congregation who issued a suggestive and challenging statement to local residents." The chief was quoted as saying, "Actually, the situation was conducive, and the community was calm, but because of this challenging statement from the Jamaah Ahmadiyah, the citizens were finally hooked [*terpancing*]." The choice of words here implies a deliberate provocation on the part of the Ahmadis.

Violence Against Shi'a and Its Media Coverage

Unlike the small Ahmadiyya congregation, Shi'a Islam had no arrival date but was always an intrinsic part of Islam in the archipelago. Perhaps even more significantly, Shi'a Islam was not specifically marked for most of Indonesia's history. The heterogeneous landscape of pre-Islamic practices mixed with various Islamic ones originating in different parts of the world, including elements that can be connected to Shi'a beliefs and practices (Muwahidah 2020). Only the twentieth century saw Shi'a Islam emerge as a clearly definable social category, increasingly imagined as internally homogeneous (Formichi 2014). Historically, debates on the alleged heterodoxy of particular Shi'a groups or individuals are not new in the region. Such discussions can be traced back to the seventeenth century, but during the reform years, a newly constructed category of homogeneous Shi'a Islam and the discussion about its Islam-ness has reached a hitherto unknown intensity. Twenty years after the end of the New Order, estimates of the number of Shi'a in Indonesia vary widely, from 1 to 5 million. Those who emphasize the threat of Shi'a tend to exaggerate the number: The State Intelligence Agency (Badan Intelijen Negara considered the number to be 1 to 2 million (Miichi 2016). These numbers themselves reflect the major shift from more fluid practices to more rigid classification since the 1980s (Formichi 2015; Formichi and M. R. Feener 2015).

The anti-Shi'a rhetoric of state institutions was shaped by this critical potential of Shi'a Islam and the exported revolutionary ideas (Zulkifli 2013). In the 1980s, the openly Shi'a Islamic boarding school Pesantren al-Khairat in Central Java was reprimanded and its newsletter halted by the Ministry of Religious Affairs (MORA). Nevertheless, a ministerial report of 1982 conceded that Shi'a Islam could not be banned per se. In 1983, the MORA circulated an internal letter reaffirming the principles of the Sunna, and asked its own staff to ensure not falling under the influence of Shi'a Islam (Formichi 2014, 7). In 1984, the central fatwa committee of the MUI released the first public statement on Shi'a Islam, urging (*menghimbau*) the Indonesian umma (*umat Islam Indonesia*) with its *ahlu sunnah wal jamaah*, to beware (*meningkatkan kewaspadaan*) the possible infiltration (*kemungkinan masuknya*) of Shi'a teaching. The recommendation highlighted theological differences from Sunni Islam as well as differences in religious and political leadership structures. The recommendation combined two key discourses, theological arguments and security narratives, subtly implying a threat to the Indonesia nation-state. Concerned about the revolutionary energy in Iran, the Suharto regime tried to curb the circulation/popularity of Shi'a publications, and the MUI found the theological arguments that underpinned this.

Over the next decade, Shi'a Islam in Indonesia lost some of its revolutionary character. Internal differences and competition were on the rise as Islamic study circles grew in the late 1980s and early 1990s, as was the visibility of variants of Islam, including Shi'a Islam (Bruinessen 1992). Then, the crumbling of the New Order in the mid-1990s and the early reform era gave Islamic intellectual debates a new boost. The publisher Mizan, closely associated with Shi'a writings, printed new editions of revolutionary literature. Under the pluralist Abdurrahman Wahid as president, Shi'a intellectuals became more confident. In 2000, Jalaluddin Rakhmat, who had long been known as a Shi'a sympathizer, founded the organization Ikatan Jamaah Ahlulbait Indonesia (IJABI), intended to be an umbrella organization. Originally aimed at representing all Shi'a in Indonesia but soon challenged by others with differing views, IJABI remains the largest Shi'a organization in the country. For more than a decade, Jalaluddin Rakhmat ran IJABI with Emilia Renita Az. Emilia Az had converted to Shi'a Islam in 2000 and founded the Organisation of Ahlulbayt for Social Support and Education, which shortly after, coinciding with her marriage to Jalaluddin Rakhmat, became IJABI's women's wing. Differences emerged between the two leaders after the death of the Lebanese Grand Ayatollah in 2010. The organizations split, and the couple eventually divorced in 2015 (S. Jones 2016). This further diversified the structural landscape of Shi'a Islam in Indonesia. A group of Sayyids, people claiming to be directly descended from the Prophet, founded the other main organization, Ahlul Bayt Indonesia (ABI), in 2010. It is much smaller than IJABI. All three organizations are involved in various da'wa activities and share a common objective, but disagreements and tensions have also characterized their generally cooperative relationships (Zulkifli 2013).

Organized opposition to Shi'a Islam has mainly come from two organizations for the past decades: the Islamic Union (Persatuan Islam, Persis) and the Indonesian Islamic Propagation Council (DDII, Dewan Dakwah Islamiyah Indonesia). Persis believes that Shi'ism is heretical and sees itself as the frontline in the fight to protect Sunni Muslims (Jones 2016). Persis is closely connected to DDII, which employs a rhetoric of self-defense (*difa'*) and forms a direct link to Saudi Arabia. The Saudi-dominated Muslim World League owns periodicals, publishing houses, and agencies that pushed the Indonesian variant of global anti-Shi'a campaigning within months after the Iranian Revolution (Zulkifli 2013). The Indonesian Shi'a discourses have since remained a site of the Saudi-Iranian struggle.

In 1997, the weakening of the right New Order regulations and the vibrant intellectual debates of the mid-1990s also gave rise to anti-Shi'a voices, which culminated in a national seminar on Shi'a Islam at Istiqlal Mosque in September 1997. The meeting was organized by Lembaga Penelitian dan Pengkajian Islam. More importantly, it received support from the MUI: Chairman K. H. Hasan Basri offered opening remarks. Attendees included members of the intelligence service Bakin, the attorney general, and members of the Ministries of Home Affairs and Religious Affairs. Members of NU and Muhammadiyah also attended, although it is unclear to what degree they supported the anti-Shi'a rhetoric (Abduh and Away 2012; Basri 2012; Hashem 1997; Rahardjo 2005).[4] Muhammadiyah and NU have—at least on the national level—retained a largely neutral if not even positive stance toward Shi'a Islam. Reformist Amien Rais held a neutral attitude (Zulkifli 2013). Nurcholish Madjid's attitude was even positive when he said, "Their Koran is the same as our Koran" (Tempo 1988) or wrote that the engagement with Shi'a Islam will lift Muslims to a higher philosophical level (Madjid 1994). At the September 1997 meeting, the Muhammadiyah representative was notably absent among the speakers (Zulkifli 2013). NU board members have likewise expressed themselves favorably and defensively for Shi'a, although different opinions could also be heard. After 1997, opposition against Shi'a Islam was more openly expressed. The early 2000s then saw attacks against a Shi'a pesantren boarding school in East Java. The police made no arrests (BBC News Indonesia 2011; Human Rights Watch 2013; Tempo 2011c). Debates about Shi'a Islam in Indonesia became a key arena not only for international rivalries, but also for struggles over authority between religious institutions and the state, as well as for competition between faith-based and rights-based arguments. In 1997, the MUI had used the call for a Shi'a ban to distance itself from the government, but in 2005, when it launched its controversial set of fatwas, the MUI decided against including a fatwa against Shi'a Islam. It is likely that it reverted to its own earlier arguments that declaring Shi'a Islam heretic would disturb Indonesian-Iranian relations. It is also likely that its members gauged that the number of people they would alienate with such a sweeping statement might be just as high as, or even higher than, the number of people such a ban would please. Nevertheless, Shi'a activist Az found that it was common knowledge that the MUI's ten criteria for misleading sects indirectly meant Shi'a: "In Indonesia, we have Majlis Ulama, saying, 'There are ten criteria of misleading or *munharif* Islam. And from there, you will know that this is Shi'a. He means . . . they mean Shi'a but they don't want to say it directly. But then at the end of the day, we know that they said that 'look at this, according to ten criteria from us, the Council of Majlis Ulama in Indonesia Shi'a is really misleading'" (Az 2015). The question as to who is practicing true Islam and who is not also affects those who are not explicitly called out: The question of proper conduct assumes more importance and affects the subjectivity of believers and nonbelievers alike.

We see a similar subtlety in Suryadharma Ali's 2012 response to the Sampang Case Solidarity Alliance, consisting of various human rights NGOs which asked him to support the vulnerable Shi'a by publicly clarifying that they are not heretical (Hidayatullah 2012): He stated that he was unable to make such a declaration since neither he, nor any other government official, was in a position to make such a judgment about any religious teaching. Instead, that was the task of scholars (Tempo 2013). Considering his earlier comments and his comments in other cases, in particular regarding the Ahmadiyya, this was an astonishing statement.

On numerous occasions, Suryadharma Ali has expressed skepticism about the religious legitimacy of Ahmadiyya and Shi'a beliefs. Various sources document him declaring that these groups' doctrines deviate from Islam. For instance, in March 2011, he remarked on the Ahmadiyya community, stating, "There are only two choices: either allow them to exist or prohibit them entirely . . . We must ban Ahmadiyya because it clearly contradicts Islam" (129). Similarly, in January 2012, following discussions with lawmakers, he publicly asserted that Shi'a teachings were "incompatible with Islam" (Human Rights Watch 2013). He also regularly connected such comments to presenting conversion as a viable solution to the problem of violence against Ahmadis and Shi'a, and a useful contribution to peacebuilding (Farabi 2024).

On the local level, however, observers have found evidence of anti-Shi'a activities and attitudes of "nearly all local offices of Muslim organizations"

(Zulkifli 2013). The widespread anti-Shi'a attitudes among local offices of Muslim organizations can be explained by local competition among Islamic groups, which was intensified by national-level discourse that spread doubts and skepticism about Shi'a Islam. In East Java, for instance, some ulama of NU, Muhammadiyah, and Persis, in collaboration with the provincial branch of MUI, met in 1992 under the framework of preventing the dissemination of Shi'a Islam in the region. This anti-Shi'a coalition lasted through the political shifts after the New Order and seems to have been strengthened by the decentralization of the reform era.

In the last days of December 2011, an unidentified group of people in the village of Nangkernang in Sampang, on the island of Madura in eastern Java set ablaze a Shi'a pesantren. At the time, five hundred Shi'a Muslims lived in the village. Newspapers reported that local authorities and the police had been warned of the planned attack three days earlier (*UCA News Indonesia* 2012b). National Human Rights Commission Chairperson Ifdhal Kasim later criticized the police for not taking any preventive measures (Tempo 2012). The few police officers present at the scene were reported to have stood by and watched (Kine 2013). The only person arrested by the police over the incident was later set free. Just a few weeks after the attack, in January 2012, the local East Java MUI branch issued a fatwa declaring Shi'a Islam deviant (JPNN 2012).[5] The East Javanese MUI legitimized their fatwa with a list of institutional, social, and doctrinal considerations. Institutionally, the fatwa was backed by preceding MUI fatwas in 1984 and 2006 as well as by other Muslim organizations in the area (Zulian 2015). Socially, the local MUI cited the imminent threat of further spreading of Shi'a Islam in the region. Finally, the scholars dedicated a lot of effort to arguing that the doctrinal differences of the local Shi'a made them incompatible with Islam in Indonesia and with the Sunna and were thus deviant and misleading (*sesat dan menyesatkan*) (Zulian 2015).

Sampang District Head Noer Tjahja subsequently demanded that all Shi'a residents may be expelled from Sampang (*UCA News Indonesia* 2012a). A second attack occurred in August 2012 in the same village. One Shi'a person was killed and another critically wounded. Dozens of people were injured and forty-nine houses were burned. Police investigated the attack and in February 2013, the Surabaya District Court sentenced one suspect in the case to eight months imprisonment for "maltreatment," according to Article 153 of the Penal Code (*Koran Madura* 2013). There were no other verdicts concerning this attack (Guntur W. 2020).

The Shi'a community in Madura experienced acts of intimidation and attacks before in 2006 and 2011. This second attack eventually led local authorities to "evacuate" the villagers to a shelter in a sports stadium in Sampang. The stadium reportedly lacked a sufficient clean water source and adequate sanitation facilities. The community of about three hundred would remain in the temporary sports stadium for another year, before being evicted to a shelter in Sidoarjo in East Java. Members of the community complained that they were neither allowed to bury their dead nor to participate in the local elections of their home area (A. Hasani 2019; Parlina and Boediwardhana 2013; *The Jakarta Post* 2018).

Some media reports covered the attack as a case concerning religion, using the old SARA acronym for this, and reported a clash (*bentrokan*) between Sunni and Shi'a (*Koran Madura* 2013). But altogether, the coverage on these attacks was extremely low, compared with coverage of other conflicts. The relatively low interest can partly be attributed to the lack of the sort of drastic images that made the Cikeusik attack on Ahmadis so visible. The other, more important reason lies in the alternative and competing framing of the attack as a local dispute whose details were portrayed as less relevant for other regions: This narrative held that the attack originated in a personal family dispute. This narrative was partly reflected in some of the media reports of the attack in 2012, in which the victims were described in their relation to one of the conflict's protagonists, the local Shi'a preacher Tajul Muluk (Detiknews 2012).

This framing also prevailed among influential Shi'a leaders. During my conversations with Rahkhmat and Az in Jakarta in early 2012, they told me the same story: A family dispute had spiraled out of control. Tajul Muluk, according to the narrative, had a disagreement with his younger brother, Roisul Hukama, over a woman whom the latter wanted to marry (Human Rights Watch 2012; Septian and Bisri 2012). After his brother's objection to the union, Roisul then joined the already existing but small anti-Shi'a campaign in Madura, which subsequently grew. In July 2011, police and Sampang officials persuaded Tajul Muluk to flee his village and provided him financial assistance to leave Nangkernang. The conflict, however, continued and culminated in the eviction of almost the entire village.

The two competing framings of this conflict—a conflict of religious freedom or between various Islamic factions versus a family dispute—seems to have overwhelmed some journalists: The details of the attacks and the minimalist legal prosecution faded from the headlines. What remained was a vague debate about the actual deviance of Shi'a Islam.

Just after the 2011 attack, on January 1, 2012, the Sampang, East Java, branch of the MUI issued a fatwa about what it described as Tajul Muluk's "deviant teachings" (Amnesty International 2012). Many who usually endorse the MUI's public statements quickly relativized the fatwa. A NU leader publicly clarified that the fatwa had been pronounced specifically for this group and did not aim at targeting Shi'a in general: "What is deviant is Tajul Muluk's Shi'a Islam, not Shi'a Islam in general" (*yang sesat itu aliran Tajul Muluk, Syiah-nya Tajul Muluk. Bukan Syiah secara keseluruhan*) (Prihandoko 2012). An even clearer distancing came officially from higher MUI members. On the same day that the local MUI branch announced their fatwa, Umar Shihab, a co-chairman of the national MUI, clearly stated that Shi'a Islam is a "school [*mazhab*] that is not deviant" (Metro TV News 2012). This episode highlights the MUI's internal divisions over the status of Shi'a Islam. On the one hand, national leaders recognized its long-standing historical presence in Indonesia and were aware that some anti-Shi'a agitation was politically motivated, both the influence of the Saudi-Iranian rivalry as well as by how this influence shaped local rivalries between religious scholars (Kayane 2020). On the other hand, the MUI also positions itself as the guardian of a unified Indonesian Islam—an aspiration that the visible presence of Shi'a communities complicates.

The ambiguities and nuances of the national debates were not influential enough to protect the East Javanese Shi'a: Two days after the local fatwa, a police report was filed against Tajul Muluk, and in March 2012, the East Java regional police charged him with blasphemy under Article 156(a) of the Indonesian Criminal Code and with "offensive actions" under Article 335 of the code. The indictment accused Tajul Muluk of telling his followers that the Quran was not the authentic text of Islam. Several months later, in July 2012, he was sentenced to two years detention under Article 156(a) (Amnesty International 2012). Tajul Muluk was accused of causing "public anxiety." Witnesses reportedly told the court that Tajul Muluk encouraged Muslims to pray three rather than five times a day, that the Quran was no longer authentic, and that followers need not make the hajj pilgrimage to Mecca (Hodal 2012). Just as in the Ahmadiyya debate, the rumored accusations suggested that Shi'a offended the core foundations of Islam.

In 2013, key MUI leaders including Ma'ruf Amin released a book with the title *Mengenal dan Mewaspadai Penyimpangan Syi'ah di Indonesia* (Recognize and be aware of Shi'a deviations in Indonesia). In the book, they discuss in detail the differences between Sunni and Shi'a notions of leadership, then list previous conflicts in order to highlight the potential to cause unrest in society, and eventually provide several pages of foundations, websites, radio stations, and other communications outlets that were either run by or suspected to be run by Shi'a or Shi'a sympathizers. In its structure, the book follows the usual double discourse of theological and security concerns and calls Muslims to be suspicious and aware of Shi'a teachings.

A letter written in 2015 by Rafani Akhyar of the MUI West Java branch that problematized the Shi'a Ashura Holiday, the commemoration of the Battle of Karbala and the death of Imam Hossein, illustrates the way in which a threat to Sunni Islam is connected to a threat to the Indonesian nation as well as the Indonesian republic: "We really understand and appreciate the defender of Ahlusunnah who worry about the rise of Shi'ah in West Java and in Indonesia in general, which could cause conflict within the Islamic umma and also poses a threat to the integrity of the Unitary Republic of Indonesia (*Negara Kesatuan Republik Indonesia*, NKRI), since the Shi'a stream, wherever they are, aim at establishing an Islamic State according to their own version" (Satrio 2015). This formulation combines theological with nationalist worries and even addresses secularists with the threat of a potential "Islamic state," once more highlighting potential ties to Iran.

This combination of theological and security arguments was echoed in statements by Athian Ali, head of the so-called National Anti-Shi'a Alliance (Aliansi Nasional Anti-Shi'ah) in 2017, when he stated that Shi'a Muslims always considered their own imams their prime authority, in whatever country they lived, thereby suggesting an inherent disloyalty among Shi'a citizens (Sulistya 2017).

In 2014, the MUI's Commission of Law Chairman Muhammad Baharun stated at an event on the island of Batam that "[Shi'a] oppose the Koranic verses and turn several friends of the Prophet into Kafirs. Their presence is an ideological threat that could destroyed the NKRI. The rise of Shi'ah destroys the unity of the state and create a fragmentation among the Islamic umma."

Because Indonesian verbs are not conjugated, Baharun's remarks can simultaneously describe a historical situation or a present process, but his reference to the Unitary Republic of Indonesia clarifies the concrete and imminent danger he wishes to paint in his comments (*TribunBatam* 2014).[6]

Comparing the two cases reveals clear patterns. From a state-centric perspective, the first parallel is police passivity. A'an Suryana (2019) has explained the police passivity in West Java and in Sampang in East Java by highlighting the close relationship that opponents of Ahmadis and Shi'a in the respective regions have with government officials and with religious authorities. Suryana reminds us that Jacqueline Hicks found that in some cases officers were neutral or even assumed mediating roles but that in other cases officials "operate[d] directly with the civil society groups that agitate[d] against Ahmadiyah" (Hicks 2014, 332). Similarly, Gerry van Klinken and Henk Schulte Nordholt underline the engineering and provocation of violence on the part of local elites in their pursuit of access to state resources (Klinken and Schulte Nordholt 2007).

A'an Suryana found that in the case of the anti-Ahmadi violence in West Java, the reason for the failure of police officers to protect Ahmadis was the alliance between various well-connected local vigilante organizations such as the Anti-Vice Movement (*Gerakan Anti Maksiat*, GIBAS) and the Combined Initiative of the Ranks of the Siliwangi Sundanese Youth (Gerakan Inisiatif Barisan Siliwangi, GIBAS) with local anti-Ahmadiyah groups and with local branches of national organizations acting against the Ahmadiyya. GAMAS and GIBAS are both based on religious and ethnic identity, respectively, and exert influence on local police (Suryana 2019).

In Sampang in East Java, the reason for police passivity was a different one. Entangled relations between the police and the local *kyai* (religious leaders) pushed police officers into the dilemma of having to choose between two authorities and sets of rules: those of the state and its rights for citizens and those of the kyai and their authority to decide over what is permissible religious practice and belief. In 2013, President Susilo Bambang Yudhoyono invited local kyai to a meeting in a hotel in Surabaya. He also invited some civil service and security officials from the central East Java government and the Sampang regency. His mission was to ask them to accept expelled Shi'a followers back into their village. He lamented that the international human rights body and the UN were breathing down his neck and that he needed the support of the kyai to resolve the problem (Suryana 2017). Politely but firmly, the kyai set their condition: the Shi'a, they demanded, were to convert back to Sunni Islam (Suryana 2018).

The police also opposed the president's wish, citing predictable conflict on a return without conversion (Suryana 2018). The kyai clearly were the highest authority in this case. Suryana argues that Indonesian presidents have little power in the face of the strong spirit to maintain a certain majoritarian social harmony (Suryana 2018).

The kyai remain a powerful political elite, despite the relative decline of their influence due to the rise of modern religious institutions such as the MUI, the digital competition from religious authorities elsewhere, and internal competition. Especially in rural Java, kyai remain part of the elite. Masdar Hilmy argues that the Sampang kyai regarded the rise of the Shi'a community around Tajul Muluk as a threat to their domination of the regional sociopolitical structure. Beyond serving as religious leaders, he argues, they offer former students patronage in economic ventures and in politics. In return, they financially support the respective pesantren (Hilmy 2015). Perhaps most importantly, Hilmy (2015) stresses the importance of kyai in the electoral process. As heads of pesantren boarding schools and wider communities, they function as crucial vote gatherers in local elections. Good relations with the kyai are thus crucial for local politicians. Some kyai are more established than others: When Muslim leaders are in competition with each other, the likely result is increased Islamist mobilization. Madura, for example, is an area marked by high competition between kyai (Pelletier 2021). This competition, Alexandre Pelletier argues convincingly, incentivizes established leaders to support Islamist mobilization and pushes "moderate" leaders into silence. In Pelletier's reading, Islamist mobilization is more successful in West Java and on Madura than in the rest of East Java because strong and established religious authorities as they exist in East Java are less likely to seek hardline alliances and rhetoric in the ways less well-established authorities do.

Competition forms the background against which episodes of violence but also othering more generally play out. It is also one of the two key factors that shape the likeliness of an identity being discriminated against because of foreignness and visibility. The Ahmadiyya and the Shi'a cases illustrate both: Each group is framed as having connections to Pakistan and Iran, respectively, and the visibility of both increased after 1998 because of public debates about their alleged deviance and the confidence concerning publicly discussing controversial beliefs that many Indonesians felt since the liberalization of the media and free speech in 1998.

The conflict in Madura illustrates this newfound confidence, the subsequent visibility, and its consequences. There was a long-established Shi'a presence in the person of Madura, but different from that of his father, Makmun, who had taught his family and the surrounding community in secrecy (*taqiyah*). Tajul Muluk preached more openly. Tajul was also generous with his resource, offering to conduct ceremonies without the common exchange of money. Within a few years, he gained many new followers and the Shi'a community grew quickly (Hilmy 2015; Pamungkas 2017).

Other religious leaders did not welcome this new popularity. Discussing a case of public conversion among Shi'a in the sports stadium in November 2012, witnessed by officials and police officers, Muslim clerics of the Islamic Boarding Schools Forum explained that the forum had been actively disseminating its teachings among Shi'a followers to "straighten out their religious understandings." Forum representative Nailul claimed that the clerics had secured permission from the East Java governor to enter the sports center and carry out their mission. "Madura has been Sunni since forever. So, it's our job to set them on the right path," Nailul was quoted as saying (*The Jakarta Post* 2012c).

A key narrative was that Shi'a Islam is somehow new and foreign, as illustrated in a statement by Abdusshomad Buchori, a local MUI leader, who reportedly said that the "Shi'a problem" (*permasalahan Syiah*) was not new but "had already entered Indonesia in 1984" (Gita Amanda 2012). He referred to the public recommendation (*tawisya*) warning against Shi'a

Islam that had only stopped short of judging Shi'a Islam as deviant. Here, he seems to refer to the MUI's own recommendation of monitoring the Shi'a in the country. Abdusshomad Buchori made this recommendation despite the long historical presence of Shi'a Islam in the region—suggesting that "the problem of" Shi'a Islam had "entered the country" in the 1980s was on one hand absurd, but it was also connected to the increasing bureaucratization and visibility of Shi'a Islam (Syarif 2023), which contributed to the construction of Shi'a Islam as a foreign and intruding problem.

What also contributed to the tense situation and the increased criminalization of Shi'a (Sofjan 2016) was the increased competition among religious leaders for followers and resources. In what we may in a simplified way imagine as a religious market, Tajul Muluk had been handing out freebies, worrying and angering the established competitors who were established enough to influence local politicians but not established enough to watch coolly as a small but growing number of people began to turn to Tajul Muluk.

Visibility and competition are often tied to security discourses of public order. This aspect becomes most apparent in cases of blasphemy and sexual morality but can also be detected in some of the arguments used against Shi'a preachers. In a newspaper report about a dialogue meeting held between representatives of IJABI, ABI, the Muhammadiyah, and the MUI in September 2012, Fahmi Salim from the Jakarta chapter of the MUI, and also an executive of Muhammadiyah, demanded that the Shi'a should "not provoke them by highlighting the differences among Sunnis and Shi'a in public." He also said, "We have previously agreed to not promote each other's religious understanding wherever the other is majority. The Shi'a community must stick to this, otherwise conflicts will be inevitable" (Aritonang 2012). This comment openly demands that minorities try to be invisible.

In their visit to the central MUI, the East Javanese MUI members made a similar argument when explaining the novelty of the Shi'a problem. They argued that in the previous couple of years, Shi'a Islam had begun to "show movement" (*syiah mulai menunjukkan pergerakannya*) and that now the case in Madura resembled a time bomb (*bom waktu*) (Gita Amanda and Ruslan 2012). A district government official in Madura, Rudy Setiadhy, reportedly said, "Yes, the government is responsible for protecting people's freedom of religion, but the local tradition also has to be respected. The Shi'a are not part of the local tradition and they are disturbing the religious harmony in the village" (Vaswani 2012). A similar argument had already been brought forward in January 2012 by MUI members from East Java in their attempt to persuade the central MUI to declare Shi'a deviant.

Other than in the Ahmadiyya case, the MUI was openly divided on the question of Shi'a Islam. Similarly, the spectrum of opinions among NU and Muhammadiyah officials was much wider on the question of whether Shi'a were deviant—as opposed to merely discussing how to deal with the Ahmadiyya's apparently established and evident deviance.

Defense

The previous sections have shown how the lines of attack against the Ahmadiyya and Shi'a mainly merged theological arguments with security discourses and highlighted the collaboration between state and religious authorities. The arguments and vocabulary used for defense differed significantly from that of the attacks, leading to a discursive situation of talking past each other, thereby delegitimizing the other's frame of reference, and further marginalization of the Ahmadis and Shi'a. In the reform period after 1998, the discourse of human rights largely replaced what remained of leftist discourse and absorbed discourses of inner-Islamic diversity and of multireligious pluralism. This would only later change in the late 2010s. In the Ahmadiyya case in the 2000s and 2010s, practically their entire defense used the terminology of human rights, not only in court, but also in the media and public debate. In almost all commentary and media coverage between 2008 and 2012, during the height of the anti-Ahmadiyya debates, intellectuals and commentators stressed minority rights, especially the rights to freedom of belief and expression. Almost all of the defenders of the Ahmadiyya in the public debates were professional human rights advocates, some of whom used an attack against an Ahmadiyya community in West Java in 2011 to advocate for the establishment of a "Human Rights Court" (Peterson and Schäfer 2021).

The high influx of funding for human rights initiatives prioritized this vocabulary over others. This included the religious and nationalist argumentation of the late Abdurrahman Wahid who was both a respected Islamic scholar and briefly president (1999–2001) and who stressed that diversity was part of Islam and of the Indonesian nation. Abdurrahman Wahid had engaged in interreligious dialogues and took steps to protect minorities, most notably lifting the ban on Confucianism as a recognized religion, but he also extended recognition and acceptance to diversity within Islam. He often used the concept of *pribumisasi Islam* (Indigenization of Islam) to encourage the integration of Islamic values with local traditions to foster harmony and mutual respect among different religious and cultural groups. Once his presidency ended and his power and influence waned, many of the discourses defending minorities prioritized the vocabulary of human rights and liberalism over the previous Islamic and nationalist repertoire.

In the mid-2000s, however, gaps developed between the discourses of pluralism and nationalism, and one important element that contributed to this gap was the rise of the vocabulary of rights, especially human rights and the right to religious freedom. In the 1990s, as mentioned, many activists had combined the rhetoric of human rights and Islam, but the 2000s saw a growing dichotomy between these two discourses. It was partly an effect of the global hegemony of human rights discourse and its intimate connection to the powers that be. This effect, of course, is not unique to Indonesia. The alienating effects that discourses of rights can have for those identified as minorities have been felt by the Copts in Egypt and other Christians in the Middle East (Mahmood 2012), the Alevis in Turkey (Dressler 2013), and the Rohingya in Myanmar (Hurd 2015), all of whom Western governments and commentators discuss as suppressed "minorities" but whose internal leadership are divided over whether this is a helpful framing or whether they should instead emphasize their national belonging rather than their religious difference (Hurd 2015). The accentuation of their "difference" often results in accelerating their exclusion from the nation. Rogers Brubaker discussed this effect in his seminal work *Ethnicity Without Groups* (2004): Enhancing a particular identity often comes at the price of neglecting another and at the potentially high price of further perpetuating the notion of a homogeneous identity that differs significantly from what is presented as "mainstream." During a conversation I had with Ahmadi students after the Jakarta launch of the novel *Maryam*, in which the non-Ahmadi author Okky Madasari writes about a Lombok Ahmadi protagonist experiencing persecution, one young Ahmadi student said to me, "You know, I really appreciate her research and her efforts to help. But when I read the novel, it made me feel different. I used to just be a normal Indonesian, and reading it makes me feel . . . different [*berbeda*]."[7]

My interlocutor reflected on the novelty and construction of her identity as an Ahmadi. For decades, Ahmadis were considered a relatively normal part of Islam in Indonesia, tolerated if not accepted by the large and powerful national organizations, recognized by the state, and only sporadically and locally problematized by critics who found their interpretation of Islam offensive.

Similarly, the relative novelty of the concept of minority itself is reflected in the Indonesian term *minoritas*. Local Indonesian languages, for instance Javanese and Makassarese, have adapted this Indonesian term to refer to those marked as a singled-out identity because the languages do not possess an equivalent concept. The term usually serves to defend those under political pressure, but it also has the effect of excluding whoever is marked as a minority from forming a majority. In other words, Indonesians become Ahmadis or Shi'a, rather than being perceived as neighbors, coworkers, or members of a particular social class. For those framed and attacked as minorities, this dynamic in Indonesian public discourse resulted in the acceleration of their marginalization.

The discourse of human rights (*hak asasi manusia*) became omnipresent. However, human rights simultaneously became increasingly associated with Western global hegemony. This threatened to drag down with them those who are defended in their name. It is unclear to what degree the human rights framework succeeded in improving the situation of the marginalized Ahmadiyya and Shi'a, but it certainly had the effect of increasing their visibility as Shi'a and that of human rights vocabulary itself. For the human rights movement, the defense of the Ahmadiyya was a site of proliferation: Almost every press article on the Ahmadiyya issue cited not only the MUI but also some human rights advocate. These defenders tried to push for an ever more prominent role of human rights in Indonesian society but remained a relatively small group.

Arguments emphasizing inner-Islamic diversity were scarce in the case of the Ahmadiyya, and slightly more pronounced for Shi'a Muslims. Abdurrahman Wahid had publicly dismissed the arguments against Ahmadiyya as propaganda before he died in 2009 (*NU Online* 2008), but for a long time after his death, very few high-authority Muslim leaders on the national stage publicly defended the Ahmadiyya and nobody primary cited arguments grounded in Islam. This hesitation can be explained by several factors, ranging from the conviction that the Ahmadis are theologically wrong to disinterest in and rejection of theological reasoning in political questions altogether. The scholar and public intellectual Najib Burhani (2021) cites theological issues as the reason for this reluctance. Two comments by Muhammadiyah leaders illustrate the balancing act they fulfil when defending the Ahmadiyya. In July 2005, Din Syamsudin said, "According to Islamic teaching, Islam also gives freedom to everyone. However, Islam also suggest[s] people to return to the right teaching. Therefore, we cannot justify the violence, let alone the destruction" (Detiknews 2005). Syamsudin here suggests that while Ahmadis must not be violently attacked, they might have deviated from the right teachings. Similarly, Ahmad Syafii Maarif said in 2010 in response to the call by Suyadharma Ali to disband the Ahmadiyya, "Even though I disagree with the Ahmadiyya ideology, they cannot be treated like this" (Widjaya 2010). Even in the defense, Maarif found it necessary to emphasize his (theological) disagreement. Another Muhammadiyah leader explained that "Shi'a and Ahmadiyah are sensitive issues [*persoalan yang sensitif*] for Muslims" and that they were being considered "opposing" [*berseberangan*] and outside mainstream Muslim beliefs (Cholid 2021).

The complex interplay of theological and security-related attacks against the Ahmadi on one side and the defenses within the idiom of human rights on the other has resulted in positioning the Ahmadiyya further outside the Indonesian umma and at the margins of the Indonesian nation. The few religious authorities who did defend the Ahmadiyya usually did so by highlighting their status as Indonesian citizens and pluralist interpretations of Indonesian nationalism. An example is the NU leader and politician Mahfud MD, a close ally of Abdurrahman Wahid. In 2011, he publicly declared that he regretted the violence and intimidation against Ahmadiyah and emphasized that the constitution "did not allow that citizens feel threatened because of their beliefs" (Antara News 2011).

This line of argument stressed that Ahmadis have a legitimate position in the Indonesian nation and should thus be protected from attacks. For instance, Ahmadi spokesperson Mubarik Ahmad once referenced Wage Soepratman, the composer of the national anthem who was awarded the title National Hero in 1971 and whose portrait graced the IDR 50,000 rupiah note printed between 1992 and 1998. He also appealed to Indonesians to remember Arief Rahman Hakim, cited as a martyr for the nation during student protests against the Indonesian Communist Party in 1966 (Abdullah 2009).

When Mubarik Ahmad made a plea for his community a few days after the Cikeusik attack, he said, "Our existence is legitimate, we're legally registered. And we are not a banned organization. We have been an officially registered legal body since 1953" (*The Jakarta Post* 2011a).

Najib Burhani's commentary in the *Jakarta Globe* in September 2012 captures the salience of nationalism in this debate: "We have to be realistic and stop expecting the 'magic' of Idul Fitri [the end of Ramadan] to reconcile those who [are] involved in conflicts over the issue of orthodoxy and heterodoxy. . . . It has never worked before and seems unlikely to work in the future if we look at this from the perspective of theology. . . . The only way to make reconciliation between mainstream Muslims and Ahmadis possible is on the basis of nationality, i.e. by accepting Ahmadis as fellow citizens and acknowledging their right to practice a different belief." Burhani here highlights nationalism as the most promising way to protect Ahmadis.

Eventually, after more than a decade of self-defense and legal and physical attacks, a group of Ahmadis sought to repeal the so-called blasphemy law on the basis of inner-Islamic diversity and pluralism in 2017 (A'yun 2019). This was seven years after the first attempt, in which Ahmadis were only partly involved, had been rejected. But the shift in strategy came too late: By then, the fronts had already hardened to such a degree that the Constitutional Court easily dismissed their attempt, almost entirely without any public debate. By then, two changes had occurred in the discourse. Most important, Indonesian nationalism was no longer first and foremost styled as multicultural and multireligious but as religious in the sense of prioritizing orthodoxy as defined by powerful religious authorities. Further, Ahmadis had been marginalized to such a degree that their attempt to be part of this religious nation was fruitless: They had become the deviant internal other.

The Shi'a case was different in some ways. Their defenders used the human rights framework and nationalism, but several authorities also pointed at arguments of diversity. The Shi'a defense was altogether more ambivalent and nuanced, as exemplified in this defending statement on Shi'a Islam by NU leader Said Aqil Siradj, when he said in 2012 that Shi'a Islam "is not deviant, just different from us" (*tidak sesat, hanya berbeda dengan kita*) (Prihandoko 2012). This comment is a rare and important embrace of religious difference, but it comes with a grain of salt: The sentence defends the Shi'a but also builds an "us" and a "we" from which Shi'a differ. With this difference comes the question who is part of this "we." Similarly, he said that "their center is actually in Iran" (*pusatnya memang di Iran*). This statement is readable in different ways, suggesting that Islam is larger than Indonesia and various interpretations had their own rights to exist but also disconnecting Shi'a from Indonesian identity.

Human rights advocates saw the public discussion on Shi'a deviance and the Madura attacks as another example of minority suppression and the restriction of religious liberty and integrated the case into their struggle for religious freedom: "It has become yet another appalling example of the lack of freedom of religion in this country," said Hendardi, chairman of the Setara Institute (Marbun 2015).

The framing of rights and minorities also characterized other voices, one of which is illustrated in the comment by Fajar Riza Ulhaq, the executive director of the Muhammadiyah-linked Ma'arif Institute (known for supporting individual rights and minorities), who said after the attacks against the Shi'a community in Sampang: "We have to act against the increasing acts of terror being meted out to minority groups. It reflects the escalating terror tactics being used against people of different faiths" (Gita Amanda 2012). Again, it is their status as a minority that their defendant highlights.

This chapter examined the marginalization of Indonesia's Ahmadiyya and Shi'a communities and identities through the Islamist Conservative Majoritarian Synthesis and showed how religious and state authorities collaborate to define and enforce Mainstream Islam in the 2000s and early 2010s. Religious and political leaders constructed Ahmadis and Shi'a as the other to bolster their own authority and position themselves at the center of an idea of Mainstream Islam. The examples showed how theological and security arguments intertwined, justifying outbreaks of violence and a blind eye on the part of onlookers and legal bans targeting the Ahmadiyya. Their opponents framed Ahmadiyya and Shi'a Muslims as threats to Islam and to national unity. State and religious leaders as well as media amplified accusations that often concerned the very heart of Islamic belief, spreading rumors and staging public "conversion" events to enforce conformity and assimilation.

The examples also showed that the defense of these identities was in this period mostly characterized by a predominance of human rights vocabulary. After 2017, these discourses then experienced a significant change as part of Jokowi's strategy of handling the rise of the Islamist Conservative Majoritarian Synthesis. This change is personified in the 2020 appointment of Yaqut Cholil Qouma, the general chairman of GP Ansor, the youth wing of NU, as minister of religious affairs. Within days of assuming his office, Yaqut Cholil Qouma promised to protect the rights of Ahmadis and Shi'a (Styawan 2020). After a brief public debate as to what this protection would entail and a skeptical comment by Anwar Abbas, the deputy chair of the MUI, who warned Yaqut and urged him to consult with senior Muslim clerics on this "theological issue [and thus] sensitive matter (*sangat sensitif, karena dia bersifat teologis*)" (Styawan 2022), Yaqut clarified his position: "I've never said I'd protect Shi'a and Ahmadiyah organizations or groups. My stance as a religious affairs minister is to protect them as citizens" (Antara and Saputri 2020; Dewi 2020; Mashabi 2020). On earlier occasions, he highlighted that national anthem composer Wage Soepratman had been an Ahmadi. With these statements, Yaqut clarified that he defended Ahmadis and Shi'a on the grounds of nationalism rather than on the grounds of diversity.

In one way, Yaqut backpedaled when he emphasized the status of Ahmadis and Shi'a as citizens, as he did not defend them in the undoubtedly weightier framework of Islam. Nevertheless, elsewhere he repeatedly emphasized diversity as an intrinsic part of Indonesian nationalism—a position missing from large swaths of the elite public discourse between 2005 and 2020. Anwar Abbas's reference to this being a "theological issue" was a reminder of those polarized debates in which a position seemed to be either tied to right-wing religio-nationalist discourses or to so-called secular nationalist– and human rights–based ones. Yaqut's choice of words is telling and interesting here: While he emphasized the status of Ahmadis and Shi'a as citizens and also said that the law was the same for everyone, he did not use the word *rights* (Polda Metro Jaya 2020). We cannot know his motivations, but in the polarized debate in which rights were often used by activists connected to foreign funding sources, it might have been a deliberate act of tactfulness to avoid a potentially divisive term and free the concept of Indonesian citizenship from the baggage of the discourse on rights.

In addition to the Ahmadiyya and Shi'a, the Islamist Conservative Majoritarian Synthesis targeted and marginalized a range of other identities in the 2000s and 2010s. The next chapter discusses the failed attempt to repeal the blasphemy law in 2010, blasphemy accusations in various cases, and the targeting of LGBTQI people.

CHAPTER 3

Patterns of Othering

Blasphemy, Classifications, and Political Homophobia

In February 2012, various media reported that then–Minister of Religious Affairs, Suryadharma Ali of the United Development Party (Partai Persatuan Pembangunan), had announced a ban on miniskirts. Suryadharma Ali had determined they were "pornographic" and promised to create an Anti-Pornography Task Force to tackle the problem. This new organization, he declared, would finally enforce the antipornography law of 2008 (Bachelard 2012; *The Jakarta Post* 2012b), which had included provisions for the implementation force (Fealy and White 2008). This force never materialized, neither after 2008 nor after 2012, but parts of the government had once again signaled to social conservatives and the Islamist far right that they saw it as their duty to monitor sexuality in realms that liberals consider private. The question of what areas of practice and behavior the state should monitor is the strongest link between the cases of supposed religious heterodoxy and those one might call public morality.

The socially conservative and Islamist-Majoritarian enforcement of religious boundaries moves from one target to another, further reducing the diversity of Islam in Indonesia and further advancing an ideal citizen model: a heterosexual Sunni Muslim who adheres to the thin religious interpretations sanctioned by a select few religious authorities. The various minorities and identities discussed in the previous and this chapter are sites where various religious and political actors compete for influence and resources and where they draw the boundaries of the constructed Mainstream Islam, reproducing the Islamist Conservative Majoritarian Synthesis.

A key year in this process was 2005, as the Council of Indonesian Islamic Scholars (MUI) enforced its notion of Mainstream Islam through its set of fatwas targeting pluralism, liberalism, and secularism. The fatwas had a major agenda-setting effect and the coming years saw a surge of accusations of blasphemy and violations of the spirit that informed the 2005 fatwa.

The previous chapter focuses on two of the most prominent variants of Islam attacked as deviant and showed how religio-nationalists have exercised border control in ways that reconfigure the Indonesian nation as majoritarian Muslim. This chapter adopts a broader and comparative approach to examining the construction of Mainstream Islam, focusing on a diverse range of identities that the Islamist Majoritarian Synthesis marginalized. It delves into how debates over public morality construct and police social boundaries, creating cycles of moral panic that shift focus from one marginalized group to another and demonstrates how exclusionary processes extend beyond but connect to theological deviance debates to encompass broader sociocultural and moral boundaries. As in the previous examples, those seeking to consolidate the center in the early 2000s pushed toward defining and marginalizing internal others, such as liberal Muslims, believers deviating from heterosexual gender norms, nonbelievers and adherents of traditional beliefs, and smaller religious organizations. The cases differ substantially from each other but show clear patterns of the process of othering: The combination of visibility and the imagined degree of foreignness are the key traits that draw suspicions of deviance and make social categories vulnerable to marginalization.

The chapter argues and shows that **visibility is a key factor of vulnerability but not a sufficient explanation for marginalization, since** even those who attempt to keep a low profile are not always shielded from persecution. The Islamist Conservative Majoritarian Synthesis can impose visibility, especially through media. Second, the cases connect the rise of social conservatism and nationalism to broader socioeconomic grievances and global influences, such as neoliberal inequality and resistance to perceived foreign cultural interventions. Third, the cases illustrate that in the early 2000s, defenders of those targeted by socially conservative Islamists and majoritarian forces predominantly relied on liberal and human rights frameworks—a strategy less effective than the later localized and culturally rooted approaches to advocacy.

In 2005, the fatwa against liberalism, pluralism, and secularism stated that religious pluralism "teaches that all religions are the same and hence the truth of every religion is relative" and that "all religious adherents will enter and coexist in heaven." The fatwa further described religious secularism as "separating world affairs from religion" and reducing religion to only "regulate the personal relationship with God, while the relationship between fellow human beings is governed only by social agreements." Religious liberalism, stated the fatwa, "understands the religious texts (Al-Qur'an & Sunnah) by using a free mind [*pikiran bebas*]." In these understandings, the fatwa stipulated, religious pluralism, secularism, and liberalism are "contrary to the religious teachings of Islam" and therefore "Muslims are forbidden to follow the understanding of pluralism, secularism and religious liberalism [*haram mengikuti paham pluralism, sekularisme dan liberalisme agama*]." The fatwa further reads, "In matters of aqidah [creed] and worship, Muslims are obliged to be exclusive, in the sense of it being haram to mix the aqidah and worship of Muslims with the aqidah and worship of followers of other religions." It differentiates such pluralism from plurality (*pluralitas*): "For Muslims living with adherents of other religions (religious plurality), in social matters unrelated to aqidah and worship, Muslims should be inclusive, in the sense of continuing to socially interact with adherents of other religions and to not harming each other."

Taking the set of fatwas as a lens for the ensuing discourses, this chapter analyses how in the 2000s and early 2010s actors of the Islamist Conservative Synthesis intensified their campaign against a broad range of identities they deemed deviant. They targeted gender pluralist Indonesians and other marginalized groups, exposing individuals who resisted conformity and accusing them of threatening moral order. In these efforts, they strategically reconfigured the boundaries of public and private spaces, using debates over morality to construct new forms of publicness. By constructing a public discourse about Mainstream Islam, they enhanced their ability to identify and amplify differences, making their campaigns of exclusion and assimilation more effective. Digital media further enabled this process, eroding distinctions between public and private life and intensifying their influence over how identity is contested and controlled.

The chapter first discusses how the small but vocal Liberal Islam Network briefly blossomed in the early 2000s but ultimately could not withstand the pushback against it. The example shows how the Islamist Conservative Majoritarian Synthesis began targeting those who differ not only in terms of their religious practice and degree of piety but also in terms of political views. This case and the discussion of aspects of transnationalism and cosmopolitanism illustrates the complicated relationship many Indonesians had to the rapid economic transformations of the 1990s: Welcomed by many as offering new chances for social mobility, the rapid privatization of national assets and other neoliberal shifts were also rejected for causing rising inequalities. The case thus demonstrates the power, limits, and effects of international discourses in postreform Indonesia: Even those activists who sought to help members of attacked minorities and identities unintentionally contributed to their discrimination in the literal sense. Discrimination derives from the Latin *discriminare*, meaning "to separate" or "to distinguish." Well-intentioned efforts to defend minorities have also contributed to marking them as distinct groups—partly because the language of defense invoked liberalism, a concept soon stigmatized, and partly because it relied on human rights, whose universality has long been contested. The case also illustrates an important shift in the discourse on diversity in Indonesia in the 2010s and alludes to later developments: Some of the activists previously involved in the Liberal Islam Network later became engaged in the discourse on Islam Nusantara (Islam of the Archipelago) that began to defend diversity from a different angle. Instead of using vocabulary emphasizing human rights and individual freedom, this new strategy indigenized the defense of diversity by highlighting local and Indonesian interpretations of Islam vis-à-vis a Middle Eastern other. This discourse, more locally rooted and less vulnerable to accusations of foreignness, then received support from President Jokowi himself and proved much more successful in terms of defending diversity and pluralism.

This chapter then discusses blasphemy. It first offers a short overview of the theological grounding of the blasphemy accusations. The Islamic imperative of "enjoining good, forbidding wrong" provides the blueprint that facilitates Islamist lobbying for state regulations in socially conservative ways. The chapter then turns to three attempts to repeal the so-called blasphemy law, of which the first attempt in 2010 by a human rights coalition was by far the most important. Its rejection firmly positioned Indonesia between an explicitly Islamist state and one in which religion belonged to a however defined private realm. The case demonstrates the strong influence of particular religious authorities on the public and judicial spheres and how Islamists made moral claims and their state interlocutors translated them into security and communitarian discourses, moving Islamist agendas from the margins to the center of society. The decision also set the stage for the 2016 demonstrations against and eventual fall of Basuki Tjahaja Purnama (Ahok). Against the background of global debates about blasphemy, the court also distinguished between public and private, showing the importance of this ongoing negotiation of public and private spaces and its intertwinement with visibility.

The two cases of the Eden Community and the East Lombok farmer Amaq Bakri, who were both convicted of blasphemy, allow a more detailed analysis of the factors visibility and foreignness. The cases illustrate the willingness of those patrolling the borders of true Islam to go after even tiny groups and widely unknown individuals who pose no serious competitive threat. At the same time, the case suggests that intentional visibility provokes official reactions. But the case of the East Lombok spiritual leader Amaq Bakri complicates this conclusion and further illustrates the complexity of the factor of public visibility: If visibility makes an organization or individual more vulnerable to accusations of deviance, does that in turn mean that those keeping a low profile will be safe? The case of Amaq Bakri shows that this would be too hasty a conclusion and that the drivers of the synthesis will occasionally force someone into visibility. The case also illustrates how digitalization facilitates this and how majoritarians employ digital media in their campaign of othering.

The marginalization of adherents of Indigenous beliefs and atheists shows that the perception of being local or foreign can become a key factor in determining the vulnerability to othering and raises the question of which identity markers become Indonesianized and which ones do not. The situation of Indigenous beliefs, classified as *aliran kepercayaan*, illustrates the association of clearly marked and neatly orthodoxified religions with modernity and the discomfort that reminders of more ambiguous practices spark among those who patrol the boundaries of religion. This case also suggests that a perception of "being local" and a lack of real or suspected ties to forces outside the nation largely protects adherents of Indigenous beliefs from attacks, and especially from attacks on them being tolerated and even encouraged by a silent majority as in the other cases. The short discussion of atheists again illustrates the high level of regulation of belief through the state, but importantly it also shows how different atheist actors formulate their space-claiming activities and what consequences these different approaches have for them. One of the most well-known cases shows how the combination of claiming a space and insulting religion creates a volatility that only needs a single spark to ignite, and that those seeking to consolidate the center stand ready to use the matches. This idea supports the book's central argument that some actors wishing to be perceived as particularly religious do not ground their identity as much in theological debates or complex religious practices as in heavily relying on producing outrage and othering.

The second part of the chapter turns to the discrimination and attacks against LGBTQI people from the mid-2010s onward as part of increasing social conservatism and heteronormativity. The case connects the notion of "foreignness" to questions of cosmopolitanism and socioeconomic disparities and suggests that some of the aggression against gender plurality channels socioeconomic grievances in ways that can be compared to the far right in Europe. In Europe and the United States, restructuring between majority and minority through migration has embedded gender, sexuality, and religion in a right-wing discourse that often—inter alia—includes anti-LGBTQI positions (Bosia and Weiss 2013).

Collectively, these examples demonstrate how the systematic enforcement of religious conformity by social conservatives targets various groups sequentially, gradually eroding Islamic pluralism in Indonesia. Several of the cases show that while visibility is a key factor, even keeping a low profile will not necessarily protect potential victims from persecution.

The Liberal Islam Network

In post-Suharto Indonesia, Liberal Islam was a movement advocating for the reinterpretation of Islamic teachings to align with democracy, pluralism, and human rights. The movement was numerically very small but gained quite some popularity among urban elites and attracted significant funding from outside and within the country. Advocates of Liberal Islam championed religious pluralism, gender equality, and the compatibility of Islam with democratic governance, while critiquing patriarchal norms and socially conservative institutions. The Liberal Islam Network (Jaringan Islam Liberal, JIL), which thrived in the early 2000s, was at the forefront of this intellectual and social movement.

The MUI strongly opposed JIL. During the opening speech at the MUI's seventh National Consultancy Meeting in 2005, then–General Chairman Sahal Mahfudh of Nahdlatul Ulama (NU) announced that the Council of Ulama would formulate several edicts to put an end to "deviant secular and liberal Islamic thoughts." He said the council was determined to win the "war of ideas against liberal Islam" and that "secularism and liberalism, two Western-influenced thoughts that have developed in Indonesia, have brought chaos to the principles of Islamic teachings" (Hicks 2014). The MUI argued that pluralism, liberalism, and secularism created social anxiety (*keresahan sosial*) within the Muslim community and that the Indonesian *umma* was facing a nonphysical war (*perang nonfisik*), or *ghazw al-fikr*, Arabic for "invasion of ideas" (Bruinessen 2015). Of the eleven fatwas issued at the meeting in 2005, the one on secularism, pluralism, and liberalism was the most controversial. It ignited "divisive passions not seen publicly within the Indonesian umma for many years" (Gillespie 2007).

While liberal and pluralist ideas have always been integral to Indonesia's mass civil society organizations, they have also faced fierce critics within them. Interreligious and prodemocratic activities thrived in the reformasi period, but both NU and Muhammadiyah were internally divided on liberal democratic values (Menchik 2016). By the mid-2000s, some observers noted the growing dominance of more conservative or exclusivist voices in both organizations. At the 2004 and 2005 national congresses of NU and Muhammadiyah, which are held every five years, there was a "purge" of liberal leadership (Bruinessen 2010). In 2005, the Muhammadiyah congress chose the more conservative Din Syamsuddin as the successor of Syafi'i Ma'arif, who had been long known for his support of democracy-related activism. At the NU congress in 2004, NU elders elected Hasyim Muzadi, who had partially campaigned on a platform of defending a middle path against fundamentalism on one side and Western liberal influences on the other. He accused liberal Islam of being too Western-influenced (Rumadi 2015).

A key figure in the formulation of the fatwas was the senior and longstanding NU leader Ma'ruf Amin, who would later, in 2019, become vice president. In 2005, he was the chairman of MUI's Fatwa Commission. In this capacity, he overruled more nuanced voices within NU, an organization in which many members pride themselves on defending traditional Southeast Asian values, including diversity. Hasyim Muzadi, who had just been elected general chairman, saw the fatwa as a backward step for Indonesia's interreligious life (Kompas 2005). Masdar F. Mas'udi, the then secretary of the Supreme Council, even asked the MUI to withdraw its fatwa on pluralism, liberalism and secularism. The Supreme Council, or Syuriah, represents the spiritual and religious leadership, while the Tanfidziyah is responsible for the operational and administrative functions of the organization. Delegates, representing regional and local NU branches, nominate and decide on the group of elder scholars on the council during the general meetings every five years. Masdar F. Mas'udi in this case feared that the MUI fatwa could escalate violence in the name of religion: "issuing such a fatwa is really risky. It could be used by people addicted to violence to justify their actions" (*NU Online* 2005a). In a written statement to the pluralist Wahid Institute, he questioned the credibility and jurisprudence of the fatwa (Ali 2019). The scholar Dawam Raharjo emphasized freedom of thought, speech, and belief in the Indonesian constitution and in the Quran and sunna (Sirry 2013). He also criticized the way MUI interpreted the meaning of *pluralism*: MUI had rejected normative religious pluralism (*pluralisme*) but tolerated the empirical existence of plurality (*pluralitas*), or diversity as an undeniable social fact.

When colleagues told me their views on this debate during my fieldwork, they pointed at the difficulty of trying to make a neat separation here: How were Muslims supposed to accept actually existing diversity but simultaneously reject pluralism as a value?

Originally, the fatwa was intended to specifically name the JIL, a numerically small but vocal network of scholars and activists around the NU figure Ulil Abshar-Abdalla, but a senior member objected, and the fatwa was thus reformulated more generally (Assyaukanie 2009b; Hasyim 2012). Liberal thought in Islam is a branch of reformist and modernist Islam. In Indonesia, their ideas were popularized in the 1970s by Nurcholish Madjid. The term *liberal Islam* became more prominent in Indonesia on the basis of two books, Leonard Binder's *Islamic Liberalism: A Critique of Development Ideologies* (1988) and *Liberal Islam: A Sourcebook*, edited by Charles Kurzman (1998). One of the key purposes of the network was to preserve tolerance and a diversity of varying interpretations of Islam. It could be argued that "liberal Islam" was a rather unfortunate label for this endeavor, but at the time, generous donations from Western agencies supported the discourse of liberalism. A group around the young intellectuals Ulil Abshar-Abdalla, Luthfi Assyaukanie, Saeful Mujani, and Ahmad Sahal used the term to respond to an apparent rise in extremist Islamist voices after Suharto's fall. The small but forceful and very visible organization formed by these scholars illustrates like few others the diversity and polarization of post-1998 public debates on Islam. JIL members disseminated their ideas through an interactive website, a mailing list, and letters to editors. The group soon established a vocal media presence, with columns and articles about Islamic teachings appearing outside specific Islamic publications. A wide-circulation newspaper group, Jawa Pos, set aside regular space for JIL activists. This was an era in which general interest in Islam in the media grew rapidly, with starkly contrasting views and ideas competing for the succession of the New Order regime. Many of the articles stressed the separation of political and religious institutions and based their arguments in interpretations of the Quran that challenged literal readings. The newspaper group names as its core values the openness of the gates of *ijtihad* (independent reasoning); an ethical-religious spirit as opposed to a literal meaning of texts; a relative, open, and plural notion of truth; standing behind minorities and the oppressed; promoting freedom of belief and faith; and the separation of heavenly from worldly authority. Scholar-activists such as Asghar Ali Engineer and Abdullahi An-Na'im are among the group's most important intellectual influences. Given that many Indonesian conservatives use the word *liberal* derogatorily, JIL chose a straightforward and provocative name.

Some see them as heirs of the legacies of both Abdurrahman Wahid and Nurcholish Madjid, reconciling and fruitfully discussing some of the tensions between traditional and modernist Indonesian Islamic thought. The group has also inspired the founding of other groups, for instance the Muhammadiyah Young Intellectual Network (Jaringan Intelektual Muda Muhammadiyah). It was established by Muhammadiyah members in 2003 in Malang, in the face of accusations of deviance from other Muhammadiyah members (Najib et al. 2023).

The accusations against JIL illustrate how religion in these public discourses on orthodoxy is "thin" even where it engages with matters of creed. According to the fatwa, there can be no pluralism in religion since religions are built on universal truth claims. Pluralism, in Ma'ruf Amin's opinion, would make all religions equal—something a true believer could not seriously accept, as the fatwa quoted illustrates (*NU Online* 2005b). The text of the fatwa composes only one and a half pages, preceded by several Quranic verses in Arabic and in Indonesian translation, spread across four pages. There are no elaborations on the process of jurisprudence. Masdar F. Mas'udi of the Supreme Council questioned the credibility and jurisprudence of the fatwa (*NU Online* 2005a). Similarly, the accusations against JIL and promoters of liberal ideas more generally were mostly vague, especially in theological terms. The theological arguments were rather weak: The cited verses revolve around historical situations between political actors at the time of the Prophet Muhammad. Even in the classic Islamic genre of the fatwa, religion here is thin: the surprisingly short wording skips the lengthy justifications and discussions that usually characterize theological debates and legal judgments and instead offers relatively straightforward interpretations of what is wrong and what is right.

Weighing at least as heavily as these accusations is the charge of foreignness, in this case the direct accusation of being an agent of foreign powers. The root of this accusation is not merely the term *liberalism* and its promoted values but predominantly the source of JIL's funding. JIL's funding was initially secured through the Asia Foundation (Gillespie 2007), the Swiss embassy, the US embassy, and other foreign organizations in the early 2000s, before local financial support was found in 2005 from, inter alia, the Freedom Institute and Goenawan Mohamad, an Indonesian intellectual. Since the first public debates on these issues and the aggressive airing of accusations JIL has claimed to be independent, but the organization's finances are—as with almost all organizations in Indonesia—not transparent (VOA ISLAM 2012).[1]

Unlike many other postcolonial societies, Indonesia has not permitted a sophisticated discussion of the advantages and dangers of foreign support.

Ulil Abshar-Abdalla and Luthfi Assyaukanie, among other public intellectuals who have in the past or present represented liberal values, are familiar with Saba Mahmood's arguments that Western forces have framed issues in Egypt in terms of religious liberty and minority rights in order to advance their own military and commercial interests (Mahmood 2012). In Indonesia, such criticism has been aimed at JIL and at LGBTQI activists and some feminist activists by their Islamist opponents. They emphasize JIL's transnational connections and the hidden agenda that foreign government manage to inject into local discourses.

The skepticism toward foreign funding and connections goes beyond topics related to religion. It even targets environmental NGOs. The banning of Greenpeace's Rainbow Warrior in 2010 and Susilo Bambang Yudhoyono's comments thereupon in 2013 illustrate this general skepticism: Yudhoyono said that a lot of suspicion among most Indonesians remained, propagated by politicians, including the notion that foreign NGOs in the country were working on their own insidious agendas and did not have Indonesia's best interests at heart (Lumanauw and Sihite 2010). Funding is usually either discussed in polemical ways (Husaini 2010) or mentioned only in passing (Gillespie 2007). Tellingly, scholarly sources on this issue are rare and weak. The academic and activist silence can largely be attributed to the aggressive way that the issue of funding is often used as a weapon against activists.

In the book *Indonesia Tanpa Liberal* (Indonesia without liberalism or liberals) (2012), the conservative thinker and commentator Artawijaya accuses JIL, which received some of its funding from Europe and the United States, of propagating humanism against religious values. Artawijaya further linked JIL to US attempts to secure its national interest in the Indonesian economy by controlling natural resources and simultaneously spreading hatred toward fundamentalists, creating a moderate, liberal, and deviant Islam (Artawijaya 2012). Similarly, Rizieq Shihab called liberal Islam in Indonesia a "foreigner's henchman": USAID, he argued, together with other international NGOs, tried to establish a network of moderate liberals with pro-American attitudes (Rizieq et al. 2011).

Such criticism is usually polemical and typically singles out identity issues rather than engaging in complex socioeconomic debates. JIL itself focused on religion and civil liberties, largely refraining from making public stances on economic questions. According to Martin van Bruinessen (2012), JIL's founders have defended political and economic liberalism, which some of them apparently see as inseparable from religious liberalism. Some Indonesians concurred with JIL's religious views but objected to the term *liberal Islam* because of its association with neoliberalism, which has similarly negative connotations in Indonesia as it does elsewhere. Despite the resilience of anti-Communist rhetoric, invocations of "the people" (*masyarakat*), condemnations of elite corruption, propagation of economic nationalism, and the rejection of capitalism and neoliberalism were central components of mainstream political rhetoric, for instance in the speeches of Prabowo Subianto and even Susilo Bambang Yudhoyono (Aspinall 2015; Carroll 2017).

JIL activists and others using the term *liberal* were thus in a tight spot: JIL was not only attacked by Islamist antiliberals but also had difficulties in forging alliances with those who disapprove of liberalism from a leftist or postcolonial perspective. "This is the criticism that pains us most," Ulil Abshar-Abdalla told me during a conversation in Jakarta in March 2012, when we were discussing the work of Saba Mahmood. He lamented the practical difficulties of integrating complex theoretical perspectives with actual political activism on the ground, especially in a discursive atmosphere. JIL is an example of the homogenization and polarization of discourses on Islamic issues, the dominance of human rights discourses in the early 2000s, and the reduction of Islamic diversity. Beyond that, JIL's difficulties highlight the dilemma that local Muslim activists face in their struggle against Islamist majoritarianism between remaining chronically underfunded but credible or well-connected/well-funded and accused of succumbing to a foreign and hostile agenda.

The early 2000s had seen what some scholars called a "Conservative Turn" (Bruinessen 2013). Observers detected reversals of the conservative trend within Muhammadiyah and NU at their respective congresses in 2010 (Bruinessen 2010). JIL was rehabilitated at the 2010 NU assembly in Makassar, only five years after it had been declared a danger to Islam, and its charismatic cofounder and leader, Ulil Abshar-Abdalla, was a candidate during the election for a leading position on the NU board. He was immensely popular among many of the younger NU members. But he was also accused of being popular with US donors. In 2011, he received the first of a series of letter bombs. Many seemed to wonder whether he was really one of the NU or if his rhetoric of liberal values threatened to erode Islam from within. Ulil himself did not get elected, and only had a very slim chance of winning to begin with, but his presence embodied the resilience of explicitly liberal ideas within NU. These rapid changes suggest that the period was not defined by a single overarching trend or its reversal. Instead, liberals navigated a winding path through an increasingly fragmented and polarized society.

Although JIL did not formally close down, it became very quiet in the mid-2010s. Using the label *liberal* had not proved a successful strategy to defend pluralism. The Indonesian political scientist Alexander Arifianto finds that JIL effectively ceased operation by as early as 2008, three years after the fatwa (Chew 2021). Ulil Abshar-Abdalla remained an outcast for many conservatives afterward, despite his continued presence as a public intellectual. He later contributed to the Indigenization of the discourse of protecting diversity, embracing the discourse of Islam Nusantara that parts of NU pushed, especially after 2015, and that tied a vision of a particular kind of Islam characterized by a restricted pluralism to Indonesian nationalism. This newly promoted term, *Islam Nusantara*, highlighted plurality and pluralism over liberalism (Suaedy 2018). It emphasized the Indonesian-ness and local roots of these values. This key difference of Indigeneity let the discourse of Islam Nusantara to thrive. As a strategy to defending diversity, albeit still controversial, it would be much more successful than the discourse of rights and liberalism.

Blasphemy

Three unsuccessful attempts to repeal the so-called blasphemy law in the 2010s show two main things: First, how the Constitutional Court acknowledged the authority of particular religious organizations and, second, how activists seeking to challenge the law used different strategies. Whereas the first attempt in 2009–10 used the framework of human rights, the second and third attempt tried alternative routes of emphasizing diversity as an aspect of Indonesian nationalism, which did not spark the same controversy. The rejections demonstrate just how much influence the hardened front of homogenizing Mainstream Islam had over the state: The Indonesian Constitutional Court's ruling fixated Indonesia as a religious state and deferred to the Muslim authorities to define the precise characteristics of this religiosity.

Enjoining Good, Forbidding Wrong: The Moral Imperative to Intervene

The main drivers of the construction of Mainstream Islam and pushing it further toward right-wing Islamist positions, the MUI and the Islamic Defenders Front (FPI), demanded more action from the state in curbing what they deemed not only un-Islamic practices but also those that were threatening to Islam. The FPI was especially clear about identifying targets. Its interruption of an interfaith meeting at the Inna Simpang Hotel in Surabaya in early 2011 illustrates the links the FPI and its network draw between social categories as diverse as the Ahmadis and LGBTQI people. At the time, FPI Executive Council (Tanfidziyah) Chairman Muhammad Mahdi al-Habsyi said he was campaigning against the meeting because it had been attended by Ahmadiyya as well as gay and lesbian groups. "They are our enemies," he reportedly said (*Tempo* 2011b). With the police present but not defusing the threats made by the FPI, the hotel gave in to the FPI's pressure and eventually dissolved the meeting. This is reminiscent of many other instances in which state authorities have stood idly by during attacks on people who were labeled taboo, such as the Cikeusik killings of three Ahmadi Indonesians in 2011 and the eviction of Shi'a in East Java in 2012. Politicians also responded to the call for more socially conservative intervention.

The aggression of these moral panics and episodes of outrage are a phenomenon of the post-Suharto era, but the laws regarding blasphemy and atheism long precede them. As it happens, the laws were rarely ever used under Suharto's New Order: Three cases were reported in three decades (Sihombing 2012). After 1998, however, there was a dramatic rise in such cases (Crouch 2011). Melissa Crouch (2017a, 239) estimates that there were more than 130 blasphemy convictions between 1998 and 2012 (Sihombing 2012), while Charlotte Setijadi (2017) counts at least 106 of them since 2005, with an extremely high conviction rate. As Adam Tyson (2021) points out, given the size of Indonesia, this is still a somewhat modest use of the blasphemy law, but it certainly marks an intensification of cases in the post-Suharto era. Most cases concerned alleged blasphemous statements against Islam, uttered by both self-identifying Muslims and Christians (Crouch 2011). Many were surrounded by heated public debates about the alleged offenses themselves and the law. Even more significantly, no blasphemy case in post-Suharto Indonesia involving religious offenses covered by Article 156a has resulted in the accused being exonerated (Crouch and Lindsey 2013).

The use of the concept of moral panic and the discussion of blasphemy shed light on the analytical limits of the differentiation between "morality" and "religiosity" (or "piety") in Indonesia. Attempts to neatly separate the language of morality from that of religion cannot seriously be undertaken, even though the two can also not be fully conflated. In many interpretations of Islam, morality is far from being a sphere limited to the individual and his or her God.

A telling anecdote illustrates the impossibility of discussing politics and morality without a view toward religion in contemporary Indonesian language use and shows how fine the nuances are and how inappropriate conceptualizing morality and religion as separate entities would be: During a discussion with an Indonesian colleague about the meaning of the different terms for various emotions of remorse, I asked about the differences between *taubat*, *sadar*, and *insaf* (the first one means "regret/repent," while the other two mean "to be aware" and "to realize," respectively). These three words were often used by opponents of the Ahmadi who sought to convert them to other variants of Islam. My interlocutor, a scholar of Islamic studies and social sciences, replied that there were no differences. The meanings, he insisted against my doubts, were all the same. I then asked whether I would use *taubat* for feelings of remorse after having done wrong toward a friend, for instance copying her work or stealing something. My interlocutor responded, "No, in that case, you would use *sadar* and *insaf* but not *taubat*." For my interlocutor, the examples of copying and stealing seem to be a transgression of more interpersonal moral boundaries than those related directly to God. Another Indonesian Muslim colleague confirms this: *Taubat* is reserved for severe sins toward God and, perhaps, in some instances against one's parents. For other wrongs or "small sins" (*dosa kecil*), she would use *insaf* or *sesal* (regret). Of course, for some others and in most *hudud* law interpretations, stealing something might also be seen as a religious transgression against God's laws and would thus by all means be worthy of *taubat* (repentance).[2]

Additionally, as Islamic studies scholar Michael Cook (2003) argues, the place of morality in Islam has always been different from other religions because it has always been predicated on a right to some kind of social intervention. In his classic study of the concept of "commanding right, forbidding wrong" (*al-amr bi 'l-ma'ruf wa 'n-nahy 'ani 'l-munkar*), Cook explains that the difference between Western and Islamic ethics is that Islam has a specific concept for interrupting the wrongdoing of others. "Forbidding wrong" (*nahi munkar*) is "the duty of one Muslim to intervene when another is acting wrong" (Cook 2003), and Surah Al Imran in the Quran seems to offer clear instruction on this: "Be a community that calls for what is good, urges what is right, and forbids what is wrong: those who do this are the successful ones" (Qur'an 3:104). "You" in this case refers to "You who believe" (Qur'an 2004, 102). The other main source of Islamic law, the collection of hadith, also offers guidance pertaining to "forbidding wrong." It stems from a time in the 660s or 670s in the city of Kufa in today's Iraq and claims to quote the Prophet: "Whoever sees a wrong [*munkar*], and is able to put it right with his hand [*an yughayyirahu bi-yadihi*], let him do so; if he can't, then with his tongue [*bilisānihi*]; if he can't, then in his heart [*bi-qalbihi*], and that is the bare minimum of faith'" (Cook 2001, 598). The internal recourse to the heart is the realm where scholars remain the furthest from any consensus.

Within the umma, there has been much debate over the succeeding centuries about whether "righting wrong" and "forbidding wrong" are the same and the exact practical implications of the question. Regarding the Quranic verse, interpretations vary as to who exactly can belong to the prescribed "community" called to forbid wrong. These discussions of the details and nuances of Quranic interpretation typically remain within the circles of ulama and are less visible in public debates.

Questions of visibility are key. Cook (2001, 79–80) quotes an old saying: "Whoever admonishes his brother in private [sirran] graces him [zaʾnahu]; whoever does so in public [alaʾniyatan] disgraces him [shaʾnahu]." The relationship between the public and the private—with concepts of what these are varying across languages and time—is tense. One basic principle is that a wrong must be public knowledge to be a valid target of duty. A hidden wrong harms only the wrongdoer and is thus beyond the scope of the duty. Yet all the cases in this book illustrate how the line between visibility and invisibility, between what may be considered public and private in the various respective conceptual vocabularies, is permanently contested.

Public debates on morality as well as the legal apparatus of the modern state tackle very similar questions: What is "wrong," and who gets to identify and thus define "wrong" and through what processes? And once finally identified, how is the "righting" of a wrong to be executed? The question debated and fought over in the postcolonial—and, in Indonesia's case, the postauthoritarian state as well—is how social intervention is best conceived of in a modern nation-state. With its more pervasive structures and more quantified knowledge, the state's presumption of latitude in enforcing morality is a particularly burning issue for religious activists worldwide. Especially in Indonesia, various movements and Islamist parties have made it a core demand that the state curb wrongdoing in areas that many liberal nation-states deem "private." Various state agencies have been responding to these calls to intervene in different ways. Other nonstate organizations, such as the FPI, have been taking matters into their own hands and have provoked reaction on the part of the state, as the accounts of violent attacks against Ahmadiyya, Shi'a, and LGBTQI Muslims show. Their references to traditions of Islamic scholarship, as the detailed case studies reveal, are for the most part narrow in scope and shallow in depth but nevertheless powerful.

The Blasphemy Law and the Efforts to Repeal It

Of all the contentious issues in Indonesia that leaders use to produce episodes of outrage and moral panic, defamation of religion is the one that is the most clearly legally regulated. Judges can apply several different clauses in cases they connect to accusations of blasphemy. The most important one is Article 156(a), which Sukarno enacted as Presidential Decree No. 1/PNPS/1965 on the Prevention of Blasphemy and Abuse of Religions. It is commonly referred to as the "blasphemy law" but Zainal Abidin Bagir points out that "defamation of religion" would be the more appropriate term (Bagir 2013). The law took effect in 1969 as Law No. 5/1969 and makes it unlawful "to, intentionally, in public, communicate, counsel, or solicit public support for an interpretation of a religion or a form of religious activity that is similar to the interpretations or activities of an Indonesian religion but deviates from the tenets of that religion." In this "act of productive intolerance" (Menchik 2016, 81), Sukarno positioned himself as the defender of those who sought a more prominent role of Islam in the newly emerging state. Already in this period, the regulation of religion was used by an otherwise not particularly religious politician to demonstrate his religious credentials in a climate of connecting nonreligiosity to Communism.

The law establishes that the government will protect its official religions by punishing those who insult approved religions and those who attempt to persuade others to adhere to unofficial religions. It also places restrictions on those within each approved religion, making it illegal to advocate "deviations from teachings of religion considered fundamental by scholars of the relevant religion." (Constitutional Court Decision No. 140/PUU-VII/2009 2010). Further, the law establishes civil and criminal penalties: The offender "shall be instructed and be warned severely to cease his/her actions" by a minister of the federal government. On the second offense, if the violation is committed by an organization or an aliran kepercayaan, the president may dissolve the organization and declare it banned, resulting in it losing the right to own property or legally practice its beliefs in public. Scholars have stated that the law's vagueness allows clerics to criminalize theological differences or disagreements (Bagir 2013).

Article 156(a) of the Criminal Code also attaches a maximum penalty of five years' imprisonment for intentionally criticizing or otherwise attempting to undermine the government's officially recognized religions. Finally, Article 28 of the 2008 Information and Electronic Transaction Law complements the blasphemy law. It makes the dissemination of information aimed at inflicting hatred based on ethnicity and religion punishable. In several publicly discussed blasphemy cases, such as the prominent 2012 Alexander Aan case of atheism, it was this 2008 law that the court eventually applied. The vague formulation of these laws is typical for blasphemy and other defamation laws, including nonreligious ones (Freedom House 2010). The state rarely enforced the 1965 Blasphemy Law before the sharp rise in cases after 1998.

In the post-Suharto era, there have been three attempts to repeal the blasphemy law—in 2009–10, 2013, and 2017. The first attempt came in the wake of the deepening polarization following the 2005 fatwa against the Ahmadiyya Community and a year after the Monas Incident in 2008, during which the FPI and others had attacked a multifaith coalition of initiatives protesting for the protection of minorities. A coalition of human rights activists and activists for the rights of religious minorities, involving seven civil society organizations and four individuals, petitioned Indonesia's Constitutional Court to invalidate the blasphemy law (National Legislative Bodies / National Authorities 1945). The applicants, many of whom were lawyers, based their challenge primarily on the constitutional rights to freedom of religion and freedom of expression, which are guaranteed respectively by Article 28E (1) and (2) of Indonesia's 1945 Constitution, and emphasized human rights and liberal values. Although motivated by the persecution of minority identities, and even though several statements by opponents and defenders of the Blasphemy Law implicitly and explicitly referred to the Ahmadiyya (Menchik 2016, 85), the Ahmadis themselves did not join the petition, nor were there any Ahmadi experts or witnesses. The coalition had found it wiser not to risk having the highly sensitive issue of the Ahmadiyya dominate the debate.

In April of the following year, nine judges reviewed the case. During the process, the judges solicited several written statements and listened to experts and public figures, including FPI chief and extremist Rizieq Shihab, who had been convicted for hate speech after the Monas incident (Yilmaz and Barton 2021). Muhammadiyah and NU representatives committed "to a limited form of pluralism," citing the existence of various religions, but excluded beliefs they deemed heterodox, most obviously the Ahmadiyya (Menchik 2016, 85). Almost without exception, the Muhammadiyah and NU supporters emphasized that freedom was a value but had its limits and that accepting organizations such as the Ahmadiyya would exceed these limits. NU representatives were Asrul Sani, Soleh Amin, and Nirsammakaru as well as Hasyim Muzadi who had called for the disbanding of the Ahmadiyya. The only NU-affiliated person who sided with those seeking to revoke the blasphemy law was M. M. Billah, the former head of the NU Institute for Human Resources Development Studies (Lembaga Kajian dan Pengembangan Sumberdaya Manusia; Lakpesdam:); in the court minutes, however, he was not identified as an NU representative, nor was his name linked to the NU. He presented himself in the court as an expert along with Luthfi Assyaukanie, Franz Magnis Suseno, and other pluralists (Aspinall and Menchik 2017). No names were explicitly mentioned for the Muhammadiyah side, but the court minutes cites the organization as rejecting the repeal of the blasphemy law.

The court's ruling would demonstrate the degree to which the judges were willing to follow the advice of and strengthen the position of religious authorities, and it would affirm Indonesia's status as a religious country. By a majority of eight to one, the court ruled that the blasphemy law was compatible with the 1945 Constitution. Its decision was informed particularly by two constitutional references—namely, to "Almighty God" (Ketuhanan Yang Maha Esa) in the Pancasila, the national foundational philosophy, and to "religious values," which, according to the judges, allowed a limitation on human rights (Constitutional Court Decision No. 140/PUU-VII/2009 2010). The judges argued that Indonesia was not secular because it is "not a state that separates religion and the state" (Amnesty International 2014a) and that the Constitution makes no provision for atheism (Constitutional Court Decision No. 140/PUU-VII/2009 2010). Instead, the court found Indonesia to be a "state that must protect its religious communities" (*negara yang harus melindungi umat yang beragama*) and stressed the importance of Indonesia's religious parent organizations (*organisasi keagamaan induk*), which work as "government partners [*mitra pemerintah*] to create religious social order" (*menciptakan ketertiban masyarakat beragama*) by protecting religious orthodoxy (*pokok-pokok ajaran agama*) from heterodoxy (*aliran sesat*) and public criticism (Constitutional Court Decision No. 140/PUU-VII/2009 2010). The term *organisasi induk keagamaan* is not extremely common in everyday Indonesian discourse but is understood and used in formal contexts, particularly in discussions about religious governance, policies, and institutional structures.

In these statements, the court endorsed a particular interpretation of the Pancasila, whose first principle, that of the Almighty God (Ketuhanan Yang Maha Esa), they presented as the main lens through which to interpret the Constitution. The court noted three reasons for its decision, which can be summarized as follows: First, the right to religious freedom, which is subject to certain limitations, is regulated in Indonesia by confining public expressions of religion to that religious orthodoxy defined by ulama, religious scholars. Second, the blasphemy law is not discriminatory because it applies to all six religions recognized in Indonesia (Islam, Catholicism, Protestantism, Buddhism, Hinduism, and Confucianism) and other religions, provided they do not violate the blasphemy law or other laws. Third, the blasphemy law is necessary because while the right to religion is an individual right, it is also a communal one. In this framework, Indonesia's main religious organizations work towards maintaining the religious social order and shield the majority's religious sensibilities in partnership with the state. Thus, the court strengthened religious authorities. In its interpretation of the law, the court used a particular definition of *religious values*: Rather than using a general definition meaning values common to most religions, such as universal principles or standards of behavior, the court defined it to mean "the tenets of religious teachings" (Peterson 2018, 6). It found that these tenets are not defined by the Ministry of Religious Affairs (then the Department of Religion) but by the relevant "religious internal parties" (67). This was an obvious reference to the MUI (Lindsey 2012) and to NU and Muhammadiyah. The court's ruling suggests that the basis of the Indonesian state is the religious orthodoxy of the majority, as defined by the respective organizations, and it also underlines the prioritization of communities over individuals, thereby strengthening majoritarian arguments.

As in the previous cases on the Ahmadiyya, the language of human rights was not simply ignored. Instead, the court had a lot to say about human rights. Legal scholar Asma Uddin (2014) even finds that the court itself used the language of human rights to justify the prioritization of religious sensibilities over individual or minority rights. In short, the court maintained that human rights were an important aspect of Indonesia's judiciary but that they were secondary to "religious values." They referred to Art 28J (2), which states, "In exercising one's rights and freedoms, every person shall defer to the limitations stipulated in statute with the sole intention of guaranteeing the acknowledgment and respect of the rights and freedoms of other persons and to fulfill just guidelines pursuant to moral considerations, religious values, security, and public order in a democratic society."

The court also drew on the distinction between public and private: It found that the absolute right to religious freedom, as guaranteed by Art28E (1) of the 1945 Constitution, was merely a private right (forum internum) rather than a public one (forum externum) and that the freedom to articulate one's belief could therefore legitimately be limited to ensure respect for the religious values of others and to protect the religious sensibilities of the public from injury (Constitutional Court Decision No. 140/PUU-VII/2009 2010). This reasoning did not explicitly reference specific cases of such injury, but less than five years earlier, in 2005 and 2006, the Muhammad cartoon controversy erupted when the Danish newspaper *Jyllands-Posten* published caricatures of the Prophet Muhammad. Many people worldwide found the cartoons offensive, sparking global protests, boycotts, and heated debates about free speech and respect for religious beliefs.

The Indonesian Constitutional Court is not alone in its emphasis of the publicness of the offense. In the Arab Middle East, as well as in Pakistan and in Malaysia, existing blasphemy laws have been used by Islamists to "project themselves as defenders of popular rights against foreign domination and despotic rule, and to mobilize broad sections of the populace in the name of religion (Krämer 2013) and by "majoritarian political actors" in their efforts toward intrareligious boundary-formation and religious national identity formation (Nelson 2018).

Finally, the judges also argued that the blasphemy law was important to curb religious conflict, citing Article 28J paragraph (2) of the 1945 Constitution, which states, "In exercising their rights and freedoms, every people are obliged to comply with the restrictions set by law for the sole purpose of guaranteeing recognition and respect for the rights and freedoms of others and to meet just demands in accordance with moral considerations, religious values, security, and public order in a democratic society." The prevention of conflict and the protection of "social order are an often-used argument in blasphemy and defamation laws. For the case of Pakistan, Matthew Nelson argued in the late 2010s that the term *public order* had experienced a shift in interpretation. Whereas in the past, religious vigilantes who would attack religious minorities in Pakistan were accused of disturbing the peace for acting against religious minorities in defiance of state authority, religious minorities later became considered a disruptive provocateur and thus a source of public disorder (European Asylum Support Office 2018). The cases discussed in this book, and the rise of blasphemy cases more generally, mark a shift in Indonesia that shows some parallels with these debates elsewhere.

As discussed in the previous chapter, one could conclude from these arguments that many opinions and practices are tolerated in Indonesia, if not accepted, as long as they remain hidden in the private realm. This argument has been made for different contexts, regions, and periods. For instance, the historian Gudrun Krämer argues that in many modern Middle Eastern countries, the principles invoked to justify interpretation include the discretionary power of the ruler to order public affairs in accordance with the broad guidelines of sharia (Ar., *siyasa shar'iyya*); the legal concept of necessity (Ar., *darura*); notions of the public good (Ar., *maslaha 'amma*); and, most far-reaching of all, the purpose or objective of sharia (Ar., *maqasid al-shari'a*) (Krämer 2013). This argument is certainly helpful in refining our understanding of what is deemed worthy of toleration and acceptance, but it would be too simplistic to rely on a neat separation between private and public. Given the centrality of the notion of public space for the modern nation-state and for our modern understanding of politics, it is not surprising that many scholars accept this explanation. And yet, feminist scholars have long been pointing out the flaws of this separation. As Nancy Fraser (1990) wrote, the "sharp separation of public and private spheres functioned as key signifiers of bourgeois difference from both higher and lower social strata" in a particular historical context of Europe of the nineteenth and early twentieth centuries. These norms later became hegemonic, sometimes imposed on, sometimes embraced by, broader segments of society—a sign of the project's success. Fraser based her observations on western Europe and North America of the late twentieth century. Others have drawn on different time periods or other geographical regions to point out the historicity and limits of the liberal normative as well as conceptual separation of private and public realms (Connelly 2002). Elsewhere, the separation between public and private realms played out very differently. A well-studied and in this context helpful example is the separation of private and public areas of Ottoman palaces. The *selamlik* (from the root word *selam*, "greeting") was the portion reserved for men and guests, similar to the *andron*, the portion of Ancient Greek houses reserved for men and male guests. In contrast, the *haremlik* was the private portion of upper-class Ottoman homes. Wandering through old Ottoman palaces today, one finds various courtyards and gardens, each dedicated to a particular sphere. The private quarters were hardly domestic in the sense that they were secluded from public life: the women took part in social, economic, and political activities from within the walls and prepared key political decisions (Schick 2010, 81), but this only underlines how complex the attempt to distinguish neatly between public and private is. Clearly, applying the dichotomy of private/public rooted in nineteenth- and early twentieth-century western Europe to other contexts causes more confusion than clarity and can obstruct more detailed analysis. Yaseen Noorani (2010) argues that two distinctions underlie this binary: an opposition between what is visible, open, or accessible to all and what is concealed and an opposition between what is collective (including political) in nature and what is personal or individual. It is worth remembering that the Joint Ministerial Decree of 2008 prohibited Ahmadiyya activities rather than the congregation itself. This allowed state actors to claim that they were still respecting the Ahmadiyya's religious freedom since Ahmadis were simply asked to conduct their activities in private. Yet many private houses of religious leaders also function as gathering spaces for religious activities, and it was in such a compound that the three Ahmadis in Cikeusik were killed in 2011. The petitioners of the 2013 judicial review of the blasphemy law were referring to similar incidents. It would be analytically short-sighted to simply echo the flawed distinction between public and private that the court and policymakers use, especially given that the publicness and privateness of spaces is never stable. As feminist scholarship has been pointing out for more than a century, these spaces are grounds of constant negotiation.

Many saw this case as a major episode in the battle of ideas about Indonesia's secular-religious character, a referendum of sorts on Indonesia's place on the spectrum between Islam and atheism. Heated public debates and angry crowds outside the court building accompanied and framed the hearings and the decision. The defenders of the blasphemy law dominated the courtroom's second floor and the courthouse's front lawn, creating a tense atmosphere (Menchik 2016, 83–84). They attacked petitioners coming out of the court building, such as the applicants' attorneys Nurkholis Hidayat and Uli Parulian Sihombing, who were encircled and kicked by FPI supporters during the recess after they had lunch. Several witnesses who took pictures of the incident were subsequently also attacked by FPI people (Ulma Haryanto 2010). The angry crowd outside the court building was not merely an interesting addition to the court's reasoning and ruling but part of it: the court conflated "public order" with "general public sentiment" (Uddin 2014). Seven years later, in the high-profile blasphemy case of Jakarta's governor, the North Jakarta District Court would argue in very similar ways (Tyson 2021).

Although their victory was not a close one, some key actors of the Islamist Conservative Majoritarian Synthesis, such as the then–Minister of Religious Affairs Suryadharma Ali, were not content with defending the status quo in the 2010 rejection of the repeal. Instead, two years later, they drew fresh attention to their cause with an action that has become a footnote of sorts to the 2010 case: a public burning of "blasphemous" books attended by religious and political authorities that demonstrates how powerful public accusations of blasphemy had become and to what degree they provoked drastic self-censorship measures in the early 2010s. The large and well-respected publishing company Gramedia Pustaka Utama, part of Indonesia's largest media conglomerate, Kompas Gramedia Group, staged the book burning in response to allegations of blasphemy in June 2012. The FPI had deemed that passages in a book by American writer Douglas Wilson insulted the prophet Muhammad and filed a complaint with the police against Gramedia for publishing the book in Indonesian. Gramedia had, they argued, thereby insulted Islam. Gramedia consequently pulled the book, *Five Cities That Ruled the World*, from its shelves on June 9, 2012. But this was not enough for the FPI. The group claimed that the book was still for sale in Indonesia a day after it was recalled and that the insults to the prophet were a formal offense, one for which simply withdrawing the books would not suffice. Spokesperson Munarman argued that "Rasulullah [i.e., Prophet Muhammad] is a symbol in Islamic teachings, and defaming religions is a crime according to the Criminal Code" (*The Jakarta Post* 2012a; Wulandari and Muhammad 2012). Gramedia publicly apologized in the Indonesian newspaper *Republika* for publishing the book. To underline this apology, the company staged a book burning outside the Kompas Gramedia complex in West Jakarta, overseen by company president director Wandi S. Brata and several MUI officials, including then–Deputy Chairman Ma'ruf Amin (Wulandari and Muhammad 2012). Altogether, two hundred copies of the book were burned in a symbolic act. Professionally photographed, dramatic images of a pile of burning books surrounded by FPI activists and formally clad, senior-looking MUI elders spread widely. The news and the images were approvingly circulated on Islamist websites. The case illustrates how widespread and powerful the notion of blasphemy was by then and how the MUI worked hand in hand with the FPI in an episode of moral outrage, or "hate spin" and "manufactured indignation" (George 2016). Its timing, not long after the Constitutional Court's decision to leave the blasphemy law untouched and the total defeat of the liberal coalition trying to bring it down, also signals that the blasphemy activists were not content with the legal victory but wanted the issue to remain in the public eye. Their strategy was successful: The circulating images boosted the public debates on blasphemy once more.

In 2013, after the failure to repeal the blasphemy law in 2010, and on the heels of the book burning, the next group of petitioners appealed to the Constitutional Court for a judicial review of the blasphemy law. Their strategy was different: The petitioners pointed at various ambiguities and inconsistencies in the law rather than declare it outright unconstitutional and violating human rights. They tried to work with the state as represented here by the court rather than outright oppose it. The most important difference to the arguments in 2009–10 was the lack of emphasis on religious freedom. In this way, they did not ask the judges or any commentators to prioritize either religion or human rights and thereby reduced the risk of further polarization. This strategy was less provocative. Given the previous controversies and the polarization that the 2010 proceedings had provoked, this seemed a wise choice. Further, in stark contrast to the activists in 2009–10, the applicants deliberately maintained a low profile. As a result, the case attracted little public attention. It was much less publicly visible. Consequently, members of Islamist organizations stayed away from the court hearings (Crouch 2013).

Partly, the difference in strategy can be explained with legal reasons, for in 2011, an amended law enabled the Constitutional Court to hear cases on the same legal provision as another as long as each case is based on new arguments. Perhaps more importantly though, the petitioners had seen the thwarted attempt in 2010 and likely adjusted their approach accordingly.

Rather than questioning all four provisions of the blasphemy law, as the petitioners in 2009–10 had done, this time the petitioners focused on Article 4, which criminalizes the offense of blasphemy. They emphasized its vagueness and vulnerability to misuse. Particularly, they pointed to the lack of a precise definition of "public" (*di muka umum*) and argued that this ambiguity makes the law particularly vulnerable to abuse. Further, they argued, the law lacks clear criteria for "hostility" (*permusuhan*), "abuse" (*penyalahgunaan*)" or "desecration" (*penodaan*) of religion and also fails to appoint an authority to determine an organization's or individual's deviance. The applicants concluded that Article 4 was thus unconstitutional and needed to either be deleted or at least restricted by the legislature. The group consisted of lawyers who collaborated with the Shi'a organization Ahlul Bayt Indonesia (ABI). The plaintiffs were Tajul Muluk, the Shi'a leader in Madura who had been violently attacked and imprisoned for blasphemy; Hassan Alaydrus, chairman of ABI; Ahmad Hidayat, the vice chairman of ABI; Umar Shahab, a Shi'a elder; and Sebastian Joe, a non-Shi'a Muslim also charged with religious blasphemy because of a Facebook post, (Amnesty International 2014b; Constitutional Court Decision No. 84/PUU- X/2012 2013). Three of the plaintiffs were ABI leaders who were worried about possible future accusations of blasphemy (Miichi and Kayane 2020).

Nevertheless, the different strategies led to similar outcomes: The Constitutional Court reaffirmed its earlier position. The judges argued that interpretations and activities deviating from the main points in the teachings of the respective religion could cause "collisions and horizontal conflicts" or "unrest, division, and enmity in the public." Granting that the "formulation cannot be said to be perfect," the judges nevertheless concluded that the Law on Prevention of Blasphemy was "still needed," because its revocation could fail to prevent "abuse and blasphemy of religion that can lead to conflict within the public."

The judges defended the use of the term "public" by noting that it appears elsewhere in the Criminal Code and is sufficiently defined in the book *Kitab the Criminal Code (KUHP) and Its Commentaries* as referring to "a place where the public goes or can hear," "a public place with a crowd," or places "where the public can see" the act in question. The law, the judges reaffirmed, was necessary to "maintain peace and public order" (*menjaga ketentraman dan ketertiban umum*). Responding to the petitioners' claim that there was a lack in clarity concerning the authority deciding over accusations of deviance, the court argued that these decisions were to be taken by the authority of the general court judges in each case. The judges explicitly referred to the 2010 decision, reemphasized that Indonesia is "a country that adheres to religious beliefs that are not separated from the state" (*Indonesia sebagai sebuah negara yang menganut paham agama tidak dipisahkan dari negara*), and pointed to the task of the Ministry of Religion to "serve and protect the growth and healthy development of religion."

The panel of justices concluded the request had no legal basis as it was "not a matter of constitutionality but a matter of how to apply the law that was under the absolute authority of the general courts." This conclusion was consistent with the government's official statement delivered for the hearing. Representatives from three government departments, the Ministry of Religious Affairs, the Ministry of Law and Human Rights, and the Attorney General's Office, disputed the applicants' claim of making new arguments and reiterated that the blasphemy law was necessary to ensure social order and harmony.

Four years later, in 2017, a group of Ahmadis of the Jemaah Ahmadiyah Indonesia organization filed yet another appeal. They continued the shift of strategy already visible in the 2013 attempt. Instead of prioritizing freedom of religion, they emphasized that the law was being used to discriminate against Ahmadis and to keep them from performing religious worship. They stated that their constitutional rights to religion and to worship were restricted and suppressed because of the joint ministerial that had effectively banned Ahmadiyah religious activities and legitimized local-level harassment. They described the domino effect of this decree in the lives of Ahmadiyya adherents: for example, being prevented from worshipping in their mosques because they were burned or sealed, their difficulties to register marriages, and their evictions from their residences.

Seven years had passed since the court had acknowledged problems in the formulation and vagueness of the law without any governmental efforts to improve the law. Therefore, the Petitioners requested that Articles 1, 2, and 3 of the blasphemy law be declared contrary to the 1945 Constitution with constitutional conditions (Anjarsari and Widiastuti 2017). They drew on human rights scholarship and Indonesian history to argue that Indonesia's peaceful diversity needed protection against foreign influxes of exclusion and violence.

The court, however, affirmed and referenced its earlier position and again argued that the implementation of the law was not to be mixed up with its constitutionality. The judges again confirmed that the law did require revision through a legislative process in the parliament but then again emphasized the decision of 2010 which had foregrounded the role of the religious "parent organizations" as "partners of the state in creating order among religious communities."

Of the three court proceedings files, the third is the longest at more than five hundred pages. In some ways it can be read as an extension and more nuanced variant of the first attempt in 2009–10, which also included a number of expert hearings and whose files comprise more than three hundred pages. The second hearing accumulated fewer than two hundred pages, trying a different route. The third attempt, then, brought together a broad range of scholarship from human rights to Indonesian history. Public intellectuals and scholars of Islam, such as Ahmad Suaedy and Najib Burhani, with a high level of theological and sociological sophistication, elaborated on how Ahmadis are part of a diverse Islamic landscape in Indonesia, often highlighting their belonging as citizens and also pointing at the danger of abuse of the blasphemy law.

However, almost ten years after the initial attempt to repeal the law, the positions had become too entrenched, even for this more sophisticated and promising route of argumentation. Several incidents in the 2010s had paved the way for further establishing orthodoxy as defined by the MUI. The arguments used in these three rejected appeals indicate the degree to which Indonesia's judiciary had begun to sympathize with Islamist ideas of more religious influence in the legal realm or how "judicial independence frequently gives way to public pressure" (M. Lim 2017, 416).

The Constitutional Court is another crucial actor in the constellation of alliances that has consolidated the center. Its decisions considered the public discourses on deviance and orthodoxy and ultimately supported a position that could be interpreted as communitarian but was largely in line with the Islamist Conservative Majoritarian Synthesis.

The Eden Community and the Case of Amaq Bakri

The two blasphemy cases involving the Eden Community (*Kaum Eden*) and Amaq Bakri, a farmer from East Lombok, offer a closer look at the roles of "visibility" and "foreignness" and show that even marginal groups and obscure individuals can become targets for those policing the boundaries of "True Islam." They further show the complexity of the notions of public and private between which the Indonesian Constitutional Court and some observers and scholars seek to differentiate. The case of the Eden Community highlights the discomfort that ambiguity can cause (Makin 2016). The Amaq Bakri case also shows the lengths these entrepreneurs would go to target even someone with no followers.

The Eden group differed significantly from the Ahmadiyya and the Shi'a: It had a very small number of followers, was geographically confined to Jakarta and had no connections with any transnational organizations. Born in the 1940s into a Muhammadiyah-oriented family in East Java, Lia Aminuddin was a married housewife with four children; in the mid-1990s, she claimed to have had an encounter with the Archangel Gabriel (*malaikat Jibril*). After the encounter, she claimed to have experienced intense spiritual purification and that she continued to receive messages from Gabriel. Later she said that her son, Ahmad Mukti Ali, was an incarnation of Jesus. For several years, she maintained a website entitled "Gabriel's Voice Worldwide. The Archangel Gabriel's Official Website on Earth through Lia Eden." Its greeting read, "Welcome to the Holy Throne of the Kingdom of Eden. This website—which belongs to the Holy Spirit, the Sovereign of the Holy Throne of the Kingdom of Eden—is the only website of the Archangel Gabriel that voices the Revelations from God the Lord of the kings in this era. His Majesty the Holy Spirit—an angel incarnate in Lia Eden—is represented in physicality by Lia Eden—Syamsuriati Lia Eden (Her Majesty the Sun Lia Eden), the Loyal and the Truthful."[3]

Between the mid-1990s and mid-2000s, Lia Eden had around one hundred followers of different religious backgrounds. Most of them were Muslims, many of them from the well-educated Jakartian middle-class and connected to the local State Islamic University Syarif Hidayatullah (Howell 2005). Before the encounter with Angel Gabriel, the group had not drawn much attention, but the inclusion of the Angel Gabriel into their teachings marked the crossing of several boundaries. Lia Aminuddin, often called Ibu (mother) Lia, had begun meddling with the monotheistic prophets. Her teachings liberally picked elements from Islam and Christianity and thereby created a degree of ambiguity that the promoters of Islamist orthodoxy were not willing to tolerate.

According to the sociologist and religious scholar Julia Howell (2005), "A somewhat quirky but socially respectable Muslim prayer group had started infringing on understandings of prophecy crucial to Muslims' understanding of the unique pre-eminence of their faith. Lia's channeling had broken, as it were, the seal of prophecy fixed by the death of the Prophet Muhammad." Small spiritual and religious extravagances might have been tolerated, but touching on the core teachings of the established religions provoked strong reactions from religious authorities, especially since Lina Eden proselytized in such a public manner online. Soon after Lia Eden had claimed her connections to the Angel Gabriel, the MUI issued an edict declaring the group deviant in 1997, supposedly reacting to questions from the umma, although these were not further specified. In this case, the MUI acted without a larger public debate. The council deemed the group's claim to be heretical and against Islam (Hasyim 2011). Before issuing its edict, the MUI's fatwa commission invited Lia Eden to "provide clarification" but the appeal went unanswered. On December 22, 1997, the MUI issued the fatwa, declaring the group to be heretical. The fatwa stated that any faith in the Angel Gabriel should be based on the Quran and hadith and that Lia Eden's claims contradicted the finality of the Quran. The council advised Lia Eden and her followers to receive religious counseling from ulama and reminded Muslims not to embrace faiths that are against the principles of the Quran and hadith.

At the time, the case did not attract widespread public attention (Hasyim 2011), and the group continued to exist and practice relatively openly but quietly. Ten years later, however, the conflict boiled up again. In early December 2005, a large crowd surrounded the group's meeting place on Jalan Mahoni in Senen in Central Jakarta. Police forcibly evacuated followers to prevent attacks by those accusing the group of heresy (Apologetics Index 2005). The next day, the police named Lia Eden and thirty-two of her followers as suspects for defamation of religion.

This interference can be read as a reaction to the group's increased visibility. Earlier that month, the Eden followers had begun to distribute flyers announcing that their house had become the Kingdom of God. In a neighbor's comment reported by *The Jakarta Post*, the violation of the public-private divide is clearly a concern: "They never bothered or intimidated us before. Sometimes Lia's followers went outside and we met them. However, they recently became active distributing several flyers to us. We just don't like the content of the flyers. They should have kept their teachings to themselves." Members of the nearby Meranti Mosque responded with their own flyers, condemning Lia Eden's teachings as heresy. They called for residents to join a gathering in front of Lia's house on December 30. On the appointed day, a crowd gathered outside: "We were just very curious in the beginning. But as more people came, many began to shout and boo at them. I think it would have ended up in violence if the police had not come quickly," a neighbor was quoted (*Religion News* 2005). Half a year later, in June 2006, the Central Jakarta District Court sentenced Lia Eden to sixteen months of detention for blasphemy. But she continued her activities. In June 2009, the same court convicted Lia Eden once more for the same offense, together with Wahyu Andito Putro Wibisono, one of her followers. The court sentenced her to two years and six months imprisonment and Wahyu Andito Putro Wibisono to two years imprisonment for contributing to Lia's religious concept used in pamphlets and online (*The Jakarta Post* 2009a).

At the time, most media articles about Lia Eden focused on presenting elements of her teachings that may be perceived as most insulting to the existing major religions. Examples are the Angel Gabriel's initiation of Ibu Lia as the Mahdi and the revelation that her son, Ahmad Mukti, was in fact Nabi Isa (the prophet Jesus). The Imam Madhi was incarnating, the angel supposedly explained to them, not just to save Indonesia from its egregious sins but to save the whole world. The news magazine *Gatra* was the first to publicize the story, and others quickly picked it up (Howell 2005). With such obviously theologically opposed teachings, no exaggerations or additional rumors were needed to present the group as deviant. Consequently, the media coverage and public discussion of the issue is much less aggressive than in all other cases. An example of the softer tone is a comment by Ma'ruf Amin on Lia Eden's release from prison: He told reporters that the MUI hoped she would now, after her time in prison, return to the true path (*kembali ke jalan yang benar*) (Taunuzi and Guna Sadat 2011). In expressing his hope for her return, he uses the word *menyimpang* rather than *sesat*. The word also means "to deviate" but leaves more space for acknowledging one's mistake and undergoing rehabilitation (Taunuzi and Guna Sadat 2011; US Department of State 2007). The MUI usually uses this term for those who are suspected of deviance but who have not yet been brought into the MUI's clarification forum to determine the status of their belief or deviance. The word is usually used for wrong deeds and sins in *fiqh*. If after this dialogue of clarification (*tabayun*), the accused keeps to his or her beliefs, the MUI uses the word *sesat* to mark the failed efforts.[4] The MUI does not seem to rigorously follow this procedure in all cases.

In the Eden case, public reactions did not reach the extremes of the Ahmadiyya and Shi'a cases, but neither were there were many supportive voices. In the news coverage of the jail sentences, only a few speakers defended the group's leaders. Luthfi Assyaukanie, one of the founders of the Liberal Islam Network, was among them. He favorably compared the case of the Eden community to the early period of Islam, when Muhammad was spreading the new belief; he also argued with the liberal stance that the state should not intervene in the status of someone's belief (Hasyim 2011). His first argument represents the rare attempt of a defense not located within the realm of liberalism, human rights, and nationalism but rather within the history of Islam itself. The second argument emphasizes the familiar line of a liberal, non-religious state.

The Lia Eden case throws into relief the risks of visibility, especially when remarks touch on the core of Islam. The importance of the prophecy had already been a key factor in the Ahmadiyya case. It was visibility, in the form of the missionary zeal of the Lia Eden congregation, that seems to have made this transgression intolerable for the MUI.

Yet how real was Lia Eden's competitive threat, and how was it perceived? The number of followers cited in all reports and articles remained at a constant seventy to one hundred people, all of them gathering in one location over ten years. This made the group manageable and indicates that neither religious nor political authorities had much reason to regard them as a growing threat, which puts them in a different category from both the opaque Ahmadiyya and the Shi'a, whose number of adherents is unclear, whose missionaries travel the country in order to attract new followers, and who themselves occasionally boast that their numbers are growing.[5] More importantly, the Eden community group had no inter- or transnational network. Lia Eden and her followers were an entirely local phenomenon. They were not only a small group that always gathered in the same place, but more important, they also had no apparent supporters who could be perceived as foreign. Yet, and this is crucial, they were also not part of the local traditional belief systems. These belief systems are somewhat more protected because of their localness. The Eden group, instead, was urban and modern rather than peripheral and a remnant of a traditional local past. This combination of factors explains why reactions to the group were comparatively mild but nevertheless led to Lia Eden's imprisonment.

The case of Amaq Bakri, however, shows that even someone far from the center and from any visibility can be dragged out into the public: in 2009, the District Court in Selong, East Lombok, tried Amaq Bakri, a seventy-year-old farmer, for having insulted religion. According to the anthropologists Kari Telle (2017), a local cleric affiliated with the Indonesian Islamic Propagation Council (Dewan Da'wah Islamiyah Indonesia) advised two preachers, who had mentioned the farmer's mystical journeys, to collect and document information on him. They took a rented video camera, posed as spiritual seekers, stayed for several days, and filmed many of their hour-long conversations. During one of the conversations, which was later uploaded to YouTube in April 2012 (Telle 2017), the two activists mentioned the word *prophet* (*nabi*), trying to encourage the old man to use this title for himself. He did not claim this title, but his descriptions of communicating with the Angel Gabriel drew accusations of deviance. Finally, the visitors asked Amaq Bakri to sign a document verifying that the material they collected indeed contained his teachings. They then handed the material to MUI officials (Telle 2017), who subsequently informed the Coordinating Board for the Monitoring of Mystical Beliefs in Society. The board organized a hearing, during which Amaq Bakri was asked to explain his understanding of Islam. The District Court eventually found him guilty for having insulted religion, and sentenced him to a year in prison. The case illustrates the eagerness with which some activists set out to find deviant beliefs and the smooth operations between various religiopolitical entrepreneurs and authorities. Perhaps more importantly, the role of digital media here once more highlights that the simple division into private and public religious activity is analytically insufficient.

Those Beyond Classification: Indigenous Believers and Atheists

From independence onward, the Indonesian state has tightly regulated religion. The first pillar of the Pancasila prescribed belief in One God, creating a hierarchy of beliefs. In addition to those who struggle with the key religious authorities in their own official religions, such as Ahmadis and Shi'a, two broad social categories of people sit awkwardly with the six officially accepted religions: those adhering to Indigenous beliefs and those who either call themselves or are by others called atheists. I suggest that the Islamist Conservative Majoritarian Synthesis regards adherents to Indigenous beliefs as "too local" to turn them into a prominent target and that the lack of the factor of "foreignness" has spared them attacks and persecution as the Ahmadis, Shi'a, and others have suffered.

Nevertheless, their being outside the officially classified religions continues to subject them to complications and restrictions. Their existence reminds others of the possibility of nuances and ambiguities and question tightly regulated religious categories. A Javanese Muslim who seeks inner peace mainly through traditional meditation techniques, celebrates local customs, and honors the spirits at special locations such as mountains or beaches questions the rules of modern homogeneity. In 2017, the Constitutional Court officially recognized aliran kepercayaan as a category, signaling a new period of regulating difference.

Atheists, on the other hand, are almost invisible if they do not seek to publicly announce their convictions and do not attempt to claim public space either in bureaucratic procedures or public debates. The experience of the few who decide to make their atheist views public and thereby claim space in a society with a high public presence of religion and belief varies depending on how they choose to be visible.

In rural areas, especially in Central and East Java, there are large numbers of people adhering to Indigenous beliefs. A growing number of Indonesians, especially in the cities and in the state apparatus, have long considered these traditional beliefs backward remains of a premodern past to be overcome by the furthering of religious teachings. For the longest period, the modern Indonesian state did not recognize belief systems outside qualified religions (*agama*). The Pancasila obliges its citizens to adhere to one of the officially accepted religions in Indonesia and distinguishes them from local and other beliefs (aliran kepercayaan). This legal distinction has concrete effects on the daily lives of citizens, for instance in the realms of marriage law and education. Despite these regulations, the formal adherence to a religion is not prescribed constitutionally beyond the Pancasila and its interpretations. Nevertheless, those not adhering to one of the accepted religions have for decades suffered numerous disadvantages because of the blank spaces in their national identity cards. Practical implications concerned mainly access to education and family law. An example is the case of Dewi Kanti, a follower of the traditional Sundanese belief system Sunda Wiwitan. In 1964, the Registry Office rejected her request to marry a Catholic man because it did not recognize her religion. Dewi Kanti's child would not be able to use the father's name. Dewi Kanti's own father, a Sunda Wiwitan leader, was once arrested for three months because he oversaw (*wali nikah*) a Sunda Wiwitan marriage in 1964 (Human Rights Watch 2013). Another example is that of Zulfa Nur Rahman, a primary school student in Semarang in North Java, who in 2016 could not be promoted to the third grade because she failed in religious studies. She had not attended the class due to her own nonofficial belief (*Tempo* 2016). In addition to these structural problems, there have been occasional attacks against Indigenous practices that some modernist Muslims consider deviant.

On a more structural level, the boundary between official religions and traditional beliefs for many decades meant that leaders of local beliefs either modified and squeezed their views and practices into the categories of the accepted world religions or accepted that their adherents fell between the cracks. It was only in 2017, in what some pluralist and liberal activists such as Guntur Romli and Andreas Harsono praised as a major step toward more religious freedom, that the Constitutional Court decided to allow followers of indigenous faiths to state their beliefs on their national identity cards (Harsono 2017). Leaders of four aliran kepercayaan from Sumba, Sumatra, and Java had filed a petition. The court declared that "the word religion in Article 61 [1] and Article 64 [1] of the Civil Administration Law contradicts the 1945 Constitution and is not legally binding" and that the same ruling applied to Article 61 [2] and Article 64 [5] of the Civil Administration Law. The court further recommended the creation of a seventh category—"adherents of a belief" (*penghayat kepercayaan*)—in addition to the six officially recognized religion to be filled into the respective column. Several religious leaders who until then had no choice but to massage their beliefs into the Hindu category welcomed this decision (Ramstedt 2019). Some scholars have called this a "seismic shift in Indonesia's religious classification system" (Aragon 2023). Others, especially legal scholars, find the ruling "muddled and inconsistent" (Butt 2020) and find that it has "created significant uncertainty" because it did not give traditional beliefs the same level of constitutional protection as official religions.

Both are true: 2017 marked the beginning of a new period in which the state would support the institutionalization of *some* diversity; however, legally, the decision has left many questions open, and practically, it had limited influence in the years since then, as only very few people have since heard of and made use of this option. In practice, many bureaucrats still create problems for individuals, usually in areas of family law or education (N. Nugroho 2020).

The MUI objected to the recognition of traditional beliefs: Anton Tabah Digdoyo, a member of the MUI Law Commission, said that recognizing Indigenous faiths was a major step backward "into the stone age" (*JawaPos.com* 2017). The MUI suggested issuing separate ID cards for adherents whose faith falls outside the officially accepted religions (*KOMPAS.com* 2018). In April 2018, Minister of Religious Affairs Lukman Hakim Saifuddin seconded this suggestion (*KOMPAS.com* 2018). This particular ID card, he announced, would not include the religion column of regular ID cards but instead would have a column called Kepercayaan (faith). The Kepercayaan column would not distinguish between various beliefs but would instead be filled in with the phrase "Kepercayaan Kepada Tuhan Yang Maha Esa" (Trust in God Almighty) or just "Kepercayaan." Lukman cited efficiency to justify this procedure, because, he argued, otherwise all ID cards would need to be reprinted (*KOMPAS.com* 2018). Of course, these distinct cards would have continued the kind of unconstitutional discrimination that the 2017 court ruling sought to end. Eventually, it became acceptable for the religious affiliation column in the normal KTP ID card to be either left empty or filled with a dash, the word *other (lainnya)*, the phrase "Kepercayaan Kepada Tuhan Yang Maha Esa" (Trust in God Almighty), or just "Kepercayaan." Only future analysis of cases based on this decision will be able to answer the question how significant this decision was.

In any case, the legal change indicated the ending of the spiral toward ever stricter interpretations of what should be acceptable belief. In some ways, it was an early indicator of a more pluralist phase that was later personified in the appointment of the NU leader Yaqut Cholil Qoumas as religious affairs minister in 2020. Within days of his appointment he vowed to uphold the rights of religious minorities (*The Jakarta Post* 2020). While adherents to Indigenous beliefs can try to squeeze into one of the accepted religions or make use of the newly formed category of kepercayaan, those who do not believe in any higher being have no alternative in the Indonesian system.

Ateisme is a concept that is even more problematic than the already controversial *sekularisme*, *pluralisme*, and *liberalisme*. Given the strong connections drawn between morality and religion, for many people in Indonesia atheism connotes immorality and connections to Communism, which after a half century is still by many considered to be pure evil. The anti-Communist massacres in 1965–66 were accompanied with a far-reaching campaign against Communists and their allies, which carried through into the New Order and has never been systematically tackled in the postauthoritarian period. In 1965, outwardly visible religiosity quickly became an expression of being anti-Communist (Bertrand 2004). The centrality of belief in one God remains enshrined in the Pancasila and was reaffirmed in the Constitutional Court's judicial review of the so-called blasphemy law in 2010.

Many atheists hide their nonbelief from family members and coworkers (Duile 2020). Moreover, Indonesian atheists face difficulties in two main legal areas: the problematic registration of religious affiliation and the danger of blasphemy accusations. Although it is legally possible to register nonadherence to religion on the Indonesian national identity card by filling in "not existent" (*tidak ada*) in the blank space provided for the category of religion, very few people choose this option (Rijkers 2020). Many bureaucrats refuse to oblige, and the danger of being discriminated against when registering at school, university, or work is considerable. Many atheists say they fear repercussions when they are known to be nonbelievers (Edgell, Gerteis, and Hartmann 2006). Even greater is the legal difficulty in the case of marriage, as is also the case for adherents of Indigenous beliefs. Indonesian law has no provision for nonreligious civil marriages. According to the marriage law of 1974, every marriage requires that a religious ceremony be led by an officially recognized religious leader in order to be recognized as legal by the state.

In the 2010s, several atheists publicly declared their positions on religion. They did so in very different ways and with respectively starkly contrasting consequences. The differences add further nuances to understanding the negotiations public and private realm and highlight the difficulties that the digitalization added to these debates.

The most high-profile case of a public accusation of atheism was that of Alexander An, usually referred to as Aan, a civil servant in the Dharmasraya regency of West Sumatra. In January 2012, an angry group of men attacked Aan violently on his way to work because they took offense to several of his Facebook posts. Rather than arresting the perpetrators, the police took Aan into protective custody. He was later charged with religious blasphemy, the propagation of atheism, and the dissemination of religious hostility. Prosecutors sought a three-and-a-half-year jail term for him, and Muslim hard-line organizations, such as the FPI, demanded his execution.

His posts combined two activities that together proved explosive: claiming a space and making insults. Both practices on their own may have been tolerable, but together, they created a tense situation that was primed to erupt with even the slightest provocation. Those seeking to consolidate the center stood ready to use the matches and publicize this case as a foil. After public attention had brought the case to the Muaro Sijunjung District Court, in June 2012, the court convicted Aan of the most serious charge and decided to drop the other two: the judge found him guilty of having violated Article 28 of the Information and Electronic Transaction Law, more precisely of "disseminating information aimed at inciting religious hatred or hostility" (Amnesty International 2012). The court sentenced Aan to two-and-a half years of imprisonment and a fine of IDR 100 million (Human Rights Watch 2013).

International and national human rights activists used his case as an example of the Indonesian state's intolerance toward atheism and cited religious freedom when calling for his unconditional release. However, the case is more complex than its interpretation by human rights activists and organizations suggests (Schäfer 2016). It serves less as an example of the real restrictions faced by atheists as for the nuances of visibility and space claiming. Alexander An was not simply imprisoned for being an atheist, or even for creating an online platform for atheists, although almost one thousand Facebook users liked his Facebook fan page Ateis Minang. Aan went much further than publicly proclaiming his disbelief and inviting others to discuss it with him by mixing his skepticism toward religion with insults. In January 2012, one of his posts read: "If God exists, why do bad things happen? . . . There should only be good things if God is merciful." He then reportedly declared that heaven, hell, angels, and devils are "myths" (*mitos*). He also posted not only an article describing Muhammad as being "attracted to his daughter-in-law" but also comic strips with offensive images (Mackinnon 2012). Years later, the Facebook page still contained images insulting Islam, such as an image of a Quran in a toilet bowl. These posts go beyond mere statements of atheism; they combine an atheist stance with insult. The sentence and the judges' reasoning indicate that Aan was punished not for his nonbelief but for "disseminating hatred." Human rights activists and some scholars have interpreted the Aan case as a straightforward example of growing intolerance and the shrinking space for expressing nonreligious views in Indonesia (I. Hasani 2016). But atheism itself, albeit uncommon and shunned, is not explicitly illegal in Indonesia. Aan's case has not changed this nor indicated any tendency toward stricter regulation of atheism. More concretely, Aan was punished for two things: posting images deemed offensive and insulting and making his atheism public. The Islamic Society Forum (Forum Umat Islam) used the case to call for more severe punishments for offenses against religion. They insisted that a prison term for Aan would not suffice: "He deserves the death penalty, even if he decides to repent. What he has done cannot be tolerated. It is important to prevent this group from spreading atheism in this country," media quoted the organization's secretary general, Muhammad al-Khaththath, in February 2012 (Al Arabiya English 2012). It cannot fully be determined whether hatred was sparked by Aan's declared disbelief or the insults he posted. During sentencing, presiding Judge Eka Prasetya Budi Dharma described Aan's actions as having caused anxiety to the community and tarnishing Islam (*keresahan dalam masyarakat dan menodai Islam*) (Constitutional Court Decision No. 140/PUU-VII/2009 2010). Using his real name rather than hiding behind anonymity further added to this visibility. By using his real name, he (whether consciously or not) presented his views as publicly viable.

Aan's case is representative of neither atheists in Indonesia nor even atheists claiming public space and hoping to improve the lives of nonbelievers. Among Indonesia's 240 million people classified as Muslim, Protestant, Catholic, Buddhist, Hindu, or Confucian, there are many who do not believe in any god. Among those, many joke about or question religious beliefs in small groups. These are nonbelievers who largely keep quiet about their views and do not make any more coordinated attempts to speak publicly about them. The space they claim is small.

In addition, there are atheist activists who campaign for their rights as nonbelievers. Many of those atheists would argue that they do not wish to convert believers to atheism but simply want to be accepted in their nonreligious identity and enjoy the same rights to marriage and education as others. With their public campaigning, they try to establish a new identity group in the religiopolitical landscape and to carve out a legitimate presence for those who wish to demonstrate their identity as atheists. A loose network of activists seeks to rehabilitate the acceptance of public nonreligiosity and often even use the term *ateis*. The activists claim not only the right to not believe in the existence of God but also the right to express this skepticism or disbelief in public. Crucially, their tone is friendly and constructive: In their Facebook groups, they wish believers a blessed Ramadan and a merry Christmas and avoid any aggressive or condescending posts. Many of them remain anonymous online but also arrange offline meetings. The online groups, discussion threads, and websites serve a double function. First, they allow like-minded people to exchange views and experiences and to organize meetings, little islands in a society that is becoming more outwardly pious. Second, online groups and websites also provide a space for atheism in a semipublic realm to educate an internet-savvy public about their perspectives. An example of this is the online forum *Anda Bertanya Ateis Menjawab* (You Ask, Atheists Respond).

Here, a group of activists "positively interact[s] with the public through [a] strongly moderated Q&A format" to "soften the devilish image of atheists" in the Indonesian public (Schäfer 2016, 261). In addition to serving as a tool of in-group communication, the internet works as a medium to give a public voice to an identity that is under pressure. Many atheist activists make use of the possibility of using pseudonyms, thereby using the internet as a semi-public space that allows them to be simultaneously visible and anonymous.

These activists are careful with their tone for good reasons: The potential to be accused of proselytization weighs heavy. Ever since the first European encounters, and especially since the days of anticolonial struggle, many Muslims have been worried about foreigners spreading Christianity, or Christianization (*kristenisasi*) (Boland 1971; Steenbrink 1998). In the postindependence period, fear of conflict through proselytization was so widespread that it was legally prohibited (Steenbrink 1998). Until today, the Proselytizing Guidelines (Ministerial Decision No. 77/1978) and the Guidelines for Overseas Aid to Religious Institutions in Indonesia (Ministerial Decision No. 20/1978) regulate and restrict the dissemination of religion. In a country that gives monotheistic belief such a central role, it is clear that this applies even more so to nonreligion. Many atheists thus keep a very low profile (Duile 2021).

As in the case of JIL, the international support that many atheist activists enjoy and have to rely on comes at the price of accusations of their being the puppets of foreign powers. In addition to the attention that Western media casts on the issue, and which especially urban and highly educated Indonesians are well aware of, support from abroad comes in two forms: the language of human rights and other atheist organizations. Both entail not only moral but also financial support, particularly in the legal realm. Locally, many view these connections skeptically and accuse local NGOs of being agents of foreign interests. As with those of the Shi'a, Ahmadiyya, and others, the cases of blasphemy and atheism are often discussed in the language of rights, especially that of minority rights. In its 2013 report "Abuses Against Religious Minorities," Human Rights Watch (2013) discusses the case of Alexander Aan at length, thereby suggesting that atheists are a religious minority in need of protection.

Atheist organizations in Indonesia not only speak the language of human rights but also focus on the right to nonbelief and are well connected to other atheist organizations abroad that argue that agnostics, humanists, and atheists are group identities that deserve state protection. They advocate for those they perceive as part of their group. In the case of Alexander Aan, the American Humanist Association—a US organization that provides legal assistance to defend the rights of nonreligious and religious minorities and actively lobbies for the separation between church and the state in the United States and abroad—internally discussed his case and vouched to assist Aan with legal support (Bulger 2012). This foreign recognition further strengthens atheism as an identity category, but also strengthens its perception as being foreign. The next case, the surge of anti-LGBTI discourses since 2016, further analyzes the complex interplay of the factors of visibility and foreignness in the reduction of ambiguity.

Restricting Pluralism: The Patriarchal Nation

Southeast Asia has a long history of gender diversity (Peletz 2006, 2009). It was mainly Western colonialism, and especially Victorian English colonialism, that introduced the omnipresence of gender binary and marginalized nonheteronormative identities. This is still visible in the law in Malaysia and Singapore law: As former English colonies, they still have laws against (male) homosexuality that were modeled after Section 377 of the Indian Penal Code introduced by the British in 1861. The Republic of Indonesia, however, which was built on Dutch law and its Napoleonic Code, does not hold on to colonial laws prohibiting same-sex intercourse. Instead, the criminalization of homosexuality is a product of the post-1998 era. It is impossible to identify a particular historical moment as the sharp turn, but some key events leading to the moment of criminalization stand out. As similar tendencies in neighboring countries indicate (Ibrahim 2016), the constriction or thinning of pluralism or increasing intolerance cannot solely be explained with the post-1998 democratization process or with what some scholars have called "the conservative turn" or increasing Islamization. Nevertheless, the post-1998 developments gave a boost to a process that was already underway, not only in the region, but globally.

The boost that intolerance toward ambiguity and diversity received in the post-1998 era is perhaps nowhere as clearly visible as in the realm of sexuality. While Indonesia had long been a heteronormative society before that, those in power largely ignored LGBTQI people. The post-1998 period then saw a brief period of euphoria, a blossoming of publicly visible sexual diversity in the form of film festivals and large gatherings. Some LGBTQI people demanded public space for their sexuality; others preferred a low profile. The newly constructed Mainstream Islam demanded opinions on what should be allowed and what should not. If there ever was a closet before the unhindered rise of the post-1998 focus on religious identity, before the communication atmosphere of the attention economy, and before the omnipresence of digital media in urban settings, the Islamist Conservative Majoritarian Synthesis dragged gender pluralist Indonesians and other members of identities deemed deviant out of their closets in order to be accused of visibility. In some sense, there was a national closet, in which some LGBTQI people did not want to hide any longer after 1998. Once they had come out and demanded their share of pubic space, others began to discuss the closet and to drag those still shielding themselves from public visibility out as well to publicly shame and assimilate them into the heterosexual morally conservative nation. The 2000s and especially the 2010s saw a rise in aggression against LGBTQI people as part of a heteronormative and patriarchal backlash (Schneider 2024).

In Aceh, the province with special autonomous status and a high prioritization of Islam in its legal regulations, the window of tolerated visibility of queer sexualities was even shorter (Ichwan 2021). Those seeking to consolidate the center discovered LGBTQI people as a vulnerable target to their accusations of moral decadence and foreign connections. Marginalizing them offered conservatives fresh opportunities to cast themselves as morally upright. They shut down old and newly found freedoms and ambivalences and further thinned pluralism on the level of speech and debate as well as on the legal level in the form of new anti-LGBTQI laws.

Majoritarian Islamists are not the only ones who pushed this development: They forged powerful alliances with conservatives of other religions and facilitated by state actors. Several states and nonstate actors have used "political homophobia" (Bosia and Weiss 2013) as part of their strategical repertoire. Especially state actors have often intentionally deployed political homophobia, a scapegoating of an other that drives processes of state building and retrenchment. Forms of political homophobia must be examined as typical tools for building an authoritative notion of national collective identity and for mobilizing around a variety of contentious issues. Their perspective transcends the boundary between state and nonstate actors in ways that are helpful for understanding the Indonesian case. On one side, politicians continued the heteronormative legacy of the New Order. On the other side, they adopted the explicitly anti-LGBTQI discourses of Islamist actors due to the increasingly top-down regulation of religion, defined and enforced by male-dominated nationalist institutions, but most crucially, the imperative to succeed in a competitive political climate shaped by elections and the attention economy. The fourfold decentralization with its heightened competition explains the timing of the public anti-LGBTQI aggression in addition to transnational developments. A view to developments in other countries confirms this: Numerous studies discuss the rise of homonationalism and heteronationalism in societies that radically reconfigure their nationalisms in late modernity, which are increasingly characterized by religio-identitarian homogenization, neoliberalism, competitive authoritarianism, and the omnipresence of a digitalized and fragmented media system. Gender and masculinity studies acknowledged the central role of competition and competitiveness even before the triumph of neoliberalism (Lipman-Blumen 1976). The case of anti-LGBTQI discourses illustrates how those seeking to consolidate the center by further marginalizing those pushed to the periphery seized the opportunity to use the foreign funding and support that many of these publicly visible events received to create the perception that LGBTQI people were somehow under foreign influence, a narrative I will discuss in more detail toward the end of this chapter. The case delves deeper into the "socially conservative" aspect of the Islamist Conservative Majoritarian Synthesis.

This section will briefly discuss how the modern Indonesian nation has promoted masculinist and heteronormative ideals and then show how the modern reduction of the tolerance toward ambiguity in the field of gender and sexuality received a fresh boost in the post-1998 period. This boost was partly facilitated by the focus on the language of rights and the selective embracing of efforts to eliminate discrimination of LGBTQI people rather than attempts to dismantle the overall patriarchic societal structure. The examples discussed in this section illustrate once more the importance of the factors of visibility and foreignness in the post-1998 aggression against LGBTQI people and how the perception of foreign connections also drove a wedge between LGBTQI activism and feminist activism that increasingly tried to portray itself as local rather than Western or internationally influenced—a discord that has further weakened both movements. None of these post-1998 developments were entirely new: They largely accelerated previous heteronormativity, adding mainly an additional layer of aggression.

The New Order regime privileged heteronormative nuclear families with few children as a "foundational element and microcosm" (Boellstorff 2005) as the "building blocks" (Dwyer 2000) of the modern Indonesian nation. The family ideal of the urbanizing developmentalist state very much resembled that of the United States or Europe in the same period: a breadwinning man and a supportive wife performing unpaid labor in the domestic sphere and supporting the community and the nation through voluntary activities in her free time. Wives, referred to and addressed as "mothers" (*ibu*), were expected to support their husbands, referred to as "fathers" (*bapak*), to enable them in their developmentalist mission. This followed the independence struggle and the short bloom of the Indonesian Communist Party, during which women were expected to assume important positions in building the Communist state. This brief period ended not only with the massacres against everyone suspected to be linked even remotely to the world's third-largest Communist Party, but also with a powerful narrative that schoolchildren grew up learning as a founding myth of the New Order. It accused the women's organization Gerwani and the youth wing of the Communist Party, Pemuda Rakyat, of torturing, performing sadistic sexual acts, and finally, killing six military generals (Larasati 2013). From 1984 until the end of the New Order, schoolchildren were required to watch the docudrama *Pengkhianatan G30S/PKI* (Treachery of G30S/PKI), which had been sponsored by the government and depicts in detail the brutal torturing and murder of the six generals killed in the coup. The official account of the New Order held that Communist women had central roles in the orchestrated killing of the generals (Wieringa 2002).

Women's organizations continued to be important during the New Order, but women were now expected to serve in the role of domestic managers of nuclear families. This definition of women as wives and mothers was epitomized in Dharma Wanita, the state-sanctioned organization for civil servants' wives. In the formal hierarchy of this nation-wide institution, the positions held by women paralleled those held by their husbands (Anthias and Nira 1989; Carol Johnson 2011; Mayer 2012; Nira 1997; Parker et al. 2018; Stokes 1998; Suryakusuma 2011). Scholars of nationalism have for four decades noted the gendered dimension of nationalism. In the 1980s, George L. Mosse (1985) posited that nationalism absorbed late nineteenth-century challenges to European social norms, such as homosexuality and bohemian, nudist, and youth movements, and channeled them into acceptable demonstrations of patriotism like the male camaraderie of the world wars and nationalistic motherhood. It is therefore useful to understand the gender dimensions of the nationalist-religious reconfiguration of the post-1998 years.

During Indonesia's postauthoritarian reform period, a continuation of the developmentalist ideal was supplemented with increased privatization and individualization, burdening women with higher responsibilities for their immediate family, including the future socioeconomic opportunities of their children. Islamist nonstate actors joined state actors in reducing (and partly pushed them to do so) women to the position of wives expected to provide reproductive labor and support for their husbands' spiritual and economic ambitions. Unlike in the New Order era, this expectation was now couched in religious and individualist terms.

The ideal of the nuclear family based on a married romantic couple has become an important marker of modernity in many Muslim societies (Huq

1999), including Indonesia. Romance here is complemented with the idea of a peaceful and serene family unit called *keluarga sakinah*, inspired by the Quranic concept *sakinah* (سكينة, tranquility, reassurance, peace). The keluarga sakinahis is based on a combination of support and negotiations and on agreements between consenting adults on their terms of marriage as determined in their Islamic marriage contract (Slama 2023; Smith-Hefner 2019). To some degree, this family concept also allows room for polygyny, albeit this is only true for a minority. One factor increasing the importance of the nuclear family in Indonesia is the rising commercialization of areas such as health and education and the decrease of services provided by the large civil society organizations NU and Muhammadiyah (Hicks 2012): As the old wider networks providing aspects of security and stability are dissolving/retreating in times of higher social and geographical mobility, it is in the interest of the state to maintain and even strengthen the functioning nuclear family.

In the neoliberal and individualizing spirit of the 1990s, this ideal became cultivated from the bottom up as well as the top down: The "Islamic books" shelves in bookstores were packed with the rapidly expanding genre of Islamic self-improvement literature. Whole sections in the shelves have since been dedicated to the ideal Muslim mother. The books are moral treatises, spiritual advice literature and self-help books that educate and instruct their readers about Islamic principles and their reader's own place in a world oriented toward Islam.

Similar literature has already existed in Arab language since the 1980s, often financed and published in Saudi Arabia. One popular example of this recent trend of Muslim self-help is the book "Don't be sad" (Ar., *La tahzan*) by the Saudi Islamic scholar Aid Al-Qarni—one of the most famous Islamic books in and outside the Muslim world and an Islamic adaptation of lifestyle guru Dale Carnegie's book *How to Stop Worrying and Start Living*. Both books offer ideas for personal development based on individual progress and achievement, popular psychology (i.e., positive thinking), and effective self- and time management and mix them with principles of virtuous behavior, self-purification, and the refinement of character (Ar. *adab, tazkiyat an-nafs, tahzib al-ahlaq*, and similar concepts). Thus, while Muslim advice literature shows parallels to the Western genre of self-help and deals with topics like happiness, success, stress, and depression, large portions of this genre are explicitly gendered and offer instructions for proper male and female behavior, family life, and child education.

Many Islamists, disappointed after the low performance of Islamist parties in 1998, had focused on Islamizing society rather than the state apparatus.

Yet because of the decentralization, political competition, and perception of Islam as morally superior, many politicians supported regulations demanded by Islamist organizations, such as dress rules. These rules often apply to both men and women, although the requirements for women are usually more elaborate. In South Tangerang (West Java), Mayor Airin Rachni Diany declared on April 24, 2013, that all Muslim staff members should wear Muslim attire on Fridays. Non-Muslim staff members were to wear their civil servant uniforms on that day, as all employees do on the other workdays. In the nearby city of Tangerang, Mayor Wahidin Halim had already announced that staff members must wear Muslim clothes as part of an effort to increase the religious atmosphere within the administration (Fidrus and Christanto 2013). In Benkulu (Sumatra), authorities announced they were considering regional legislation on the protection of women and children that would include rules on a stricter dress code and banning "sexy clothing" in public in order to counter "sexual violence and rape against women and children" (Constance Johnson 2017). Victims of violence are here reframed as potential provocateurs. Restrictive measures are often supported with the language of care, cure, and prevention rather than punishment, as the following examples of campaigns to lead homosexual people "back" to heterosexuality illustrate.

The nuclear family is an important element not only of the nation-state but also of neoliberalism. In the well-researched case of the United States, the collaboration between free-market neoliberals and social conservatives has partly been explained with the shared value of family responsibility and kinship obligations (Cooper 2017). In this reading, the poor law tradition is revived in the form of household debt. The family thus serves as an alternative to the twentieth-century welfare state, with private debt obligations of family being foundational to socioeconomic order. Neoliberals and social conservatives can thus agree on the bonds of family as a necessary complement to market freedom. Similarly, in Indonesia, the state tries to trace family members of homeless people or other people in need (Hegarty 2016).

Like social conservatives elsewhere, for instance in Malaysia and the United States, the Islamist Conservative Majoritarian Synthesis couched their proposed measures against gender pluralism in a terminology of care, cure, and containment rather than persecution and aggression (Thajib 2022). This discourse of care (*peduli*) makes anti-gender pluralism more acceptable to a greater number of otherwise tolerant people, particularly as it holds the constructive element of inviting the culprits to return to the right path, similar to the cases of the Ahmadiyya, Shi'a, and other deviants. Respective programs to prevent deviance from heteronormativity have already been underway for several years in neighboring Malaysia and are likely to find imitation in Indonesia.

A New Wave of Anti-LGBTQI Activism and Legislation

Compared to neighboring Singapore and Malaysia and to Western societies, Indonesia has been relatively tolerant of homosexuality. Before the 2016 surge of new aggression against LGBTQI people, scholars described Indonesia as a "heteronormative, but yet not punitively homophobic state" (Bennett and Davies 2014, 12) and as "a context where heterosexism has historically held a dominant cultural position without homophobia's aid (Boellstorff 2004). In the early 2000s, the anthropologist Tom Boellstorff described how neither anger nor aggression were common reactions to gay advances or the sight of gay couples in Indonesia as compared to Western societies, where many homosexual couples and transgender people continue to fear for their safety in the public sphere. Historical work stresses the important roles transgender people played in rituals, overseeing sacred ceremonies that were of critical importance to local societies and polities (Peletz 2006).

After 1998, with the rise of civil society and of the rights discourse, many, especially urban people with diverse sexual orientations and gender expressions began to adopt Western terminologies—such as terms of self-identification as LGBTQI (lesbian, gay, bisexual, transgender, queer, and intersex). Partly inspired by the enthusiasm for new freedoms and the growing discourses of human and minority rights, they also began demanding greater acceptance and normalization of their sexualities. Part of these space-claiming activities, which combined the celebratory with the political, was the LGBTQI film festival in Jakarta that allowed many LGBTQI activists to connect to a growing transnational "community" of people challenging heterosexual gender norms.

These activities led to greater visibility. In the early 2000s, Indonesian state actors supported steps toward women's sexual equality and rights on a legal and policy level (Bennett and Davies 2014, 6). At the same time, right-wing Islamists stirred moral panics that many conservatives from other religions chimed into. By the mid-2010s, scholars saw "in the reform era the seesaw of progressive versus conservative sexual values oscillating through an expanding array of technologies and social sites" (Bennett and Davies 2014, 8). These new freedoms framed in terms of "rights," and with them the old previous freedoms, ultimately became constrained by the mid-2010s (Ridwan and Wu 2018; Rodríguez and Murtagh 2022; Thajib 2022).

Especially in the post-1998 era and the short rise of the LGBTQI rights movement, many Indonesians began to perceive gender pluralism as something foreign rather than local. There has been the widespread assumption among Indonesians "that gay men and women are products of the executive, jet-setting classes" (Boellstorff 2005, 29). Of course, this is far from the truth, and many, if not most, Indonesians who do not adhere to heterosexual gender norms live even more precariously because they face discrimination in the workplace. In Boellstorff's view, these accusations prove that organized forces such as Gay International (Massad 2002) are not necessary for a globalization, as people often assume transnational connections regardless. Boellstorff highlights that transnational categories can then become localized and uses the categories *gay* and *lesbi* as Indonesian terms that signify specific Indonesian identities. With this argument on the dynamics between transnational and national concepts, Boellstorff built on heated debates in US and European scholarship on this topic, which had previously mostly focused on Middle Eastern societies. In those debates on the influence of Gay International (Massad's term for global LGBTQ rights advocacy efforts, which he argues impose Western sexual identities on non-Western societies) on the heterosexualization of previously more tolerant or gender-fluid societies, Joseph Massad (2002, 372) argued that international actors undertook efforts "to impose a European heterosexual regime on Arab men." Others accused Massad of neglecting empirical scholarship on existing sexual diversity in the region (Schmitt 2003).

My argument on how the aspect of foreignness and internationalism contributes to the anti-LGBTQI aggressions is that while Boellstorff is right to emphasize the Indonesian character of the *gay* and *lesbi* identities and the modest socioeconomic circumstances of LGBTQI Indonesians (contrary to their opponents' perception), the fact remains that the terms themselves, even while being Indonesian concepts, sound very much like English terms and showcase their transnational influences in a way comparable to many other terms in these debates: *ateis, sekuralisme, pluralisme,* liberalism—all of these barely conceal their origin in Western lexicons of modernity, a point that their detractors are keen to emphasize.

Further, the English-sounding initialism LGBTQI is used globally, and terminology thus carries a constant and repeated tinge of foreignness. Framing the defense of gender pluralist individuals primarily in terms of rights, rather than local history, especially in public debates, reinforced the perception of gender pluralists as connected to foreign interests. Recalling that "gay men and lesbians have not always existed. Instead, they are a product of history, and have come into existence in a specific historical era" (D'Emilio 2007), *gay* and *lesbi* as Indonesian terms offer a window into how LGBTQI identities became constructed in Indonesia at a particular historical moment.

Familiarity with the unglamorous, often violent, and vulnerable reality of lives on the margins of heteronormativity blinds many researchers to seeing the degree to which many Indonesians not consciously acquainted with LGBTQI people often associate them with what they call a culture of hedonism (*budaya hedon, hedonisme*) and decadence (*dekadensi*). Occasionally, this is accusingly linked to capitalism. An example is an article titled "LGBT Scenario of Global Capitalism Destroying a Generation" on the Islamist website Panjimas, which circulated on various social media (Susmiyati 2016). These accusations, generalizing and conspiracy-theoretic as they are, are not entirely without basis. "LGBT Marketing" and "pinkwashing" (Rao 2015) have been targeting homosexual and transgender consumers for a long time, making them and their spending resources publicly visible to a large audience. While the vast majority of gender pluralist Indonesians are not part of an affluent upper middle class connected to global markets, public discourses connect them to distinctly pro-LGBTQI images and practices abroad. Viewed in that light, they are part of something larger, a transnational identity. Whether or not gender pluralist Indonesians have actual cosmopolitan and transnational connections does not matter to the public discourse portraying them as thriving on such connections and thereby potentially threatening the national cohesion. Further, there are real material aspects: In the example of the Q! Queer Film Festival, most of the festival's venues were foreign-funded cultural institutes. Hence the accusations by FPI leaders that "the colonialists [were] purposely corrupting and destroying Indonesia's next generation" are rooted in actual material foreign support that can be measured precisely. It cannot be denied that foreignness is a powerful accusation in the debates on deviance as part of the nationalist reconfiguration.

The law that authorities use against those they accuse of homosexuality is the antipornography law established in 2008, even though this law did not target particular sexualities. The bill outlaws "pornographic images and acts," broadly defining pornography as "man-made sexual materials in the form of drawings, sketches, illustrations, photographs, text, voice, sound, moving pictures, animation, cartoons, poetry, conversations and gestures." Crucially and controversially, it also prohibits public performances with the potential to "incite sexual desire." The bill calls for harsh penalties for those in violation of the laws. Anyone caught "displaying nudity" in public could spend up to ten years in prison and be fined up to $500,000. When parliament voted for the bill in 2008, it turned into law a decade-long public debate that attracted much national and international coverage. The bill was originally drafted in 1999, but in its formulations contradicted too many local (often Hindu or Christian) traditions. After controversies surrounding the gyrating hip motions used by dangdut pop singer Inul Daratista in her famous "drilling" dance after one of her concerts was aired in 2003 and the launching of an Indonesian version of *Playboy Magazine* in 2006, the Prosperous Justice Party (Partai Keadilan Sejahtera, PKS) revived the draft. Significantly reduced, it eventually was supported by about four hundred members of parliament in 2008, with around one hundred speaking out against it. One of its starkest features is the vagueness of the offense. The condemnation of Inul Daratista's dance, whose concerts the MUI demanded be banned, clarified that any law prohibiting pornography would have to cover a broad range of images and "actions" to satisfy its proponents.

The law has since been applied eclectically in several high-profile cases, some of which included pop stars and politicians. Despite these cases, it is probably gay men who have felt the threat of the vaguely defined law the most. The vague formulation of the law has been capitalized by police forces who throughout the 2010s have increasingly been raiding hotels and private residence, targeting and arresting groups of men for allegedly engaging in sex parties in these closed premises (Renaldi 2017).

Violence against homosexual and transgender people, conducted and accepted by the state, by organizations, and also by individuals, is not an entirely new phenomenon. In recent decades, especially transgender people, especially *waria* (male-to-female transvestites), have frequently been pushed to work in the dangerous sex industry. One of my Indonesian interlocutors, an offshore drilling worker in Balikpapan, an oil town in Kalimantan, told me in the early 2000s that he was very unhappy about his brother, whose group of friends, every now and then when they were drunk, drove across the town to beat up waria sex workers at night, mainly out of boredom and frustration. Accounts of such violence have been documented for many decades, constituting just the tip of the iceberg of undocumented violence, and it would be difficult to assess where and when such violence first arose and during what phases it increased. However, apart from the everyday violence against transgender sex workers and other forms of structural discrimination, there was still more room for gender pluralism in Indonesia in the early 2000s than there had been twenty years later.

Several milestones mark the path toward this new level of hostility and criminalization. In November 2000, a group of 150 men calling themselves part of the Gerakan Pemuda Ka'bah (Ka'bah Youth Movement) broke into a gathering of waria who were observing National Health Day with an event in the Central Javanese town Kaliurang. The event was sponsored by several health organizations as well as the local Indonesian-French Institute and had been held across Indonesia since the early 1990s without any major interruptions. The attackers arrived on motorcycles and in jeeps, many of them clad in the typical white robes and turbans associated with violent Islamism, and beat up many of the participants. Afterward, fifty-seven men were arrested, but all were soon released without charges being filed (Boellstorff 2005, 466). In March 2010, parallel to the hearings to repeal the blasphemy law, a similarly sized group stormed through a hotel in Surabaya that was the planned venue for a conference of the International Lesbian, Gay, Bisexual, Transgender and Intersex Association (ILGA). Days earlier, the Surabaya Police had announced not to issue a permit for the conference after objections raised by the MUI and the Muhammadiyah. The police declared the event too "vulnerable" (*rawan*) for an official permit (*Liputan6* 2010). For the participants and rights activists, the state's inability to protect the conference from attacks showed the state's weakness at best, but mostly it proved to them the state's unwillingness to uphold its constitution for those who deviate from gender and sexual norms (Human Rights Watch 2016). Only half a year later, a similar mixture of aggression and nonprotection blocked parts of the Q! Queer Film Festival in Jakarta and other cities, marking the beginning of the end of Asia's largest LGBTQI film festival. The annual festival, held between 2002 and 2017, screened several dozen films at various venues. In 2010, several days into the festival, the FPI staged an aggressive protest outside two of the screening venues, the German Goethe Institute and the Dutch Erasmus Huis. The choice of locale most likely confirmed their narrative of gender diversity being mainly the product of promotion through foreign agents and interests. A group of several dozen FPI men, clad in long white gowns and white turbans, rallied just outside the gate of the Goethe Institute. Two filmmakers later turned their footage of the protest into a short documentary (Ucu and Lucky 2010). The opponents carried FPI flags and printouts of film stills showing homosexual couples. Pumping their fists into the air, the crowd echoed the anger of their speaker, who was screaming his anger into a microphone: "The colonialists are purposely corrupting and destroying Indonesia's next generation!" Other film shots focused on the scared organizers of the festival. In almost comic desperation, one of the organizers reports of a phone call by the FPI: "They are demanding money and food from us!" A visibly annoyed policeman demanded the organizers accept a petition by the FPI, acting more like a conflict mediator between two legitimate parties than a police officer protecting the freedoms of a liberal political system. Several screenings were interrupted but the festival continued. Similar scenes were happening in other places of the country. One of my interlocutors reported of disturbed screenings in Yogyakarta, where the protesting FPI crowd was much larger than the small audience it managed to disperse: "We were only a small group watching a film. The protesters outnumbered us by far. Nobody understood what made them so angry."

Since the early 2010s, police have justified banning LGTQI events because of previous attacks on similar events by organizations like FPI. The Jakarta film festival officially ceased to exist in 2017 amid what has constituted the strongest surge of rhetoric, policies, and new bylaws against gender pluralism. The surge was sparked in 2016, by a politician's apparently thoughtless comment. The comment and the subsequent reactions to it unleashed a whole campaign against people of nonheteronormative sexual orientations and resulted in comments by the MUI reaffirming its anti-LGBTQI fatwa of 2014, which in turn inspired drafts for a national law criminalizing nonheteronormative relationships—Indonesia was preparing to criminalize homosexuality on the national level, for the first time in its history. The Indonesian debate was boosted by US debates that played out to a large degree on Twitter and other digital media: When the US Supreme Court held in a 5–4 decision that the Fourteenth Amendment requires all states to grant same-sex marriages and recognize same-sex marriages granted in other states, the Human Rights Campaign (HRC), the largest LGBTQI civil rights organization in the United States, launched its campaign for marriage equality using the hashtag #LoveWins. The HRC "wanted to build a drumbeat across the country and win over hearts and minds around the globe, encouraging a conversation both on and off line." HRC used digital networks and encouraged users to participate with their own images in the campaign. #LoveWins was a global trend throughout the day, trending on Facebook, Instagram and Twitter, gaining over 1.4 million photos on Instagram and 7 million tweets (Shorty Awards, n.d.). Many Indonesians participated online and were part of a larger global campaign. This campaign and the US Supreme Court decision were crucial for the Indonesian debates, as they made it very difficult for many to continue pretending that homosexuality was just a phase that would be ended by heterosexual marriage (Thajib 2022).

Within Indonesia, since decentralization in 1999, human rights organizations have been documenting anti-gender pluralist bylaws in individual provinces, such as the South Sumatra Provincial Ordinance on the Eradication of Immoral Behavior (No. 13/2002), which classifies homosexual acts and anal sex performed by men as "immoral behavior"; the Banjar South Kalimantan District Ordinance on Social Order (No. 10/2007), which mentions "abnormal" homosexual and heterosexual acts in its definition of "prostitution" and prohibits the formation of organizations "leading to immoral acts" that are "unacceptable to the culture of [local] society" (the latter explained with examples of lesbian and gay organizations "and the like"); and several other similar regulations in Tasikmalaya, West Java, the Riau island of Batam, and Padang Panjang in West Sumatra (Human Rights Watch 2016).

Those seeking to consolidate the center of Mainstream Islam threw themselves into this new other. Islamist majoritarian activist organizations, such as the FPI, used the seemingly marginal media comment by Muhammad Nasir, the then minister of higher education, to spark a storm of aggression against people outside the heteronormative gender order. "The LGBT community should not be allowed to grow or be given room to conduct its activities," Muhammad Nasir had said in an interview. He found that they "corrupted the nation's morals" (*LGBT ini tidak sesuai dengan tataran nilai dan kesusilaan bangsa Indonesia. Saya melarang. Indonesia ini tata nilainya menjaga kesusilaan*). A storm of protest rolled up against this, mostly in digital networks, such as Twitter. When the minister half-heartedly rowed back on Twitter, it was already too late. While he asserted that "it is an individual's right to be gay or lesbian, but the academic atmosphere must not be disrupted," others had taken up the issue. Various actors, most of them well-known right-wing Islamists, whipped up a new wave of aggressive anti-LGBTQI rhetoric. The initialism became widely known in the public and has since been used in many different situations in Indonesian daily life, way beyond the circles of activism and politicians (Braunschweiger 2016).

Information ministry spokesman Ismail Cawidu requested social media platforms to remove any emojis "that smack of LGBT" (*The Guardian* 2016). He said it was a gesture of respect for "religious values and norms." The popular Japan-based mobile chat application LINE acquiesced on February 12. Adding insult to injury, it apologized for failing to "filter culturally sensitive content." The Indonesian Broadcasting Commission first banned the broadcast of a LGBTQI campaign, then forbade portraying gender pluralism as "normal" and finally prohibited the broadcast of effeminate men (Braunschweiger 2016). Several ministers declared alternative sexualities to be diseases. Vice President Jusuf Kalla instructed the United Nations Development Program to cut funding to LGBTQI rights education programs. Indonesia's Coordinating Political, Legal, and Security Affairs Minister Luhut Pandjaitan publicly spoke out about the need to respect the rights of LGBT people, but he dampened his apparent support by adding that he believed homosexuality was the result of a chromosomal condition that required "curing" (*The Jakarta Post* 2016a). A new series of regulations and bylaws institutionalized discrimination against LGBTQI people by criminalizing same-sex relations, "immoral behavior," and gender nonconformity, thereby providing a legal basis for harassment, arbitrary arrests, and abuse by authorities (Human Rights Watch 2016).

The MUI used the opportunity to emphasize that it had issued a respective fatwa calling for the criminalization of LGBTQI activities back in 2014 (*The Jakarta Post* 2016b). The fatwa had asked (*diminta*) the government to prohibit the existence of homosexuals, whether lesbian or gay or other communities of a sexually deviant orientation (*kamunitas* [sic] *homoseksual, baik lebi* [sic] *maupun gay, serta komunitas lain yang memiliki orientasi seksual menyimpang*). The council had further demanded heavy penalties and support of rehabilitation programs in order to curb the spreading (*meluasnya*) of LGBTQI identities (Majelis Ulama Indonesia 2014). At the point of being issued in 2014, the fatwa was mainly discussed among specialist circles, now it became more publicly visible. What many referred to as "LGBT" had become a problem of national(ist) concern. With the MUI's call for an outright criminalization of LGBTQI identification and its amplification by the wave of anti-LGBTQI comments by several senior politicians, the discourses against gender pluralism reached a new level of aggression (Wijaya 2022).

It may be helpful here to consider the discussions of the "punitive turn" in the United States and other Western societies, even though they do not map onto other regions easily. For the United States and parts of Europe, scholars attested to a rapid increase in incarceration and a decline of the rehabilitative ideal (Bell 2011). A main difference to Southeast Asia is that "the new punitiveness" in the United States and parts of Europe and Australia targets mainly the poor (Wacquant 2009). In Southeast Asia, there has been a similar tendency of the rise of neoliberalism coinciding with a rise of a more punitive climate. Reports state that the prison population increased sharply from 2000 to 2019: In 2019, approximately 1.19 million people in Southeastern Asia were detained in prison, a rise of 120 percent since 2000 (United Nations 2022). Despite this more punitive climate, the target groups do not always include gender pluralists. In Thailand and in the Philippines, queer people were largely spared, while others, such as drug users in the Philippines, were subjected to killings and prosecution. Singapore retains the colonial Section 377, despite loosening its tight grip of law enforcement on the topic. In Brunei, Indonesia, and Malaysia, the state increasingly enforces heteronormativity through punitive means (Yulius 2018). This punitive trend does not easily map onto neat patterns of socioeconomic background: Those deemed deviant are not part of an ethnicized identity, such as Black Americans or Muslims in Europe. Ahmadis, Shi'a, and LGBTQI people are found in all economic backgrounds. However, the political systems in Indonesia and Malaysia allow most wealthy offenders to escape punishment, including the offense of deviance. The anthropologist Michael Peletz discusses the "elective affinities" between neoliberalism and the punitive turn. He argues that interpretations of the paradigmatic Quranic injunction to enjoin good and forbid evil (*amar maaruf, nahi munkar*) first began to assume prominence in official parlance in the late 1970s, and into the early 1990s, it centered on the enjoining good (*amar maaruf*) half of the equation before the emphasis began to be placed on the forbidding of evil (*nahi munkar*) half: on harsh, punitive sanctions geared ostensibly toward deterrence (Peletz 2020, 615, 616). He outlines the simultaneous neoliberal restructuring of Malaysia and Indonesia that went hand in hand with the described punitive turn.

The process was facilitated by the crucial factors of visibility and foreignness. The latter is also connected to the previously mentioned accusations of decadence and hedonism, which intertwine with anticapitalist and antineoliberal rhetoric even beyond social conservatives.

Neoliberalism and the Accusations of Cosmopolitanism

This section explains the accusations of decadence and hedonism against the background of the complex relationship of neoliberalism and publicly visible homosexuality. One accusation leveled against gender pluralists is the corruption of youth and the erosion of the nuclear family. The young generation, so goes the accusation, is lured into a hedonistic and luxurious lifestyle that threatens cultural values (Jansen 2025). This became most publicly apparent in the protests against a concert by the US pop singer Lady Gaga in May 2012. The pop star, whose fame has closely been tied to her pro-LGBTQI activism and also involved cooperating with global companies, such as Google (Deflem 2017), had scheduled a show in Jakarta. The FPI demanded that politicians prohibit the show. Posters at demonstrations showed portraits of the singer, crossed out and reading, "Kafir." Hizbut Tahrir argued that the concert was part of the "development of materialistic values based on the ideology of capitalism, at the center of society" (*berkembangnya nilai-nilai materialisme di tengah-tengah masyarakat yang bersumber ideologi kapitalisme*). The MUI also sent a letter to the chief of police, strongly recommending canceling the concert. The council stated that the concert would be contrary to the principles of the nation (*prinsip-prinsip kehidupan berbangsa dan bernegera*) and the Pancasila, to the 1945 Constitution, and to religious norms (*norma agama*). Lady Gaga as an icon of pornography and liberalism (*ikon pornografi dan liberalisme*) should not, the council stated, be given room to deplete the nation's energy (*menguras energi bangsa*) by causing "horizontal conflicts" (*konflik horizontal*) that would disturb tranquility and order (*mengusik ketenangan dan menggangu ketenangan dan ketertiban masyarakat*). Indulging in hedonism (*mengumbar hedonisme*), the council argued, would destroy social solidarity and a sense of national belonging (*mematikan kesetiakawanan sosial dan rasa solidaritas sebagai warga bangsa*), especially at a time when many Indonesians were facing economic hardship (*masyarakat Indonesia dalam kondisi kesulitan ekonomi*). This line of argument again evoked the endangerment of community cohesion and social order. It also partly places the responsibility for poverty and unemployment on the shoulders of those who insist on their excessive (*mengumbar*) lifestyles. This individualization of societal problems would later be picked up again by the proponents of the family resilience bill.

These accusations are a refinement of the general accusation of hedonism and decadence: Not only are these portrayed as wrong, but they are portrayed as a double threat of being possible at the cost of poorer Indonesians and at potentially corrupting the youth and the future of the national community. The ways in which this argumentation mixes social conservatism with questions of economic precarity and solidarity show how the discourse transgresses categorizations of left-and-right and thus addresses a broad range of people and their anxieties about a quickly changing and increasingly unequal society. Comparable to nationalist populism in Western Europe, which has won many voters over from left-wing to right-wing parties, the frustration and anger that feeds much of the hatred toward singled-out minorities cannot be understood without acknowledging its corrective elements (Kaltwasser 2012). There are many who feel left behind by the jet-setting cosmopolitan class that they see embodied in LGBTQI people. The literature on cosmopolitanism and communitarianism posits that there has been a widening gap between elites culturally and economically oriented toward global connections and masses that are rooted/committed to local, regional, or national spheres/contexts (De Wilde et al. 2019). In the realm of cultural capital, opinions and habits pertaining to questions of gender fluidity and rigidity are split into the two different camps. In some countries, it might be fair to speak of urban cosmopolitan elites and rural communitarian masses, but in many other countries, such as India and Indonesia, urban elites themselves are often deeply split between cosmopolitan and communitarian outlooks, wherein there are often simultaneously nationalist and (right-wing) religious viewpoints. A body of literature that emerged after what many observers called the rise of populism highlights the masculinist features/characteristics of this populism (Eksi and Wood 2019). Across the globe, nationalist-authoritarian circles have cultivated "gender" or "gender ideologies" as one of their primary enemies. In Indonesia, the public debates are arguably less crude than in Turkey and Hungary, but some of the practices in the form of legal criminalization and violent attacks are on a similar level. Just as liberals in Western Europe and the United States have eventually begun to see rapidly rising inequalities as one of multiple source of the discontent expressed in nationalist populism (Manow 2018) and as Vedi Hadiz (2015) has explained variants of these sentiments as "Islamic Populism" in Indonesia and Turkey, it is important to acknowledge that social conservative actors target LGBTQI people who are portrayed and perceived as cosmopolitan—even if the lived realities of the people in this group are much more diverse than this simplistic portrayal indicates. It is less the empirical reality and more opponents' perceptions that inform the sentiments at stake here.

This chapter took the 2005 fatwa against secularism, pluralism, and liberalism as a lens and analyzed the discourses it was part of and further boosted, from atheism, blasphemy, and Indigenous beliefs to the wave of anti-LGBTQI activism that has further contributed to the reduction of diversity in the reconfiguring of the nation as socially conservative Sunni Muslim.

The failed attempt to repeal the blasphemy law in 2010 illustrates how the Indonesian Constitutional Court takes its cues from the MUI and other conservative religious authorities and firmly rejects the notion of a "secular" Indonesia without fully committing to an "Islamic" state, however defined. The attacks against and lack of widespread support for the small but highly visible Liberal Islam Network—some of whose founding members were important figures within the NU—shows how liberalism had a short blossoming period but quickly lost its ground in the postreform period. A part of the group of intellectuals who supported Liberal Islam later lent their voices to the Islam Nusantara discourse on Southeast Asian Islam, promoted by a faction within the NU after 2015. The Islam Nusantara discourse (Suaedy 2018) attracted the support of Jokowi in the late 2010s and saw much more success than the discourse on rights.

One key question is to what degree this discourse will extend its definition of diversity to gender pluralism. This chapter showed that the acceptance and tolerance of gender pluralism has been shrinking since colonialism and that a brief post-1998 window of greater visibility of a certain segment of LGBTQI activism in urban spheres was followed by an antidiversity backlash.

All of these explanatory factors relate to negotiations of visibility and the limits of the analytical distinction between private and public. The flaws of this distinction shimmers through the various allegations of corrupting the youth in the examples of the Q! Queer Film Festival and the Lady Gaga controversy, and it is most obvious in the 2016 wave of anti-LGBTQI aggression. Many comments and the MUI fatwa itself specifically addressed the public character of LGBTQI activities and their potential to "spread" sexual deviance.

In the 2000s and 2010s, the intensified focus on religious identity, the dynamics of the attention economy, and the spread of digital media in urban spaces redefined the boundaries of visibility. Gender pluralist Indonesians and others labeled as deviant faced increasing public scrutiny. Some actively sought recognition and demanded inclusion in public discourse, challenging societal norms. Others, unwillingly exposed, were subjected to public condemnation and pressures to conform to heteronormative, morally conservative ideals. The rise of digital media has amplified this dynamic, eroding distinctions between private and public spaces and intensifying the negotiation of identity under constant observation.

CHAPTER 4

Bottom-Up vs. Top-Down Centralization
Indonesia and Malaysia in Comparative Perspective

In 2011, Ainul Yakin, the leader of the main Ahmadiyya community in Kampong Nakhoda, Batu Caves, just outside Kuala Lumpur, gave me a tour of the mosque compound. As we walked around the walls encircling the yard and the garden, he greeted several of his neighbors. Some smiled back, some asked about his guest, others made a point of throwing us disapproving glances in response to Ainul's wide and demonstrative smile. Officially, this was not a mosque: The community was not allowed to call it such. In April 2009, a few months after the Indonesian joint ministerial decree had banned Ahmadiyya activities, Malaysian official religious authorities crafted their own version of restrictions for their Ahmadiyya community. The Selangor Islamic Religious Council forbade Ahmadis to call their places of worship "mosques" or to hold large assemblies in them. Henceforth, they were to call them *pusat*, which translates as centers or headquarters. Shortly thereafter, in 2011, Selangor Islamic Religious Council officers arrived to install large bright orange warning signs around the Kampong Nakhoda compound reading, "Ahmadis are outside Islam" in Malay. The congregation shifted to meeting in people's homes. During one such meeting, an elegantly dressed elderly man told me how shameful he found it to conduct their meetings in these circumstances and to hold Friday prayers in a garage-like place. At the same time, since it had only been a few weeks since the attack against Ahmadis in West Java, during which three people were killed, one of the community leaders expressed worry about his Indonesian brothers and sisters in faith: "In Indonesia, they live in fear now. Here, we are protected by the state and the police."

This type of gratitude for the tight grip of the Malaysian state on religious authorities and society more generally puzzled me. Many other marginalized Muslims, such as Shi'a or Sufis, whom I had spoken to had expressed worry about the government and its tight control. The numbers of these communities are tiny and the congregations barely visible, but the Malaysian state closely watches and regulates its religious authorities and communities through a network of laws, state religious authorities, undercover informants, and the ever-present threat of detention. While Ahmadis and Shi'a Muslims in Indonesia try to persuade the police to protect them from aggressive organizations such as the Islamic Defenders Front, in Malaysia the state itself enforces the restrictions—while simultaneously protecting the minorities from outbursts of physical violence through extremist organizations. The result is that the number of physically violent attacks carried out by extremist organizations against Shi'a and Ahmadiyya communities in Malaysia is close to zero. In Indonesia, by contrast, human rights organizations have been documenting hundreds of violent incidents since the fall of Suharto in 1998 (Human Rights Watch 2013).

In Indonesia, the mainstreaming of Islam—meaning both the homogenization and bureaucratization of what is accepted as proper Islam as well as the growing importance of Islam in this homogenized form—is driven forward by the actions of different religious and political actors competing for resources and support. The result of the competition is that it encourages Islamist groups and parties to make more and more ambitious majoritarian claims to be the single proper expression of Islam in the country. In Malaysia, meanwhile, the mainstreaming of Islam is similarly driven by formalized political competition (Hamayotsu 2012). From early on, state actors strategically used Islam became as an important resource in consolidating their decades-long capture of the state apparatus.

The comparison of Indonesia and Malaysia complicates a commonly accepted, but mistaken, view of how democratization functions in Indonesia. In the standard view of liberal Western commentators, the mainstreaming of Islam in Indonesia has been the result of open debate, with the citizens reclaiming their Islamic identities after decades of authoritarian clampdown. However, in Malaysia, a society where speech and expression are severely repressed, a similar mainstreaming has taken place. It is therefore the pressure of competitive electoral logic that has accelerated the mainstreaming of Islam in Indonesia rather than the opening of the public sphere. Together, the two cases of Indonesia and Malaysia illustrate how competition—electoral but also more existential competition for state resources—accelerates Islamization and the construction of Mainstream Islam in different ways: bottom up and decentralized in Indonesia; centralized and top down in Malaysia. More important, the comparison also helps us understand how the mainstreaming of Islam in each country has meant the end of more pluralistic and capacious understandings of Islam and replaced them with an exclusivist, majoritarian Islam that, in both countries, is increasingly more threatening to emerging religious minorities. The main difference is that in Malaysia the state disciplines and detains irksome minorities, while in Indonesia, the oppression comes from nonstate organizations who are in fierce competition for access to resources.

This chapter begins by tracing the historical and colonial legacies that influenced the regulation of Islam in both countries and then contrasts the decentralized, bottom-up competition contributing to the dynamics of constructing Mainstream Islam in Indonesia during the democratization period with Malaysia's top-down, heavily state-controlled developments. The chapter then outlines the implications of these systems for religious minorities, which are similar but also show some differences, for instance concerning the question of who the perpetrators of various kinds of violence are. These examples demonstrate how both nations converge toward exclusivist majoritarian Islam despite their divergent political contexts.

The Malaysian scholar Farish Noor has called Indonesia and Malaysia "twins, separated at birth" (Shah 2009). The two countries share hundreds of years of history and the same language but followed different trajectories after colonial treaties resulted in the present-day nation-states. The borders are porous: thousands of students and domestic workers cross the borders by boat and plane, books and pop songs are shared between the two Malay-speaking societies, and fatwas travel as fast as moral panics.

The homogenization of religion in both countries shares the same roots: In both the Netherlands East Indies and in British Malaya, religious authorities returning from the Middle East had spread stricter interpretations of Islam that various elites then mobilized in different ways. In Indonesia, anti-colonialists further mobilized Islam and nationalism against the Dutch. The Indonesian nationalist leaders chose the regional lingua franca Malay rather than Javanese as the national language in an attempt to counter and overcome the ethnic divisions of the Dutch colonialists. After a short electoral democratic phase, during which the populist leader Sukarno tried to merge Islam, nationalism, and Communism, the military regime under Suharto from 1965 onward replaced cultivated a nonreligious developmentalist nationalism in which the state defined and regulated religion but suppressed its public visibility. Religious organizations and citizens were similarly repressed under the oligarchic regime between 1965 and 1998. Only once electoral democracy, an open media system, and decentralization incentivized religious and political authorities to compete with each other for followers, votes, and other forms of public support did the mainstreaming of Islam take shapes that increased pressure on those who were now increasingly defined as religious minorities vis-à-vis a constructed mainstream majority instead of just being part of internally diverse societies.

Malaysia's independence deepened the colonial ethnic and religious divisions. The difference resulted in a relatively straightforward marriage between Islam and ethnic nationalism in Malaysia and a much more complicated trajectory in the Indonesian case. While in Indonesia the complicated range of forces of the Islamist Conservative Majoritarian Synthesis drove the construction of a homogenizing Mainstream Islam, Malaysian homogenization of Islam has been top down since colonial days.

Indonesia's independence was won in a bloody four-year-long war. By contrast, Malay independence was the result of negotiations with the British. In August 1957, the queen's representative, the Duke of Gloucester, presented the English-educated Malay nobleman Tunku Abdul Rahman with the legal documents establishing independence. A stadium had especially been built to celebrate the occasion. The group of cooperating elites who received independence from the colonial rulers was dominated by the United Malays National Organisation (UMNO) which claimed to represent all those whom the British had filed in their census as "Malay."

While Indonesia's government in the first years after independence was largely democratic—there were relatively open legislative elections in 1955—the Malaysian political system was from its early days a competitive authoritarian system: Elections were not free and fair, but the opposition did have a slight chance at winning. UMNO formed a coalition, the Barisan Nasional (BN, or the National Front), with two other ethnic-based parties, the Malaysian Chinese Association and the Malaysian Indian Congress. Not only the main parties, but society more generally was and remains structured along ethnic lines (Holst 2013). The omnipresent categories of the Malaysian racialized system are "Malay," "Chinese," "Indian," and "Other," simplifying a vastly more dynamic and complex society. At the time of independence, around half of the population was officially designated Malay, 37 percent Chinese, and 11 percent Indian, whereas the rest were either "natives of Sabah," "natives of Sarawak," or simply fell outside the conventional categories altogether. The proportion has since tilted toward a numerical Malay majority. This UMNO-led coalition would dominate the government for the next sixty years and the ethnoreligious party used the federal and state bureaucracies to ensure its monopoly on defining the legally and socially accepted variant of Sunni Islam.

Under the UMNO's authoritarian grip, no large explicitly Islamic civil society organizations were ever able to establish themselves in Malaysia, where no equivalent to the Nadhlatul Ulama or Muhammadiyah exist. Instead, UMNO faced a serious Islamist opposition party, the Parti Islam Se-Malaysia, or the Islamic Party of Malaysia (PAS). UMNO and PAS have for decades been involved in a holier-than-thou race targeting Malay votes (Mueller 2014; Noor 2014b; Tayeb and Weiss 2024).

PAS was established in 1951 by former UMNO supporters advocating for the formation of an Islamic state in Malaysia. A party that initially promoted Malay-Muslim rights and interests, it remained small and relatively weak until the leadership of Burhanuddin al-Helmy, who drew inspiration from global struggles of decolonization and Pan Arab nationalism. Burhanuddin grafted together elements of Islamist, nationalist, socialist, and reformist thought (Noor 2014a). Under Burhanuddin, PAS changed its direction from ethnonationalism toward an *umma*centric universalism. But despite notable successes in the 1959 and 1969 elections, the overall electoral results signaled the predominance of race in Malaysian politics. Burhanuddin failed to win popular support through his pan-Islamic orientation in the 1964 elections. In the 1970s, the new PAS President Asri Muda shifted the party back toward ethnonationalism and controversially joined the BN coalition in 1973. This alliance came at a high cost for PAS, which was seriously weakened as a political force by the time it left the coalition four years later.

By withdrawing from more explicitly universalist conceptions of Islam, the PAS left a vacuum that gave rise to new Islamist organizations, such as the Muslim Youth Movement of Malaysia and Darul Arqam, and other international Islamist networks, such as the Tablighi Jemaat. Inspired by the Egyptian Muslim Brotherhood, a group of students established the Muslim Youth Movement of Malaysia (ABIM) in 1971. They promoted Islam through charity work and education programs aimed at the poor. Its second president was the founding leader Anwar Ibrahim, who would become one of the country's most important politicians. The Darul Arqam movement was a highly successful and rapidly growing group of middle-class Muslims. UMNO eventually shut the movement down. The Tablighi Jemaat remained relatively small in numbers and did not provoke the state's wrath to the same degree as other organizations (Noor 2009; Reetz 2009).

Over time, the competition for Malay votes became even more important than in the early days, because those classified as Malays and Muslims grew numerically. Fertility rates of those classified as Malay were higher than other groups', resulting in a higher percentage of Malay voters.

UMNO and PAS politicians regularly accuse each other of not practicing Islam properly. Both use religious language to weaken the opponents' credibility. For example, in 2009, the senior PAS cleric Nik Aziz publicly accused UMNO of practicing false Islam and that consequently only PAS voters would go to heaven. In response, then–Deputy Prime Minister Muhyiddin Yasin called for the National Fatwa Council and other ulama to issue a statement declaring Nik Aziz's view as deviant. "I do not want to resort to politics," Yasin said, in a statement that can be taken as typical. "This is about religion, faith, and religious doctrines" (Bernama 2009b). The National Fatwa Council followed suit and issued a statement condemning Nik Aziz's comment as against Islamic teachings (Bernama 2009a). Similar accusations have for decades been part of the rivalry between UNMNO and PAS. This illustrates that competition was a central part of Malaysian politics despite its authoritarian character. Islam, as a key element of defining Malayness, was a central ingredient of that competition.

One of the main differences between Indonesia and Malaysia was the BN government's continuation of many key colonial practices, most importantly, perhaps, the racial categorization and soldering together of ethnic and religious identity. All Malaysian citizens would paternally inherit their racial and religious categorizations, as reflected on their birth certificates. In Indonesia, the newly independent government rejected all of the Dutch ethnic categorizations and only documented religion on birth certificates. In Malaysia, racial categorization had a bearing on an individual's access to education, housing, credit loans, and the job market. Several policies continue to benefit the *bumiputera*, or "sons of the soil," which include diverse Indigenous groups as well as the Malay Muslim majority (designated as Indigenous by the government's version of Malaysian history). Those classified as Malays form the largest group of bumiputera. UMNO presented itself as the savior of the Malays, who would—so their political line runs—otherwise be outperformed and outnumbered by the economically successful Chinese minority. The local elites who inherited the colonial state claimed to represent all those categorized as Malay and immediately set out securing privileges for this category from those categorized Chinese, Indian, or other. The British had encouraged the immigration of thousands of Chinese and South Asians who upon independence turned into second-class citizens with fewer rights than those classified as locals.

Connected to this, the government also positioned itself as the champion of Islam and the only potent preserver of national unity and peace. Islam and Malay identity had formed their special relationship under the colonial rule: The British had offered the Malay sultans autonomy in matters of religion and culture in return for power in almost all other realms. Islam and Malay culture subsequently merged and became inseparable. The seeds were planted for the rising importance of religious and cultural matters. Malay identity thus became intimately bound to Islam. This turned Islam into a central element of Malay, Malayan, and later Malaysian nationalism. The constitution defines "Malay" in Article 160(2) as a person who professes to be a Muslim, habitually speaks Malay, and adheres to Malay customs. Malayness was something a non-Malay could enter into (*masuk Melayu*) and, with more difficulty, leave. As the criteria of language and customs became more blurred over the course of the postwar decades—partly because many Malaysians of Chinese and Indian immigrant backgrounds were educated in Malay schools and spoke the language fluently—a person's Muslim-ness assumed a more important role over time.

"Malay Unity" is one of the key narratives that the UMNO relied on for its political strength, combined with the idea that these internally united "Malays" are under threat. The government coalition for decades imagined and presented Malaysia as multireligious but ultimately belonging to "the Malays," a category styled as particularly homogeneous, with differences and variety within this category glossed over. In reality, within the Malay category, universalist and ethnic interpretations of Islam have been competing since before independence. From the early days of the current political system, the authoritarian government that mobilized religionational identity faced an Islamist opposition that would during some periods emphasize universalist and transethnic Islam and during other periods flaunt its ethnic identity and ambitions. Competition concerning Islam shaped society from the first day onward, leading to a much faster and more encompassing mainstreaming of Islam than that which occurred in Indonesia. In Malaysia, assimilation was even more important in this construction of Mainstream Islam than in Indonesia, mainly because of the different demographic landscape and the connection to ethnicity. Those styling themselves as the representatives of the Malays needed every vote of their narrow segment of the electorate, despite their gerrymandering practices (Ostwald 2017).

During the colonial era, Islam was originally managed by state (*negeri*) governments, but with independence from the British came centralization of Islam at the federal level. In sharp contrast to Indonesia, where the political leaders tried to curb the influence of religious authorities, the early UMNO leaders assigned the religious authorities to respectable positions within the political system. The UMNO leaders did not compete with the Malay royalty but instead pushed for the intertwinement of race, religion, and royalty and crafted a system in which the sultans held high symbolic power and retained the final say in many matters but left daily operational power to the political leadership and the religious authorities who became part of the bureaucracy. In 1962, Tunku Abdul Rahman's government centralized the funds for the Haj pilgrimage; a decade later, the Department of Education created its own religious division.

In the realm of law, the Malaysian state went far beyond anything ever seriously considered in Indonesia. It created what many consider a dual law system. The restructuring of the legal system along Islamized lines began in the mid-1970s and would experience another boost in 1988, when the so-called syariah courts were established. In 1976, a constitutional amendment replaced each iteration of "Muslim law" with "Islamic law" and thereby lent the laws a new level of legitimacy. Every mention of "Muslim courts" was amended to "syariah courts" (Moustafa 2018). In a thorough move toward inventing a new tradition, the same semantic shift soon appeared in statutory law. In this way, the government succeeded in presenting the so-called Shariah Courts as a faithful rendering of the Islamic legal tradition, even though this particular variant of Anglo-Muslim law was only a few decades old at the time and sharia practices much more diverse than this codification suggested (Daniels 2017). What had been a British colonial governing tool continued as such, but now had been injected with a revitalized aura of Islamic traditionalism. This shift from "Muslim" to "Islamic" and its claim to represent continuing Islamic traditions can also be found outside the legal realm in the corporate sector, where members of the newly emerging Muslim middle classes and business elite began to work toward the agenda of Islamizing their own immediate environments. They decorated libraries and other buildings with Arabic letters; established halal restaurants, beauty parlors, and hotels; and supported the spread of supposedly "Islamic" banking (Fischer 2009).

In assessing Indonesia's complex legal system, legal scholars are divided. Some, especially anthropologists, emphasize its legal pluralism, a mix of old Dutch legal provisions, post-1998 liberal institutions, and religious and customary law (Benda-Beckmann, Benda-Beckmann, and Griffiths 2013). Other legal scholars, such as the Indonesian lawyer Adnan Buyung Nasution, argue that the post-1998 system has a clear hierarchy of liberal institutions, with legally flawed local sharia laws (Nasution 2016). In either view, the many local legal regulations in Indonesia that explicitly showcase their Sharia-related character are subordinate because they are regional laws. Concerning the mainstreaming of Islam in the legal sphere, Malaysia went much further. The highly publicized and influential case of Lina Joy illustrates what this inflexibility would come to mean for Malaysian citizens. Lina Joy was a Malaysian woman of Javanese Malay descent who was raised a Muslim but later converted to Catholicism. She applied for her change of name and of religion to be recognized in her official records in order for her to marry a non-Muslim. The name change was granted, but the National Registration Department refused her application to change her religious affiliation on the basis that she had to obtain a certificate of conversion from the Shariah-based courts, which had jurisdiction over the matter. This was not possible since the Shariah-based courts were more likely to detain her and send her for religious rehabilitation rather than issue a certificate of conversion. She therefore filed an application for judicial review against the government, claiming a violation of her religious freedom. The High Court rejected her application, stating that since the plaintiff "is a Malay," by definition, "she cannot renounce her Islamic religion" but "remains in the Islamic faith until her dying days" (Hussin 2008). A competing interpretation was that a person who converts out of Islam is no longer regarded as a Malay. The court's interpretation of the clause affirmed Islam as part of a group's ethnic identity (Neo 2014).

Conversion out of Islam is not common in Indonesia and would cause much controversy in most families, but it is neither impossible nor illegal. In 2021, Sukmawati Sukarnoputri, the daughter of Indonesia's first president, Sukarno, and the sister of former President Megawati Sukarnoputri, officially left Islam and converted to Hinduism. She attracted the wrath of some but was overall left alone. The mainstream newspapers covered her conversion only as a curiosity.

In Malaysia, conversions out of Islam are only possible if they are conducted off the radar of public debates. The dual law system and the control the authorities exercise over Islam are largely owed to the influence of one man. In the 1980s, the peak of the global da'wah movement in the aftermath of the Iranian Revolution coincided with the first appointment of prime minister as Mahathir Mohamad, a former physician who had long sought higher positions in the party and who would deeply shape the country in his following twenty-two years in power and far beyond. He continued the tendency of further centralization of matters pertaining to Islam, but he expanded the process in a much greater scale. Mahathir Islamized the bureaucracy and bureaucratized Islam: Islamic authorities began to occupy key positions in state institutions, which would in turn regulate Islamic teaching and practice to a much higher degree. The emancipatory and anticolonial potential of

Islam that contributed to the growing mobilization resources of Islamists and Muslim majoritarians in Indonesia played out differently in Malaysia: It was harvested by the Malay rulers, most of all Mahathir. Despite the obviously increasing Islamization of Malaysian society, elements of a siege mentality became exacerbated. Malay ethnonationalists, first and foremost the UMNO party, framed Malay identity as threatened and endangered by external and internal forces. The government urged Malays to be wary because along with Malayness, they declared that Islam itself was under threat.

In 1982, as part of his strategy of ring-fencing the growing da'wah movement, Mahathir recruited Anwar Ibrahim, the head of the Muslim Youth Movement of Malaysia, into UMNO. Anwar's cooption was Mahathir's masterstroke and shocked Anwar's liberal supporters. Anwar moved up the political ranks quickly. Six years later, in 1988, Mahathir used constitutional amendments to considerably weaken the independence of the courts. Simultaneously, Mahathir's government further intensified the tendencies of greater uniformity in the administration of Muslim Laws. The 1988 constitutional amendment of Article 121(1A) allowed for the expansion of the Islamic judicial and legal systems. The Shariah Courts now held the authority to exercise separate jurisdiction over matters concerning Islam that were outside the realm of the civil courts. The now-consolidated dual legal system would become the site of many controversies over the coming decades.

In the 1990s, several new Malaysian bureaucratic bodies further regulated Islam. The respective sultans remained the heads of the religion of Islam, except in the states Penang, Melaka, Sabah, Sarawak, and the Federal Territories, where the Malaysian king, the Yang di-Pertuan Agong, is the head of Islam. The Yang di-Pertuan Agong and the respective sultans continue to hold the highest positions in matters relating to Islamic affairs, but their duties were increasingly supplemented with various advising bodies.

The Department of Islamic Advancement of Malaysia (Jabatan Kemajuan Islam Malaysia, JAKIM) became the central institution for planning and coordinating on the federal level. On the state level, Islamic Religious Councils and Islamic Religious Affairs Departments now enforced the respective state laws. On this point, the Malaysian bureaucratization of Islam thus differs sharply from Indonesia: Indonesia (except for the autonomous region of Aceh) never established any authority comparable to Malaysia's state councils and departments. Indonesian nationalism is rooted in the idea of multireligiosity, and so the Islamic bureaucratic institutions have only grown very slowly over time. However, in the 2000s and 2010s, the MUI, the Council of Indonesian Islamic Scholars, imitated and adapted institutions and control mechanisms in other countries, including Malaysia. MUI developed in such a way that it can be described as a "transformation into the Indonesian version of JAKIM" (Menchik 2022).

In each Malaysian state, the institutional bodies differ to some degree. In Selangor, the state surrounding the capital Kuala Lumpur, a Fatwa Committee is solely responsible for issuing fatwas. The committee consists of the mufti, the deputy mufti, the state legal adviser, two members of the council, an officer of the Islamic Religious Department, between two and seven fit and proper persons appointed by the council, and an officer of the Mufti's Department who serves as its secretary. These religious authorities are state employees. One of their tasks is formulating fatwas, which in Indonesia are issued only by the semigovernmental MUI, by civil society organizations, or by individual religious figures with no connection to the state. The Malaysian Mufti in Selangor calls for a meeting to prepare his fatwa and then submits it to the Selangor Islamic Religious Council, which publishes the fatwa in the *Gazette*. In Kelantan and Johore, by contrast, the assent of the respective sultan is required before a fatwa can be officially published. In the Federal Territories, however, muftis do not need the consent of the sultans to formulate and publish a fatwa in the *Gazette*. Once published, the fatwa becomes binding on every Muslim in the State of Selangor. In this sense, Malaysian fatwas differ considerably from fatwas in most other Muslim countries, where they usually remain nonbinding legal opinions.

UMNO's co-optation of Anwar culminated in Mahathir making him his deputy prime minister in 1993, but unbridgeable differences broke the alliance between the two men. In September 1998, Mahathir had Anwar removed from his posts and eventually had him imprisoned on allegations of corruption and sexual misconduct. After his arrest, Anwar appeared in court and pleaded innocent to charges of corruption and sodomy. A photo of Anwar with a black eye, incurred from a beating by then–Inspector General of Police Rahim Noor, and one hand raised became key symbols of the political opposition. Anwar's imprisonment marked the birth of Malaysia's own reform movement, but it would never succeed in initiating changes comparable to those that transpired in Indonesia after 1998. Under Anwar's leadership, several opposition members formed an alternative multi-ethnic coalition, the People's Pact/Alliance (*Pakatan Rakyat*, PR), a successor to the Alternative Front, (*Barisan Alternatif*, BA, 1999–2008), an earlier coalition of opposition parties including PAS and other parties and organizations. This coalition was a major achievement in the otherwise fragmented opposition, which broadly consists of two camps: the Islamist camp, associated with PAS, and a more liberal camp that couches much of its criticism of the government in the language of human rights. This multiethnic opposition alliance marked a serious challenge to Barisan Nasional's ethni-based model. Unlike previous communal opposition efforts, this formation rejected racialized politics for shared democratic principles. The coalition's ability to unite despite ideological differences between PAS and secular parties demonstrated alternative arrangements, offering voters a viable choice that transcended traditional ethnicized loyalties and religious divisions.

The polarization between Islam and human rights that only developed in Indonesia in the early 2000s after a period of joined forces against Suharto's authoritarianism in the 1990s already characterized the Malaysian debates that followed Mahathir's 1988 constitutional reforms. Anwar was popular, in part, because he was one of the few individuals who successfully melded the rhetoric of human rights with that of Islam and Malay privileges. For example, in his 1977 speech as president of ABIM, he praised Islam as a tolerant religion, stating that discrimination would contradict the goal of unity and of integrating various different communities in tolerance, friendship, and mutual respect (Ibrahim 1977). At the same time, he continued to call for greater press freedom and openly criticized the narrative of Asian values (Ibrahim 2005). Among his supporters, Anwar featured as the uncrowned prince of Malaysian politics for two decades. During the periods that he was not imprisoned, Anwar toured the world on invitations of human rights and developmental organizations, giving speeches about the need for liberal rights in Malaysia.

Anwar was imprisoned in April 1999 after a trial for sodomy and corruption that human rights organizations heavily criticized. He was released in 2004 and four years later returned to parliament after a by-election caused by his wife Wan Azizah's resignation from her own position. The by-election took place in Anwar's hometown in the state of Penang. When I visited the town during the days ahead of the by-election, Anwar's mood was confident, and the atmosphere was festive. A local journalist joked that the English had the Glastonbury music festival, and Malaysians had hopeful elections. Optimism was in the air among his supporters, which were a diverse mix of middle-class Malaysians tired of the corrupt regime under UMNO.

Anwar made a comeback as leader of the opposition from 2008 to 2015 and was prominent because of his ability to bring together opposition parties into the Pakatan Rakyat (Alliance of the People) coalition in the 2008 and 2013 general elections. In 2015, Malaysia's Federal Court upheld Anwar Ibrahim's conviction for sodomy, affirming the five-year prison sentence imposed by the Court of Appeal (Leong and Hamza 2015). While Anwar was still in prison, he forged a new collaboration.

Three years later, in 2018, to the confusion of many, former Prime Minister Mahathir joined the opposition coalition, renamed Pakatan Harapan

(Alliance of Hope). The surprising reconciliation between Anwar and Mahathir—now aged seventy-one and ninety-three, respectively, gave rise to the hope that the duo would free the country from the highly corrupt rule of Najib Razak, whose involvement in the 1MDB scandal had fueled widespread discontent. The scandal centered on 1Malaysia Development Berhad (1MDB, with "Berhad" meaning "limited"), a state investment fund Najib established in 2009 as prime minister to promote economic development. By 2015, investigations revealed it had become a vehicle for massive corruption, with over $4.5 billion allegedly stolen—leading to Najib's 2018 election defeat, his 2019 arrest, and ongoing prosecutions that have ensnared his wife, Rosmah Mansor, and key allies into the 2020s.

Ahead of the 2018 elections, the opposition coalition promised that its candidate, Mahathir, would soon hand over power to Anwar. The opposition coalition won, and for the first time in Malaysian history, UMNO did not govern the country. However, the change of government did not lead to a regime change; most of the authoritarian laws continued to be implemented. Power gradually shifted back to UMNO, partly due to the fragmented state of Pakatan Harapan and the inability of the sudden renegotiation of privileges to fundamentally challenge the entrenched ethnicized societal structures (Hamayotsu 2013). Eventually, in 2020, Mahathir resigned. He never handed power over to Anwar, nor did he fulfill the hopes for change: The two men had not been able to resolve their competition in the harmonious way that many of their supporters had hoped for.

Throughout these power struggles, the authoritarian state structures remained in place. Unlike in Indonesia, the Malaysian reform movement never managed to create a freer climate among the civil society. In Indonesia, the reform movement had broken open the civil society landscape and broadened the spectrum of actors, but in Malaysia, the opposite was the case: Restrictive laws remained in place or were minimally tweaked and modified.

Malaysian state actors have been at the forefront of repressing pluralism and of marginalizing non-Sunni practices of Islam and practices that the state considers deviant, and they succeeded in extending their powers into civil society itself: shortly after the 2008 general election, the former UMNO-member and Malay rights activist Ibrahim Ali established the "Mighty Native Organisation" Perkasa in order to protect the constitutional privilege of the Malays. In the 2010s, Perkasa won the support of many UMNO politicians, eventually serving as the practical extension of UMNO into civil society. Perkasa's tone and actions are more extreme than UMNO and comprises around 700,000 members. Examples of their verbal aggressions include repeatedly accusing Chinese and Christian Malaysians of wanting to take over the country (Chooi 2011, 2012), publicly mocking Hindu gods (Su-Lyn and Ding 2013), and calling for the burning of Bibles (Shankar 2013).

In contrast to Indonesia, where a complicated range of many different actors formed the Islamist Conservative Majoritarian synthesis, the Malaysian state is centralized and regulates religion in a top-down fashion through institutions such as JAKIM and state-sanctioned fatwas. The state's control is exemplified by its treatment of the Ahmadiyya community, forced to rename their places of worship and subjected to degrading warnings labeling them "outside Islam." Both cases underscore how competition—whether grass-roots or institutional—reinforces a homogenized Islam that marginalizes minorities.

State Control of Religion: Monopolizing the Interpretation of Islam

Monopolizing the interpretation of Islam and the representation of modern Malayness has been a cornerstone of Malaysia's authoritarian regime. The country's mosques are key sites of production of Sunni Malay subjects. All mosques are registered and governed by the respective Islamic religious councils, which are responsible for preparing, publishing, and distributing *khutbas* (sermons) to every certified imam. Khutbas that have not been prepared and published by the councils are not allowed to be delivered. The *khatib* or imams thus cannot read any khutbas that they themselves may have written. State shariah laws call for stringent action against imams who deliver khutbas that are not prepared by the religious authorities. For example, Section 97 of the Shariah Criminal Offences Enactment, State of Sabah 1995, states: "Whomsoever reads a khutba on a Friday that was not prepared or approved by the Council has committed an offence, and, if convicted, is punishable by a fine not exceeding MYR 2000 or imprisonment for no longer than one year or both."

The khutba writers are public officials and civil servants in the governmental religious departments who received their education from state or national religious schools before training in local and foreign universities. They are decidedly different from the preindependence religious authorities coming from *pondok* (traditional religious boarding schools) and work more independently. Once part of the khutba unit, they are responsible for composing khutbas every week. They may employ university lecturers or certified teachers of Islamic studies as external contributors. After that, a special committee of Muslim bureaucrats and local ulama evaluates and verifies each khutba. The khutba, similar to the fatwa, has become completely absorbed by the state religious bureaucracy.

Similar to the Sunnification process in Turkey, the Malaysian state has brought key religious areas under its control and transformed them to serve their own ideas of shaping society. Besides their efforts in constructive sites such as the education system and mosques, state authorities also draw on a range of punitive measures to ensure their monopoly of interpreting Islam and using Islam as an instrument of rule. Most commonly, authorities employ legal provisions to curb the activities of actors they deem deviant. This ranges from using the aforementioned provisions that specifically address religion to employing other legal requirements, such as withholding police permits to hold assemblies in public halls and private properties. The threat of being accused of religious deviance is often more powerful than its actual enforcement.

To legitimize its authoritarian posture, UMNO has, over decades, cultivated fears of various others, including non-Muslim minorities, non-Malays, the opposition, and the West. Malays, and Islam with them, were presented as under threat by non-Muslims.

Another key site of religious bureaucracy and regulation that has no equivalent in Indonesia are the so-called faith rehabilitation centers. In these centers, in different parts of the country, Malaysians voluntarily and involuntarily receive education about the government-sanctioned version of Islam. They are called Pemulian Akidah (Faith Rehabilitation Center), Pusat Pemantapan Akidah (Faith Strengthening Center), and Pusat Pemurnian Akidah (Faith Purification Center) (PPA) in Malay and State Islamic Moral Rehabilitation Centers in English, usually abbreviated to "rehabilitation center." It is not clear how many of these centers exist—the state heavily restricts access to them to outsiders—but at least three have been listed in official reports and newspaper coverage: one in Jelebu, in the state of Negeri Sembilan; one in Ulu Yam Bharu, in the state of Selangor; and another one in Sabah, in East Malaysia. The Jelebu PPA was founded in 1996 under the jurisdiction of the federal JAKIM, and the one in Ulu Yam Bharu has been in operation since 2000 under the management of the Selangor Islamic Religious Council. The Jelebu facility was reportedly closed after the few inmates were moved to the internment camp in Kamunting, which operated under the Internal Security Act. One widely reported case of a detainee of the Ulu Yam Bharu center was Revathi Massosai, a Hindu Malaysian woman. She was officially registered as Muslim but had been raised Hindu by her grandmother. When Revathi married a Malaysian registered as Hindu and gave birth to a baby daughter, the authorities noticed her official registration as Muslim and charged her with apostasy. Shortly after, in 2007, she was sent for "rehabilitation" at Ulu Yam, during which she was allowed to see neither her baby daughter nor her husband. It was only after six months of detention that Revathi was released. The existence of these camps and of their shadowy recruitment and detention methods serve to discipline and censor the Muslim public. They thereby shape Islam and Malaysian society more generally, and in much deeper ways, than a cursory glance would suggest.

Public debates in Malaysia focus much less on diversity within Islam than on questions of dress, gender roles, and sexuality involving cases of *khalwat* (intimacy, proximity, dating). The authorities make the accusation of offending Islam sparingly in order to maintain the notion of Islamic unity, but some of the laws get enforced in relatively unpredictable ways. In Selangor, for instance, the religious authorities became known for their strict enforcement of provisions that ensure the state's right to define proper Islamic practice. The officers have regularly conducted raids, for instance, in hotels during Valentine's Day, to catch nonmarried couples. Every February, newspapers publish blurred images of the faces of people caught during such raids. In 2009, the case of Kartika Dewi Shukarno made international headlines. Two years earlier, the thirty-two-year-old mother of two had been caught drinking a beer in a hotel bar in Pahang. The Sharia Court sentenced her to six strokes of the cane. Once international media reported the case, the Malaysian authorities were in a dilemma: They wanted to uphold their Islamic credentials but also not anger international investors and jeopardize the image as a major tourist destination. They indefinitely postponed the caning and later turned it into a community service. Kartika Shukarno herself repeatedly expressed frustration over the media coverage and said that she regretted her actions and would have preferred to be caned to end the long and humiliating debate about her offense. "I hope this community service will serve as a lesson to others to stay away from alcohol," a heavily censored newspaper quoted her (Theborneopost.com 2010). This public repentance is likely what saved her from a more violent treatment in the media.

The raids affect different classes differently, with raids usually focused on poorer neighborhoods. During my fieldwork in the mid- and late 2000s, I found that those who can afford to frequent more exclusive venues have little to fear after the vocal public outcry following the raids in high-end clubs in the early 2000s. Since then, the religious authorities have left high-end venues alone. Finely adjusted to the conditions of the global market, the UMNO-led government demonstrates its power to enforce its rules to its domestic audience but takes care not to risk disturbing the wealthier middle-classes and their consumption habits.

It is not only breaking the rules of "good Islam"—as defined by UMNO—that will provoke punishment by Malaysian authorities. Another type of trouble arises from following the rules so well that the need for UMNO's existence is called into question. Perhaps the most striking and dramatic case is that of Darul Arqam (The House of Arqam).[1] The movement (known in its early years simply as Al Arqam) was hugely successful in building and maintaining its own autonomous structures in the 1970s and '80s. It began as a relatively small study group circle (*halaqah*) in Datok Keramat, a predominantly Malay lower-middle-class suburb in Kuala Lumpur in 1968. The founder, Ashaari Mohammad, an ex-government religious teacher, developed the movement through self-purification and soul-searching activities. The group soon developed into a self-contained community that practiced strict adherence to an Islamic code. They developed their own home-based and—to a large extent—self-enclosed economy, focusing on halal food (Kamarulnizam 2003). Al Arqam was critical of capitalism and the Malay habit of depending for subsidy from the government. So in the commune, the residents demonstrated self-reliance and economic independence by cooperating to produce vegetables, noodles, cakes, and soya sauce for sale in the open market (Hassan 2006). Early recruits were mostly young, first generation rural migrants who were beginning to form the upcoming Malay middle class (Nagata 1980).

A Darul Arqam settlement set up in 1973 in Sungei Penchala in the outskirts of Kuala Lumpur comprised a mosque, a lecture hall, dormitories, offices, a school, houses, and shops. This form of urban spiritualism, solidarity, and communal living rapidly became very popular throughout the country from the 1970s onward. Members organized courses on Islamic education, established businesses, printed their own publications, planned missionary activities, and built schools as well as their own medical facilities. Members did not officially register in the movement but participated in the organization's lifestyle and activities. Some observers estimate that between 10,000 and 12,000 members were part of the organization before 1994, with another 200,000 sympathizers and supporters (Kamarulnizam 2003). Urban youth flocked in large numbers to the self-contained villages (Hamid 2005). In the 1980s, Darul Arqam expanded internationally, and by the 1990s, the organization had burgeoned into a self-styled business empire with an extensive global network whose influence penetrated into mainstream sociopolitical circles. Darul Arqam sponsored students of various fields for higher education in Egypt, Iraq, Pakistan, Jordan, and Uzbekistan. The organization also established its own international school in Thailand and university in Pekan Baru, Indonesia. Through trade missions, Darul Arqam managed to set up investment subsidiaries abroad. Darul Arqam's overseas branches operated, inter alia, a restaurant and a tailor shop in Tashkent, Uzbekistan; an animal husbandry project in Ningxia, China; catering and perfume industries in Pakistan; a double-decker executive coach in Thailand; a food packaging and distribution company in Singapore; and in Indonesia, in addition to the private university in Pekan Baru, soy sauce and shoe factories in Tasek Malaya and a hairdressing saloon, grocery stores, and tailor shops in Jakarta and Medan (Hamid 2006).

With their own education, health care, and welfare systems for members, Darul Arqam quickly became perceived as a threat by the government. Foreign observers in the 1980s characterized the movement, much like the Gülen movement in Turkey (though on a considerably smaller scale), as a "state within a state" (Hamid 2006). The UMNO-led government curbed the growth of movement in 1994, in part by planting a series of negative articles into the heavily state-controlled mainstream media. Security forces also raided the communal villages and confiscated properties, universities and state agencies suspended jobs and scholarships, state organizations encouraged social boycotts, and authorities restricted oversees traveling for Darul Arqam members. Finally, the authorities detailed the organization's leaders under the Internal Security Act and followed this with a mass arrests of members for offenses such as failing to register marriages and distributing illegal publications. On August 5, 1994, the National Fatwa Council issued a fatwa banning the movement and forced the members to repent, citing mostly security-related issues and deviance from established teachings (Hamid 2005). With its success, Darul Arqam had come too close to what the UMNO has for decades claimed as its exclusive domain. Twenty days later, the Ministry of Home Affairs declared the group unlawful under the Societies Act (1966). Many members had to undergo special classes at the state's Islamic Centre, which later became the Department of Islamic Development. Thai police took the organization's leader, Ashaari, who was living in exile in Thailand at that time, into custody and handed him over to their Malaysian counterparts. Subsequently, the Malaysian authorities detained him and several of his aides under the Internal Security Act until October of the same year. After several weeks of detention, Ashaari appeared on National Television. His beard was shaven and his characteristic green robe and turban were no longer visible. He confessed to deviating from Islamic teachings and would refrain from doing so again in the future (Cult Education Institute 2006). Afterward, Ashaari remained under house arrest and was barred from visitors except for immediate family members (Means 2009). He spent the next ten years in Labuan, a small island thirty miles off the coast of Brunei. The authorities shut down the communal settlements of Darul Arqam and prohibited all former members from reviving the movement. Ashaari died in 2010. Parts of the movement continued to operate clandestinely, and in later years several other much smaller religious organizations and movements made headlines when the authorities shut them down on the pretext of security and religious purity. However, the rise of an Islamist movement like Darul Arqam was not repeated and seems unlikely in Malaysia's near future.

The efforts to clamp down on religious movements concerns not only Muslim organizations but also less clearly defined ones. In 2005, the authorities dismantled buildings of the Sky Kingdom group. Around the mid-1980s, the Sky Kingdom commune was formed in Besut in the state of Terengganu (*Daily Express* 2016). In 1995, the members began their signature building projects. The most famous of these would be a gigantic pot to symbolize the purification power of water. Two years later, the Terrenganu Local Religious Affairs council (Jawatankuasa Fatwa Majlis Agama Islam dan Adat Melayu Terengganu) issued a fatwa against the group and arrested four adherents for renouncing Islam. They were eventually freed on grounds that as ex-Muslims, they no longer fell under the Sharia courts' jurisdiction. Such flexibility would not be possible anymore a decade later (Liow 2009; *The Telegraph* 2016).

In 2001, the main leader, a Malay-born man called Ayah Pin renounced Islam (*Astro Awani* 2016). The Sharia court accused him of contravening Section 25 of the Enakmen Pentadbiran Hal Ehwal Agama Islam, 1986 (Administration of Islamic Religious Affairs, 1986), stating that his teachings and beliefs were false, deviant, corrupting, and threatening to the public peace (*membawa ancaman kepada ketenteraman orang awam serta merosakkan akidah*) (Fandom, n.d.). He pleaded guilty to the charge of "belittling Islam" (*menghina Islam*), and was imprisoned for eleven months and fined MYR 2,900 (*Astro Awani* 2016). The Religious Affairs Office hoped that Ayah Pin's arrest would prevent the movement's growth. However, the Sky Kingdom continued to attract new followers, mostly from university students and Indigenous groups (D. Lim and Siong Yee 2007).

On July 18, 2005, as a rare incident of nonstate violence, a group of masked vigilantes vandalized the Sky Kingdom's headquarters, smashing windows and torching buildings (theage.com.au 2005). Two days later, fifty-eight followers were arrested, and on July 31, three of Ayah Pin's four wives were also arrested (*Astro Awani* 2016; *Sun2Surf Malaysian Source for News &*

Lifestyle 2005). Ayah Pin escaped arrest and became a fugitive wanted by the Malaysian authorities (*Astro Awani* 2016). Forty-five members initially faced charges of failing to observe the government fatwa (i.e., for continuing to be members of a sect declared as deviant), which carries a fine up to RM 3,000 or two years in prison. One of those arrested faced an additional charge of "humiliating Islam" (Aglionby 2005).

On August 1, 2005, officials of the Besut Land and District Office destroyed various buildings, citing Section 129 of the National Land Code concerning unauthorized construction with land confiscation (Fandom, n.d.). The titular land owner is Ayah Pin's first wife, who apparently failed to appear in court for a hearing on the matter. On September 1, 2005, at a hearing, a trial date for forty-five followers accused of violating the government fatwa was set for three days beginning on December 18 that year. All of the accused were represented by Wan Haidi Wan Jusoh of Ubaidullah Aziz and Co., who unsuccessfully petitioned the court to order his name blacked out by the media. The group had previously experienced great difficulty in attracting legal representation, presumably owing to attorneys' fear of reprisals or negative publicity.

As of 2007, after wide media coverage, the original Hulu Besut commune, now down to twenty-four members, had reportedly chosen a new leader and was weary of visitors, routinely turning off the commune's lights whenever a car would approach at night (Cari Gold 2006; *The Star* 2006). From 2009 onward, Ayah Pin seems to have been residing in exile across the Thai border, making visits to his home community until his death of natural causes in 2016. Another key figure of the commune, Kamariah Ali, was born Muslim and was denied the permission to leave Islam to avoid being imprisoned for apostasy in 2011 (*BBC News* 2011).

While Malaysia clamps down on civil organizations, centralizing the regulation of Islam through the state apparatus, in Indonesia it is mainly civil society actors, facilitated by state actors, that regulate Islam. In Malaysia, institutions like JAKIM and state religious councils monopolize the interpretation and enforcement of Islamic norms, suppressing independent religious movements and discouraging dissent. In contrast, Indonesia's post-1998 democratization and decentralization empowered religious civil organizations to play a significant role in defining and regulating religious beliefs and practices. The result is a stark contrast: Malaysia's top-down, authoritarian approach to Islam fosters strict homogenization, while Indonesia's bottom-up, competitive environment allows for a more dynamic, albeit fragmented, religious landscape.

As part of the Malaysian government's ongoing effort to monopolize interpretations of Islam, it has entered deeply into the linguistic fray and attempted to police the very language of the populace. In the mid-2000s, a heated debate in Malaysia grew around the word *Allah*. The term, of Arabic origins, means "the God" and both Muslims and Christians in Egypt and other Middle Eastern countries use the term. Indonesian Christians also use the Arabic term to refer to God. In Malaysia, by contrast, only very few Christians speak Malay (Yue-Yi 2013). For this tiny numerical minority, the state's monopoly over terminology became exceedingly difficult to navigate when in 2007, the federal court judges Seri Mohamed Apandi Ali, Abdul Aziz Abd Rahim, and Mohd Zawawi Salleh prohibited the publisher of the main Catholic church newspaper *The Herald* from using the term *Allah* to refer to God (*Deutsche Welle* 2013). The judges referred to a government directive of 1986 that ostensibly prohibited the use of the words *Allah* (God), *Kaabah* (Islam's holiest place in Mecca), *Solat* (prayer), and *Baitullah* (House of God) in all non-Islamic religious publications (I. Lim 2021). The judges reasoned that allowing the paper to use the term would mislead Muslims and ultimately encourage misguided conversions to Christianity, thereby leading to social unrest. Malay-speaking Christians argued that they had been using the term for hundreds of years. Many Christian Malaysians, especially in the eastern part of Malaysia, were not ethnically classified as Malay but could only speak the Malay language. Still, the government persisted in prohibiting the use of Allah in Bibles. In 2009, a lower court ruled in favor of *The Herald* and allowed the newspaper to use the word, in a decision that prompted a spike in religious tensions between Muslims and Christians. Dozens of churches and a few Muslim prayer halls were attacked and burned.

In 2013, the decision was overturned by the Court of Appeal, which reinstated the ban (Gomes 2021). The High Court decided in favor of the church in 2010, but a three-judge bench at the Court of Appeal overturned the decision in 2013 (Hamid and Razali 2015). UMNO capitalized on this debate during the 2013 election campaign. UMNO's campaign stirred old fears: Malays were under threat. Ibrahim Ali, the head of Perkasa, deliberately played up the Allah controversy to swing Malay votes toward UMNO. In 2014, the Federal Court upheld the ban. Around the same time, the media discussed whether the Perkasa leader Ibrahim Ali had indeed called for the burning of all Bibles containing the word, and whether such a call should be investigated or was within the range of the acceptable. This debate was informed by the strong will on the part of UMNO and its allies to maintain and emphasize Islam as an exclusive feature of ethicized Malay identity rather than as a universalist religion (Neo 2014). For the UMNO and its allies, global developments in and connections to Islam have mattered less than an explicitly Malay-ized interpretation of Islam in which the UMNO itself deploys officers for boundary-patrolling practices. Similarly, religious authorities in each state maintain lists of deviant teachings for their respective states. These lists are not publicly available but can sometimes be obtained upon request, as interlocutors told me during my fieldwork. State governments have listed several small congregations and Sufi orders as deviant (*sesat*) and then surveilled them and prohibited individual activities. These controls and regulations ensure assimilation and maintaining the public image of Malayness and Islam as homogeneous and united.

Controversial Identities in Malaysia

Minorities in Malaysia can, as in Indonesia, be grouped into non-Muslim minorities and Muslim minorities, whereas the latter category also includes Muslims challenging heterosexual gender norms. A key difference lies already in the term: Whereas many different commentators in Indonesia call the identities discussed in the previous chapters "minorities," Malaysians usually reserve the term for non-Malays due to the image of Malays as united and homogeneous. Each of these categories faces different problems. In both countries, those challenging rigid definitions of orthodoxy face the strongest aggression. Ahmadi parents in Malaysia told me about their children's dilemma in navigating school exams in which they have to declare their own variant of Islam wrong and un-Islamic in order to pass. Shi'a and some Sufi children face similar situations. The Malaysian state commands a wide range of instruments to bring Muslims back in line. Most of these instruments were either created or sharpened in the 1980s, when the central and state governments required the registering of all public religious schools, standardized the curriculum for religious schools and Islamic subjects, and broadcasted religious campaigns via national media.

Over time, the homogenization intensified: Authorities have, especially since the 2000s, regularly raided Ahmadiyya and Shi'a mosques, or so-called centers (*pusat*). Sometimes tucked away in backyards, behind commercial buildings and sometimes just a small part of a larger complex, they were largely left alone for decades. When I searched for the main Shi'a mosque in Selangor, it took me over an hour to eventually discover it at the top of a normal business building. Once I made my way to the top, a locked door blocked my way. I had to call my contact on his cell phone, and he in turn called the congregation inside, since they would not pass on their number before meeting me. The community leader later explained to me that they were worried about raids and kept a low profile. At the same time, they had recently distributed plastic roses, sweets, and invitations to a Shi'a festivity to important neighbors in order to win their support. They share this delicate balancing of beneficial visibility and a low profile and questions of negotiating the boundaries between what is public and what is private with the Indonesian communities (Schäfer 2015).

The difference between the ways Indonesian and Malaysian minorities relate to the state shows itself in the way minorities organize their gatherings and how open they are to strangers: Malaysian Muslims know that the state determines the definition and contours of Islam, and consequently, many Muslims are wary of new members to their religious circles. They fear government agents and being discovered to have breached some rule or law and being sent to a rehabilitation camp. Organizations regularly lobby and use legal means to get their name off the lists of deviant groups. Sometimes, they are successful, sometimes not. In Selangor, for example, the community of Bahai successfully convinced the authorities to take them off the list of deviant teachings after years of personal meetings and of providing evidence that their religion really was too far from Islam to be considered a deviance.[2] At the same time, the feminist organization Sisters in Islam, which seeks to improve the situation of Muslim women through lobbying and legal counseling and by combining the framework of human rights and Islam, remained on the Selangor list despite attempts to legally challenge this and despite better connections to high-level politicians. The difference can, to some degree, be explained by the low profile of the Bahai and the visibility of Sisters in Islam—some of whose key figures have connections to high-profile members of the government—but perhaps more importantly by the use of "Islam" on the part of Sisters in Islam compared to the Bahai community's insistence that they did not claim any connection to Islam. The state offers protection from nonstate violence through its system of intimidation and threats, but it also demonstrates the boundaries of toleration to those who deviate from the state-sanctioned variant of Islam.

While in Indonesia, it was mainly nonstate actors who drove aggression and violence while state actors tolerated and facilitated it, in the Malaysian case state actors themselves oppressed minorities. Simultaneously, they promised some protection from nonstate aggressors (Yi Lih 2018).[3] It is usually the offices of the state religious departments who conduct raids, often during religious holidays, sometimes together with police officers. Media, especially the Malay-language media, which is heavily biased towards the government (J. Abbott 2011), widely publicizes images from the raids and sends a clear signal to everyone: The official religious authorities are watching closely and will not hesitate to step in if believers deviating from the state-sanctioned variants of faith cross certain boundaries of visibility.

In the case of queer Muslims, this does not mean that violence against them does not occur or is punished by the authorities. Also, the public accusations against queer people are similar to the ones voiced in Indonesia and concern hedonism and spreading "a Western lifestyle" (Qantara.de 2021; Duffy 2019). Similar to the Q! Queer Film Festival in Jakarta in the late 2010s, the Sexual Independence (Seksualiti Merdeka) festival was first held in 2008 and then prohibited in the early 2010s. The PAS Youth chief Nasrudin Hassan Tantawi said about the movement: "The gay and lesbian culture is a deviated culture and should not be fought for or practiced by any human being, especially Muslims" (*Asia One* 2011). Homosexual activities have remained outlawed in Malaysia since the British colonial period. The sodomy trials against Anwar Ibrahim show the aggressive potential within the state apparatus against homosexuals, but overall, Malaysian state actors prioritize reeducation programs and self-censorship over encouraging nonstate violent aggressions against LGBTQI.

Popular preachers, both those who are part of the state bureaucracy and freelancing ones, condemn efforts to fight for LGBTQI rights but show compassion for homosexual Muslims and demand that others help them on their journey toward heterosexuality rather than attack them (Zulkffli and Ab Rashid 2016). The "right path" rhetoric is reminiscent of similar rhetoric in the conversion ceremonies of Ahmadiyya and Shi'a in Indonesia. Since 2011, for instance, JAKIM has organized a three-day Mukhayyam camp eight times a year, where queer people are lured to improve their socioeconomic situation through trainings but, in reality, have to listen to conservative religious talks that frame their sexuality as a mental illness in need to be cured and have to join cross-country trekking, climbing, and running through mud among other physical activities, presumably to enhance their masculinity. Participants report having to wear male clothes despite their preference for female clothes. JAKIM claims to regularly "heal" hundreds of participants (Jain and Ghoshal 2018). Here in the Malaysian case, state authorities oversee this intended process of "healing" that elsewhere socially conservative nonstate actors drive forward, such as in Indonesia and the United States (Bjork-James 2019; Pauly and Carnell 2024; Schäfer 2024; Thajib 2022; Weiss and Bosia 2013). In Malaysia, particular medical centers offer to "heal" LGBTQI-identifying people. With the same aim, teachers and parents send youth to camps for reeducation. Human rights organizations have documented the devastating impact these efforts have on individuals (Human Rights Watch 2022a; Human Rights Commission of Malaysia 2019).

Similar to the Indonesian case and to other minoritized identities, publicness and visibility and the open demand for rights have an effect on the degree to which authorities restrict sexual freedoms. Some politicians from the opposition, such as Wan Azizah Wan Ismail stated that homosexual practices should not be prosecuted if they remain private (Jayne 2018). Compared to those of Indonesia, Malaysian authorities remain largely in control of violence. Despite attempts to challenge religious authorities, as illustrated by the example of Darul Arqam, such competitors of UMNO were either integrated into the state bureaucracy or prohibited and extinguished.

The example of Malaysia shows that the increased pressure on minorities in Indonesia cannot solely be explained by the rise of new religiopolitical entrepreneurs, even though they are an important part of the explanation. Similar pressure on Ahmadis, Shi'a, and LGBTQI people in Malaysia has existed for decades.

Competition was central to the mainstreaming of Islam in both Indonesia and Malaysia in different ways. In Indonesia, the post-1998 electoral democratization and decentralization pushed actors into competition who had formerly been somewhat united against the nonreligious authoritarian military regime. In Malaysia, competition for Muslim votes was an intrinsic part of the political system from the beginning on and manifested itself in the struggle between the different Islam-oriented parties.

If the Indonesian case has demonstrated that electoral democratization can push an Islamist-nationalist synthesis, Malaysia demonstrates that the rise of this synthesis—which in the Malaysian case has the additional ethnic component of being Malay-Muslim nationalism—does not result from open public debates or widespread public participation. The Malaysian state apparatus, with its colonial laws for the repression of dissidents and its media censorship, has for decades ensured low levels of political participation. The example of Malaysia instead suggests that rather than the open debate, it is mainly the pressure for competition along identitarian lines that drives the mainstreaming of Islam in the sense of marginalizing minorities and reducing the spectrum of accepted and tolerated Islamic beliefs and practices. The outbidding race draws on homogenized identities of religion that lend themselves well to being mobilized in nationalist ways. In Malaysia, the British legacy of ethnic plurality and categorization enforced the nationalist framing of religion earlier than in Indonesia. Despite the very different political and societal structures in the two countries, competition among religious and political actors for public support functioned similarly against the background of homogenizing and thin religion.

Conclusion

This book has focused on the postreformation period, especially on the years between 2005 and 2017, and analyzed how this period of democratization and decentralization saw rising aggression against minoritized identities, such as Ahmadiyya, Shi'a, LGBTQI people and others. Indonesia's experience differed from those of other societies in some aspects but shows strong parallels in others. After the celebrations of globalization, the rise of supranational institutions, and what many commentators perceived as the victory of Western liberalism in the 1990s and early 2000s, the aftermath of the 2008 socioeconomic crisis saw the return of forces that had once previously been thought to be on the wane, or even extinct, such as political strongmen, nationalism, and authoritarian religiosity.

Indonesia's variant of this rise holds a few lessons and questions about the relationship between democracy and conflict. One key characteristic of the Indonesian case has been what I have called the Islamist Conservative Majoritarian Synthesis. This concept highlights the broad range of actors that have contributed to the increased proximity between nationalism and religion and the long-lasting effects of their actions and discourses.

Together, the various actors of this synthesis accelerated the construction of Mainstream Islam, a variant of homogenization as part of modernity and simultaneously the product of bureaucratization and competitive decentralization. This homogenization includes the assimilation and othering of those constructed as deviant, who, in the case of post-1998 Indonesia comprised a broad range of identities, including Ahmadiyya, Shi'a, LGBTQI people, and others.

Indonesia's bottom-up dynamics in constructing Mainstream Islam stand in contrast to the centralized approaches seen in Turkey, Poland, and Russia. While Turkey consolidated state control over religious institutions, blending nationalism and Islam into a top-down project, Indonesia's fragmented and competitive post-1998 democracy allowed nonstate actors—religious authorities, political elites, and vigilante groups—to forge exclusionary alliances that pushed conservative Islam to the center. Similarly, Russia, Poland and Hungary have witnessed top-down religious nationalism, with ruling parties instrumentalizing Christianity to construct national identities that marginalize internal others. The Indonesian case, however, highlights the dangers of decentralization, where political competition at various levels amplifies religious exclusion through alliances with socially conservative forces.

One of the reasons why the concept of Mainstream Islam is so essential is that it grasps the increased importance of orthodoxy as a religious variant of nationalism. Various actors and interests—from traditionalist clerics to pop preachers and politicians—promulgate Mainstream Islam and drive it forward. In this book, I have adopted Sudipta Kaviraj's (2010) concept of thin religion to explain why the synthesis of religion and nationalism has been so fruitful. The religion at work in this transformation is thin: instead of engaging with the complexities and ambivalences that characterize spirituality and belief, it instead focuses on consolidating a relatively narrow and straightforward set of religious rules.

Other than in better-studied cases such as Turkey, India, and Hungary, Indonesia's post-1998 rise of Mainstream Islam was *facilitated*, rather than hindered, by the twin processes of liberal democratization and decentralization. In the post–Cold War landscape, several formerly autocratic or one-party governments experimented with democratization—only to pull back from the brink once they tasted the results—as in the case of Algeria in 1991. In other cases, brief periods of democratization were followed by phases of rapid autocratization, such as in the cases of Hungary, Russia, and Turkey. But in Indonesia, the state stuck for a long period with an electoral democratization program that allowed hitherto marginal Islamists to grow beyond even their own expectations. The new electoral competition since the introduction of free elections in 1998, boosted by one of the most ambitious and encompassing decentralization initiatives worldwide, had the unintended effect of fueling money politics that would undermine democratization. In this climate, religious virtue-signaling thrived, especially after the reduced political influence and visibility of Islam under Suharto's New Order. The most important outcome of what I have called the fourfold decentralization process was that in the 2000s, with free speech, freedom of assembly, and blooming competition amid growing socioeconomic inequality, Islamists began to thrive. Politicians in need of moral credentials began to court religious entrepreneurs, and conservative nationalists and Islamists forged fruitful alliances. The discourse about who belongs and who does not belong to the community of Muslims became the most important factor in determining the contours and limits of the political community. We can thus learn from the Indonesian case under what conditions the interaction between religion and modernity feeds into nationalism and subsequent conflict.

The leading Indonesian forces that have constructed the discourse of Mainstream Islam have been not primarily state actors and their clearly locatable allies but instead a complex and internally shifting assemblage of actors—religious authorities, media celebrities, activists—most of whom forge short-term alliances of convenience with specific state actors and politicians. These alliances between political and religious leaders are volatile. Jokowi's embrace of a majoritarian religious cleric as his running mate in 2019 illustrated that Indonesia's religiopolitical camps allow for spontaneous alliances possible at the highest level. Likewise, the quick rehabilitation of Rizieq Shihab (the previously imprisoned leader of the Islamic Defenders Front in the mid-2010s), his appearance on the same stage as Jokowi at the antiblasphemy rally in December 2016, and his subsequent flight to self-exile in Saudi Arabia less than half a year later, escaping investigations into fabricated accusations of pornography and rumors he insulted the Pancasila and Sukarno, show how fragile the alliances are.

This lack of reliable alliances has made the political art of identifying common enemies all the more important: Political and religious leaders support and outbid each other in their search for new culprits of alleged heterodoxy or slander of values they define as Islamic. Patrolling the border of religion has become a key practice that compensates for a lack of core values and policy programs as well as for the lack of long-lasting and strong networks. The Indonesian case thus shows how religion and nationalism work together and how various alliances of actors have consolidated a new center position in Indonesian politics by identifying new internal others, whose political fate and marginalization have been detailed in this book.

In contrast to cases such as Malaysia, India, Turkey, and Russia, where mainly state actors aided by religious allies identify, discipline, and detain irksome minorities, in Indonesia, the oppression comes from nonstate organizations who are in fierce competition for access to resources. Indonesian politicians have used references to Islam to outbid each other in the race for constituencies and resources. Outpourings of anti-Westernism figure in every presidency, but the main sites in the struggle to define the nation and Indonesian-ness are two minoritized identities: non-Muslims, such as Christians, and Muslims who are

CONCLUSION

treated as being defective or incomplete, such as Ahmadis and Shi'a, LGBTQI Muslims, and others. The marginalization and persecution of these internal others is a key element holding the internally diverse synthesis together and cohering the center in this new phase of Indonesian nationalism. The Indonesian experience complicates assumptions that democratization inherently fosters pluralism, as competitive political systems may incentivize actors to appeal to majoritarian sentiments to consolidate power.

However, the comparison with Malaysia showed that it would be too hasty a conclusion to blame democratization, for Malaysia has experienced a similar rise of Mainstream Islam without the experience of electoral democratization and a free media system. The closer look at Malaysia in chapter 4 showed that it was *political competition* that pushed the merging of nationalism and religion.

Similarly, in Indonesia, the 2000s and 2010s were characterized by fierce political competition for resources, prompting ever more exclusionary rhetoric and policy making on the part of politicians and religious authorities. A country that, as late as the early 1990s, was still characterized by the diversity of its Muslim currents and groupings and by a relatively stable and predictable landscape of oligarchs, had transformed into a winner-takes-all type of religiopolitical contest in which a pop preacher could rapidly rise to fame and fall from grace within weeks.

Those seeking to consolidate the center through border patrolling, assimilation, and othering targeted a very broad range of identities. Those pushed to the margins of society—Ahmadis and Shi'a Muslims, LGBTQI people, liberals, atheists, and members of smaller sects and organizations—belong to very different social categories and communities. In chapters 2 and 3, I have identified a set of main factors that explain why some identities get attacked more than others. The main factors are the visibility of people labeled with a particular identity category and the ways in which this category is framed as "foreign." To understand this, regional distinctions are key: in West Java, ethnic and modern organizations shape the social structure, while in East Java, religious leaders from the large Muslim civil society organization Nahdlatul Ulama hold decisive authority, with officials often deferring to them during disagreements. Outside Java, diverse identities challenge Java-centric visions of the nation. Yet amid these local dynamics, a new class of religious entrepreneurs has gained influence at the national level, promoting a Sunni-Muslim nationalist identity rooted in modernist-conservative ideals.

As an intrinsic part of postcolonial Indonesia, which still upholds the Pancasila as the national motto, these internal others have never been excluded outright from the Indonesian nation, but they remain at its margins. If they were in slightly awkward positions a few decades ago, their belonging to the Indonesian nation was not questioned and contested to the degree it is now.

CONCLUSION

Their position is always precarious, and their situation depends on any given specific political constellation. The Islamist Conservative Majoritarian Synthesis pushed them to the margins in a period in which the fragile national identity sought self-assurance amid the insecurities and anxieties of globalization and democratization with their increased social mobility. A greater wealth gap nourished more consumption while oligarchic networks chipped away at elections and other forms of political participation.

In the period after Suharto, being Indonesian has been increasingly defined as being a good Muslim, defined by religious authorities supported by the state apparatus. The fresh conservative Islamist-nationalist synthesis managed to push the emerging political "mainstream" toward majoritarian notions of Islam and has changed Indonesia's religious nationalism. This new religious nationalism calls for tighter regulation in the realm of belief, prioritizes Muslims adhering to Islam as defined by the most powerful religious authorities, and marginalizes those deemed deviant.

Decentralization and competition shaped four key realms of Indonesian politics: elections, religious authorities, civil society, and media. The large-scale decentralization program that between 1999 and 2001 meant to wrestle the high concentration of power out of the hands of the remaining elite in Jakarta and foster democracy had the unintended effect of unleashing corruption on a grand scale. It incentivized local politicians and community leaders to exchange benefits for votes, thereby spreading predatory behavior downward. This decentralization coincided with rapid economic development and consumption, with the fragmentation of established religious authorities and the rise of new ones, and with a fast-growing media landscape.

My analysis has expanded the notion of informal politics by placing religious authorities, influential civil-society organizations, and the structures of Indonesian media front and center. The cases of othered minorities discussed in this book illustrate that the shifts within the larger political system are not secondary conditions in which Indonesian postreform democratization and authoritarianization occurred but a core part of these processes. Together, the twin forces of decentralization and competition contributed to the reconfiguration of Indonesian nationalism. All four aspects of Indonesia's decentralization—elections, the increased visibility of Islam and religious authorities, media, and civil society—were characterized by increasing competition for resources.

Indonesia's experience demonstrates how competitive electoral systems and an unregulated media landscape can exacerbate identity-based exclusion. Unlike India, where Hindu nationalist forces led by the BJP mobilized through strong central leadership and a media ecosystem aligned with the party's agenda, Indonesia's fragmentation allowed local actors to define and enforce religious boundaries. In Hungary and Poland, populist leaders use state-controlled media to craft exclusionary narratives, targeting LGBTQI people, migrants, and minoritized religious identities to consolidate majoritarian identities. In the United States, bottom-up mobilization of evangelical movements combined with elite political alliances has similarly shaped exclusionary politics, particularly targeting gender, sexuality, and religious pluralism. Indonesia's trajectory adds a vital dimension to this pattern: It reveals how decentralization and unregulated competition, rather than centralization alone, can drive the homogenization of religious and national identity.

An irony of this process of constructing Mainstream Islam is that it was facilitated by not only competition among political and religious leaders but also identity-based discourses that originally aimed to defend the newly identified minorities. By defending these minorities as just that—minorities—rather than as full claimants to the fruits of the Indonesian nation, the human rights discourse has had the unintended consequences of solidifying the majoritarian mainstream/minority distinction.

What are the lessons Indonesia holds for the relationship between religion, democracy, and conflict elsewhere? The rise of Mainstream Islam in Indonesia shares parallels with identity politics elsewhere but offers a unique lesson: Religious nationalism can thrive without a central strongman. Turkey's Recep Tayyip Erdoğan, India's Narendra Modi, and Hungary's Viktor Orbán have centralized power to impose majoritarian identities through state apparatuses. In contrast, Indonesia's pluralistic erosion resulted from decentralized competition where alliances between political actors, religious authorities, and media figures fostered homogenization. This bottom-up process demonstrates how democratization, decentralization, and neoliberal economic reforms can inadvertently facilitate identity-based exclusion.

Indonesia has thus not been understood in this book as an outlier or as the moderate exception within an otherwise intrinsically undemocratic Muslim world. Instead, Indonesia has appeared in this book as the world's largest Muslim electoral democracy and as a country that has provided social scientists with one of the major tutorials about modern nationalism.

The post-Suharto period demonstrates how electoral competition and decentralization paired with free media in an attention economy can incentivize political elites to adopt increasingly exclusionary positions, appealing to majority identities while marginalizing minorities. This dynamic broadens our understanding of how electorally competitive systems can often exacerbate, rather than mitigate, identity-based exclusion. The erosion of Indonesia's pluralist vision raises pressing questions about how multicultural and diverse democracies can sustain pluralism.

Acknowledgments

This book draws on my PhD fieldwork in the late 2000s and early 2010s and took so long to complete that I cannot adequately thank everyone who helped me to bring it on its way. First of all, I am grateful to the many activists and religious leaders who made time in their schedules to meet me and answer naive questions from a student while they had more urgent matters to handle. At Humboldt University in Berlin, Frederik Holst, Sumit Mandal, Anthony Milner, Farish Noor, and Ingrid Wessel encouraged me to pursue my questions in a PhD and set standards that I have since tried, but only sometimes managed, to reach. During my time in Malaysia, Norani Othman taught me to try to be clear while keeping complexity in sight, and the people at Sisters in Islam showed me how they translated theological debates into advocacy. In Yogyakarta, Pak Gatot and his family warmly hosted me; I will always be grateful to them, especially to Alia Damaihati, for letting me feel at home in Yogya. My sincere thanks also go to Moch Nur Ichwan, Noorhaidi Hassan, and Fatima Husein at the Islamic State University Sunan Kalijaga for their invaluable mentorship. During my short stays in Melbourne, Alberto Gomes, Gerhard Hoffstaedter, Nicole Lamb, and Dirk Tomsa, helped me rearrange my thoughts—thank you.

My time at the Berlin Graduate School of Muslim Cultures and Societies at Freie Universität in Berlin was profoundly shaped by interdisciplinary discussions with my fellow PhD candidates, especially Sarah Albrecht, Zeynep Aydoğan, Till Grallert, Sabine Hanisch, Ebtisam Hussein, Ellinor Morack, Benedikt Pontzen, Rune Steenberg Reyhé, Usman Shah, Ruth Streicher, and Torsten Wollina. I especially benefited from sharing an office with Syafiq Hasyim, who invited me to join the Nahdlatul Ulama Muktamar in Makassar in 2010 and from whom I learned not only about Indonesia but also how to refine my questions. I am also grateful to my advisors Cilja Harders and Birgit Krawietz as well as Schirin Amir-Moazami, Ulrike Freitag, Nico Kaptein, Gudrun Krämer, Mirjam Künkler, Antje Missbach, Nadja-Christina Schneider, and Thomas Stodulka.

In Makassar and Jakarta, the group around Ulil Abshar-Abdalla and Luthfi Assyaukanie were wonderful hosts, and I am thankful to the many leaders of minoritized organizations who made time to speak with me.

ACKNOWLEDGMENTS

During my postdoc at Columbia University, I was lucky to learn from Manan Ahmed, Karen Barkey, Michael Buehler, Khairudin Aljunied, Sudipta Kaviraj, Mirjam Künkler, Duncan McCargo, and the late Alfred Stepan. I am also grateful for the conversations with Shi-Yan Chao, Michael Griffiths, Ann Marie Murphy, Sanjay Pinto, and Margaret Scott and for my friendships and discussions with Manja Herrmann, Katharina Ivanyi, Ana Keilson, Patrick Koch, Daniel Mahla, Owen Miller, Intan Paramaditha, and Justin Reynolds.

I extend my gratitude to the colleagues who gave me the opportunity to present earlier versions of this project at workshops and colloquia hosted by Berkeley, Cornell, Yale, the Max Planck Institute of Social Anthropology, New York University, NYU Shanghai, and the Austrian Academy of Sciences. I am also deeply appreciative of the insightful discussions and feedback I received from colleagues during conference panels and other academic events, with special thanks to Ja Ian Chong, Laura Coppens, Wikke Jansen, Dominik Müller, Geoffrey B. Robinson, Tansen Sen, Ahmad Suaedy, Ferdiansyah Thajib, Azmil Tayeb, and Hew Wai Weng.

In Hong Kong, Hsiung Ping-Chen at the Chinese University kindly hosted me, and Thomas Patton, Mark Thompson, and Sharon Wai-yee Wong helped me connect my project to wider Southeast Asian studies and anthropology.

Back in Berlin, I was fortunate to have my own research group on democracy and religion in Indonesia and Turkey funded by the VolkswagenStiftung. I am grateful to the foundation and to the group of politically engaged and academically rigorous researchers and students, especially Leona Pröpper and Mutmainna Syam, who helped me with their questions and expertise, as well as Zeynep Balcioğlu, Ela Ezgi Benli, Dissa Paputungan-Engelhardt, Nadira Chairani, Müşerref Çetinkaya, Bahar Çatı, Jessy Petsy Ismoyo, Mehmet Keserli, Lea Ebeling, and several cohorts of curious and engaged student interns. I am also very grateful to Merlyna Lim, who spent several weeks with us as a visiting professor and whose reflections on knowledge and its conditions of production continue to inspire me. I thank Sabine Achour, Sophia Hoffmann, Norma Osterberg-Kaufmann, and Susanne Pickel for connecting my work on Indonesia to German debates. My non-Indonesianist colleagues and friends helped me put my work into perspective; thank you Nushin Atmaca, Elisabeth Becker, Tobias Berger, Anna Dobrucki, Marie Huber, Lena Neuberger, Marion Thimm, Carolin Weser, Thorsten Zander, and Alexander Ziegler.

Over the years, Karen Barkey demanded that I finish this book. I'll be forever grateful for her steadfast friendship, for helping shape its arguments, and for generously reading multiple iterations of all sections of the manuscript until they began to resemble chapters. For their detailed readings and critical feedback on earlier versions of the manuscript, I extend my sincere gratitude to Alexander Arifianto, Moch Nur Ichwan, John Sidel, Martin Slama, and Verena Meyer. I am also grateful to Chris Chaplin, Christine Holike, Leyla Jagiella, Kai Kresse, Sushmita Nath and Ferdiansyah Thajib for their comments on earlier versions of individual chapters. Thanks to Ron Hassner for his comments on the manuscript and streamlining the publication of the book. Willemina Don provided invaluable expertise in developmental editing. I am also grateful to two reviewers, one of whom offered a review so encouraging and constructive that it served as a reminder of the best aspects of academia. Any errors and shortcomings of course remain solely my responsibility.

My deepest gratitude goes to my family and friends. My grandparents Dieter and Frauke and my grandmother Waltraud visited us in Singapore when my family was living there in the 1990s and ever since patiently listened to my Southeast Asia stories. My brother, Lennart, cooked comforting meals when I returned home to the grays of Berlin. I am especially grateful to those who helped care for my children, allowing me to dedicate time to this book. Angenette and Bob Meaney once traveled all the way to Singapore to babysit on campus during a workshop. I am deeply thankful to my parents, Gaby and Frithjof Schäfer, for their unwavering support and to Thomas Meaney, whose thoughtful comments on various sections I was able to trade for sessions of dinner cooking and dishwashing. I dedicate this book to my children—Levin, Lila, and Clara—from whom I borrowed countless hours in pursuit of this work. This is for you. *Ma'af*, we rarely get to choose the gifts our parents bestow on us.

Notes

Introduction

1. The novel *Maryam* by Okky Madasari was published by in 2012 by Gramedia Pustaka Utama. It was translated into English and released under the title of *The Outcast* in March 2014. The interview took place at the book launch in Jakarta on March 7, 2012.

2. Bauman actually uses the term *ambivalence* but largely means what others have called *ambiguity*.

1. Between Homogenization and Decentralization

1. I am grateful to Moch Nur Ichwan for highlighting this.

2. For a classic discussion of why soft law is in many instances preferred to hard law, see Kenneth W. Abbott and Duncan Snidal (2000).

2. The Making of Mainstream Islam

1. Interview conducted in Jakarta in March 2012.

2. Laporan Sementara Pemantauan Kasus Penyerangan Penganut Ahmadiyah di Kampung Peundeuy, Desa Umbulan, Kecamatan Cikeusik, Kabupaten Pandeglang, Provinsi Banten Pada Minggu 6 Februari 2011, Komnas HAM: Jakarta 2011.

3. Satu Keluarga Mantan Ahmadiyah di Pangandaran Kembali ke Islam, Monday, 07 January 2019, https://jabar.kemenag.go.id/portal/read/satu-keluarga-mantan-ahmadiyah-di-pangandaran-kembali-ke-islam.

4. Attendees included Moh. Dawam Anwar (Khatib Syuriah NU); KH. Irfan Zidny, MA (Ketua Lajnah Falakiyah Syuriah NU); Thohir Al-Kaff (Yayasan Al-Bayyinat); Nabhan Husein (Dewan Dakwah Islamiyah Indonesia); KH. A. Latif Mukhtar (Ketua PERSIS); Hidayat Nur Wahid (Ketua Yayasan Al-Haramain); Syu'bah Asa (Wakil Pimpinan Redaksi Panji Masyarakat).

5. The exact wording is: "Mengukuhkan dan menetapkan keputusan MUI-MUI daerah yang menyatakan bahwa ajaran Syi'ah (khususnya Imamiyah Itsna Asyariyah atau yang menggunakan nama samara Madzhab Ahlul Bait dan semisalnya) serta ajaran-ajaran yang mempunyai kesamaan dengan faham Syi'ah Imamiyah Itsna Asyariyah adalah SESAT DAN MENYESATKAN." Suryadharma Ali stated that the conflict in Sampang was not an intergroup conflict between Sunni and Shi'a but a family conflict.

6. "Mereka telah menentang ayat Alquran dan mengafirkan para sahabat rasulullah. Keberadaan mereka adalah ancaman ideologi, yakni merusak NKRI. Munculnya Syi'ah merusak persatuan negara dan menjadikan perpecahan umat Islam."

7. The novel *Maryam* by Okky Madasari was published by in 2012 by Gramedia Pustaka Utama. It was translated into English and released under the title of *The Outcast* in March 2014. The interview took place at the book launch in Jakarta on March 7, 2012.

3. Patterns of Othering

1. To escape accusations of foreign influence, some liberal and progressive activists occasionally omit mention of their sponsors. I once attended the film launch of an Indonesian-Malaysian feminist film, after which the filmmaker explained to me that the German foundation that had financed parts of the work had agreed to not have their name displayed at the screenings. Similarly, the founders of a large feminist conference in 2009 in Kuala Lumpur were only named in passing, and I caused visible discomfort when I asked the organizers about the funding.

2. *Hudud*, literally meaning "edge, border, or limit," is the word often used in Islamic legal literature for the bounds of acceptable behavior and the punishments for a certain fixed set of serious crimes.

3. The website http://www.liaeden.info was online between 2006 and 2011.

4. Syafiq Hasyim, personal communication, March 2010.

5. Karen Barkey (1994) makes a similar argument for religious organizations in the Ottoman Empire: The ruling elite largely left contained organizations alone but pursued and restricted those who ventured further and broadened their spatial outreach. In Indonesian, the verb *bergerak*, "to move or stir," is often used to describe this process.

4. Bottom-Up vs. Top-Down Centralization

1. Arqam ibn Abi'l-Arqam (c. 597–675) was a companion of Muhammad. He was the owner of the house where the early Muslim community held its meetings.

2. A member of the congregation told me about the process of explaining their beliefs and practices to the authorities until they took the Bahai off the list.

3. This of course does not mean that there is no nonstate violence against queer people; such violence is well documented (Human Rights Watch 2022b).

References

Abbott, Jason P. 2011. "Electoral Authoritarianism and the Print Media in Malaysia: Measuring Political Bias and Analyzing Its Cause." *Asian Affairs: An American Review* 38 (1): 1–38. https://doi.org/10.1080/00927678.2010.520575.

Abbott, Kenneth W., and Duncan Snidal. 2000. "Hard and Soft Law in International Governance." *International Organization* 54 (3): 421–56.

Abduh, Umar, and K. Away. 2012. *Mengapa Kita Menolah Syi'ah; Kumpulan Makalah Seminar Nasional Sehari Tentang Syi'ah*. Lembaga Penelitian dan Pengkajian Islam.

Abdullah, Taufiq. 2009. *Indonesia: Towards Democracy*. Institute of Southeast Asian Studies.

Ádám, Zoltán, and András Bozóki. 2016. "State and Faith: Right-Wing Populism and Nationalized Religion in Hungary." *Intersections. East European Journal of Society and Politics* 2 (1). https://doi.org/10.17356/ieejsp.v2i1.143.

Al Arabiya English. 2012. "Indonesian Atheist's Arrest Sparks Tension Online." February 2, 2012. https://english.alarabiya.net/articles/2012/02/02/192028.

The Age. 2005. "Bulldozers Etch Boundaries of Religious Freedom." August 20, 2005. https://www.theage.com.au/world/bulldozers-etch-boundaries-of-religious-freedom-20050820-ge0q5g.html.

Aglionby, John. 2005. "Bruising Their Religion: John Aglionby Asks What Lies Behind Malaysia's Ambiguous Clampdown on the Sky Kingdom Sect." *The Guardian*, July 5, 2005. https://www.theguardian.com/world/2005/jul/05/malaysia.

Akmaliah, Wahyudi. 2020. "The Demise of Moderate Islam: New Media, Contestation, and Reclaiming Religious Authorities." *Indonesian Journal of Islam and Muslim Societies* 10:1–24. https://doi.org/10.18326/ijims.v10i1.1-24.

Akuntono, Indra. 2015. "Jokowi Tanda Tangani Keppres 22 Oktober Jadi Hari Santri." *KOMPAS.com*, October 15, 2015. https://nasional.kompas.com/read/2015/10/15/16195371/Jokowi.Tanda.Tangani.Keppres.22.Oktober.Jadi.Hari.Santri.

Alatas, Ismail Fajrie. 2021. *What Is Religious Authority?: Cultivating Islamic Communities in Indonesia*. Princeton Studies in Muslim Politics 84. Princeton University Press. https://doi.org/10.2307/j.ctv1b3qqfw.

Albertus, Michael, and Victor Menaldo. 2018. *Authoritarianism and the Elite Origins of Democracy*. Cambridge University Press.

Alfitri. 2008. "Religious Liberty in Indonesia and the Rights of 'Deviant' Sects." *Asian Journal of Comparative Law* 3 (1): 3. https://doi.org/10.2202/1932-0205.1062.

Alfitri. 2018. "Religion and Constitutional Practices in Indonesia: How Far Should the State Intervene in the Administration of Islam?" *Asian Journal of Comparative Law* 13, no. 2 (2018): 389–413. https://doi.org/10.1017/asjcl.2018.20.

Ali, Ahmad. 2019. "Mengokohkan Status Non-Muslim Sebagai Warga Negara." [Affirming the Status of Non-Muslims as Citizens]. *NU Online*, March 5, 2019. https://www.nu.or.id/opini/mengokohkan-status-non-muslim-sebagai-warga-negara-7nJN9.

REFERENCES

Almanar, Alin. 2016. "Jakarta Police Issue Official Warning Against 'Acts of Treason' During Anti-Ahok Protests." *Jakarta Globe*, November 22, 2016. https://jakartaglobe.id/news/jakarta-police-issue-official-warning-acts-treason-anti-ahok-protests.

Al-Tanwir. 2017. "Dikotomi Sunni-Syiah Tidak Relevan Lagi" [The Sunni-Shia dichotomy is no longer relevant]. April 9, 2017. https://www.altanwir.net/menjawab/wawancara-dr-jalaluddin-rakhmat-dikotomi-sunni-syiah-tidak-relevan-lagi.

Alvarez, Sonia E. 2009. "Beyond NGO-ization? Reflections from Latin America." *Development* 52 (2): 175–84.

Amiq, Amanda Gita. 1998. "Two Fatwas on Jihad Against the Dutch Colonization in Indonesia: A Prosopographical Approach to the Study of Fatwa." 5 (3). https://doi.org/10.15408/sdi.v5i3.740.

Amnesty International. 2011. "Indonesia: Ahmadiyya Community at Risk in Indonesia." ASA 21/008/2011. March 16, 2011. https://www.amnesty.org/en/documents/asa21/008/2011/en/.

Amnesty International. 2012. "Amnesty International Public Statment Indonesia: Shi'a Leader Imprisoned for Blasphemy Must Be Released." ASA 21/025/2012. July 12, 2012. https://www.amnesty.org/en/wp-content/uploads/2021/06/asa210252012en.pdf.

Amnesty International. 2014a. "Indonesia: New Administration Must End the Criminalization of Beliefs Through Oppressive Blasphemy Laws." November 21, 2014. https://www.amnesty.org/en/latest/news/2014/11/indonesia-new-administration-must-end-criminalization-beliefs-through-oppre/.

Amnesty International. 2014b. *Prosecuting Beliefs: Indonesia's Blasphemy Laws*. Amnesty International London. https://www.amnesty.org/en/wp-content/uploads/2021/06/asa210302014en.pdf.

Amnesty International. 2018. "Homes of Religious Minority Destroyed by Mob." ASA 21/8453/2018 Indonesia. May 22, 2018. https://www.amnesty.org/es/wp-content/uploads/2021/05/ASA2184532018ENGLISH.pdf.

Amrullah, Amri. 2013. "Korban Aliran Sesat Berhak Terima Zakat" [Victims of heresy are entitled to Receive Zakat]. *Republika*, September 3, 2013. https://www.republika.co.id/berita/dunia-islam/fatwa/13/09/03/msjd87-korban-aliran-sesat-berhak-terima-zakat.

Andarini, Rindang Senja. 2014. "Jurnalisme Damai Dalam Pemberitaan Ahmadiyah Pada Harian Jawa Pos." *Interaksi: Jurnal Ilmu Komunikasi* 3, no. 1 (2014): 85–93.

Anderson, Benedict R. O'G. 1983. *Imagined Communities: Reflections on the Origin and Spread of Nationalism*. Verso.

Anjarsari, Lulu, and Yuniar Widiastuti. 2017. "Ahmadiyya Adherents Revise Petition of Judicial Review of Blasphemy Law." *Mahkamah Konstitusi RI*, September 11, 2017. https://en.mkri.id/news/details/2017-09-11/Ahmadiyya+Adherents+Revise+Petition+of+Judicial+Review+of+Blasphemy+Law.

Antara and Maya Saputri. 2020. "Menag Yaqut Klarifikasi Soal Perlindungan Bagi Ahmadiyah Dan Syiah" [Minister of Religion Yaqut Clarifies About Protection for Ahmadiyah and Shia]. *Tirto*, December 26, 2020. https://tirto.id/menag-yaqut-klarifikasi-soal-perlindungan-bagi-ahmadiyah-dan-syiah-f8xL.

Antara News. 2009. "Jamaah Ahmadiyah Tobat Massal Di Monas." [Ahmadiyah congregation mass repentance in Monas]. June 1, 2009. https://www.antaranews.com/berita/142663/jamaah-ahmadiyah-tobat-massal-di-monas.

Antara News. 2011. "Mahfud: Kalau Ahmadiyah Salah, Biar Tuhan Menghukumnya." [Mahfud: If Ahmadiyah is wrong, let God punish them]. March 8, 2011. https://www.antar Abdullah anews.com/berita/249099/mahfud-kalau-ahmadiyah-salah-biar-tuhan-menghukumnya.

Anthias, Floya, and Yuval-Davis Nira, eds. 1989. *Women-Nation-State:* Macmillan.

Antique and Zaky Al-Yamani. 2011. "Sosialisasi SKB 3 Menteri Jadi Prioritas" [Socialization of SKB 3 Ministers Becomes Priority]. *Viva News*, February 7, 2011. https://www.viva.co.id/berita/nasional/203409-pemprov-banten-pacu-sosialisasi-skb-3-menteri.

Apologetics Index. 2005. "Eden Community / Kingdom of Eden / Salamullah / Lia Eden / Lia Aminuddin / Kaum Eden." Accessed May 25, 2023. https://www.apologeticsindex.org/74-lia-eden-salamullah.

Appadurai, Arjun. 2006. *Fear of Small Numbers: An Essay on the Geography of Anger:* Duke University Press.

Aragon, Lorraine V. 2023. "Religious Pluralism in Indonesia: 7. Regulating Religion and Recognizing 'Animist Beliefs' in Indonesian Law and Life." In *Threats and Opportunities for Democracy*, edited by Chiara Formichi. Cornell University Press.

Arifianto, Alexander R., and Adri Wanto. 2015. "The 2015 NU Muktamar: Further Conservative Turn in Indonesian Islam?—Analysis." *Eurasia Review*, September 3, 2015. https://www.eurasiareview.com/03092015-the-2015-nu-muktamar-further-conservative-turn-in-indonesian-islam-analysis/.

Aritonang, Margareth S. 2012. "Govt Has Role in Irreconcilable Shia-Sunni Split: Dialogue." *The Jakarta Post*, September 19, 2012. https://www.thejakartapost.com/news/2012/09/19/govt-has-role-irreconcilable-shia-sunni-split-dialogue.html.

Artawijaya. 2012. *Indonesia Tanpa Liberal: Membongkar Misi Asing Dalam Subversif Politik Dan Agama*. [Indonesia Without Liberals: Exposing Foreign Missions in Political and Religious Subversion]. Pustaka Al Kautsar.

Artharini, Isyana. 2017. "Kewajiban Berjilbab Bagi Siswi Non-Muslim Di Sekolah Negeri 'Bukan Hanya Di Banyuwangi.'" [Obligation of Hijab for Non-Muslim Students in Public Schools "Not Only in Banyuwangi"]. *BBC News Indonesia*, July 18, 2017. https://www.bbc.com/indonesia/indonesia-40635043.

Asia Foundation. 2016. "Understanding Social Exclusion in Indonesia: A Meta-Analysis of Proram Peduli's Theory of Change Documents." https://www.slideshare.net/slideshow/understanding-social-exclusion-in-indonesia-65145738/65145738.

Asia One. 2011. "Opinions Split over Sexuality Movement." November 3, 2011. Retrieved via Internet Archive's Wayback Machine. http://web.archive.org/web/20171030121647/http://www.asiaone.com/print/News/AsiaOne%2BNews/Malaysia/Story/A1Story20111103-308502.html.

Aspinall, Edward. 2010. "Assessing Democracy Assistance: Indonesia." Unpublished manuscript, last modified August 10, 2020. https://www.files.ethz.ch/isn/130783/IP_WMD_Indonesia_ENG_jul10.pdf.

Aspinall, Edward. 2013. "A Nation in Fragments." *Critical Asian Studies* 45 (1): 27–54. https://doi.org/10.1080/14672715.2013.758820.

Aspinall, Edward. 2015. "Oligarchic Populism: Prabowo Subianto's Challenge to Indonesian Democracy." *Indonesia*, no. 99: 1–28.

Aspinall, Edward, and Ward Berenschot. 2019. *Democracy for Sale: Elections, Clientelism, and the State in Indonesia:* Cornell University Press.

Aspinall, Edward, and Jeremy Menchik. 2017. "Islam and Democracy in Indonesia: Tolerance Without Liberalism." *Indonesia* (104): 183–85. http://www.jstor.org/stable/10.5728/indonesia.104.0183.

Aspinall, Edward, and Marcus Mietzner. 2010. *Problems of Democratisation in Indonesia. Elections, Institutions and Society.* Institute of Southeast Asian Studies.

Aspinall, Edward, and Marcus Mietzner. 2019. "Southeast Asia's Troubling Elections: Nondemocratic Pluralism in Indonesia." *Journal of Democracy* 30 (4): 104–18. https://doi.org/10.1353/jod.2019.0055.

Assyaukanie, Luthfi. 2009a. "Fatwa and Violence in Indonesia." *Journal of Religion and Society* 11.

Assyaukanie, Luthfi. 2009b. *Islam and the Secular State in Indonesia.* Institute of Southeast Asian Studies (ISEAS).

Astro Awani. 2016. "'Sky Kingdom' Cult Leader Ayah Pin Dies." *Astro Awani*, April 23, 2016. https://www.astroawani.com/berita-malaysia/sky-kingdom-cult-leader-ayah-pin-dies-103473.

Atkinson, Jane Monnig. 1983. "Religions in Dialogue: The Construction of an Indonesian Minority Religion." *American Ethnologist* 10 (4): 684–96. http://www.jstor.org/stable/644056.

A'yun, Qurrata Rafiqa. 2019. "Blasphemy on the Rise." *Inside Indonesia*, January 20, 2019. https://www.insideindonesia.org/blasphemy-on-the-rise.

Az, Emilia Renita. 2015. *Islam in Indonesia with Sister Emilia Renita Az*. Imam Hussein TV 3, August 15, 2015. https://youtu.be/nYXRMTuomx8?t=532.

Aziz, Alam Nasru. 2011. "Solusi MUI: Bubarkan Ahmadiyah." [MUI's solution: Dissolve the Ahmadiyya]. *KOMPAS.com*, February 17, 2011. https://nasional.kompas.com/read/2011/02/17/21460279/solusi.mui.bubarkan.ahmadiyah.

Bachelard, Michael. 2012. "'You Know What Men Are Like': Indonesia to Ban Mini-Skirts over Links to Rape." *The Age*, March 29, 2012. Retrieved via Internet Archive's Wayback Machine. https://web.archive.org/web/20120329144900/http://www.theage.com.au:80/world/you-know-what-men-are-like-indonesia-to-ban-miniskirts-over-links-to-rape-20120329-1vz7q.html.

Bagir, Zainal Abidin. 2013. "Defamation of Religion Law in Post-Reformasi Indonesia: Is Revision Possible?" *Australian Journal of Asian Law* 13 (2): 153–68. https://papers.ssrn.com/sol3/papers.cfm?abstract_id=2228476.

Barkey, Karen. 1994. *Bandits and Bureaucrats: The Ottoman Route to State Centralization.* Cornell University Press.

Barkey, Karen, Sudipta Kaviraj, and Vatsal Naresh. 2021. *Negotiating Democracy and Religious Pluralism: India, Pakistan, and Turkey.* Oxford University Press.

Baso, A. 1999. *Civil Society Versus Masyarakat Madani: Arkeologi Pemikiran "Civil Society" Dalam Islam Indonesia.* [Civil Society Versus Masyarakat Madani: An Archaeology of "Civil Society" Thought in Indonesian Islam]. Pustaka Hidayah.

Basri, Hasan. 2012. "Mengapa Kita Menolak Syiah, LPPI." [Why we reject Shi'a]. *Fakta.com*, January 5, 2012. http://fakta-faktual.blogspot.com/2012/01/bahaya-syiah-melebihi-ekstasi-dan.html.

Bauer, Thomas. 2021. *A Culture of Ambiguity: An Alternative History of Islam:* Columbia University Press.

Bauman, Zygmunt. 1991. *Modernity and Ambivalence.* Cornell University Press.

Bayat, Asef. 2007. *Islam and Democracy: What Is the Real Question?* ISIM paper 8. https://scholarlypublications.universiteitleiden.nl/handle/1887/12452.
BBC News Indonesia. 2011. "Pesantren Syiah Dibakar Di Madura" [Shia Islamic boarding school burned in Madura]. December 29, 2011. https://www.bbc.com/indonesia/berita_indonesia/2011/12/111229_madura.
BBC News. 2011. "Malaysian 'Teapot Cult' Woman Loses Islam Legal Bid." July 19, 2011. https://www.bbc.com/news/world-asia-pacific-14199815.
Beck, Herman L. 2005. "The Rupture Between the Muhammadiyah and the Ahmadiyy." *Bijdragen tot de taal-, land- en volkenkunde* 161 (2–3): 210–46.
Beittinger-Lee, Verena. 2013. *(Un) Civil Society and Political Change in Indonesia: A Contested Arena:* Routledge.
Bell, Emma. 2011. *Criminal Justice and Neoliberalism.* Springer.
Benda-Beckmann, K. von, F. von Benda-Beckmann, and A. Griffiths. 2013. *The Power of Law in a Transnational World: Anthropological Enquiries:* Berghahn Books.
Bennett, Linda Rae, and Sharyn Graham Davies. 2014. *Sex and Sexualities in Contemporary Indonesia: Sexual Politics, Health, Diversity and Representations.* Routledge.
Berenschot, Ward, and Gerry van Klinken. 2018. "Informality and Citizenship: The Everyday State in Indonesia." *Citizenship Studies* 22 (2): 95–111. https://doi.org/10.1080/13621025.2018.1445494.
Bernama. 2009a. "Fatwa Council: Only Allah Decides Heaven or Hell." *The Nut Graph*, August 19, 2009. https://www.thenutgraph.com/fatwa-council-only-allah-decides-heaven-hell/.
Bernama. 2009b. "Nik Aziz Denies 'Heaven' Statements; Fatwa Council to Clarify." *The Nut Graph*, August 18, 2009. https://thenutgraph.com/nik-aziz-denies-heaven-statements-fatwa-council-to-probe/.
Bertrand, Jacques. 2004. *Nationalism and Ethnic Conflict in Indonesia.* Cambridge Asia-Pacific Studies. Cambridge University Press.
Binder, Leonard. 1988. *Islamic Liberalism: A Critique of Development Ideologies.* University of Chicago Press.
Bjork-James, Sophie. 2019. "Christian Nationalism and LGBTQ Structural Violence in the United States." *Journal of Religion and Violence* 7 (3): 278–302.
Boellstorff, Tom. 2004. "The Emergence of Political Homophobia in Indonesia: Masculinity and National Belonging." *Ethnos* 69 (4): 465–86. https://doi.org/10.1080/0014184042000302308.
Boellstorff, Tom. 2005. *The Gay Archipelago: Sexuality and Nation in Indonesia.* Princeton University Press.
Boland, B. J. 1971. *The Struggle of Islam in Modern Indonesia.* Verhandelingen van het Koninklijk Instituut voor Taal-, Land- en Volkenkunde 59. Nijhoff.
Bonasir, Rohmatin. 2018. "Apa Yang Membuat Jemaah Ahmadiyah Sembahyang Di Masjid Sendiri, Tidak Bersama Muslim Lain?" [What Makes Ahmadiyya Pilgrims Pray in Their Own Mosque, Not with Other Muslims?]. *BBC News Indonesia*, February 21, 2018. https://www.bbc.com/indonesia/dunia-42791329.
Borneo Post Online. 2010. "Kartika's Caning Sentence Commuted to Community Service." April 2, 2010. https://www.theborneopost.com/2010/04/02/kartika%E2%80%99s-caning-sentence-commuted-to-community-service/.

Bosia, Michael J., and Meredith L. Weiss. 2013. "Political Homophobia in Comparative Perspective." In *Global Homophobia*, edited by Meredith L. Weiss and Michael J. Bosia. States, Movements, and the Politics of Oppression. University of Illinois Press.

Bourchier, David M. 2019. "Two Decades of Ideological Contestation in Indonesia: From Democratic Cosmopolitanism to Religious Nationalism." *Journal of Contemporary Asia* 49 (5): 713–33. https://doi.org/10.1080/00472336.2019.1590620.

Braunschweiger, Amy. 2016. "Interview: Indonesia's LGBT Community Under Threat." Human Rights Watch, August 11, 2016. https://www.hrw.org/news/2016/08/11/interview-indonesias-lgbt-community-under-threat.

Brubaker, Rogers. 1994. "Nationhood and the National Question in the Soviet Union and Post-Soviet Eurasia: An Institutionalist Account." *Theory and Society* 23 (1): 47–78. http://www.jstor.org/stable/657812.

Brubaker, Rogers. 2004. *Ethnicity Without Groups*. Harvard University Press.

Bruinessen, Martin van. 1992. Gerakan Sempalan Di Kalangan Umat Islam Indonesia: Latar Belakang Sosial-Budaya. [Sectarian Movements in Indonesian Islam: Social and Cultural Background]. *Ulumul Qur'an* 3 (1): 16–27.

Bruinessen, Martin van. 1996. "Islamic State or State Islam? Fifty Years of State-Islam Relations in Indonesia." In *Indonesien Am Ende Des 20. Jahrhunderts*, edited by Ingrid Wessel. Abera-Verlag. https://dspace.library.uu.nl/bitstream/1874/20759/1/bruinessen_96_islamicstateorstateislam.pdf.

Bruinessen, Martin van. 2010. "New Leadership, New Policies?" *Inside Indonesia* June 16, 2010. https://www.insideindonesia.org/new-leadership-new-policies..

Bruinessen, Martin van. 2012. "Indonesian Muslims and Their Place in the Larger World of Islam." In *Indonesia Rising: the Repositioning of Asia's Third Giant*, edited by Anthony Reid. ISEAS, pp. 117–140.

Bruinessen, Martin van. 2011b. *What Happened to the Smiling Face of Indonesian Islam? Muslim Intellectualism and the Conservative Turn in Post-Suharto Indonesia*. 222 vols. RSIS Working Papers.

Bruinessen, Martin van, ed. 2013. *Contemporary Developments in Indonesian Islam*. Institute of Southeast Asian Studies.

Bruinessen, Martin van. 2015. "Ghazwul Fikri or Arabization? Indonesian Muslim Responses to Globalization." In *Southeast Asian Muslims in the Era of Globalization*, edited by Ken Miichi and Omar Farouk. Palgrave Macmillan.

Buehler, Michael. 2016. *The Politics of Shari'a Law: Islamist Activists and the State in Democratizing Indonesia*. Cambridge University Press.

Buehler, Michael. 2023. "Do Discriminatory Laws Have Societal Origins? The Diffusion of Anti-Ahmadiyah Regulations in Indonesia." *Politics and Religion* 16 (3): 468–91. https://doi.org/10.1017/S1755048323000081.

Bulger, Matthew. 2012. "The Story of Alexander Aan: An Indonesian Atheist Fears for His Life." *The Humanist*, May 17, 2012. https://thehumanist.com/news/international/the-story-of-alexander-aan-an-indonesian-atheist-fears-for-his-life/.

Burhani, Ahmad Najib. 2012. "Time to Forgive and Live in Harmony with Ahmadiyah." *Jakarta Globe*. September 7.

Burhani, Ahmad Najib. 2013. "Liberal and Conservative Discourses in the Muhammadiyah: The Struggle for the Face of Reformist Islam in Indonesia." In

Contemporary Developments in Indonesian Islam, edited by Martin van Bruinessen. Institute of Southeast Asian Studies.

Burhani, Ahmad Najib. 2014a. "Conversion to Ahmadiyya in Indonesia: Winning Hearts Through Ethical and Spiritual Appeals." *Sojourn: Journal of Social Issues in Southeast Asia* 29 (3): 657–90.

Burhani, Ahmad Najib. 2014b. "Hating the Ahmadiyya: The Place of "Heretics." In Contemporary Indonesian Muslim Society." *Contemporary Islam* 8 (2): 133–52. https://doi.org/10.1007/s11562-014-0295-x.

Burhani, Ahmad Najib. 2019a. "Between Social Services and Tolerance: Explaining Religious Dynamics in Muhammadiyah." In *Between Social Services and Tolerance: Explaining Religious Dynamics in Muhammadiyah*, edited by Ahmad N. Burhani. Trends in Southeast Asia: ISEAS–Yusof Ishak Institute. https://www.cambridge.org/core/product/0E2A2BDD12B3F1AD57DE55D9CF138260.

Burhani, Ahmad Najib. 2019b. "Torn Between Muhammadiyah and Ahmadiyah in Indonesia." *Indonesia and the Malay World* 48 (140): 60–77. https://doi.org/10.1080/13639811.2019.1663678.

Burhani, Ahmad Najib. 2021. "'It's a Jihad': Justifying Violence Towards the Ahmadiyya in Indonesia." *TRaNS: Trans-Regional and-National Studies of Southeast Asia* 9 (1): 99–112.

Bush, Robin. 2015. "Religious Politics and Minority Rights During the Yudhoyono Presidency." In *The Yudhoyono Presidency: Indonesia's Decade of Stability and Stagnation*, edited by Edward Aspinall, Marcus Mietzner, and Dirk Tomsa. ISEAS–Yusof Ishak Institute.

Butt, Simon. 2020. "Constitutional Recognition of 'Beliefs' in Indonesia." *Journal of Law and Religion* 35 (3). https://doi.org/10.1017/jlr.2020.39.

Caeiro, Alexandre. 2006. "The Shifting Moral Universes of the Islamic Tradition of Ifta: A Diachronic Study of Four Adab Al-Fatwa Manuals." *Muslim World* 96: 661–85.

Cari Gold. 2006. Pemimpin Baru 'Kerajaan Langit' Muncul. *Harian Metro Edisi Timur*, October 3, 2006. https://carigold.com/forum/threads/pemimpin-baru-%E2%80%98kerajaan-langit%E2%80%99-muncul.9060/.

Carroll, Toby. 2017. "Capitalism, Contradiction and the Onward March of Variegated Neoliberalism in Southeast Asia." In *The Political Economy of Emerging Markets: Varieties of BRICS in the Age of Global Crises and Austerity*, edited by Richard Westra. Routledge.

Cederroth, Sven. 1996. "From Ancestor Worship to Monotheism: Politics of Religion on Lombok." *Temenos—Nordic Journal of Comparative Religion* 32: 7–36.

Chaplin, Chris. 2017. "Islam and Citizenship." *Inside Indonesia*, August 8, 2017. https://www.insideindonesia.org/editions/edition-129-jul-sep-2017/islam-and-citizenship.

Chaplin, Chris. 2021. *Salafism and the State: Islamic Activism and National Identity in Contemporary Indonesia*. NIAS Press.

Chew, Amy. 2021. "Can Indonesia's More Moderate Ulema Council Help Stem a Rise in Islamic Extremism?" *South China Morning Post*, January 2, 2021. https://www.scmp.com/week-asia/politics/article/3116158/can-indonesias-more

-moderate-ulema-council-help-stem-rise?fbclid=IwAR0DaM4tmgLUzir5CiL LoHWTLp4lKLoXUmEAj_xJVjg54vVpICwc9w680ps.

Cholid, Idham. 2021. "Antara Menteri Agama, Syiah, Dan Ahmadiyah" [Between the Ministers of Religion, Shiites, and Ahmadis]. *Tempo*, January 12, 2021. https://www.tempo.co/kolom/antara-menteri-agama-syiah-dan-ahmadiyah-549065.

Chooi, Clara. 2011. "DAP Claims Umno Backing Perkasa's Crusade Threat Against Christians." *The Malaysian Insider*, May 16, 2011. Retrieved via Internet Archive's Wayback Machine. https://web.archive.org/web/20110517225305/http://www.themalaysianinsider.com/malaysia/article/dap-claims-umno-backing-perkasas-crusade-threat-against-christians/.

Chooi, Clara. 2012. "Growing Chinese Clout May Cause New May 13, Says Ibrahim Ali." *Malaysian Insider*, December 14, 2012. Retrieved via Internet Archive's Wayback Machine. https://web.archive.org/web/20130606195122/http://www.themalaysianinsider.com/malaysia/article/growing-chinese-clout-may-cause-new-may-13-says-ibrahim-ali.

Choudry, Aziz, and Dip Kapoor, eds. 2010. *Learning from the Ground Up*. Palgrave Macmillan.

Choudry, Aziz, and Dip Kapoor, eds. 2013. *NGOization: Complicity, Contradictions and Prospects*. Zed Books.

Cleland, Jamie, Chris Anderson, and Jack Aldridge-Deacon. 2018. "Islamophobia, War and Non-Muslims as Victims: An Analysis of Online Discourse on an English Defence League Message Board." *Ethnic and Racial Studies* 41 (9): 1541–57. https://doi.org/10.1080/01419870.2017.1287927.

CNN Indonesia. 2016. "FULL—Kapolri, GNPF MUI & MUI Kompak Tentang Aksi 2 Desember." Streamed on YouTube, November 28, 2016. https://www.youtube.com/watch?v=g2J2UdmxULI.

Connelly, James. 2002. "Raymond Geuss, Public Goods, Private Goods." *Philosophy in Review* 22: 277–78.

Constitutional Court Decision No. 140/PUU-VII/2009. 2010. https://www.mkri.id/public/content/persidangan/putusan/putusan_sidang_Putusan%20PUU%20140_Senin%2019%20April%202010.pdf.

Constitutional Court Decision No. 84/PUU-X/2012. 2013. https://www.mkri.id/public/content/persidangan/putusan/putusan_sidang_84%20PUU%202012-telah%20ucap%2019%20September%202013.pdf.

Cook, Michael. 2001. *Commanding Right and Forbidding Wrong in Islamic Thought*. Cambridge University Press.

Cook, Michael. 2003. *Forbidding Wrong in Islam*. Themes in Islamic History 3. Cambridge University Press.

Cooper, Melinda. 2017. *Family Values: Between Neoliberalism and the New Social Conservatism*. MIT Press.

Crouch, Melissa. 2011. "Law and Religion in Indonesia: The Constitutional Court and the Blasphemy Law." *Asian Journal of Comparative Law* 7:1–46. https://doi.org/10.1017/S2194607800000582.

Crouch, Melissa. 2013. *Law and Religion in Indonesia: Conflict and the Courts in West Java*. Routledge.

Crouch, Melissa. 2014. "Proselytization, Religious Diversity and the State in Indonesia: The Offense of Deceiving a Child to Change Religion." In *Proselytizing and the Limits of Religious Pluralism in Contemporary Asia*, edited by Juliana Finucane and R. M. Feener. Springer Singapore.

Crouch, Melissa. 2017a. "Pluralism, Transnationalism and Culture in Asian Law: 10 Negotiating Legal Pluralism in Court: Fatwa and the Crime of Blasphemy in Indonesia." In Pluralism, Transnationalism, and Culture in Asian Law, edited by Gary F. Bell. ISEAS Publishing.

Crouch, Melissa. 2017b. "Ahok, Indonesia's 'Nemo,' Sentenced to Jail." *Asia and the Pacific Policy Society*, May 10, 2017. https://www.policyforum.net/ahok-indonesias-nemo-sentenced-jail/.

Crouch, Melissa, and Tim Lindsey. 2013. "Cause Lawyers in Indonesia: A House Divided." In "Cause Lawyers in Asia," special issue, *Wisconsin International Law Journal* 31 (3): 620–45.

Cult Education Institute. 2006. "Malaysia: Heretical Islamic Cult Returns." *Spero News*, December 5, 2006. https://culteducation.com/group/807-al-arqam/1641-malaysia-heretical-islamic-cult-returnss.html.

Curran, James. 2011. *Media and Democracy*. Routledge.

Daily Express. 2016. "Cult Leader Ayah Pin Dies." April 24, 2016. https://www.dailyexpress.com.my/news.cfm?NewsID=109076.

Daniels, Timothy. 2017. "Living Sharia: Law and Practice in Malaysia." University of Washington Press.

Davies, William. 2017. "Elite Power Under Advanced Neoliberalism." *Theory, Culture & Society* 34 (5–6): 227–50. https://doi.org/10.1177/0263276417715072.

Davies, William. 2018. *Nervous States: How Feeling Took Over the World*. London: Jonathan Cape.

Deflem, Mathieu. 2017. *Lady Gaga and the Sociology of Fame: The Rise of a Pop Star in an Age of Celebrity*. Palgrave Macmillan.

D'Emilio, John. 2007. "Capitalism and Gay Identity." In *Culture, Society and Sexuality*. Routledge.

Detiknews. 2005. "Muhammadiyah Soal Ahmadiyah" [Muhammadiyah About Ahmadiyah]. July 18, 2005. https://news.detik.com/berita/d-404996/muhammadiyah-soal-ahmadiyah-.

Detiknews. 2007. "Inilah 10 Kriteria Aliran Sesat." *detikcom*, November 6, 2007. https://news.detik.com/berita/d-849046/inilah-10-kriteria-aliran-sesat.

Detiknews. 2011a. "BAZ Bandung Lunasi Utang Jemaat Ahmadiyah Yang Tobat" [BAZ Bandung Pays Off the Debt of the Repentant Ahmadiyya Congregation]. March 21, 2011. https://news.detik.com/berita-jawa-barat/d-1597367/baz-bandung-lunasi-utang-jemaat-ahmadiyah-yang-tobat.

Detiknews. 2011b. "Gubernur Banten: Penyerangan Terhadap Warga Ahmadiyah Adalah Musibah" [Banten Governor: Attacks on Ahmadiyya Residents Is a Disaster]. February 7, 2011. https://news.detik.com/berita/d-1562139/gubernur-banten-penyerangan-terhadap-warga-ahmadiyah-adalah-musibah?nd771108bcj=.

Detiknews. 2011c. "Komnas HAM Temukan Pelanggaran Pada Kasus Cikeusik" [Komnas HAM Finds Violations in the Cikeusik Case]. February 23, 2011. https://news.detik.com/berita/d-1577104/komnas-ham-temukan-pelanggaran-pada-kasus-cikeusik-.

Detiknews. 2012. "Kronologi Kekerasan yang Dialami Warga Syiah di Sampang" [Chronology of Violence Experienced by Shia Residents in Sampang]. August 27,

2012. https://news.detik.com/berita/d-1999831/kronologi-kekerasan-yang-dialami-warga-syiah-di-sampang.

Dewan, Angela. 2010. "Followers of Ahmadiyah Face Pressure in Indonesia." *Voice of America*, August 10, 2010. https://www.voanews.com/east-asia/followers-ahmadiyah-face-pressure-indonesia.

Dewi, Nurita. 2020. "MUI Imbau Menag Hati-Hati Bicara Afirmasi Hak Beragama Syiah Dan Ahmadiyah" [MUI Urges Minister of Religion to Be Careful in Speaking Affirmations of Shia and Ahmadiyya Religious Rights]. *Tempo*, December 25, 2020. https://nasional.tempo.co/read/1417619/mui-imbau-menag-hati-hati-bicara-afirmasi-hak-beragama-syiah-dan-ahmadiyah.

De Wilde, Pieter, Ruud Koopmans, Wolfgang Merkel, Oliver Strijbis, and Michael Zürn. 2019. *The Struggle over Borders: Cosmopolitanism and Communitarianism*. Cambridge University Press.

Dhakidae, Daniel. 1991. "The State, the Rise of Capital and the Fall of Political Journalism: Political Economy of Indonesian News Industry." PhD diss., Cornell University.

Dhyatmika, Wahyu. 2014. "Who Owns the News in Indonesia?" *NiemanReports*, December 12, 2014. https://niemanreports.org/articles/who-owns-the-news-in-indonesia/.

Dipa, Arya. 2017. "No Merry Idul Fitri Celebration for Ahmadiyah Followers in Depok." *The Jakarta Post*, June 24, 2017. https://www.thejakartapost.com/news/2017/06/24/no-merry-idul-fitri-celebration-for-ahmadiyah-followers-in-depok.html.

Douglas, Mary. 1966. *Purity and Danger: An Analysis of Concepts of Pollution and Taboo*. Routledge & Kegan.

Dressler, Markus. 2013. *Writing Religion: The Making of Turkish Alevi Islam*. Oxford University Press.

Duffy, Nick. 2019. "Malaysia PM Mahathir Mohamad: Gays Shouldn't Get Married Because They Can't Have Kids." *Pink News*, June 17, 2019. https://www.thepinknews.com/2019/06/17/malaysia-pm-mahathir-mohamad-gays-married-cant-have-kids/.

Duile, Timo. 2020. "Being Atheist in the Religious Harmony State of Indonesia." *Asia Pacific Journal of Anthropology* 21 (5): 450–65. https://doi.org/10.1080/14442213.2020.1829022.

Duile, Timo 2021. "Social Media in Research on a Marginalized Identity: The Case of Atheism in Indonesia." *Austrian Journal of South-East Asian Studies* 14(1): 121–128.

Dursun, Çiler. 2003. "Türk-İslâm Sentezi İdeolojisi Ve Öznesi" [Ideology and Subject of the Turkish-Islamic Synthesis]. *Doğu-Batı* 7 (25): 59–82.

Deutsche Welle. 2013. "Malaysia Paper Can't Use 'Allah.'" October 14, 2013. https://www.dw.com/en/malaysia-court-bans-use-of-word-allah-by-christian-newspaper/a-17155592.

Dwi, Agnes R., Akhol Firdaus, Zaini Apridon, Azhari Aiyub, Dewi Nova, Indra Listantiantara, M. Bahrun, M. Irfan, Rochmond Onasis, and Syarif Abadi. 2012. "The Condition of Freedom of Religion/ Belief in Indonesia 2011." In *The Condition of Freedom of Religion/Belief in Indonesia 2011*, edited by Ismail Hasani and Bonar Tigor Naipospos. Jakarta: Pustaka Masyarakat Setara, 2011. http://setara-institute.org/wp-content/uploads/2016/04/laporan-KBB-2011-ENGLISH.pdf.

Dwyer, Leslie. 2000. "Spectacular Sexuality: Nationalism, Development and the Politics of Family Planning in Indonesia." In *Gender Ironies of Nationalism: Sexing the Nation*, edited by Tamar Mayer. Routledge.

Edgell, Penny, Joseph Gerteis, and Douglas Hartmann. 2006. "Atheists as 'Other': Moral Boundaries and Cultural Membership in American Society." *American Sociological Review* 71 (2): 211–34. https://doi.org/10.1177/000312240607100203.

Eksi, Betul, and Elizabeth A. Wood. 2019. "Right-Wing Populism as Gendered Performance: Janus-Faced Masculinity in the Leadership of Vladimir Putin and Recep T. Erdogan." *Theory and Society* 48 (5): 733–51. https://doi.org/10.1007/s11186-019-09363-3.

Engesser, Sven, Nicole Ernst, Frank Esser, and Florin Büchel. 2017. "Populism and Social Media: How Politicians Spread a Fragmented Ideology." *Information, Communication & Society* 20 (8): 1109–26. https://doi.org/10.1080/1369118X.2016.1207697.

European Asylum Support Office. 2018. "EASO COI Meeting Report: Pakistan 16–17 October 2017." Unpublished manuscript, last modified March 24, 2023. https://www.ecoi.net/en/file/local/1426168/90_1520500210_easo-pakistan-meeting-report-october-2017.pdf.

Fairclough, Norman. 2010. *Critical Discourse Analysis: The Critical Study of Language.* 2nd ed. Routledge.

Fakhruroji, Moch. 2019. "Digitalizing Islamic Lectures: Islamic Apps and Religious Engagement in Contemporary Indonesia." *Contemporary Islam* 13 (2): 201–15. https://doi.org/10.1007/s11562-018-0427-9.

Fandom. n.d. "Ariffin Mohammad." Religion Wiki. Accessed December 30, 2022. https://religion.fandom.com/wiki/Ariffin_Mohammed.

Farabi, Nadia. 2024. "Addressing the Challenges of Heresy in Peacebuilding: Evidence from the Ahmadiyya and Shia in Indonesia." *Conflict, Security & Development*, 1–19. https://doi.org/10.1080/14678802.2024.2436544.

Fealy, Greg. 2008. "Consuming Islam: Commodified Religion and Aspirational Pietism in Contemporary Indonesia." In *Religious Life and Politics in Indonesia*, edited by Greg Fealy and Sally White. ISEAS Publishing.

Fealy, Greg, and Virginia Hooker, eds. 2006. *Voices of Islam in Southeast Asia*. Singapore.

Fealy, Greg, and Sally White, eds. 2008. *Expressing Islam: Religious Life and Politics in Indonesia*. Paper presented at the 25th Annual Indonesia Update Conference held at Australian National University, September 7–8, 2007. Institute of Southeast Asian Studies.

Feener, R. Michael, and Mark E. Cammack, eds. 2007. *Islamic Law in Contemporary Indonesia: Ideas and Institutions*. Harvard Series in Islamic Law. Cambridge, MA: Harvard University Press.

Fenwick, Stewart. 2016. *Blasphemy, Islam and the State: Pluralism and Liberalism in Indonesia*. Taylor & Francis.

Fidrus, Multa, and Dicky Christanto. 2013. "S Tangerang Staff to Wear Muslim Attire Once a Week." *The Jakarta Post*, April 24, 2013. https://www.thejakartapost.com/news/2013/04/24/s-tangerang-staff-wear-muslim-attire-once-a-week.html.

Firmansyah, Teguh. 2015. "Muhammadiyah Tolak Hari Santri Nasional, Ini Alasannya." [Muhammadiyah Rejects National Santri Day, Here's Why]. *Republika*, October 17, 2015. https://www.republika.co.id/berita/dunia-islam/islam-nusantara/15/10/17/nwceor377-muhammadiyah-tolak-hari-santri-nasional-ini-alasannya.

REFERENCES

Fischer, Johan. 2009. *Proper Islamic Consumption: Shopping Among the Malays in Modern Malaysia*. Nordic Institute of Asian Studies Press.

Fitzgerald, Timothy. 2000. *The Ideology of Religious Studies*. Oxford University Press.

Fleuß, Dannica, and Gary S. Schaal. 2019. "What Are We Doing When We Are Doing Democratic Theory?" *Democratic Theory* 6 (2): 12–26.

Florentin, Vindry. 2018. "Jokowi: Peran Ulama Dan Santri Menjaga Bhinneka Tunggal Ika." [Jokowi: The Role of Ulama and Santri in Maintaining Unity in Diversity]. *Tempo*, October 21, 2018. https://www.tempo.co/politik/jokowi-peran-ulama-dan-santri-menjaga-bhinneka-tunggal-ika-805215.

Formichi, Chiara. 2014. "Shaping Shi'a Identities in Contemporary Indonesia Between Local Tradition and Foreign Orthodoxy." *Die Welt Des Islams* 54, no. 2 (2014): 212–236, https://doi.org/10.1163/15700607-00542p04.

Formichi, Chiara. 2015. "From Fluid Identities to Sectarian Labels: A Historical Investigation of Indonesia's Shi'I Communities." *Al-Jami'ah: Journal of Islam Studies* 52 (1): 101. https://doi.org/10.14421/ajis.2014.521.101-126.

Formichi, Chiara. 2020. "Performing Shi'ism Between Java and Qom: Education and Rituals." In *Shi'a Minorities in the Contemporary World: Migration, Transnationalism and Multilocality*, edited by Oliver Scharbrodt and Yafa Shanneik. Edinburgh University Press.

Formichi, Chiara, and Michael R. Feener, eds. 2015. *Shi'ism in Southeast Asia: 'Alid Piety and Sectarian Constructions*. Hurst & Company.

Foucault, Michel. (1984) 1992. *The History of Sexuality*. Vol. 2, *The Use of Pleasure*. Penguin Books.

Fox, Colm. 2018. "Candidate-Centric Systems and the Politicization of Ethnicity: Evidence from Indonesia." *Democratization* 25 (7): 1190–1209. https://doi.org/10.1080/13510347.2018.1461207.

Fox, Colm, and Jeremy Menchik. 2011. "The Politics of Identity in Indonesia: Results from Campaign Advertisements." *APSA 2011 Annual Meeting Paper*. https://ink.library.smu.edu.sg/soss_research/2254/.

Fraser, Nancy. 1990. "Rethinking the Public Sphere: A Contribution to the Critique of Actually Existing Democracy." *Social Text* 25/26:56–80.

Freedom House. 2010. "Policing Belief: The Impact of Blasphemy Laws on Human Rights—Malaysia." News release, October 21, 2010. RefWorld database. UNHCR. https://www.refworld.org/docid/4d5a700a2.html.

Frenkel-Brunswik, Else. 1949. "Intolerance of Ambiguity as an Emotional and Perceptual Personality Variable." *Journal of Personality* 18: 108–43. https://doi.org/10.1111/j.1467-6494.1949.tb01236.x.

Fuchs, Christian. 2020. *Nationalism on the Internet: Critical Theory and Ideology in the Age of Social Media and Fake News*. Routledge.

Gaffar, Abdul. 2013. "Jamaah Ahmadiyah Indonesia (JAI) Dalam Perspektif Kekerasan Negara: Dua Kasus Dari Surabaya Jawa Timur Dan Lombok NTB." [Jamaah Ahmadiyah Indonesia (JAI) in the Perspective of State Violence: Two Cases from Surabaya East Java and Lombok NTB]. *Sociology of Islam* 3 (2). https://doi.org/10.15642/jsi.2013.3.2.%p.

Gellner, Ernest. 1983. *Nations and Nationalism*. New Perspectives on the Past. Cornell University Press.

George, Cherian. 2017. *Hate Spin: The Manufacture of Religious Offense and Its Threat to Democracy.* Information Policy Series. MIT Press.

George, Cherian, and Gayathry Venkiteswaran. 2019. *Media and Power in Southeast Asia.* Cambridge University Press.

Gillespie, Piers. 2007. "Current Issues in Indonesian Islam: Analysing the 2005 Council of Indonesian Ulama Fatwa No. 7 Opposing Pluralism, Liberalism and Secularism." *Journal of Islamic Studies* 18 (2): 202–40.

Gita, Amanda. 2012. "MUI Jatim Desak MUI Pusat Keluarkan Fatwa Syiah Sesat" [East Java MUI Urges Central MUI to Issue Heretical Shi'a Fatwa]. *Republika*, January 24, 2012. https://www.republika.co.id/berita/dunia-islam/islam-nusantara/12/01/24/lyasld-mui-jatim-desak-mui-pusat-keluarkan-fatwa-syiah-sesat.

Gita, Amanda, and Heri Ruslan. 2012. "MUI Jatim Desak MUI Pusat Keluarkan Fatwa Syiah Sesat." [East Java MUI Urges Central MUI to Issue Fatwa on Shia Deviant]. *Republika*, January 24, 2012. https://www.republika.co.id/berita/dunia-islam/islam-nusantara/12/01/24/lyasld-mui-jatim-desak-mui-pusat-keluarkan-fatwa-syiah-sesat.

TheGlobalEconomy.com. n.d. "Indonesia: Household Debt to GDP." Accessed October 5, 2021. https://www.theglobaleconomy.com/Indonesia/household_debt_gdp/.

Göle, Nilüfer. 1997. "Secularism and Islamism in Turkey: The Making of Elites and Counter-Elites." *Middle East Journal* 51 (1): 46–58.

Gomes, Robin. 2021. "Malaysian Court: Use of 'Allah' by Christians Not Unlawful." *Vatican News*, March 13, 2021. https://www.vaticannews.va/en/world/news/2021-03/malaysia-high-court-use-allah-word-christians-legal.html.

Gorski, Philip. 2017. "Why Evangelicals Voted for Trump: A Critical Cultural Sociology." *American Journal of Cultural Sociology* 5: 338–354. https://doi.org/10.1057/s41290-017-0043-9https://doi.org/10.1057/s41290-017-0043-9.

Govil, Nitin, and Anirban Kapil Baishya. 2018. "The Bully in the Pulpit: Autocracy, Digital Social Media, and Right-Wing Populist Technoculture." *Communication, Culture and Critique* 11 (1): 67–84. https://doi.org/10.1093/ccc/tcx001.

Gualtieri, Antonio R. 1989. *Conscience and Coercion: Ahmadi Muslims and Orthodoxy in Pakistan.* Essay Series 9. Guernica.

The Guardian. 2016. "Indonesia Bans Gay Emoji and Stickers from Messaging Apps." February 12, 2016. https://www.theguardian.com/world/2016/feb/12/indonesia-bans-gay-emoji-and-stickers-from-messaging-apps.

Guntur W., Yovinus. 2020. "Indonesia: Shia Uprooted by Violence on Madura Island Long to Go Home." *Benar News*, May 20, 2020. https://www.benarnews.org/english/news/indonesian/shia-home-05202020164016.html.

Hadiz, Vedi R. 2010. *Localising Power in Post-Authoritarian Indonesia: A Southeast Asia Perspective.* Stanford University Press.

Hadiz, Vedi R. 2015. *Islamic Populism in Indonesia and the Middle East.* Cambridge University Press.

Hadiz, Vedi R. 2021. "Indonesia's Missing Left and the Islamisation of Dissent." *Third World Quarterly* 42 (3): 599–617. https://doi.org/10.1080/01436597.2020.1768064.

Hadiz, Vedi R., and Richard Robison. 2004. *Reorganising Power in Indonesia: The Politics of Oligarchy in an Age of Markets:* Routledge.

Hallaq, Wael B. 1996. "Ifta and Ijtihad in Sunni Legal Theory." In *Islamic Legal Interpretation: Muftis and Their Fatwas*, edited by Muhammad K. Masud, Brinkley Messick, and David Powers. Harvard Studies in Islamic Law. Harvard University Press.

Hallaq, Wael B. 2009. *An Introduction to Islamic Law.* Cambridge: Cambridge University Press.

Hamayotsu, Kikue. 2012. "Once a Muslim, Always a Muslim: The Politics of State Enforcement of Syariah in Contemporary Malaysia." *South East Asia Research* 20 (3): 399–421. https://doi.org/10.5367/sear.2012.0114.

Hamayotsu, Kikue. 2013. "Towards a More Democratic Regime and Society? The Politics of Faith and Ethnicity in a Transitional Multi-Ethnic Malaysia." *Journal of Current Southeast Asian Affairs* 32 (2): 61–88. https://doi.org/10.1177/186810341303200204.

Hamid, Ahmad Fauzi Abdul. 2005. "'The Banning of Darul Arqam in Malaysia." *Review of Indonesian and Malaysian Affairs* 39 (1): 87–128.

Hamid, Ahmad Fauzi Abdul. 2006. "Southeast Asian Response to the Clampdown on the Darul Arqam Movement in Malaysia, 1994-2000." *Islamic Studies* 45 (1): 83–120.

Hamid, Ahmad Fauzi Abdul. 2014. "Jokowi's Populism in the 2012 Jakarta Gubernatorial Election." *Journal of Current Southeast Asian Affairs* 33 (1): 85–109. https://doi.org/10.1177/186810341403300105.

Hamid, Ahmad Fauzi Abdul, and Che Hamdan Che Mohd Razali. 2015. "The Changing Face of Political Islam in Malaysia in the Era of Najib Razak, 2009–2013." *Sojourn: Journal of Social Issues in Southeast Asia* 30 (2): 301–37. http://www.jstor.org/stable/24779957.

Harsono, Andreas. 2011. "Penyerang Cikeusik" [Cikeusik Striker]. http://www.andreasharsono.net/2011/05/penyerang-cikeusik.html.

Harsono, Andreas. 2016. *Indonesia Religious Discrimination Harms Education Rights.* https://www.hrw.org/news/2016/08/29/indonesia-religious-discrimination-harms-education-rights.

Harsono, Andreas. 2017. "Pemerintah Indonesia Cabut Ancaman Tuntutan Penodaan Terhadap Minoritas Agama: Mahkamah Konstitusi Mengakui 'Kepercayaan Asli' dalam KTP." *Human Rights Watch*, November 7, 2017. https://www.hrw.org/id/news/2017/11/08/311118.

Hasan, Noorhaidi. 2006. *Laskar Jihad: Islam, Militancy, and the Quest for Identity in Post-New Order Indonesia.* Cornell University Press.

Hasani, Asip. 2019. "Hundreds of Displaced Shia Eligible to Vote." *The Jakarta Post*, April 16, 2019. https://www.thejakartapost.com/news/2019/04/16/hundreds-of-displaced-shia-eligible-to-vote.html.

Hasani, Ismail. 2016. "The Decreasing Space for Non-Religious Expression in Indonesia: The Case of Atheism." In *Religion, Law and Intolerance in Indonesia*, edited by Tim Lindsey and Helen Pausacker, 1st ed. London: Routledge. https://doi.org/10.4324/9781315657356.

Hashem, O. 1997. "Jawaban Lengkap Atas Seminar Sehari Tentang Syi'ah." [Complete Answers to the Day Seminar on Shi'a]. *Bangil: YAPI.* September 1997. https://simpatisansyiah.files.wordpress.com/2016/08/omar-hashem-jawaban-lengkap-atas-seminar-sehari-tentang-syiah.pdf.

Hassan, Sharifah Zaleha Syed. 2006. "Political Islam in Malaysia: The Rise and Fall of Al Arqam." *Asian Cultural Studies* 15: 43–55.

Hasyim, Syafiq. 2011. *The Council of Indonesian Ulama (Majelis Ulama Indonesia, MUI) and Religious Freedom*. IRASEC Discussion Papers, no. 12. https://irasec.com/IMG/UserFiles/Files/04_Publications/Notes/The_Council_of_Indonesian_Ulama_Majelis_Ulama_Indonesia_MUI_and_Religious_Freedom.pdf.

Hasyim, Syafiq. 2016. The Council of Indonesian Ulama (MUI) and 'Aqīda-Based Intolerance: A Critical Analysis of Fatwas on Ahmadiyya and "Sepilis." In *Religion, Law and Intolerance in Indonesia*, edited by Tim Lindsey and Helen Pausacker. London: Routledge.

Hasyim, Syafiq. 2013. *The Council of Indonesian Ulama (Majelis Ulama Indonesia, MUI) and Its Role in the Shariatisation of Indonesia*. Institute of Islamic Studies, Freie Universität Berlin.

Hasyim, Syafiq. 2014. "Challenging a Home Country: A Preliminary Account of Indonesian Student Activism in Berlin, Germany." 7 (2): 183–98.

Hasyim, Syafiq. 2015. "Majelis Ulama Indonesia and Pluralism in Indonesia." *Philosophy & Social Criticism* 41 (4–5): 487–95. https://doi.org/10.1177/0191453714566547.

Hasyim, Syafiq. 2018. "Islam Nusantara' and Its Discontents." *RSIS Commentary*, no. 134. https://hdl.handle.net/10356/87868.

Hasyim, Syafiq. 2023. *The Shariatisation of Indonesia: The Politics of the Council of Indonesian Ulama (Majelis Ulama Indonesia, MUI)*. Brill.

Hefner, Robert W. 2000. *Civil Islam: Muslims and Democratization in Indonesia*. Princeton Studies in Muslim Politics. Princeton University Press.

Hefner, Robert W. 2019. "Whatever Happened to Civil Islam? Islam and Democratisation in Indonesia, 20 Years On." *Asian Studies Review* 43 (3): 375–96. https://doi.org/10.1080/10357823.2019.1625865.

Hegarty, Benjamin. 2016. "Seeking a 'Zone of Safety.'" *New Mandala*, April 19, 2016. https://www.newmandala.org/seeking-a-zone-of-safety/.

Helmke, Gretchen, and Steven Levitsky. 2004. "Informal Institutions and Comparative Politics: A Research Agenda." *Perspectives on Politics* 2 (4): 725–40.

Heta News. 2023. "Dinilai Diskriminasi, Aturan Pencatatan Perkawinan Bagi Penduduk Beragama Non-Islam Diuji" [Deemed Discriminatory, Marriage Registration Rules for Non-Islamic Religious Residents Challenged in CourtTransl]. *Heta News*, September, 23, 2023. https://www.hetanews.com/article/274091/dinilai-diskriminasi-aturan-pencatatan-perkawinan-bagi-penduduk-beragama-non-islam-diuji.

Hicks, Jacqueline. 2012. "The Missing Link: Explaining the Political Mobilisation of Islam in Indonesia." *Journal of Contemporary Asia* 42 (1): 39–66. https://doi.org/10.1080/00472336.2012.634640.

Hicks, Jacqueline. 2014. "Heresy and Authority: Understanding the Turn Against Ahmadiyah in Indonesia." *Southeast Asia Research* 22 (3): 321–39.

Hidayatullah. 2012. "Menag: Pemerintah Tidak pada Kapasitas Menilai Sesat atau Tidak" [Minister of Religious Affairs: The Government Doesn't Have the Capacity to Judge Whether or Not It Is Heretical]. *Hidayatullah.com*, August 28, 2012. https://hidayatullah.com/berita/nasional/2012/08/28/61969/menag-pemerintah-tidak-pada-kapasitas-menilai-sesat-atau-tidak.html.

Hill, David T., and Krishna Sen. 1997. "Wiring the Warung to Global Gateways: The Internet in Indonesia." *Indonesia*, no. 63: 67–89. https://doi.org/10.2307/3351511.

Hill, David T., and Krishna Sen, eds. 2005. *The Internet in Indonesia's New Democracy*. Asia's Transformations. RoutledgeCurzon.

Hilmy, Masdar. 2015. "The Political Economy of Sunni-Shi'ah Conflict in Sampang Madura." *Al-Jami'ah: Journal of Islam Studies* 53 (1): 27–51.

Hirschman, Charles. 1987. "The Meaning and Measurement of Ethnicity in Malaysia: An Analysis of Census Classifications." *Journal of Asian Studies* 46 (3): 555–82.

Hodal, Kate. 2012. "Indonesia Jails Shia Cleric for Blasphemy." *The Guardian*, July 12, 2012. https://www.theguardian.com/world/2012/jul/12/indonesia-jails-shia-cleric-blasphemy.

Hoesterey, James Bourk. 2016. *Rebranding Islam: Piety, Prosperity, and a Self-Help Guru*. Studies of the Walter H. Shorenstein Asia-Pacific Research Center. Stanford University Press.

Hoesterey, James Bourk. 2022. "Globalization and Islamic Indigenization in Southeast Asian Muslim Communities." *Islam Nusantara* 3 (2): 1–20. https://doi.org/10.47776/islamnusantara.v3i2.370.

Holst, Frederik. 2007. "(Dis-)Connected History—the Indonesia-Malaysia Relationship." In *Indonesia—The Presence of the Past: A Festschrift in Honour of Ingrid Wessel*, edited by Eva Streifeneder and Antje Missbach. Regiospectra Verlag Berlin.

Holst, Frederik. 2013. *Ethnicization and Identity Construction in Malaysia*. Routledge.

Hooker, M. B. 2003. *Indonesian Islam: Social Change through Contemporary Fatawa*. Honolulu: University of Hawaii Press.

Hooker, M. B., and Virginia Hooker. 2006. "Sharia." In *Voices of Islam in Southeast Asia*, edited by Greg Fealy and Virginia Hooker, 137–206. Singapore: ISEAS Publishing.

Howell, Julia D. 2005. "Muslims, the New Age and Marginal Religions in Indonesia: Changing Meanings of Religious Pluralism." *Social Compass* 52 (4): 473–93. https://doi.org/10.1177/0037768605058151.

Howell, Julia D. 2011 [1982]. "Indonesia: Searching for Consensus: Religion and Societies: Asia and the Middle East." In *Religion and Societies*, edited by Carlo Caldarola. De Gruyter.

Human Rights Commission of Malaysia. 2019. "Study on Discrimination Against Transgender Persons Based in Kuala Lumpur and Selangor: Right to Education, Emplozment, Healthcare, Housing and Dignity." Human Rights Commission of Malaysia. https://www.ohchr.org/sites/default/files/Documents/Issues/SexualOrientation/SocioCultural/NHRI/Malaysia_Human_Rights_Commission.pdf.

Human Rights Watch. 2012. "Indonesia: Shia Cleric Convicted of Blasphemy." *Human Rights Watch*, July 12, 2012. https://www.hrw.org/news/2012/07/12/indonesia-shia-cleric-convicted-blasphemy.

Human Rights Watch. 2013. "In Religion's Name: Abuses Against Religious Minorities in Indonesia." *Human Rights Watch*, February 28, 2013. https://www.hrw.org/report/2013/02/28/religions-name/abuses-against-religious-minorities-indonesia.

Human Rights Watch. 2016. "'These Political Games Ruin Our Lives': Indonesia's LGBT Community Under Threat." August 10, 2016. https://www.hrw.org/report/2016/08/10/these-political-games-ruin-our-lives/indonesias-lgbt-community-under-threat#_ftn22.

Human Rights Watch. 2017. "Indonesia: Journalists Under Assault." April 26, 2017. https://www.hrw.org/news/2017/04/27/indonesia-journalists-under-assault.

Human Rights Watch. 2022a. "'I Don't Want to Change Myself': Anti-LGBT Conversion Practices, Discrimination, and Violence in Malaysia." August 10, 2022. https://www.hrw.org/report/2022/08/10/i-dont-want-change-myself/anti-lgbt-conversion-practices-discrimination-and.

Human Rights Watch. 2022b. "Malaysia: State-Backed Discrimination Harms LGBT People: Criminalization, Conversion Practices Threaten Safety, Dignity." https://www.hrw.org/news/2022/08/10/malaysia-state-backed-discrimination-harms-lgbt-people?utm_source=chatgpt.com.

Humprecht, Edda, Michael Amsler, Frank Esser, and Peter van Aelst. 2024. "Emotionalized Social Media Environments: How Alternative News Media and Populist Actors Drive Angry Reactions." *Political Communication* 41 (4): 559–87. https://doi.org/10.1080/10584609.2024.2350416.

Huntington, Samuel P. 1984. "Will More Countries Become Democratic?" *Political Science Quarterly* 99 (2): 193–218.

Huq, Maimuna. 1999. *New Media in the Muslim World: The Emerging Public Sphere*. Edited by Dale F. Eickelman and Jon W. Anderson. Indiana Series in Middle East Studies. Indiana University Press.

Hurd, Elizabeth Shakman. 2015. *Beyond Religious Freedom: The New Global Politics of Religion*. Princeton University Press.

Husaini, Adian. 2010. *Pluralisme Agama—Musuh Agama-Agama*. [Religious Pluralism—The Enemy of Religions]. Ketua Dewan Da'wah Islamiyah Indonesia.

Hussin, Iza. 2008. "Islam, Ethnicity and the Problem of Mixed Legality: Two Malaysian Cases." *Yearbook of Islamic and Middle Eastern Law Online* 14 (1): 83–93. https://doi.org/10.1163/22112987-91000208.

Ibrahim, Anwar. 1977. "Islam—Penyelesaian Kepada Masalah Masyarakat Majmuk" (*Islam—Solutions to the Problems of a Multicultural Society*). Ucapan Dasar, Muktamar ABIM. Cited in Peletz, Michael G. 2005. *Remaking Muslim Politics: Pluralism, Contestation, Democratization*. Princeton: Princeton University Press.

Ibrahim, Anwar. 2005. "Media Freedom in South-East Asia—Shattering the Myth." Speech, Society of Publishers in Asia 2005 Awards for Editorial Excellence Gala Dinner, Hong Kong, May 26, 2005. https://www.sopasia.com/wp-content/uploads/2012/01/Anwar-Speech.pdf.

Ibrahim, Nur Amali. 2016. "Homophobic Muslims: Emerging Trends in Multireligious Singapore." *Comparative Studies in Society and History* 58 (4): 955–81.

Ichsan, A. Syalaby. 2013. "712 Warga Ahmadiyah Ucapkan Syahadat" [712 Ahmadiyya Confess]. *Republika*, May 21, 2013. https://republika.co.id/berita/dunia-islam/islam-nusantara/13/05/21/mn4lm2-712-warga-ahmadiyah-ucapkan-syahadat.

Ichwan, Moch Nur. 2005. "'Ulamā,' State and Politics: Majelis Ulama Indonesia After Suharto." *Islamic Law and Society* 12 (1): 45–72.

Ichwan, Moch Nur. 2012. "The Local Politics of Orthodoxy: The Majelis Ulama Indonesia in the Post-New Order Banten." *Journal of Indonesian Islam* 6 (1). https://jiis.uinsby.ac.id/index.php/JIIs/article/view/103.

Ichwan, Moch Nur. 2013. "Towards a Puritanical Moderate Islam: The Majelis Ulama Indonesia and the Politics of Religious Orthodoxy." In *Contemporary Developments in Indonesian Islam: Explaining the "Conservative Turn,"* edited by Martin van Bruinessen. ISEAS–Yusof Ishak Institute.

Ichwan, Moch Nur. 2016. "MUI, Gerakan Islamis, Dan Umat Mengambang." [MUI, Islamist Movements, and the Floating Umma]. *Maarif* 11 (2): 87–104.

Ichwan, Moch Nur. 2021. "Forbidden Visibility: Queer Activism, Shariʻa Sphere and Politics of Sexuality in Aceh." *Studia Islamika* 28 (2).

Ichwan, Moch Nur, and Martin Slama. 2022. "Reinterpreting the First Pillar of the Nation: (Dis)Continuities of Islamic Discourses About the State Ideology in Indonesia." *Politics, Religion & Ideology* 23 (4): 457–74. https://doi.org/10.1080/21567689.2022.2139687.

International Crisis Group. 2008. "Indonesia: Implications of the Ahmadiyah Decree." Briefing no. 78, Asia, July 7, 2008. https://www.crisisgroup.org/asia/south-east-asia/indonesia/indonesia-implications-ahmadiyah-decree.

Jäger, Siegfried. (1993) 2004. *Kritische Diskursanalyse: Eine Einführung.* Edition DISS. Unrast.

Jain, Sagaree, and Neela Ghoshal. 2018. "Malaysia Should Find 'Right Path' on LGBT Rights." Human Rights Watch, August 7, 2018. https://www.hrw.org/news/2018/08/07/malaysia-should-find-right-path-lgbt-rights.

The Jakarta Post. 2009a. "Cult Leader Lia Eden Gets Two and a Half Years for Religious Blasphemy." June 2, 2009. https://culteducation.com/group/1014-gods-kingdom-of-eden/11971-cult-leader-lia-eden-gets-two-and-a-half-years-for-religious-blasphemy.html.

The Jakarta Post. 2009b. "Muhammadiyah Intellectuals Need Meaningful Dialog." November 22, 2009. http://muhammadiyahstudies.blogspot.com/2009/11/muhammadiyah-intellectuals-need.html.

The Jakarta Post. 2010. "Discourse: 'Sharia' Rules a Manipulation of Religious Norms: Senior Cleric."

The Jakarta Post. 2011a. "Ahmadis Make Plea for No Ban." February 15, 2011. https://www.thejakartapost.com/news/2011/02/15/ahmadis-make-plea-no-ban.html.

The Jakarta Post. 2011b. "Heavier Sentence Sought for Ahmadi Man." August 3, 2011. https://www.thejakartapost.com/news/2011/08/03/heavier-sentence-sought-ahmadi-man.html.

The Jakarta Post. 2012a. "Gramedia Burns Books 'Defaming' Prophet." June 14, 2012. https://www.thejakartapost.com/news/2012/06/14/gramedia-burns-books-defaming-prophet.html.

The Jakarta Post. 2012b. "Next in Line, Anti-Porn Task Forces for Provinces, Regencies." March 17, 2012. Retrieved via Internet Archive's Wayback Machine. https://web.archive.org/web/20120316175749/http://www.thejakartapost.com/news/2012/03/14/next-line-anti-porn-task-forces-provinces-regencies.html.

The Jakarta Post. 2012c. "Sampang Shiites Forced to Convert to Sunni: Kontras." November 6, 2012. https://www.thejakartapost.com/news/2012/11/06/sampang-shiites-forced-convert-sunni-kontras.html.

The Jakarta Post. 2016a. "Luhut Agrees LGBTs Need Rights Protected but Says They Are Diseased." February 16, 2016. https://www.thejakartapost.com/news/2016/02/16/luhut-agrees-lgbts-need-rights-protected-says-they-are-diseased.html.

The Jakarta Post. 2016b. "MUI Wants Law to Ban LGBT Activities." February 17, 2016. https://www.thejakartapost.com/news/2016/02/17/mui-wants-law-ban-lgbt-activities.html.

The Jakarta Post. 2018. "Kontras Condemns Police for Obstructing Burial of Sampang Shiite." June 18, 2018. https://www.thejakartapost.com/news/2018/06/15/kontras-condemns-police-for-obstructing-burial-of-sampang-shiite.html.

The Jakarta Post. 2020. "New Religious Affairs Minister Vows to Protect Shia, Ahmadiyah." December 26, 2020. https://www.thejakartapost.com/news/2020/12/25/new-religious-affairs-minister-vows-to-protect-shia-ahmadiyah.html.

Jansen, Wikke. 2025. *Queer Mobilities in Indonesia: Religion, Activism, and Everyday Life.* Liverpool University Press.

JawaPos.com. 2017. "Aliran Kepercayaan Muncul Di KTP, MUI: Negeri Ini Mundur Ke Zaman Batu." [Beliefs appear on ID cards, MUI: This Country is Back to the Stone Age]. https://www.jawapos.com/nasional/01115534/aliran-kepercayaan-muncul-di-ktp-mui-negeri-ini-mundur-ke-zaman-batu.

Jayne, Tamara. 2018. "Wan Azizah: LGBT Lifestyle Can Exist in Malaysia If They Don't 'Glamourise' It." *Says,* August 20, 2018. https://says.com/my/news/dpm-lgbt-lifestyle-can-exist-if-kept-private-and-not-glamourised.

Johnson, Carol. 2011. "Gendering the Nation-State: Canadian and Comparative Perspectives, Yasmeen Abu-Laban, Ed., Vancouver: UBC Press.

Johnson, Constance. 2017. *Indonesia: Province Drafts Regulation Banning Provocative Clothing.* Library of Congress. https://www.loc.gov/item/global-legal-monitor/2017-12-28/indonesia-province-drafts-regulation-banning-provocative-clothing/.

Jones, Carla. 2010. "Materializing Piety: Gendered Anxieties About Faithful Consumption in Contemporary Urban Indonesia." *American Ethnologist* 37 (4): 617–37. https://doi.org/10.1111/j.1548-1425.2010.01275.x.

Jones, Sidney. 2016. "The Anti-Shi'a Movement in Indonesia." Institute for Policy Analysis of Conflict. Report no. 27, April 27, 2016. http://file.understandingconflict.org/file/2016/04/IPAC_Report_27.pdf.

Jordan, Lisa, and Peter van Tuijl. 2012. *NGO Accountability: Politics, Principles and Innovations.* Taylor & Francis.

JPNN. 2011. "18 Pengikut Ahmadiyah Tobat" [18 Ahmadiyah Followers Repent]. *JPNN.com,* March 31, 2011. https://www.jpnn.com/news/18-pengikut-ahmadiyah-tobat?page=2.

JPNN. 2012. "Konflik Sampang Bukan Soal Sunni Dan Syiah" [The Sampang Conflict Is Not About Sunnis and Shiites]. *JPNN.com,* August 28, 2012. https://www.jpnn.com/news/konflik-sampang-bukan-soal-sunni-dan-syiah.

Jurriens, Edwin, and Ross Tapsell, eds. 2017. *Digital Indonesia: Connectivity and Divergence.* ISEAS–Yusof Ishak Institute.

Kahin, George McTurnan. 1952. *Nationalism and Revolution in Indonesia.* Cornell University Press.

Kaldor, Mary. 2003. "The Idea of Global Civil Society." *International Affairs* 79 (3): 583–593.

Kaltwasser, Cristóbal Rovira. 2012. "The Ambivalence of Populism: Threat and Corrective for Democracy." *Democratization* 19 (2): 184–208.

Kamarulnizam, Abdullah. 2003. *The Politics of Islam in Contemporary Malaysia*. Universiti Kebangsaan Malaysia.

Kaptein, Nico J.G. 2004. "The Voice of the 'Ulamâ': Fatwa and Religious Authority in Indonesia." *Archivesde sciences sociales des religions*, no. 125 (January–March): 115–30.

Karaman, Hayreddin. 2014. "İslam, Demokrasi Ve Medine Vesikası." [Islam, Democracy and the Council of Medina]. *Yeni Şafak*, May 28, 2014. https://www.yenisafak.com/yazarlar/hayrettin-karaman/islam-demokrasi-ve-medine-vesikasi-53922.

Kaviraj, Sudipta. 2010. "On Thick and Thin Religion: Some Critical Reflections on Secularisation Theory." In *Religion and the Political Imagination*, edited by Ira Katznelson and Gareth S. Jones. Cambridge University Press.

Kayane, Yuka. (2020). "Understanding Sunni-Shi'a sectarianism in contemporary Indonesia: A different voice from Nahdlatul Ulama under pluralist leadership." *Indonesia and the Malay World*, 48 (140), 78–96. https://doi.org/10.1080/13639811.2020.1675277.

Kholid, Idham. 2015. "Usai Kirab, Massa Menuju Istiqlal Untuk Deklarasi Hari Santri Oleh Jokowi." [After the Kirab, the crowd headed to Istiqlal for the declaration of Santri Day by Jokowi]. *Detiknews*, October 22, 2015. https://news.detik.com/berita/d-3050618/usai-kirab-massa-menuju-istiqlal-untuk-deklarasi-hari-santri-oleh-jokowi.

Kine, Phelim. 2013. "Putting a Smiley Face on Indonesia's Religious Intolerance." *HuffPost*, August 20, 2013. https://www.huffpost.com/entry/washingtons-statue-of-hyp_b_3785936.

Kine, Phelim. 2014. "Indonesia's Growing Religious Intolerance." Human Rights Watch, December 14, 2014. https://www.hrw.org/news/2014/12/04/indonesias-growing-religious-intolerance.

Klinken, Gerry van, and Henk Schulte Nordholt, eds. 2007. *Renegotiating Boundaries: Local Politics in Post-Suharto Indonesia*. Leiden–Boston: Brill. https://library.oapen.org/handle/20.500.12657/34661.

Kompas. 2005. "Fatwa MUI memicu kontroversi." [MUI fatwa triggers controversy], July 30, 2005. https://www.mail-archive.com/ppiindia@yahoogroups.com/msg25783.html. Accessed May 22, 2025.

KOMPAS.com. 2018. "Tak Akan Ada E-KTP Khusus Warga Penghayat Kepercayaan." [There Will Be No Special e-ID Card for People of Indigenous Faiths]. January 20, 2018. https://nasional.kompas.com/read/2018/01/20/11243591/tak-akan-ada-e-ktp-khusus-warga-penghayat-kepercayaan#.

Koran Madura. 2013. "Pelaku Kerusuhan Syiah Sampang, Saniwan Dihukum Delapan Bulan" [Perpetrators of the Sampang Shia Riot, Saniwan Sentenced to Eight Months]. February 6, 2013. https://www.koranmadura.com/2013/02/pelaku-kerusuhan-sampang-saniwan-dihukum-delapan-bulan/.

Krämer, Gudrun. 2013. "Modern but Not Secular: Religion, Identity and the Ordre Public in the Arab Middle East." *International Sociology* 28 (6): 629–44. https://doi.org/10.1177/0268580913503875.

Krämer, Gudrun, and Sabine Schmidtke. 2006. *Speaking for Islam: Religious Authorities in Muslim Societies*. Social, Economic, and Political Studies of the Middle East and Asia. Brill.

Künkler, Mirjam. 2011. "Zum Verhältnis Staat-Religion und der rolle islamischer intellektueller in der indonesischen Reformasi." In *Religion in Diktatur und Demokratie: Zur Bedeutung Religiöser Werte, Praktiken und Institutionen in politischen Transformationsprozessen*, edited by Simon Fuchs and Stephanie Garling. Lit Verlag.

Künkler, Mirjam. 2018. "The Bureaucratization of Religion in Sotheast Asia: Expanding or Restricting Religious Freedom?" *Journal of Law and Religion* 33 (2): 192–96. https://doi.org/10.1017/jlr.2018.38.

Künkler, Mirjam, John Madeley, and Shylashri Shankar, eds. 2018. *A Secular Age Beyond the West: Religion, Law and the State in Asia, the Middle East and North Africa*. Cambridge Studies in Social Theory, Religion and Politics. Cambridge University Press.

Kurzman, Charles, ed. 1998. *Liberal Islam: A Sourcebook*. Oxford University Press.

La Batu, Safrin. 2017. "Jokowi Accused of Promoting Secularism." *The Jakarta Post*, March 27, 2017. https://www.thejakartapost.com/news/2017/03/27/jokowi-accused-of-promoting-secularism.html.

Lane, Max. 2001. "How the IMF Gang Wrecked Indonesia." *Socialist Worker*, September 14, 2001. https://socialistworker.org/2001/377/377_08_Indonesia.php.

Lang, Sabine. 2013. *NGOs, Civil Society, and the Public Sphere*. Cambridge University Press.

Larasati, Rachmi Diyah. 2013. *The Dance That Makes You Vanish: Cultural Reconstruction in Post-Genocide Indonesia*. University of Minnesota Press.

Lauth, Hans-Joachim. 2000. "Informal Institutions and Democracy." *Democratization* 7: 21–50.

Leong, Trinna, and Al-Zaquan Amer Hamzah. 2015. "Malaysia's Anwar Jailed for Five Years After Losing Appeal in Sodomy Trial." Reuters, February 11, 2015. https://www.reuters.com/article/world/malaysias-anwar-jailed-for-five-years-after-losing-appeal-in-sodomy-trial-idUSKBN0LD2F5/.

Lewis, Bernard. 1996. "Islam and Liberal Democracy: A Historical Overview." *Journal of Democracy* 7 (2): 52–63.

Lim, Danny, and Tong Siong Yee. 2007. "Pie in the Sky." *Sun2Surf Malaysian Source for News & Lifestyle*, February 19, 2007. Retrieved via Internet Archive's Wayback Machine. https://web.archive.org/web/20070219062618/http://www.sun2surf.com/article.cfm?id=10057.

Lim, Ida. 2021. "Explainer: High Court's 96-Page Judgment on Why Malaysia's 1986 'Allah' Ban Was Quashed in Jill Ireland's Case." *Malay Mail*, March 24, 2021. https://www.malaymail.com/news/malaysia/2021/03/24/explainer-high-courts-96-page-judgment-on-why-malaysias-1986-allah-ban-was/1960449.

Lim, Merlyna. 2012. "The League of Thirteen: Media Concentration in Indonesia." Research report. Tempe, AZ: Participatory Media Lab at Arizona State University. https://merlyna.wordpress.com/wp-content/uploads/2019/02/lim_the_league_of_thirteen_media_2012.pdf.

Lim, Merlyna. 2017. "Freedom to Hate: Social Media, Algorithmic Enclaves, and the Rise of Tribal Nationalism in Indonesia." *Critical Asian Studies* 49 (3): 411–27. https://doi.org/10.1080/14672715.2017.1341188.

Lim, Merlyna. 2018. "Challenging Technological Utopianism." *CJC* 43 (3). https://cjc.utppublishing.com/doi/full/10.22230/cjc.2018v43n3a3393.

Lindsey, Tim. 2012. "Monopolising Islam: The Indonesian Ulama Council and State Regulation of the 'Islamic Economy.'" *Bulletin of Indonesian Economic Studies* 48 (2): 253–74. https://doi.org/10.1080/00074918.2012.694157.

Liow, Joseph Chiyong, ed. 2009. *Piety and Politics: Islamism in Contemporary Malaysia*. Oxford University Press.

Lipman-Blumen, Jean. 1976. "Toward a Homosocial Theory of Sex Roles: An Explanation of the Sex Segregation of Social Institutions." *Signs: Journal of Women in Culture and Society* 1 (3, Part 2): 15–31.

Liputan6. 2010. "Polisi Tak Beri Izin Kongres Lesbian-Gay." March 24, 2010. https://www.liputan6.com/news/read/269247/polisi-tak-beri-izin-kongres-lesbian-gay.

Liputan6. 2011a. "Enam Jemaat Ahmadiyah Kembali Memeluk Islam" [Six Ahmadiyya Congregations Return to Islam]. April 8, 2011. https://www.liputan6.com/news/read/328483/enam-jemaat-ahmadiyah-kembali-memeluk-islam.

Liputan6. 2011b. "Enam Orang Ahmadiyah Masuk Islam" [Six Ahmadis Convert to Islam]. March 10, 2011. https://www.liputan6.com/news/read/323644/enam-orang-ahmadiyah-masuk-islam.

Lombok Today. 2016. "10 KK Pengikut Ahmadiyah Bertobat." [10 Families of Ahmadiyah Followers Repent]. March 29, 2016. https://lomboktoday.co.id/2016/03/29/10-kk-pengikut-ahmadiyah-bertobat-1921.html.

Luizard, Pierre-Jean. 2002. *La formation de l'Irak contemporain: Le rôle politique des ulémas chiites à la fin de la domination ottomane et au moment de la construction de l'Etat irakien*. New ed. CNRS Editions.

Lumanauw, Novi, and Ezra Sihite. 2010. "SBY Now Welcoming of Foreign NGOs: SBY's New Stance Belies His Administration and Party's Hostility to Foreign NGOs." *Jakarta Globe*, June 10, 2010.

Mackinnon, Ian. 2012. "Atheist Indonesian in Protective Custody After Being Beaten by Mob." *The Telegraph*, January 20, 2012. https://www.telegraph.co.uk/news/worldnews/asia/indonesia/9027145/Atheist-Indonesian-in-protective-custody-after-being-beaten-by-mob.html.

Mackintosh-Smith, Tim. 2019. *Arabs: A 3,000-Year History of Peoples, Tribes and Empires*. Yale University Press.

Madjid, Nurcholish. 1994. "Menatap Masa Depan Islam."[Looking to the Future of Islam]. *Jurnal Ilmu dan Kebuduyaan Ulumul Qur'an* V (1).

Mahmood, Saba. 2012. "Religious Freedom, the Minority Question, and Geopolitics in the Middle East." *Comparative Studies in Society and History* 54 (2): 418–46. https://doi.org/10.1017/S0010417512000096.

Majelis Ulama Indonesia. 2005. "Fatwa Majelis Ulama Indonesia Nomor: Aliran Ahmadiyah." 11/MUNAS VII/MUI/15/2005. July 28, 2005. https://almanhaj.or.id/2330-fatwa-majelis-ulama-indonesia-aliran-ahmadiyah.html.

Majelis Ulama Indonesia. 2014. "Fatwa Majelis Ulama Indonesia: Lesbian, Gay, Sodomi, Dan Pencabulan." 57 Tahun 2014. December 31, 2014. Retrieved via Internet Archive's Wayback Machine. https://web.archive.org/web/20190403134704/https://lampung.kemenag.go.id/files/lampung/file/file/MUI/xdob1460683589.pdf.

Makin, Al. 2016. *Challenging Islamic Orthodoxy: Accounts of Lia Eden and Other Prophets in Indonesia*. Popular Culture, Religion and Society. A Social-Scientific Approach 1. Springer International.

REFERENCES

Malaka, Tan. (1925) 2019. *Menuju Republik Indonesia*. [Toward the Republic of Indonesia]. Sega Arsy.

Mamdani, Mahmood. 2002. "Good Muslim, Bad Muslim: A Political Perspective on Culture and Terrorism." *American Anthropologist* 104 (3): 766–75. https://doi.org/10.1525/aa.2002.104.3.766.

Mamdani, Mahmood. 2004. *Good Muslim, Bad Muslim: America, the Cold War, and the Roots of Terror*. Pantheon Books.

Mandal, Sumit K. 2017. *Becoming Arab: Creole Histories and Modern Identity in the Malay World*. Asian Connections. Cambridge University Press.

Mandaville, Peter, Farish A. Noor, Alexander Horstmann, Dietrich Reetz, Ali Riaz, Animesh Roul, Noorhaidi Hasan, Ahmad Fauzi Abdul Hamid, Rommel C. Banlaoi, and Joseph C. Liow, eds. 2009. *Transnational Islam in South and Southeast Asia*. National Bureau of Asian Research.

Manow, Philip. 2018. *Die Politische Ökonomie des Populismus*. [*The Political Economy of Populism*]. Suhrkamp Verlag.

Marbun, Julkifli. 2015. "Setara: Tolikara Incident Violated Human Right of Religious Freedom." *Republika*, July 21, 2015. https://en.republika.co.id/berita/en/national-politics/15/07/21/nrsyzy-setara-tolikara-incident-violated-human-right-of-religious-freedom?.

Marwick, Alice, and Rebecca Lewis. 2017. "Media Manipulation and Disinformation Online." Data & Society Research Institute Report. May 15, 2017. Last modified November 16, 2021. https://datasociety.net/library/media-manipulation-and-disinfo-online/.

Mashabi, Sania. 2020. "Menag Yaqut Akan Lindungi Hak Beragama Warga Syiah Dan Ahmadiyah" [Minister of Religion Yaqut Will Protect Religious Rights of Shia and Ahmadiyya Residents]. *KOMPAS.com*, December 26, 2020. https://nasional.kompas.com/read/2020/12/26/09561771/menag-yaqut-akan-lindungi-hak-beragama-warga-syiah-dan-ahmadiyah.

Massad, Joseph. 2002. "Re-Orienting Desire: The Gay International and the Arab World." *Public Culture* 14 (2): 361–86.

Massad, Joseph. 2008. *Desiring Arabs*. Chicago University Press.

Masuzawa, Tomoko. 2005. *The Invention of World Religions: Or, How European Universalism Was Preserved in the Language of Pluralism*. Chicago University Press.

Mayer, Tamar. 2012. *Gender Ironies of Nationalism: Sexing the Nation*. Routledge.

Mazzoleni, Gianpietro. 1995. "Towards a 'Videocracy'?" *European Journal of Communication* 10 (3): 291–319. https://doi.org/10.1177/0267323195010003001.

McAllister, Ian. 2012. "Lauri Karvonen, the Personalisation of Politics: A Study of Parliamentary Democracies." *Australian Journal of Political Science* 47 (3): 523–24. https://doi.org/10.1080/10361146.2012.704891.

McDaniel, June. 2010. "Agama Hindu Dharma Indonesia as a New Religious Movement: Hinduism Recreated in the Image of Islam." *Nova Religio: The Journal of Alternative and Emergent Religions* 14 (1): 93–111. https://doi.org/10.1525/nr.2010.14.1.93.

McGlynn Scanlon, Megan, and Tuti Alawiyah. 2015. "The NGO Sector in Indonesia: Context, Concepts and an Updated Profile." Cardno report prepared for the Department of Foreign Affairs and Trade. https://www.ksi-indonesia.org/assets/uploads/original/2020/02/ksi-1580493585.pdf.

Means, Gordon Paul. 2009. *Political Islam in Southeast Asia*. Lynne Rienner.

Menchik, Jeremy. 2014. "Productive Intolerance: Godly Nationalism in Indonesia." *Comparative Studies in Society and History* 56 (3): 591–621. https://doi.org/10.1017/S0010417514000267.

Menchik, Jeremy. 2016. *Islam and Democracy in Indonesia: Tolerance Without Liberalism*. Cambridge Studies in Social Theory, Religion and Politics. Cambridge University Press.

Menchik, Jeremy. 2022. "The Politics of the Fatwa: Islamic Legal Authority in Modern Indonesia." *Indonesia* 114 (1): 75–97.

Metro TV News. 2012. "MUI: Syiah Tak Sesat." [MUI: Shiites Are Not Lost]. January 1, 2012. https://www.metrotvnews.com/read/newsvideo/2012/01/01/142507/MUI-Syiah-Tak-Sesat/6.

Meyer, Thomas, and Lewis P. Hinchman. 2002. *Media Democracy: How the Media Colonize Politics*. Polity Press.

Meyer, Verena. 2024. "Grave Matters: Ambiguity, Modernism, and the Quest for Moderate Islam in Indonesia." *Journal of the American Academy of Religion* 92 (1): 160–79. https://doi.org/10.1093/jaarel/lfae061.

Mietzner, Marcus. 2012. "Indonesia's Democratic Stagnation: Anti-Reformist Elites and Resilient Civil Society." *Democratization* 19 (2): 209–29.

Mietzner, Marcus. 2015. "Reinventing Asian Populism: Jokowi's Rise, Democracy, and Political Contestation in Indonesia." Policy Studies 72. https://www.eastwestcenter.org/publications/reinventing-asian-populism-jokowis-rise-democracy-and-political-contestation-in.

Mietzner, Marcus, and Burhanuddin Muhtadi. 2019. "The Mobilisation of Intolerance and Its Trajectories: Indonesian Muslims' Views of Religious Minorities and Ethnic Chinese." In *Contentious Belonging*, edited by Greg Fealy and Ronit Ricci. ISEAS Publishing.

Mietzner, Marcus, and Burhanuddin Muhtadi. 2020. "The Myth of Pluralism: Nahdlatul Ulama and the Politics of Religious Tolerance in Indonesia." *Contemporary Southeast Asia* 42 (1): 58–84. https://doi.org/10.1355/cs42-1c.

Miichi, Ken. 2016. "Minority Shi'a Groups as a Part of Civil Society in Indonesia." *Middle Eastern Institute*, August 20, 2016. https://www.mei.edu/publications/minority-shia-groups-part-civil-society-indonesia.

Miichi, Ken, and Yuka Kayane. 2020. "The Politics of Religious Pluralism in Indonesia: The Shi'a Response to the Sampang Incidents of 2011–12." *TRaNS: Trans-Regional and -National Studies of Southeast Asia* 8 (1): 51–64. https://doi.org/10.1017/trn.2019.12.

Millie, Julian, Dede Syarif, and Moch Fakhruroji. 2019. "Islamic Preaching and State Regulation in Indonesia." *CILIS Policy Papers* 18. Melbourne: Centre for Indonesian Law, Islam and Society, Melbourne Law School. https://law.unimelb.edu.au/centres/cilis/research/publications/cilis-policy-papers/islamic-preaching-and-state-regulation-in-indonesia

Moore, Sally Falk. 1987. "Explaining the Present: Theoretical Dilemmas in Processual Ethnography." *American Ethnologist* 14 (4): 727–36.

Mosse, George L. 1985. *Nationalism and Sexuality Respectability and Abnormal Sexuality in Modern Europe*. New York: Howard Fertig.

Moustafa, Tamir. 2018. *Constituting Religion. Islam, Liberal Rights, and the Malaysian State*. Cambridge University Press.

Mudzhar, M. Atho'. 1993. *The Fatwas of the Council of Indonesian Ulama: A Study of Islamic Legal Thought in Indonesia, 1975–1988*. INIS.

Mueller, Dominik. 2014. *Islam, Politics and Youth in Malaysia: The Pop-Islamist Reinvention of PAS*. Routledge.

Mujani, Saiful. 2020. "Intolerant Democrat Syndrome: The Problem of Indonesian Democratic Consolidation." *Jurnal Politik* 6 (1): 5. https://doi.org/10.7454/jp.v6i1.1006.

MUI Digital. 2024. "Ketua MUI Bidang Fatwa Sampaikan 10 Kriteria Aliran Sesat." [Head of MUI Fatwa Division Presents 10 Criteria for Deviant Sects]. *Majelis Ulama Indonesia*, March 26, 2024. https://www.mui.or.id/baca/berita/ketua-mui-bidang-fatwa-sampaikan-10-kriteria-alirat-sesat.

Muwahidah, Siti Sarah. 2020. "For the Love of Ahl Al-Bayt: Negotiating Shi'ism in Indonesia." PhD diss., Emory University. https://etd.library.emory.edu/concern/etds/j9602186x.

Nadhirah, Hanny. 2023. "Mewujudkan Hak Pendidikan Agama Untuk Semua Siswa." [Realizing the Right to Religious Education for All Students]. Program Studi Agama dan Lintas Budaya, Universitas Gadjah Mada. October 24, 2023. https://crcs.ugm.ac.id/mewujudkan-hak-pendidikan-agama-untuk-semua-siswa/.

Nagata, Judith. 1980. "Religious Ideology and Social Change: The Islamic Revival in Malaysia." *Pacific Affairs* 53 (3): 405–39.

Najib, Muhammad Ainun., Dudung Abdurrahman, Ahmad Muttaqin. "From Resistance to Accommodation: The Emergence and Controversy of Jaringan Intelektual Muda Muhammadiyah (JIMM)". *Religio: Jurnal Studi Agama-agama* 13, no. 2 (2023): 209–229. DOI:10.15642/religio.v13i2.2467.

Nandy, Ashis. 1988. "The Politics of Secularism and the Recovery of Religious Tolerance." *Alternatives* 13(2):177–94. https://doi.org/10.1177/030437548801300202.

Nashih, Nashrullah. 2013. "Ratusan Jamaah Ahmadiyah Tasikmalaya Bertobat." [Hundreds of Ahmadiyya Members in Tasikmalaya Repent]. *Republika*, May 20, 2013. http://www.republika.co.id/berita/dunia-islam/islam-nusantara/13/05/20/mn3810-ratusan-jamaah-ahmadiyah-tasikmalaya-bertobat.

Nashrullah, Nashih. 2019. "Peran NU Dan Muhammadiyah Diapresiasi Di Eropa." [Role of NU and Muhammadiyah Appreciated in Europe]. *Republika*, June 22, 2019. https://www.republika.co.id/berita/dunia-islam/islam-nusantara/19/06/22/pthnnu320-peran-nu-dan-muhammadiyah-diapresiasi-di-eropa.

Nasrudin, Dede A. 2008. *Koreksi Terhadap Pemahaman Ahmadiyah Dalam Masalah Kenabian*. [Corrections to Ahmadiyya Understanding of the Issue of Prophethood]. Irsyad Baitus Salam.

Nasution, Adnan Buyung. 2016. "Religious Freedom, Minority Rights and the State of Democracy in Indonesia." In *Religion, Law and Intolerance in Indonesia*, edited by Tim Lindsey and Helen Pausacker. London: Routledge. https://doi.org/10.4324/9781315657356.

National Human Rights Commission of the Republic of Indonesia (Komisi Nasional Hak Asasi Manusia Republik Indonesia). 2015. Laporan Akhir Tahun Pelapor Khusus Kebebasan Beragama Dan Berkeyakinan2015 [Year-end report by the Special Rapporteur on Freedom of Religion and Belief]. Accessed May 20, 2025. https://www.komnasham.go.id/files/20150908-pelapor-khusus-kebebasan-beragama-$DFNW.pdf.

National Legislative Bodies / National Authorities. 1945. Constitution of the Republic of Indonesia (Last Amended 2002). UNHCR, RefWorld. Accessed March 20, 2023. https://www.refworld.org/docid/46af43f12.html.

Nawawi, Imam. 2014. *Riyad as Salihin: The Gardens of the Righteous*. Blue Dome.

Nelson, Matthew. 2018. "Religious Freedom and Public Order: Fundamental-Rights Lawfare and the Construction of Majoritarian Identities in Pakistan and Malaysia." Centre of South Asian Studies: Seminars, November 15, 2018. https://sms.cam.ac.uk/media/2865906.

Neo, Jaclyn L. 2014. "What's in a Name? Malaysia's 'Allah' Controversy and the Judicial Intertwining of Islam with Ethnic Identity." *International Journal of Constitutional Law* 12 (3): 751–68. https://doi.org/10.1093/icon/mou050.

Nira, Yuval-Davis. 1997. *Gender and Nation*. SAGE Publications.

Noer, Deliar. 1973. *The Modernist Muslim Movement in Indonesia, 1900–1942*. Oxford University Press.

Noor, Farish A. 2009. "Islamist Networks and Mainstream Politics in South and Southeast Asia." In *Transnational Islam in South and Southeast Asia: Movements, Networks, and Conflict Dynamics*, edited by Ali Riaz, Alexander Horstmann, Farish A. Noor, Noorhaidi Hasan, Animesh Roul, Dietrich Reetz, Rommel C. Banlaoi, Ahmad Fauzi Abdul Hamid, Joseph Chinyong Liow, and Peter Mandaville. NBR Project Report, April 1, 2009. The National Bureau of Asian Research. https://www.nbr.org/publication/islamist-networks-and-mainstream-politics-in-south-and-southeast-asia/.

Noor, Farish A. 2011. "Understanding Anti-Malaysianism in Indonesia." *Aliran*, October 16, 2011.

Noor, Farish A. 2014a. "Introduction. Islamism in a Mottled Nation: The Story of PAS." In *The Malaysian Islamic Party PAS 1951–2013*. Amsterdam University Press.

Noor, Farish A. 2014b. *The Malaysian Islamic Party PAS 1951–2013: Islamism in a Mottled Nation*. Amsterdam University Press.

Noor, Nina Mariani. 2017. *Ahmadi Women Resisting Fundamentalist Persecution: A Case Study on Active Group Resistance in Indonesia*. Globethics.net Theses No. 27. Geneva: Globethics.net. https://core.ac.uk/download/582408168.pdf.

Noorani, Yaseen. 2010. "The Moral Transformation of Femininity and the Rise of the Public-Private Distinction in Colonial Egypt." In *Culture and Hegemony in the Colonial Middle East*, edited by Yaseen Noorani. Palgrave Macmillan.

NU Online. 2005a. "Fatwa MUI Diminta Dicabut." August 2, 2005. https://www.nu.or.id/warta/fatwa-mui-diminta-dicabut-0xx1I.

NU Online. 2005b. "MUI Jelaskan Fatwa Soal Pluralisme Dan Ahmadiyah Kepada DPR." [MUI Explains Fatwa on Pluralism and Ahmadiyya to DPR]. August 31, 2005. https://www.nu.or.id/warta/mui-jelaskan-fatwa-soal-pluralisme-dan-ahmadiyah-kepada-dpr-nijrt.

NU Online. 2008. "Gus Dur: Silakan Mempropogandakan Ahmadiyah Salah!" [Please, the Propaganda Against the Ahmadiyah Is Wrong!]. June 9, 2008. Retrieved via Internet Archive's Wayback Machine. https://web.archive.org/web/20220731093716/https://jurnal.kominfo.go.id/index.php/jppki/article/view/581.

NU Online. 2011. "Polri Duga Ada Provokasi Dari Kelompok Ahmadiyah" [Police Suspected There Was Provocation from the Ahmadiyah Group]. February

7, 2011. https://www.nu.or.id/post/read/26729/polri-duga-ada-provokasi-dari-kelompok-ahmadiyah.

Nugraha, Irwan. 2013. "20 Orang Tinggalkan Ahmadiyah" [Twenty People Leave Ahmadiyya]." *KOMPAS.com*, May 20, 2013. https://regional.kompas.com/read/2013/05/20/18551599/Puluhan.Jemaah.Ahmadiyah.Tasik.Tobat.

Nugroho, Nd. 2020. "60 Ribu Warga Jawa Timur Kantongi KTP Penghayat Kepercayaan." [Sixty Thousand East Java Residents Hold Belief Practitioner ID Cards]. Jatimnet.com. March 12, 2020. https://jatimnet.com/60-ribu-warga-jawa-timur-kantongi-ktp-penghayat-kepercayaan.

Nugroho, Yanuar, Leonardus K. Nugraha, Shita Laksmi, Mirta Amalia, Dinita Andriani Putri, and Dwitri Amalia. 2013. "Media and the Vulnerable in Indonesia: Accounts from the Margins." Report series. Engaging Media, Empowering Society: Assessing Media Policy and Governance in Indonesia Through the Lens of Citizens' Rights. Centre for Innovation Policy and Governance. https://cipg.or.id/wp-content/uploads/2015/06/MEDIA-3-Media-Vulnerable-2012.pdf.

OECD. 2018. *A Broken Social Elevator? How to Promote Social Mobility.* https://www.oecd.org/en/publications/broken-elevator-how-to-promote-social-mobility_9789264301085-en.html.

Okafor, Obiora Chinedu. 2006. *Legitimizing Human Rights NGOs: Lessons from Nigeria.* Africa World Press.

Olle, John. 2009. "The Majelis Ulama Indonesia Versus 'Heresy': The Resurgence of Authoritarian Islam." In *State of Authority: The State in Society in Indonesia*, edited by Gerry van Klinken and Joshua Barker. 95–116. Ithaca, NY: Cornell University Press. https://doi.org/10.7591/9781501719448-005.

Ostwald, Kai. 2017. "Malaysia's Electoral Process: The Methods and Costs of Perpetuating UMNO Rule." October 6, 2017. SSRN. https://papers.ssrn.com/sol3/papers.cfm?abstract_id=3048551.

Ottaway, Marina, and Thomas Carothers. 2000. *Funding Virtue: Civil Society Aid and Democracy Promotion.* Carnegie Endowment for International Peace.

Pabbajah, M. Taufiq Hidayat, Hasse Jubba, Irwan Abdullah, and Juhansar Andi Latief. 2021. "From the Scriptural to the Virtual: Indonesian Engineering Students Responses to the Digitalization of Islamic Education." *Teaching Theology & Religion.* https://doi.org/10.1111/teth.12581.

Pamungkas, Cahyo. 2015. "Social Resilience of Minority Group: Study on Syiah Refugees in Sidoarjo and Ahmadiyah Refugees in Mataram." *Ulumuna* 19 (2): 251–78.

Pamungkas, Cahyo. 2017. *Mereka Yang Terusir: Studi Tentang Ketahanan Sosial Pengungsi Ahmadiyah Dan Syiah Di Indonesia.* Yayasan Pustaka Obor Indonesia.

Panggabean, Samsu Rizal. 2016. "Policing Sectarian Conflict in Indonesia: The Case of Shi'ism." In *Religion, Law and Intolerance in Indonesia.* Routledge.

Pariser, Eli. 2011. *The Filter Bubble: What the Internet Is Hiding from You.* Penguin Press.

Parker, Andrew, Mary Russo, Doris Sommer, and Patricia Yaeger. 2018. *Nationalisms & Sexualities.* Routledge.

Parlina, Ina. 2013. "Gamawan Describes FPI as an 'Asset' to the Nation." *The Jakarta Post*, October 25, 2013. https://www.thejakartapost.com/news/2013/10/25/gamawan-describes-fpi-asset-nation.html.

Parlina, Ina, and Wahyoe Boediwardhana. 2013. "Sampang Shiites Evicted from Madura." *The Jakarta Post*, June 21, 2013. https://www.thejakartapost.com/news/2013/06/21/sampang-shiites-evicted-madura.html.

Pauly, Madison, and Henry Carnell. 2024. "First They Tried to 'Cure' Gayness. Now They're Fixated on 'Healing' Trans People." *Mother Jones*. July 2024. https://www.motherjones.com/politics/2024/05/conversion-therapy-lgbtq-anti-trans-gay-gender-affirming-care.

Peletz, Michael G. 2006. "Transgenderism and Gender Pluralism in Southeast Asia Since Early Modern Times." *Current Anthropology* 47 (2): 309–40. https://doi.org/10.1086/498947.

Peletz, Michael G. 2009. *Gender Pluralism: Southeast Asia Since Early Modern Times*. Routledge.

Pelletier, Alexandre. 2021. "Competition for Religious Authority and Islamist Mobilization in Indonesia." *Comparative Politics* 53, no. 3: 525–47.

Pemberton, John. 1994. *On the Subject of Java*. Cornell University Press.

Peterson, Daniel. 2018. "Blasphemy, Human Rights, and the Case of Ahok." In *The Asian Yearbook of Human Rights and Humanitarian Law*, edited by Javaid Rehman and Ayesha Shahid. Brill/Nijhoff.

Peterson, Daniel. 2020. *Islam, Blasphemy, and Human Rights in Indonesia the Trial of Ahok*. Routledge Contemporary Southeast Asia Series. Routledge.

Peterson, Daniel, and Saskia Schäfer. 2021. "Who Are Indonesia's Islamist Majoritarians and How Influential Are They?" In *Religion and Identity Politics: Global Trends and Local Realities*, edited by Mathew Mathews and Melvin Tay. World Scientific Publishing.

Pintak, Lawrence, and Budi Setiyono. 2011. "The Mission of Indonesian Journalism: Balancing Democracy, Development, and Islamic Values." *International Journal of Press/Politics* 16 (2): 185–209. https://doi.org/10.1177/1940161210391784.

Pisani, Elizabeth. 2014. *Indonesia Etc. Exploring the Improbable Nation*. W. W. Norton.

Pitakasari, Ajeng Ritzki. 2011. "Alhamdulillah . . . Jamaah Ahmadiyah Sekecamatan Cisurupan Bertaubat" [Alhamdulillah . . . The Ahmadiyya Jamaat of Cisurupan Subdistrict Repents]. *Republika*, March 30, 2011. https://www.republika.co.id/berita/nasional/hukum/lix7zf/dunia-islam/islam-nusantara/11/03/30/liv23u-alhamdulillah-jamaah-ahmadiyah-sekecamatan-cisurupan-bertaubat.

Polda Metro Jaya. 2020. *Webinar Silaturahmi Nasional Lintas Agama*. Streamed live on YouTube, December 26, 2020. https://www.youtube.com/watch?v=Z1aEgNmn8fQ&ab_channel=PoldaMetroJaya.

Poskota News. 2016. "MUI: Fatwa Itu Rekomendasi Ke Pemerintah." [MUI: Fatwas are recommendations to the government]. *Poskota News*, December 20, 2016. http://poskotanews.com/2016/12/20/mui-fatwa-itu-rekomendasi-ke-pemerintah/.

Prihandoko. 2012. "NU: Syiah Tidak Sesat, Hanya Berbeda" [NU: Shia Are Not Astray, Just Different]. *Tempo*, August 29, 2012. https://nasional.tempo.co/read/1519333/wakil-ketua-mpr-audit-seluruh-bumn-penerima-modal-pmn.

Przeworski, Adam. 2018. *Why Bother with Elections?* Polity.

Purbo, Onno W. 2017. "Narrowing the Digital Divide." In *Digital Indonesia: Connectivity and Divergence*, edited by Edwin Jurriens and Ross Tapsell. ISEAS–Yusof Ishak Institute.

Putra, Idhamsyah Eka, Ali Mashuri, and Esti Zaduqisti. 2015. "Demonising the Victim: Seeking the Answer for How a Group as the Violent Victim Is Blamed." *Psychology and Developing Societies* 27 (1): 31–57. https://doi.org/10.1177/0971333614564741.

Putro, Galang Aji. 2016. "Kapolri: Fatwa MUI Bukan Hukum Positif, Ormas Jangan Buat Masyarakat Takut." [Police Chief: MUI fatwas are not positive law, mass organizations should not scare the public]. *Detiknews*, December 19, 2016. https://news.detik.com/berita/d-3374898/kapolri-fatwa-mui-bukan-hukum-positif-ormas-jangan-buat-masyarakat-takut.

Qantara.de. 2021. "Malaysia Seeks Stricter Sharia Laws for "Promoting LGBT Lifestyle." *Qantara.de*, 2021. https://qantara.de/en/article/pride-month-2021-malaysia-seeks-stricter-sharia-laws-promoting-lgbt-lifestyle.

Qur'an. 2004. Oxford University Press.

Rahardjo, Dawam. 2005. "Kala MUI Mengharamkan Pluralisme" [When the MUI Forbids Pluralism]. *Koran Tempo*, August 1, 2005. https://m.tempo.co/read/news/2005/08/01/05564630/kala-mui-mengharamkan-pluralisme.

Rakhmani, Inaya. 2014. "Mainstream Islam: Television Industry Practice and Trends in Indonesian Sinetron." *Asian Journal of Social Science* 42 (3–4): 435–66. https://doi.org/10.1163/15685314-04203009.

Rakhmani, Inaya. 2016. *Mainstreaming Islam in Indonesia: Television, Identity, and the Middle Class*. Palgrave Macmillan.

Ramstedt, Martin, ed. 2004. *Hinduism in Modern Indonesia: A Minority Religion Between Local, National, and Global Interests*. Routledge.

Ramstedt, Martin. 2019. "Politics of Taxonomy in Postcolonial Indonesia: Ethnic Traditions Between Religionisation and Secularisation." *Historical Social Research* 44 (3): 264–89.

Rao, Rahul. 2015. "Global Homocapitalism." *Radical Philosophy* 194: 38–49. https://www.radicalphilosophy.com/article/global-homocapitalism.

Rathje, Steve, Jay J. van Bavel, and Sander van der Linden. 2021. "Out-Group Animosity Drives Engagement on Social Media." *Proceedings of the National Academy of Sciences* 118 (26): e2024292118. https://doi.org/10.1073/pnas.2024292118.

Redman, Eva-Lotta E., ed. 2008. *Conflict, Violence, and Displacement in Indonesia*. Cornell University Press.

Reetz, Dietrich. 2009. *Migrants, Mujahidin, Madrassa Students: The Diversity of Transnational Islam in Pakistan*. NBR Project Report, April 2009, 53–77. The National Bureau of Asian Research (NBR).

Regional Office of the Ministry of Religious Affairs, Jambi Province. 2011. "MUI Jambi Tolak Ahmadiyah" [Jambi MUI Rejects Ahmadiyah]. News release. March 29, 2011. https://jambi.kemenag.go.id/news/499/mui-jambi-tolak-ahmadiyah.html.

Reis, Jack. 1997. *Ambiguitätstoleranz: Beiträge Zur Entwicklung Eines Persönlichkeitskonstruktes*. Asanger.

Religion News (blog). 2005. "Sect Leader, Followers Arrested." December 30, 2005. https://www.religionnewsblog.com/13122/Sect-leader--followers-arrested.

Renaldi, Adi. 2017. "This Law Is at the Center of Indonesia's LGBT Arrests." *VICE*, May 24, 2017. https://www.vice.com/en/article/this-law-is-at-the-center-of-indonesias-lgbt-arrests/.

Republic of Indonesia. 2014. *Undang-Undang Republik Indonesia Nomor 33 Tahun 2014 tentang Jaminan Produk Halal (UU JPH)* [Law of the Republic of Indonesia Number 33 of 2014 concerning Halal Product Assurance]. Jakarta: President of the Republic of Indonesia.

REFERENCES

Rheingold, Howard. 2014. *Net Smart: How to Thrive Online*. MIT Press.

Ridwan, Rinaldi, and Joyce Wu. 2018. "'Being Young and LGBT, What Could Be Worse?' Analysis of Youth LGBT Activism in Indonesia: Challenges and Ways Forward." *Gender & Development* 26 (1): 121–38. https://doi.org/10.1080/13552074.2018.1429103.

Rijkers, Monique. 2020. "Menjadi Ateis Di Negeri Religius Indonesia." [Becoming Atheist in the Religious Country of Indonesia]. *Deutsche Welle*, March 21, 2020. https://www.dw.com/id/menjadi-ateis-di-negeri-religius-indonesia/a-52757730.

Rinaldo, Rachel. 2013. *Mobilizing Piety: Islam and Feminism in Indonesia*. Oxford University Press.

Rizieq, Al-Habib Muhammad, Aru Syaif Assadullah, Rahimi Sabirin, and M. Shodiq Ramadhan. 2011. *Hancurkan Liberalisme: Tegakkan Syariat Islam*. 1st ed. Jakarta: Suara Islam Press.

Robinson, Francis. 2009. "Crisis of Authority: Crisis of Islam?" *Journal of the Royal Asiatic Society* 19 (03): 339. https://doi.org/10.1017/S1356186309009705.

Robinson, Geoffrey B. 2018. *The Killing Season: A History of the Indonesian Massacres, 1965–66*. With the assistance of E. D. Weitz. Princeton University Press.

Rodríguez, Diego García, and Ben Murtagh. 2022. "Situating Anti-LGBT Moral Panics in Indonesia." *Indonesia and the Malay World* 50 (146): 1–9. https://doi.org/10.1080/13639811.2022.2038871.

Ropi, Ismatu. 2017. *Religion and Regulation in Indonesia*. Springer.

Rudnyckyj, Daromir. 2012. "Spiritual Economies: Islam and Neoliberalism in Contemporary Indonesia." *Cultural Anthropology* 24 (1): 104–41.

Rumadi. 2015. *Islamic Post-Traditionalism in Indonesia*. ISEAS–Yusof Ishak Institute.

Saat, Norshahril. 2015. "Nahdlatul Ulama's 33rd Congress: Ma'ruf Amin's Rise and Its Impact on Indonesia's Traditionalist Islam." *ISEAS Perspective*, no. 48. Singapore: ISEAS–Yusof Ishak Institute. https://www.iseas.edu.sg/wp-content/uploads/pdfs/ISEAS_Perspective_2015_48.pdf.

Saat, Norshahril, and Ahmad Najib Burhani, eds. 2020. *The New Santri: Challenges to Traditional Religious Authority in Indonesia*. ISEAS–Yusof Ishak Institute.

Sapiie, Marguerite Afra. 2017. "Govt Takes over Halal Label." *The Jakarta Post*, October 14, 2017. https://www.thejakartapost.com/news/2017/10/14/govt-takes-over-halal-label.html.

Satrio, Abu Luthfi. 2015. "Maklumat MUI Jabar: Syiah Ancaman NKRI, Melarang Asyuro Wewenang Pemerintah" [MUI Jabar Information: Shiites Threaten NKRI, Prohibit Asyuro Government Authority]. *Hidayatullah*, October 21, 2015. https://www.hidayatullah.com/berita/nasional/read/2015/10/21/81498/maklumat-mui-jabar-syiah-ancaman-nkri-melarang-asyuro-wewenang-pemerintah.html.

Schäfer, Saskia. 2015. "New Practices of Self-Representation: The Use of Online Media by Ahmadiyya and Shia Communities in Indonesia and Malaysia." In *New Media Configurations and Socio-Cultural Dynamics in Asia and the Arab World*, edited by Nadja-Christina Schneider and Carola Richter. Nomos.

Schäfer, Saskia. 2016. "Forming 'Forbidden' Identities Online: Atheism in Indonesia." *ASEAS, Austrian Journal of South-East Asian Studies* 9 (2): 253–68. https://doi.org/10.14764/10.ASEAS-2016.2-5.

Schäfer, Saskia. 2018. "Ahmadis or Indonesians? The Polarization of Post-Reform Public Debates on Islam and Orthodoxy." *Critical Asian Studies* 50 (1): 16–36. https://doi.org/10.1080/14672715.2017.1404925.

REFERENCES

Schäfer, Saskia. 2019. "Democratic Decline in Indonesia: The Role of Religious Authorities." *Pacific Affairs* 92 (2): 235–55. https://doi.org/10.5509/2019922235.
Schäfer, Saskia. 2024. "Political Homophobia: The Rise of Anti-Queer Rhetoric in Indonesia and Turkey." *Journal of Language and Politics* 23. https://doi.org/10.1075/jlp.22050.sch.
Schick, Irvin Cemil. 2010. *The Harem as Gendered Space and the Spatial Reproduction of Gender*. Duke University Press.
Schmitt, Arno. 2003. "Gay Rights Versus Human Rights: A Response to Joseph Massad." *Public Culture* 15 (3): 587–91. https://muse.jhu.edu/pub/4/article/47188.
Schneider, Kristina. 2024. *"Unity in Diversity Is Not for Us": Lesbi and Trans Men Navigating Gender, Desire, and Islam in Java, Indonesia*. Göttingen: Universitätsverlag Göttingen. https://doi.org/10.17875/gup2024-2640.
Schroeder, Ralph. 2019. "Digital Media and the Entrenchment of Right-Wing Populist Agendas." *Social Media + Society* 5 (4): 205630511988532. https://doi.org/10.1177/2056305119885328.
Scott, James C. 1998. *Seeing Like a State: How Certain Schemes to Improve the Human Condition Have Failed*. Yale University Press.
Sebastian, Leonard C., Syafiq Hasyim, and Alexander R. Arifianto, eds. 2020. *Rising Islamic Conservatism in Indonesia: Islamic Groups and Identity Politics*. Routledge.
Şen, Mustafa. 2010. "Transformation of Turkish Islamism and the Rise of the Justice and Development Party." *Turkish Studies* 11 (1): 59–84. https://doi.org/10.1080/14683841003747047.
Septian, Anton, and Musthofa Bisri. 2012. "Love Before Religion." *Asia Views*, January 11, 2012. http://www.asiaviews.org/index.php?option=com_content&view=article&id=33936:love-before-religion&catid=1:headlines&Itemid=2.
Setijadi, Charlotte. 2017. *Ahok's Downfall and the Rise of Islamist Populism in Indonesia*: ISEAS–Yusof Ishak Institute.
Sevea, Teren. 2024. "Keramat: Muḥammad's Heirs and Nodes of a Multi-Centered Islam in Southeast Asia." *International Journal of Islam in Asia* 4 (1–2): 48–74. https://doi.org/10.1163/25899996-20241068.
Shah, Shanon. 2009. "Living with the Ahmadiyah." *The Nut Graph*, September 29, 2009. https://thenutgraph.com/living-with-the-ahmadiyah/.
Shaikh, Farzana. 2018. "Pakistan's Quest for Identity: Contesting Islam." *The Conversation*, May 6, 2018. https://theconversation.com/pakistans-quest-for-identity-contesting-islam-95571.
Shankar, Athi. 2013. "Burn 'Allah' Bibles, Perkasa Chief to Muslims: Proclaiming He Is Not Instigating Communal Tensions, Ibrahim Ali Says It's the Only Way to Stop Non-Muslims from Stirring Sensitivities." *FMT news*, January 19, 2013. Retrieved via Internet Archive's Wayback Machine. https://web.archive.org/web/20160328032918/http://www.freemalaysiatoday.com/category/nation/2013/01/19/burn-allah-bibles-perkasa-chief-tells-muslims/.
Shorty Awards. n.d. "From the 8th Annual Shorty Awards HRC's #LoveWins Hashtag Goes Viral; Celebrates Marriage Equality Victory." Accessed March 27, 2023. https://shortyawards.com/8th/hrcs-lovewins-hashtag-goes-viral-celebrates-marriage-equality-victory.
Sidel, John T. 2006. *Riots, Pogroms, Jihad: Religious Violence in Indonesia*. Cornell University Press.

REFERENCES

Sidel, John T. 2021. *Republicanism, Communism, Islam: Cosmopolitan Origins of Revolution in Southeast Asia*. Cornell University Press.

Sihombing, Uli Parulian. 2012. *Ketidakadilan Dalam Beriman: Hasil Monitoring Kasus-Kasus Penodaan Agama Dan Ujaran Kebencian Atas Dasar Agama Di Indonesia*. [Injustice in Faith: Results of Monitoring Cases of Blasphemy and Religious Hatred in Indonesia]. With assistance from Siti Aminah, Muhammad Khoirul Roziqin. Indonesian Legal Resource Center.

Sila, Muhammad Adlin. 2020. "Revisiting Nu-Muhammadiyah in Indonesia." *Indonesia and the Malay World* 48 (142): 304–22. https://doi.org/10.1080/13639811.2020.1823150.

Sila, Muhammad Adlin. 2021. *Being Muslim in Indonesia: Religiosity, Politics and Cultural Diversity in Bima*. Amsterdam University Press.

SINDOnews. 2019. "Satu Keluarga Penganut Ahmadiyah di Pangandaran Masuk Islam" [An Ahmadiyya Family in Pangandaran Converts to Islam]. January 7, 2019. https://daerah.sindonews.com/artikel/jabar/3923/satu-keluarga-penganut-ahmadiyah-di-pangandaran-masuk-islam.

Sirry, Mun'im. 2013. "Fatwas and Their Controversy: The Case of the Council of Indonesian Ulama (MUI)." *Journal of Southeast Asian Studies* 44 (1): 100–17.

Skjerdal, Terje S. 2003. "Research on Brown Envelope Journalism in the African Media." *African Communication Research* 3 (3): 367–407. https://ccms.ukzn.ac.za/Files/articles/ACR/Bribery%20and%20corruption%20in%20African%20journalism.pdf#page=7.

Slama, Martin. 2017. "Social Media and Islamic Practice: Indonesian Ways of Being Digitally Pious." In *Digital Indonesia: Connectivity and Divergence*, edited by Edwin Jurriens and Ross Tapsell, 146–62. Books and Monographs. ISEAS–Yusof Ishak Institute.

Slama, Martin. 2018. "Practising Islam Through Social Media in Indonesia." *Indonesia and the Malay World* 46 (134): 1–4. https://doi.org/10.1080/13639811.2018.1416798.

Slama, Martin. 2019. "Jokowi and the Preachers: An Ambiguous Pre-Election Relationship." *New Mandala*, April 8, 2019. https://www.newmandala.org/jokowi-and-the-preachers-an-ambiguous-pre-election-relationship/.

Slama, Martin. 2021. "Tracing Digital Divides in Indonesian Islam: Ambivalences of Media and Class." *Cyberorient* 15 (1): 290–313. https://doi.org/10.1002/cyo2.15.

Slama, Martin. 2023. "Conspicuous Pilgrimages and the Politics of Public/Private: Social Media Representations of Indonesia's Muslim Middle Class." In *The "Crossed-Out God" in the Asia-Pacific: Religious Efficacy of Public Spheres*, edited by Julian Millie. Springer Nature Singapore.

Smith, Matt Baillie, and Katy Jenkins. 2011. "Disconnections and Exclusions: Professionalization, Cosmopolitanism and (Global?) Civil Society." *Global Networks* 11 (2): 160–79.

Smith-Hefner, Nancy J. 2019. *Islamizing Intimacies: Youth, Sexuality, and Gender in Contemporary Indonesia*. University of Hawai'i Press.

Sodikin, Amir. 2016. "Fatwa MUI, Hukum Positif, Dan Hukum Aspiratif." [MUI Fatwa, Positive Law, and Aspirational Law]. *KOMPAS.com*, December 22, 2016. https://nasional.kompas.com/read/2016/12/22/17262341/fatwa.mui.hukum.positif.dan.hukum.aspiratif.

Soedirgo, Jessica. 2018. "Informal Networks and Religious Intolerance: How Clientelism Incentivizes the Discrimination of the Ahmadiyah in Indonesia." *Citizenship Studies* 22 (2): 191–207. https://doi.org/10.1080/13621025.2018.1445490.

Soedirgo, Jessica. 2020. The threat of small things: Patterns of repression and mobilization against micro-sized groups in indonesia. Ph.D. diss., University of Toronto (Canada), https://www.proquest.com/dissertations-theses/threat-small-things-patterns-repression/docview/2425651647/se-2. Accessed May 22, 2025.

Sofjan, Dicky. 2016. "Minoritization & Criminalization of Shia Islam in Indonesia." *Journal of South Asian and Middle Eastern Studies* 39 (2): 29–44. https://dx.doi.org/10.1353/jsa.2016.0002.

Solahudin, Dindin, and Moch Fakhruroji. 2020. "Internet and Islamic Learning Practices in Indonesia: Social Media, Religious Populism, and Religious Authority." *Religions* 11 (1). https://doi.org/10.3390/rel11010019.

Spohr, Dominic. 2017. "Fake News and Ideological Polarization." *Business Information Review* 34 (3): 150–60. https://doi.org/10.1177/0266382117722446.

The Star. 2006. "Former Inspector Takes over Sky Kingdom Sect." September 26, 2006. https://www.thestar.com.my/news/nation/2006/09/26/former-inspector-takes-over-sky-kingdom-sect/.

Steenbrink, Karel A. 1998. "Muslim-Christian Relations in the Pancasila State of Indonesia." *Muslim World* 88 (3–4): 320–52. https://doi.org/10.1111/j.1478-1913.1998.tb03664.x.

Stepan, Alfred. 2000. "Religion, Democracy, and the 'Twin Tolerations.'" *Journal of Democracy* 11 (4): 37–57. https://doi.org/10.1353/jod.2000.0088.

Stokes, Patricia R. 1998. "Gendered Nations: Nationalisms and Gender Order in the Long Nineteenth Century—International Comparisons: Berlin, March 25–28, 1998." *Historical Social Research / Historische Sozialforschung* 23, no. 4 (86): 149–59.

Strassler, Karen. 2019. *Demanding Images.* Democracy, Mediation, and the Image-Event in Indonesia. Duke University Press.

Styawan, Aji. 2020. "New Religious Affairs Minister Vows to Protect Shia, Ahmadiyah." *The Jakarta Post*, December 26, 2020. https://www.thejakartapost.com/news/2020/12/25/new-religious-affairs-minister-vows-to-protect-shia-ahmadiyah.html.

Styawan, Aji. 2022. "Prove It, Groups Say of Minister's Religious Inclusivity Promise." *The Jakarta Post*, December 27, 2022. https://www.thejakartapost.com/news/2020/12/27/prove-it-groups-say-of-ministers-religious-inclusivity-promise.html.

Suaedy, Ahmad. 2016. "The Inter-Religious Harmony (KUB) Bill Vs Guaranteeing Freedom of Religion and Belief in Indonesian Public Debate."

Suaedy, Ahmad. 2018. "Gus Dur, Islam Nusantara, & Kewarganegaraan Bineka: Penyelesaian Konflik Aceh & Papua 1999–2001. Jakarta: Gramedia Pustaka Utama."

Subijanto, Rianne. 2025. *Communication Against Capital: Red Enlightenment at the Dawn of Indonesia*. Ithaca, NY: Southeast Asia Program Publications, Cornell University Press.

Sudibyo, Agus, and Nezar Patria. 2013. "The Television Industry in Post-Authoritarian Indonesia." *Journal of Contemporary Asia* 43 (2): 257–75. https://doi.org/10.1080/00472336.2012.757434.

Sulistya, Rahma. 2017. "Annas: Pemerintah Diminta Berhati-Hati Dengan Ajaran Syiah." [Annas: Government Asked to Be Careful with Shia Teachings]. *Republika*, September 7, 2017. https://www.republika.co.id/berita/ovwn50282/annas-pemerintah-diminta-berhatihati-dengan-ajaran-syiah.

Su-Lyn, Boo, and Emily Ding. 2013. "Zul Noordin Asks Why Hindu Gods Did Not Stop Flood." *The Malaysian Insider*, March 30, 2013. Retrieved via Internet Archive's Wayback Machine. https://web.archive.org/web/20130331002238/http://www.themalaysianinsider.com/malaysia/article/zul-noordin-asks-why-hindu-gods-did-not-stop-flood/.

Sunandar, Wahyu. 2011. *Fatwa Majelis Ulama Indonesia (MUI) tentang Nikah Beda Agama dan Respon para Pemuka Agama terhadapnya*. Thesis, Fakultas Ushuluddin dan Filsafat, UIN Syarif Hidayatullah Jakarta. https://repository.uinjkt.ac.id/dspace/handle/123456789/4082.

Sunstein, Cass R. 2003. *Why Societies Need Dissent*. Harvard University Press.

Sunstein, Cass R. 2018. *#Republic: Divided Democracy in the Age of Social Media*. Princeton University Press.

Sun2Surf Malaysian Source for News & Lifestyle. 2005. "58 Followers of Ayah Pin Arrested." July 21, 2005. Retrieved via Internet Archive's Wayback Machine. http://web.archive.org/web/20090912190159/www.sun2surf.com/article.cfm?id=10254.

Suprapto, Hadi. 2011. "Ramai-Ramai Melarang Ahmadiyah" [Many Prohibit Ahmadiyah]. *Viva News*, March 5, 2011. https://www.viva.co.id/ragam/fokus/207831-ramai-ramai-melarang-ahmadiyah.

Suryakusuma, Julia. 2011. *State Ibuism: The Social Construction of Womanhood in New Order Indonesia*. Forewords by David Reeve and Robert Cribb. Komunitas Bambu.

Suryana, A'an. 2017. "Discrepancy in State Practices: The Cases of Violence Against Ahmadiyah and Shi'a Minority Communities During the Presidency of Susilo Bambang Yudhoyono." *Al-Jami'ah J. Islam Stud.* 55 (1): 71–104. https://doi.org/10.14421/ajis.2017.551.71-104.

Suryana, A'an. 2018. "Indonesian Presidents and Communal Violence Against Non-Mainstream Faiths." *South East Asia Research* 26 (2): 147–60. https://doi.org/10.1177/0967828X18769393.

Suryana, A'an. 2019. "State Officials' Entanglement with Vigilante Groups in Violence Against Ahmadiyah and Shi'a Communities in Indonesia." *Asian Studies Review* 43 (3): 475–92. https://doi.org/10.1080/10357823.2019.1633273.

Suryanto. 2011. "Dimyati: Ahmadiyah, Bubarkan Atau Agama Sendiri" [Dimyati: Ahmadiyah, Disband or Own Religion]. *Antara News*, February 11, 2011. https://www.antaranews.com/berita/245673/dimyati-ahmadiyah-bubarkan-atau-agama-sendiri.

Susmiyati, M. Pd. I. 2016. "LGBT Skenario Kapitalis Global Hancurkan Generasi." [LGBT Global Capitalist Scenario to Destroy a Generation]. *Panjimas*, March 12, 2016. https://www.panjimas.com/citizens/2016/03/12/lgbt-skenario-kapitalis-global-hancurkan-generasi/.

Syarif, Dede. 2023. "Minority Islam in Indonesia's Public Square: The Shia Emergence and Its Effects." In *The "Crossed-Out God" in the Asia-Pacific: Religious Efficacy of Public Spheres*, edited by Julian Millie. Springer Nature.

Talbot, Ian. 2016. *A History of Modern South Asia: Politics, States, Diasporas*. Yale University Press.

Tampubolon, Hans David. 2011. "Police Protection Not Enough for Ahmadis." *The Jakarta Post*, February 9, 2011. http://www.thejakartapost.com/news/2011/02/09/%E2%80%98police-protection-not-enough-ahmadis%E2%80%99.html.

Tapsell, Ross. 2010. "Stopping the Flow." *Inside Indonesia*, July 10, 2010. https://www.insideindonesia.org/stopping-the-flow.

Tapsell, Ross. 2012. "Old Tricks in a New Era: Self-Censorship in Indonesian Journalism." *Asian Studies Review* 36 (2): 227–45. https://doi.org/10.1080/10357823.2012.685926.

Tapsell, Ross. 2014. "Platform Convergence in Indonesia: Challenges and Opportunities for Media Freedom." *Convergence* 21 (2): 182–97. https://doi.org/10.1177/1354856514531527.

Tapsell, Ross. 2017. *Media Power in Indonesia: Oligarchs, Citizens and the Digital Revolution*. Media, Culture and Communication in Asia-Pacific Societies. Rowman & Littlefield.

Taunuzi, Iwan, and Anwar Guna Sadat. 2011. "MUI Harap Lia Eden Kembali Ke Ajaran Islam." *Tribunnews.com*, April 15, 2011. https://www.tribunnews.com/nasional/2011/04/15/mui-harap-lia-eden-kembali-ke-ajaran-islam.

Tayeb, Azmil, and Meredith L. Weiss. 2024. "Islamist Government in Malaysia Under PAS: Ideology, Policies, and Competition." *Asian Studies Review*, 1–21. https://doi.org/10.1080/10357823.2024.2383682.

The Telegraph. 2016. "Ariffin Mohammed, Cult Leader—Obituary." May 5, 2016. https://www.telegraph.co.uk/obituaries/2016/05/05/ariffin-mohammed-cult-leader--obituary/.

Telle, Kari. 2017. "Faith on Trial: Blasphemy and 'Lawfare' in Indonesia." *Ethnos* 13 (2): 1–19. https://doi.org/10.1080/00141844.2017.1282973.

Tempo. 1988. "Menuduh Quran Yang Beda." [Accusing a Different Quran]. January 23, 1988. https://www.tempo.co/politik/menuduh-quran-yang-beda-1058789.

Tempo. 2011a. "Enam Jamaah Ahmadiyah Tewas Diserang Warga Cikeusik." February 6, 2011. https://nasional.tempo.co/read/311404/enam-jamaah-ahmadiyah-tewas-diserang-warga-cikeusik.

Tempo. 2011b. "FPI Surabaya Bubarkan Diskusi Lintas Agama." [FPI Surabaya Disperses Interfaith Discussion]. January 13, 2011. https://nasional.tempo.co/read/306097/fpi-surabaya-bubarkan-diskusi-lintas-agama.

Tempo. 2011c. "Shia Islamic Boarding School Set on Fire in Madura." December 30, 2011. https://en.tempo.co/read/374513/shia-islamic-boarding-school-set-on-fire-in-madura.

Tempo. 2012. "Komnas HAM Anggap Polisi Tak Serius Lindungi Syiah." [Komnas HAM Considers Police Not Seriously Protecting Shia]. August 28, 2012. https://nasional.tempo.co/read/426002/komnas-ham-anggap-polisi-tak-serius-lindungi-syiah.

Tempo. 2013. "Wawancara Menteri Agama Soal Syiah Di Sampang." [Interview with the Minister of Religion on Shiites in Sampang]. July 27, 2013. https://nasional.tempo.co/read/500167/wawancara-menteri-agama-soal-syiah-di-sampang.

Tempo. 2016. "Sekolah Tolak Tuntutan Siswa Penganut Kepercayaan Naik Kelas." [School Rejects Student's Demand to Be Promoted to the Next Grade]. July 31, 2016. https://nasional.tempo.co/read/792074/sekolah-tolak-tuntutan-siswa-penganut-kepercayaan-naik-kelas.

Tempo. 2017. "Minister Supports Ahmadiyah Followers to Have ID Cards." July 24, 2017. https://en.tempo.co/read/894079/minister-supports-ahmadiyah-followers-to-have-id-cards.

Thajib, Ferdiansyah. 2022. "Discordant Emotions: The Affective Dynamics of Anti-LGBT Campaigns in Indonesia." *Indonesia and the Malay World* 50 (146): 10–32. https://doi.org/10.1080/13639811.2022.2005312.

Tjoe, Yenny. 2018. "Two Decades of Economic Growth Benefited Only the Richest 20%. How Severe Is Inequality in Indonesia?" *The Conversation*, August 28, 2018. http://theconversation.com/two-decades-of-economic-growth-benefited-only-the-richest-20-how-severe-is-inequality-in-indonesia-101138.

TribunBatam. 2014. "Waspadai Aliran Syi'ah Yang Mengancam Keutuhan NKRI." [Beware of the Shi'a Sect that Threatens the Integrity of the Republic of Indonesia]. February 3, 2014. https://batam.tribunnews.com/2014/02/03/waspadai-aliran-syiah-yang-mengancam-keutuhan-nkri?page=2.

Tribunnews.com. 2014. "Jokowi: Hari Santri Nasional Permintaan Para Santri." [Jokowi: National Santri Day is a Request from the Santri]. July 4, 2014. https://www.tribunnews.com/nasional/2014/07/04/jokowi-hari-santri-nasional-permintaan-para-santri.

Tuğal, Cihan. 2009. *Passive Revolution: Absorbing the Islamic Challenge to Capitalism*. Stanford University Press.

Tyson, Adam. 2021. "Blasphemy and Judicial Legitimacy in Indonesia." *Politics and Religion* 14 (1): 182–205. https://doi.org/10.1017/S1755048319000427.

UCA News Indonesia. 2012a. "Bupati Sampang Diduga Provokator Serangan Atas Syiah." December 5, 2012. https://indonesia.ucanews.com/2012/12/05/bupati-sampang-diduga-provokator-serangan-atas-syiah/.

UCA News Indonesia. 2012b. "Komnas HAM: Polisi Biarkan Penyerangan Syiah" [Komnas HAM: Police Allow Shia Attacks]. August 29, 2012. https://indonesia.ucanews.com/2012/08/29/komnas-ham-polisi-biarkan-penyerangan-syiah/.

Ucu, Agustin, and Kuswandi Lucky. 2010. *FPI Mob Threatens Q! Film Festival Jakarta 2010*. Posted on YouTube, May 30, 2016. https://www.youtube.com/watch?v=dYF10YZMXxc.

Uddin, Asma T. 2014. "The Indonesian Blasphemy Act: A Legal and Social Analysis." In *Profane: Sacrilegious Expression in a Multicultural Age*, edited by Christopher S. Grenda, C. Beneke, and D. Nash. University of California Press.

Ulma Haryanto. 2010. "FPI Attacks Four People at Constitutional Court Building." *Jakarta Globe*, March 24, 2010. https://www.asia-pacific-solidarity.net/news/2010-03-24/fpi-attacks-four-people-constitutional-court-building.html.

Ungsuchaval, Theerapat. 2020. "NGOization." In *Global Encyclopedia of Public Administration, Public Policy, and Governance*, edited by Ali Farazmand. Springer International.

United Nations. 2022. "New Publication: Regional Snapshot 2—Prison Population in South-Eastern Asia." United Nations Office on Drugs and Crime, June 1, 2022. https://coekostat.unodc.org/coekostat/en/news/new-publication_-regional-snapshot-2--prison-population-in-south-eastern-asia-.html.

USAID. 2018. "U.S. Overseas Loans and Grants: Obligations and Loan Authorizations." Accessed September 2023. https://pdf.usaid.gov/pdf_docs/PBAAJ820.pdf.

US Department of State. 2007. "2007 Report on International Religious Freedom." Unpublished manuscript, last modified March 24, 2023. https://2009-2017.state.gov/j/drl/rls/irf/2007/index.htm.

Vaswani, Karishma. 2012. "Shia Muslims: Indonesian Villages Burned Down." BBC, December 26, 2012. https://www.bbc.com/news/av/world-asia-20843259.

Viva News. 2011. "MUI Tetap Anggap Ahmadiyah Menyimpang" [MUI Still Considers Ahmadiyah Deviant]. February 8, 2011. https://www.viva.co.id/berita/nasional/203463-mui-tetap-anggap-ahmadiyah-menyimpang.

VOA ISLAM. 2011. "Gubernur Banten Juga Larang Segala Aktivitas Ahmadiyah" [Banten Governor Also Bans All Ahmadiyya Activities]. March 3, 2011. https://www.voa-islam.com/read/indonesiana/2011/03/03/13600/gubernur-banten-juga-larang-segala-aktivitas-ahmadiyah/.

VOA ISLAM. 2012. "JIL & Kelompok Liberal Mulai Kere-Meredup, Kini Mulai Saweran." [JIL & Liberal Groups Start to Fade, Now Asking for Donations]. March 8, 2012. https://www.voa-islam.com/read/indonesiana/2012/03/08/18077/jil-kelompok-liberal-mulai-keremeredup-kini-saweran/.

VOA ISLAM. 2016. "KH Ma'ruf Amin: Fatwa MUI Bisa Dijadikan Rujukan Regulasi Nasional." [KH Ma'ruf Amin: MUI Fatwa Can Be Used as a Reference for National Regulations]. December 21, 2016. http://www.voa-islam.com/read/indonesiana/2016/12/21/48035/kh-ma'ruf-aminfatwa-mui-bisa-dijadikan-rujukan-regulasi-nasional/#sthash.ycrKr7tt.Y6GGvDGh.dpbs.

Voll, John O., and John L. Esposito. 1994. "Islam's Democratic Essence." *Middle East Quarterly* 1 (4): Fall 1994. https://www.meforum.org/middle-east-quarterly/islams-democratic-essence.

Wacquant, Loic. 2009. *Punishing the Poor: The Neoliberal Government of Social Insecurity*. Politics. History, and Culture. Duke University Press.

Wahid Institute. 2011. "Lampu Merah Kebebasan Beragama." http://www.wahidinstitute.org/wi-eng/images/upload/dokumen/laporan_kebebasan_beragama_wahid_institute_2011.pdf.

Wahid Institute. 2012. "Kebebasan Beragama Dan Intoleransi 2012." http://www.wahidinstitute.org/wi-eng/images/upload/dokumen/laporan_kebebasan_beragama_dan_berkeyakinan_wi_2012.pdf.

Wahid Institute. 2013. "Kebebasan Beragama / Berkeyakinan Dan Intoleransi." http://www.wahidinstitute.org/wi-eng/images/upload/dokumen/laporan_kbb_2013_wi.pdf.

Wanandi, Jusuf. 2002. "Islam in Indonesia: Its History, Development and Future Challenges." *Asia-Pacific Review* 9 (2): 104–12. https://doi.org/10.1080/1343900022000036115.

Weiss, Meredith L., and Michael J. Bosia. 2013. *Global Homophobia: States, Movements, and the Politics of Oppression*. University of Illinois Press.

REFERENCES

White, Jenny B. 2014. *Muslim Nationalism and the New Turks*. New edition, with a new afterword by the author. Princeton Studies in Muslim Politics. Princeton University Press.

Widjaya, Ismoko. 2010. "Syafii Maarif: Menteri Agama Tidak Bijak." [Syafii Maarif: Minister of Religious Affairs is Not Wise]. *Viva News*, August 31, 2010. https://www.viva.co.id/berita/nasional/174493-menteri-agama-coba-dengar-ulama-lain.

Wieringa, Saskia. 2002. *Sexual Politics in Indonesia*. Springer.

Wijaya, Callistasia Anggun. 2016. "Tito Booed as He Addresses Anti-Ahok Protesters." *The Jakarta Post*, December 2, 2016. https://www.thejakartapost.com/news/2016/12/02/tito-booed-as-he-addresses-anti-ahok-protesters.html.

Wijaya, Hendri Yulius. 2022. "Digital Homophobia." *Indonesia and the Malay World* 50 (146): 52–72. https://doi.org/10.1080/13639811.2022.2010357.

Wilson, Ian Douglas. 2008. "As Long as It's Halal: Islamic Preman in Jakarta." In *Expressing Islam: Religious Life and Politics in Indonesia*, edited by Greg Fealy and Sally White. Papers Presented at the Twenty-Fifth Annual Indonesia Update Conference, Australian National University, September 7–8, 2007. Indonesia update series. ISEAS.

Wilson, Ian Douglas. 2015. *The Politics of Protection Rackets in Post-New Order Indonesia: Coercive Capital, Authority and Street Politics*. Asia's Transformations. Taylor and Francis.

Wilson, Ian Douglas. 2017. "Jakarta: Inequality and the Poverty of Elite Pluralism." *New Mandala*, April 19, 2017.

Winters, Jeffrey. 2011. *Oligarchy*. Cambridge University Press.

Winters, Jeffrey. 2013. "Oligarchy and Democracy in Indonesia." *Indonesia* 96: 11–33. https://doi.org/10.5728/indonesia.96.0099.

Winters, Jeffrey A., Chris Manning, Jonathan Pincus, and Vedi R. Hodiz. 2000. "The Political Economy of Labor in Indonesia." *Indonesia*, no. 70: 139–49. https://doi.org/10.2307/3351500.

Wirz, Dominique S. 2018. "Does Consistency Matter? Perception and Persuasiveness of Value Appeals in Populist Communication." *Studies in Communication and Media* 7 (1): 59–88. https://doi.org/10.5771/2192-4007-2018-1-58.

World Bank. n.d. "Gini Index (World Bank Estimate)—Indonesia." Accessed May 22, 2025. https://data.worldbank.org/indicator/SI.POV.GINI?locations=ID.

Wulandari, Indah, and Dijbril Muhammad. 2012. "Gramedia Musnahkan Buku Penista Rasulullah." *Republika*, June 13, 2012. https://news.republika.co.id/berita/nasional/umum/12/06/13/m5jw42-gramedia-musnahkan-buku-penista-rasulullah.

www.foreignassistance.gov. n.d. "Indonesia: Foreign Assistance." Accessed May 22, 2025. https://foreignassistance.gov/cd/indonesia/.

Yilmaz, Ihsan, and Greg Barton. 2021. *"Populism, Violence, and Vigilantism in Indonesia: Rizieq Shihab and His Far-Right Islamist Populism."* Deakin University, 2021. https://hdl.handle.net/10536/DRO/DU:30162408.

Yi Lih, Beh. 2018. "A Brutal Assault and Rising Fear in Malaysia's LGBT Community." Reuters, August 24, 2018. https://www.reuters.com/article/us-malaysia-lgbt-idUSKCN1L9009.

Yue-Yi, Hwa. 2013. "'Allah' Issue: The Battle over Bahasa." *The Nut Graph*, January 21, 2013. https://thenutgraph.com/allah-issue-the-battle-over-bahasa/.

Yulius, Hendri. 2018. "Rethinking the Mobility (and Immobility) of Queer Rights in Southeast Asia: A Provocation." Heinrich Böll Stiftung, December 26, 2018. https://www.boell.de/en/2018/12/26/rethinking-mobility-and-immobility-queer-rights-southeast-asia-provocation.

Zulian, Pradana Boy. 2018. *Fatwa in Indonesia: An Analysis of Dominant Legal Ideas and Mode of Thought of Fatwa-Making Agencies and Their Implications in the Post-New Order Period*. Religion and Society in Asia. Amsterdam: Amsterdam University Press.

Zulkarnain, Iskandar. 2005. *Gerakan Ahmadiyah Di Indonesia:* PT LKiS Pelangi Aksara.

Zulkffli, Mohd Asyraf, and Radzuwan Ab Rashid. 2016. "A Discursive Psychological Analysis of Islamic Sermons on Homosexuality." *International Journal of Applied Linguistics and English Literature* 5 (6): 190–98.

Zulkifli. 2013. *The Struggle of the Shi'is in Indonesia*. ANU Press. http://doi.org/10.22459/SSI.11.2013.

Index

Aa Gym (Abdullah Gymnastiar), 46–47, 54, 71, 72
Aan (Alexander An), 126, 144–48
Abdurrahman Wahid (Gus Dur), 33, 40, 41, 47–48, 59–60, 75, 94, 104, 106–7, 119
Aburizal Bakrie, 65
Aceh, 32, 149
activists: defense strategies, 73, 80–81, 86, 104–8, 139 (*see also* blasphemy law, attempts to repeal). *See also* feminist activists; freedom of religion; human rights; minority rights
Ahlul Bayt Indonesia (ABI), 94, 103, 134
Ahmadiyya, 4, 9, 11, 16, 22–24, 34, 42, 53, 55, 73–93, 96, 98, 100–101, 104–9, 122–23, 125–27, 131, 135–36, 165–66, 178, 186, 189, 191–92, 194
Ahmad Mustofa Bisri (Gus Mus), 49
Ahmad Suaedy, 136
Ahok (Basuki Tjahaja Purnama), 2, 8, 16–17, 42, 44, 53–55, 57, 71, 72, 114
aliran kepercayaan, 37, 115, 141–43
aliran sesat, 25–26, 82–83
Alternative Front (BA), 175–76
Amaq Bakri (East Lombok farmer), 115, 136, 140
ambiguity, 17–18, 34–35, 99, 136–41, 148, 150
Amien Rais, 50, 59, 95
Anderson, Benedict, 15, 31–32
An-Na'im, Abdullahi, 80, 118
anticolonialism, 8, 12, 14, 21, 32, 35, 38, 168
Anti-Vice Movement (GIBAS), 101
Anwar Ibrahim, 169, 174–77, 188
Appadurai, Arjun, 18, 78
Arabic, 2, 12, 37, 41, 49, 60, 92, 116, 119, 172, 185
Arabs, 12, 14, 18–20
Arifianto, Alexander, 121–22
Artawijaya, 120

Aspinall, Edward, 11, 27, 58, 62
assimilation, 4, 6, 79–80, 85, 109, 112–13, 149, 171, 186, 191–92, 194
Assyaukanie, Luthfi, 118, 120, 127, 139, 197
atheists, 23, 112, 115, 126, 128, 143–48, 164, 194
Australia, 22, 59–62, 161
Ayah Pin, 183–84
Az, Emilia Renita, 94, 96, 98
Azyumardi Azra, 40–41, 59, 73

Bahai, 187
Bahasa Indonesia, 32
Bakor Pakem (Coordinating Board for the Monitoring of Mystical Beliefs in Society), 83, 140
Bali, 33, 36
Banten, 84–85, 90–91
Barisan Nasional (BN), 168
Barkey, Karen, 202n5
Bauer, Thomas, 18
Bauman, Zygmunt, 17
Berenschot, Ward, 11, 27, 58
blasphemy law, 64, 99, 112, 125–26, 134–40, 144–48; attempts to repeal, 6, 16, 107–8, 114, 122, 126–33, 164; theology of, 114–15, 122–25
Boellstorff, Tom, 154–55
British Malaya, 167–68, 170–71
Brubaker, Rogers, 105
Bruinessen, Martin van, 13, 48, 120
Brunei, 161
Buddhism, 31, 36, 128, 146
Burhani, Najib, 106–7
Burhanuddin al-Helmy, 169

Catholicism, 31, 36, 128, 146, 173, 185
censorship, 24, 27, 64, 189. *See also* press freedom

243

Chinese Indonesians, 33, 38
Chinese Malaysians, 168, 170–71, 177–78
Christianity, 33–34, 38, 73, 82, 105, 123, 137, 147, 177–78, 185. *See also* Catholicism; Protestantism
citizenship rights, 11, 21–22, 40, 110; national identity cards, 16, 89, 142–43
civil society, 4–5, 20, 34, 47, 184; decentralization, 57–63, 177, 195. *See also* Muhammadiyah; Nahdlatul Ulama
colonialism, 18, 148; in Malaysia, 167–68, 170–71. *See also* anticolonialism; Dutch colonial rule
Communism, 14, 37, 77, 126, 144, 150–51
communitarianism, 114, 136, 163
competition, 23–24, 27, 166–67, 189, 191–96; decentralization and, 23–24, 38–39, 189, 192–96; elections and, 4, 23–24, 46, 101–2, 189, 195–96; in Malaysia, 166–67, 170–71, 175–77, 189–90, 194; political-religious alliances and, 40, 51, 70–71, 190, 195; small groups and, 139–40
Confucianism, 36, 82, 104, 128, 146
Constitutional Court (Indonesia), 4, 164; on blasphemy law, 6, 24, 122, 126–36, 144; on Indigenous beliefs, 142
consumerism and consumption, 23, 28, 195
conversion, 16, 84–85, 89–91, 96, 101–2, 173, 185
Cook, Michael, 124–25
Coordinating Board for the Monitoring of Mystical Beliefs in Society (Bakor Pakem), 83, 140
corruption, 11, 27, 35, 39, 51, 66, 177, 195
cosmopolitanism, 13, 35, 40, 72, 113–14, 116, 156, 163
Council of Indonesian Ulama (Majelis Ulama Indonesia, MUI), 3, 6, 70, 143, 174–75; Ahmadiyya and, 9, 53, 55, 74, 76–78, 81–92, 126–27; blasphemy law and, 122, 129, 133, 137–39; fatwas, 9, 22, 26, 48, 52–53, 55–56, 72, 78, 82–84, 112–13, 116–17, 126–27, 159–61, 164, 175; founding of, 37–38; influence of, 20–21, 39, 41, 49, 51–57, 67, 83; LGBTQI Muslims and, 159–62; Shi'a and, 77–78, 95–97, 102–4
Crescent Star Party, 39
Crouch, Melissa, 123

Darul Arqam (The House of Arqam), 169, 181–83, 189
Dasan Bangik, 89
Davies, William, 55
da'wah movement, 7, 173–74
decentralization, 7, 10–11, 17, 27, 97, 167–68; competition and, 23–24, 38–39, 189, 192–96; fourfold, 11, 28, 34, 57–72, 149, 192–93. *See also* civil society; elections; media; religious authorities
democracy, 12, 26–27, 58, 59–62, 66, 191–96. *See also* elections
Department of Islamic Advancement of Malaysia (JAKIM), 174–75, 178–79, 184, 188
deviant social categories, 9, 19, 22–26, 37, 74, 76, 80, 82–83. *See also* Ahmadiyya; *aliran sesat*; atheists; LGBTQI Muslims; marginalization and othering; Shi'a
digital media, 11; anti-LGBTQI rhetoric, 160, 164; atheism and, 144–47; politics and, 65–69; public-private divide and, 113, 140
Din Syamsuddin, 49, 50, 106, 117
diversity. *See* nationalism; pluralism
Douglas, Mary, 17, 78
dress regulations, 15, 153, 180
Dutch colonial rule, 12, 19, 38, 148, 167, 170

East Java, 23, 95–99, 101, 102, 141, 194, 201n5
economic development, 24, 28, 195
Eden Community, 115, 136–40
education, 19, 68, 70, 141–43, 146
Egypt, 8, 35, 105, 120, 169, 181, 185
Eka Prasetya Budi Dharma, 146
elections, 4, 7, 10, 16–17, 34, 166; 2019 presidential, 2–3, 50; competition and, 4, 23–24, 46, 101–2, 189, 195–96; decentralization, 57–58, 195; media and, 63–69
Erdoğan, Recep Tayyip, 196
Europe, 55, 116, 161, 163
extremists, 2–3, 19–20, 42, 57, 67, 118, 127, 166

family law, 142–43, 162–63
fatwas, 26; against Ahmadis, 9, 53, 55, 74, 78, 83–84, 126–27; anti-Ahok, 53, 56; defined, 52; against interfaith marriage, 9, 55, 83; in Malaysia, 74, 170, 175, 178, 182–84; political influence of, 53–55; against secularism, pluralism, and

INDEX

liberalism, 9, 48, 56, 83, 112–13, 116–17, 164; against Shi'a, 97–99
Felix Siauw, 47, 50
feminist activists, 120, 150, 187
foreign influence, 23, 59–63, 78, 102–3, 108, 112, 115–16, 119–20, 135–41, 147–50, 154–62, 194, 202n1 (chap. 3)
Foucault, Michel, 26
Fraser, Nancy, 130
freedom of religion, 73, 76, 80, 104–6, 127, 128–29, 133, 143
free speech, 33, 102, 129, 193

gender, 6, 35, 116, 148–63, 180. *See also* heteronormativity; women
George, Cherian, 55
Gerakan Pemuda Ka'bah (Ka'bah Youth Movement), 157
Gerakan Reformis Islam, 89
Gerwani, 151
Goenawan Mohamad, 119
Göle, Nilüfer, 8
Golkar Party, 65, 84, 85, 87
Gramedia Pustaka Utama, 132
Gülen movement, 182

Habibie, Bacharuddin Jusuf, 38, 41, 61
hadith, 124, 137–38
Hadiz, Vedi, 17, 62–63, 163
Hajj Fund Management Agency, 57
Hajj Supervisory Commission (KPHI), 57
halal industry, 35, 56–57
hardline Islamists, 2–3, 5, 8, 10, 19, 47, 49, 82, 102
Hasyim Muzadi, 48, 117, 127
Hefner, Robert, 13
heterodoxy, 10, 77, 80, 93, 107, 111, 127–28, 193
heteronormativity, 112, 115, 148–64
Hicks, Jacqueline, 100
Hill, David T., 68
Hinduism, 31, 36, 82, 128, 142, 146, 173, 179
Hizbut Tahrir, 13, 25, 47, 81, 162
homosexuality: criminalization of, 148, 159–61. *See also* LGBTQI Muslims
Howell, Julia, 137
Hulu Besut commune (Malaysia), 184
humanism, 120, 147–48
human rights, 16, 73, 76, 80–81, 85–86, 96, 104–6, 109, 114, 121–22, 127–30, 133, 135–36, 139, 145–48, 159, 176, 187, 196

Hungary, 10, 163, 192, 196

Ibrahim Ali, 177, 185
identity discourses, 2, 5–6, 9–11, 13, 196; boundary patrolling, 22–24 (*see also* deviant social categories); hierarchies, 22, 82–83; modernity and, 17; social cohesion and, 78–79, 162. *See also* Mainstream Islam; marginalization and othering; religious nationalism
Ikatan Jamaah Ahlulbait Indonesia (IJABI), 94, 103
India, 10, 192, 193, 195, 196
Indian Malaysians, 168, 170–71
Indigenous beliefs, 15, 36–37, 83, 115, 140, 141–48, 164
Indonesia: Constitution (1945), 33, 40, 127–30, 135, 142, 162; as diverse and multireligious, 1, 3, 10, 12–13, 15–19, 22, 31–34, 40–41, 104–5, 107, 109, 114, 122, 135–36, 174; geographical boundaries, 32; independence, 12, 32, 168; national identity, 5–6, 33, 129, 142–44, 192, 195–96; national language, 32–33; reform period (post-1998), 4, 24–25, 27, 38–39, 177; religious nationalism, 8–17, 24, 34, 39–43, 85, 87, 108, 195
Indonesian Association of Muslim Intellectuals (ICMI), 38
Indonesian Islamic Propagation Council (DDII), 95, 140
inequalities, 22; digital divide, 68; socioeconomic, 17, 24, 55, 112, 114, 116, 162–63
informal politics, 26–28, 195
Information and Electronic Transaction Law, 64, 126, 145
internationalism. *See* foreign influence
internet. *See* digital media
Iran, 77, 95, 96, 102, 108, 173
Islam: center-periphery discourse, 12, 20; certification of, 34–35, 56–57; nationalism and, 14–15 (*see also* religious nationalism); polarization of discourses on, 34, 50, 59, 67, 109–10, 118, 121, 126, 133, 176; study groups, 61, 71; "true Islam," 9, 23, 84–85, 87, 136. *See also* Islamist Conservative Majoritarian Synthesis; Mainstream Islam

INDEX

Islamic Boarding Schools Forum, 102
Islamic Defenders Front (FPI), 2, 6, 39–40, 42, 73–74, 76, 81, 89, 91, 122–23, 125, 127, 132–33, 144, 156, 159–60, 162, 166, 193
Islamic law, 13, 39, 40, 51, 124, 172–73. *See also* blasphemy law; family law; fatwas; marriage law; Sharia law
Islamic Society Forum (FUI), 89, 145–46
Islamic Union (Persis), 95, 97
Islamism: defined, 8; nationalism and, 14, 40; Turkish, 21–22, 45–46
Islamist Conservative Majoritarian Synthesis, 9–11, 21–25, 43–57, 191–96. *See also* Mainstream Islam; marginalization and othering; religious authorities; social conservatism
Islamization: Arabization and, 19–20; competition and, 167; conservative turn and, 148; defined, 3, 5, 7–8, 43–44; in Malaysia, 174; pluralist, 77; Sunni privilege and, 44
Islam Nusantara (Islam of the Archipelago), 49, 51, 114, 122, 164
Istiqlal Mosque, 1–2, 7, 95

Jäger, Siegfried, 26
Jakarta, 25
Jakarta Charter, 7, 40
Jalaluddin Rakhmat, 77, 94
Java, 23, 25, 37, 142, 194. *See also* East Java; West Java
Jawa Pos Group, 65, 118
Jemaah Ahmadiyah Indonesia (JAI), 74–75, 135
Jokowi (Joko Widodo), 2–4, 7, 8, 10, 33, 42–43, 48–49, 63–65, 71, 109, 114, 164, 193
journalism, 27, 64, 66, 87

Kalla, Jusuf, 48, 160
Kaviraj, Sudipta, 14, 32, 192
Kemalism, 45
K. H. Hasan Basri, 95
Klinken, Gerry van, 27, 100
Kompas Gramedia Group, 65

leftists, 45–46, 63, 80, 104, 121, 163
legal system, 172–73. *See also* Islamic law
LGBTQI Muslims (lesbian, gay, bisexual, transgender, queer, and intersex), 3, 4, 23–24, 115–16, 120, 122–23, 125, 148–64, 188–89, 191–92, 194
Lia Aminuddin (Lia Eden), 136–40

Liberal Islam Network (JIL), 48, 113–14, 116–22, 139, 147, 164
liberalism, 4, 6, 14, 38, 80, 139, 162, 191; fatwa against, 9, 48, 56, 83, 112–13, 116–17, 164
Lina Joy, 173
Luhut Pandjaitan, 160
Lukman Hakim Saifuddin, 143

Ma'arif Institute, 108
Madura, 97–98, 102, 108
Mahathir Mohamad, 173, 176–77
Mahfud MD, 107
Mainstream Islam, 4–11, 31–72; bottom-up construction of, 17–21, 29, 72, 152, 167, 184, 192–96 (*see also* decentralization); bureaucratization and, 3, 7, 19, 28, 43, 58, 71, 89, 103, 166, 174, 191; competition and, 166–67, 189, 191–96; defined, 3–5; homogenization of belief, 3–5, 9–10, 17–19, 23–24, 34, 36, 40, 43–57, 70–72, 79, 121–22, 141, 150, 166–68, 178, 184, 186, 189–91, 196; minorities and, 111–12 (*see also* Ahmadiyya; atheists; LGBTQI Muslims; Shi'a). *See also* Islamist Conservative Majoritarian Synthesis; orthodoxy
Malaysia, 25; Ahmadiyya in, 165–66, 178, 186, 189; authoritarianism and repression, 168–77, 189; blasphemy laws, 129; British colonialism in, 167–68, 170–71; centralized and top-down regulation of Islam, 165–90; competition in, 166–67, 170–71, 175–77, 189–90, 194; fatwas, 74, 170, 175, 178, 182–84; independence, 168; LGBTQI people in, 148, 153–54, 161; religious nationalism, 10, 12; Shi'a in, 166, 186–87, 189
Maluku, 33–34
Manajemen Qolbu (Management of the Heart), 46–47, 71
Mandal, Sumit, 20
marginalization and othering, 3, 4, 9, 22–26, 71, 113, 191–96; mechanisms of, 68, 76, 78–80, 85–89, 91–92, 112; media and, 67, 86–87; visibility and, 102–3, 108, 112, 115–16, 120, 136–41, 145–46, 148–50, 154–63, 189, 194. *See also* deviant social categories; violence
marriage law, 9, 15–16, 37, 55, 83, 141–44, 146, 159, 173

Ma'ruf Amin, 3, 26, 49, 51, 53–55, 87–88, 99, 117, 119, 132, 139
Masdar F. Mas'udi, 117, 119
Mathla'ul Anwar, 37
Mecca, 12, 19, 43, 99, 185
media, 4, 34; on attacks against Ahmadiyya, 83–93; on attacks against Shi'a, 98–104; on blasphemy cases, 138–39; decentralization, 11, 57, 63–69, 149–50, 168, 195; elections and, 63–69; Western, 147–48. *See also* censorship; digital media; journalism; press freedom
Media Group, 65
Megawati Sukarnoputri, 41
Menchik, Jeremy, 15, 50
Middle East, 12, 19, 114, 129–30. *See also* Iran; Saudi Arabia
Mietzner, Marcus, 50, 62
Ministry of Culture, 37
Ministry of Home Affairs, 95
Ministry of Law and Human Rights, 135
Ministry of Religious Affairs (MORA), 36–38, 50, 56–57, 70–72, 74, 83, 90–91, 93–94, 129, 134–35
minority rights, 33, 44, 72, 104–10, 143, 147–48, 150, 154–55, 158–60, 164. *See also* citizenship rights; human rights
Mirza Ghulam Ahmad, 74, 81, 88, 92
modernity, 5, 14, 17, 21, 32, 34–35, 115, 118, 151–52
Modi, Narendra, 196
Monas Incident, 89, 127
moral panics, 112, 123, 154. *See also* public morality
Mubarik Ahmad, 86, 107
Muhammad (Prophet), 88, 119, 129, 132, 137, 139, 145, 202n1 (chap. 4)
Muhammadiyah, 20, 37, 41, 43, 47, 50–51, 60–61, 74, 81, 95, 97, 103–4, 117, 121, 127, 129, 152
Muhammadiyah Young Intellectual Network, 119
Muslim Brotherhood, 8, 169
Muslim World League, 74, 95
Muslim Youth Movement of Malaysia (ABIM), 169, 174, 176

Nahdlatul Ulama (NU), 20, 25, 37, 41, 43, 47–50, 60–61, 81, 95, 97, 104, 108, 116–17, 121, 122, 127, 129, 152, 164, 194
Najib Burhani, 136
Najib Razak, 177

National Anti-Shi'a Alliance, 100
National Awakening Party, 47
national belonging, 6, 24, 105, 136, 162. *See also* marginalization and othering
nationalism, 10, 17; diversity and, 1, 3, 10, 12–13, 15–19, 22, 31–34, 40–41, 104–5, 107, 109, 114, 122, 135–36, 174; gendered dimension of, 151, 163; religious, 8–17, 24, 34, 39–43, 85, 87, 108, 195; right-wing, 67
National Santri Day, 50
Nelson, Matthew, 130
neoliberalism, 23, 35, 46, 60, 114, 120–21, 152, 153, 161, 162–63, 196
New Order. *See* Suharto's New Order
NGOs (nongovernmental organizations), 24, 58–63, 120
Noor, Farish, 167
nuclear family, 150–53, 162
Nurcholish Madjid, 59, 95, 118–19

1MDB (1Malaysia Development Berhad), 177
Organisation of Ahlulbayt for Social Support and Education, 94
orthodoxy, 4, 7, 21–22, 24, 69, 72, 107–8, 115, 119, 128–29, 136–37, 186, 192. *See also* Mainstream Islam
othering. *See* marginalization and othering
Ottoman Empire, 6, 202n5

Pakatan Harapan (Alliance of Hope), 176–77
Pakistan, 81, 102, 129–30
Pancasila, 15, 16, 36–38, 40–41, 128, 141–42, 144, 162, 194
Pancasila Day, 73
Parti Islam Se-Malaysia (PAS), 169–70, 175, 188
patriarchal norms, 13, 35, 116, 148–50
patronage networks, 11, 27, 58, 101
Peletz, Michael, 161
Pelletier, Alexandre, 102
Pemuda Rakyat, 151
People's Pact/Alliance (PR), 175–76
Perindo, 65
Perkasa, 177, 185
Persatuan Islam, 37
Persatuan Tarbiyah Islamiyah, 37
pesantren (Islamic boarding schools), 43, 50, 93–95

piety, 7–8, 13, 22, 37–39, 43, 46–47, 71–72, 81, 83, 113, 123
pilgrimage management, 56–57
pluralism, 9–10, 16, 20, 40–41, 63, 73, 80, 104–5, 107, 114, 116–22, 127, 172, 194, 196; fatwa against, 9, 48, 56, 83, 112–13, 116–17, 164
plurality, 10, 18, 113, 116–17, 122, 190
Poland, 10, 192, 196
political homophobia, 149
politics: formal, 2, 11, 27; informal, 26–28, 41, 57, 195; religion and, 25–26, 40 (*see also* religious authorities). *See also* civil society; competition; elections; *specific political leaders*
populism, 17, 55, 64, 67, 163, 167, 196
pornography, 111, 156–57, 162
postcolonialism, 8, 10
Prabowo Subianto, 3, 48, 121
press freedom, 24, 27, 64. *See also* censorship
Prosperous Justice Party (PKS), 39, 92, 156
Protestantism, 31, 36, 43, 128, 146
public morality, 21, 39, 41, 52, 72, 103, 111–14, 122–25, 143–44
public-private divide, 113–15, 125, 129–31, 138, 140, 164, 187
punitiveness, 51, 55, 72, 126, 161, 179–80

Q! Queer Film Festival, 154, 156, 158, 164, 188
Qum School, 77
Quran, 42, 43, 91–92, 99, 118, 124–25, 137–38, 145

Ratu Atut Chosiyah, 84–85, 90–91
rehabilitation, 139, 153, 179–80, 187, 188–89
religion: defamation of, 125–26 (*see also* blasphemy law); hiearchies of, 35–36; politics and, 25–26, 40; religious identity, 9–10, 16, 32, 83, 164, 196; "thin religion," 14, 23, 32, 111, 119, 190, 192. *See also* Buddhism; Catholicism; Christianity; Confucianism; Hinduism; Islam; Mainstream Islam; Protestantism
religionization *(agamaisation)*, 37
religious authorities, 4; alliances with political leaders, 10, 13, 25–26, 40, 44, 51, 70–71, 91, 101–2, 109, 190, 192–95 (*see also* Islamist Conservative Majoritarian Synthesis); decentralization, 57, 69–71, 195;

pop preachers, 23–24, 28, 46–47, 51, 70–71, 188; use of term, 69–70. *See also* Council of Indonesian Ulama; Muhammadiyah; Nahdlatul Ulama
religious nationalism, 8–17, 34, 39–43, 85, 87, 108, 192, 195–96
rights, discourses of. *See* citizenship rights; freedom of religion; human rights; minority rights; press freedom
right-wing groups, 21, 25, 42, 45–50, 55, 67, 109, 116, 122, 154, 160, 163. *See also* extremists; hardline Islamists
Rizieq Shihab, 3, 54–55, 120, 127, 193
Russia, 192–93

Saba Mahmood, 120, 121
Saeful Mujani, 118
Sahal Mahfudh, 116
Said Aqil Siradj, 48–49, 108
Sambelia H. Bukhari, 90
Saudi Arabia, 19, 34–35, 62–63, 95
Schulte Nordholt, Henk, 100
secularism, 3, 14; fatwa against, 9, 48, 56, 83, 112–13, 116–17, 164
security discourses, 19–20, 80–81, 92–95, 100, 103, 109
Selangor Islamic Religious Council, 165, 175
self-help books, 152
Sen, Krishna, 68
Şen, Mustafa, 45
Seri Mohamed Apandi Ali, 185
Setara Institute, 34, 76, 108
Setijadi, Charlotte, 123
sexuality, 21, 39, 71, 157–58, 180, 188
Sharia law: in Indonesia, 7, 21, 51–53, 83, 92, 130; in Malaysia, 172–74, 178, 180, 183
Shariati, Ali, 77
Shi'a, 4, 9, 14, 23–24, 34, 42, 73, 75–82, 93–109, 125, 166, 186–87, 189, 191, 192, 194, 201n5
Singapore, 22, 148, 154, 161
Sisters in Islam, 187
Sky Kingdom commune (Malaysia), 183–84
social cohesion, 78–79, 162
social conservatism, 3–5, 13, 34, 111, 153, 162–63, 192–94. *See also* Islamist Conservative Majoritarian Synthesis
social intervention, 52, 72, 122–25. *See also* public morality
social mobility, 8, 72, 114, 195
Societies Act (Malaysia), 182

Soedirgo, Jessica, 79
Stepan, Alfred, 13
Sufis, 166, 186
Suharto's New Order (1966–98), 1, 4, 7, 12–13, 15, 21, 32–33, 37–38, 51, 58, 61, 64, 66, 73, 80, 123, 150–51, 167, 168, 192
Sukarno, 1, 37, 46, 126, 167
Sukmawati Sukarnoputri, 173
Sulawesi, 25, 68
Sumatra, 142
Sunni Islam, 44; in Indonesia, 6, 18, 20–22, 24, 40, 77–78, 94–95, 98–103, 111, 164, 169, 194 (see also Mainstream Islam); in Malaysia, 177–79; in Turkey, 21, 44–45
Suryadharma Ali, 6, 42, 80, 90, 91, 96, 106, 111, 132, 201n5
Suryana, A'an, 100–101
Surya Paloh, 65
Suseno, Franz Magnis, 127
Syafi'i Ma'arif, 50, 117
Syarikat Islam, 37

Tablighi Jemaat, 169
Tajul Muluk, 98–99, 101–3, 134
Taman Mini Indonesia Indah, 31–33, 38
Tanjung Priok Massacre, 61
Tan Malaka, 14
Tapsell, Ross, 65
Telle, Kari, 140
Tengku Zulkarnain, 42–43
"thin religion," 14, 23, 32, 111, 119, 190, 192
Tito Karniavan, 53–55
transnationalism, 78, 113–14, 120, 154–56. *See also* foreign influence
Tuğal, Cihan, 45
Tunisia, 35
Tunku Abdul Rahman, 168, 172
Turkey, 6, 10, 18, 22, 35, 44–45, 163, 182, 192–93, 196
Turkish-Islamic Synthesis, 21–22, 45–46, 72

Ubaidullah Aziz and Co., 184
Uddin, Asma, 129

Ulil Abshar-Abdalla, 48, 118, 120–22
Uli Parulian Sihombing, 132
United Development Party, 42, 85, 111
United Kingdom, 67. *See also* British Malaya
United Malays National Organisation (UMNO), 168–82, 185–86, 189
United States, 10, 20, 22, 34–35, 67, 116, 119, 121, 153, 159, 161, 163, 196; USAID, 59–62, 120

violence, 4, 9, 33–34, 78–79, 191–96; against Ahmadiyya and Shi'a, 4, 9, 14, 34, 42, 75–76, 79–104, 107, 108, 122–23, 125, 131, 165–66, 191, 201n5; against LGBTQI Muslims, 4, 115–16, 122–23, 125, 149, 157–58, 188–89, 191; police responses to, 73–74, 79–80, 95, 100–101, 123, 158
visibility: of Islam, 3–4; marginalization and, 102–3, 108, 112, 115–16, 120, 136–41, 145–46, 148–50, 154–63, 189, 194; public-private divide and, 114–15, 125, 164, 187

Wage Soepratman, 107, 109
Wahabi Islam, 63
Wahdah Islamiyah, 40, 54
Wahid Institute, 75, 117
Western societies, 8, 17–18, 106, 147–48, 154–56, 191. *See also* Europe; United States
West Java, 23, 88–90, 92, 102, 194
Wilson, Ian, 17
Winters, Jeffrey, 11
women, 35, 71, 116, 151, 153–54, 180
world religions, 6, 36, 44

Yang di-Pertuan Agong, 174
Yaqut Cholil Qoumas, 109–10, 143
Yenny Zannuba Wahid, 75
Yudhoyono, Susilo Bambang, 4, 6, 8, 39–42, 53, 101, 120–21

www.ingramcontent.com/pod-product-compliance
Lightning Source LLC
Chambersburg PA
CBHW030536230426
43665CB00010B/911